gilbert
LAW SUMMARIES

CORPORATIONS

Thirteenth Edition — 1989-90

Jesse H. Choper
Dean and Professor of Law
University of California, Berkeley

Melvin A. Eisenberg
Professor of Law
University of California, Berkeley

HARCOURT BRACE LEGAL AND PROFESSIONAL PUBLICATIONS, INC.

EDITORIAL OFFICES: 176 W. Adams, Suite 2100, Chicago, IL 60603

gilbert
LAW SUMMARIES

REGIONAL OFFICES: New York, Chicago, Los Angeles, Washington, D.C.

Distributed by: **Harcourt Brace & Company** 6277 Sea Harbor Drive, Orlando, FL 32887 (800)787-8717

PROJECT EDITOR
Maureen A. Mitchell, B.A., J.D.
Attorney At Law

QUALITY CONTROL EDITOR
Ann R. Kerns, B.S.

SUMMARY OF CONTENTS

gilbert
capsule summary
corporations

C. **DISREGARD OF CORPORATE ENTITY**
1. **In General:** Since a corporation is a distinct legal entity, shareholders are normally shielded from corporate obligations. In certain instances, however, the corporate entity will be disregarded .... [26]
2. **Suits by Corporate Creditors Against Shareholders:** This is the most common situation for disregarding the corporate entity, and it is called "piercing the corporate veil." Shareholders are usually liable under either the alter ego or undercapitalization theories .... [27]
    a. **Alter ego:** This theory applies when, in reality, *no separate entity* is maintained, *e.g.,* domination and control of corporate finances and business by a shareholder (individual or other corporation), commingling of assets, lack of corporate formalities. Note that statutory close corporations are permitted more flexibility regarding corporate formalities .... [28]
    b. **Undercapitalization:** If the corporation was organized without sufficient capital to meet obligations reasonably expected to arise, the corporate veil may be pierced .... [33]
3. **Piercing Corporate Wall Between Affiliated Corporations:** This occurs when a plaintiff with a claim against one corporation attempts to satisfy the claim against the assets of an affiliated corporation under common ownership. For liability to be imposed, usually the corporations must be operated as a *common, intermingled enterprise* .... [35]
4. **Use of Corporate Form to Evade Statutory or Contract Obligations:** The corporate form may be ignored where it is used to evade a statutory or contractual obligation. The issue is whether the contract or statute was intended to apply to the shareholders as well as the corporation .... [36]
5. **Disregard of Corporate Entity in Favor of Corporation or Its Shareholders:** Only *third parties*, not the corporation or its shareholders, are generally allowed to disregard the corporate entity .... [37]

D. **SUBORDINATION OF SHAREHOLDER DEBTS—"DEEP ROCK" DOCTRINE**
Upon a corporation's insolvency, debts to shareholders may be subordinated to claims of other creditors. Where subordination occurs, shareholder loans are treated as if they were *invested capital* (stock) .... [38]
1. **Grounds:** Major factors in determining whether to subordinate include fraud, mismanagement, undercapitalization, commingling, excessive control, and other equitable reasons .... [41]

II. **ORGANIZING THE CORPORATION**

A. **GENERAL CORPORATION LAWS**
Generally, corporations are created under and according to statutory provisions of the state in which formation is sought .... [42]

B. **FORMALITIES IN ORGANIZING CORPORATION**
1. **Articles (Certificate) of Incorporation:** State law governs the content of the articles, which are filed with the secretary of state. Usually, the articles *must* specify the corporate name, number of shares authorized, address of the corporation's initial registered office and name of initial registered agent, and the name and address of each incorporator. Optional provisions may include provisions concerning the management and powers of the corporation, shareholder liability for corporate debt, and any provision that is required or permitted in the bylaws .... [43]
    a. **Purpose clause:** Under most statutes, no elaborate purpose clause is needed. It is sufficient to state that the purpose of the corporation is to engage in any lawful business activity .... [46]

III. PROMOTERS

A. INTRODUCTION

1. **Definition:** A promoter participates in the formation of the corporation, usually arranging compliance with the legal requirements of formation, securing initial

V. MANAGEMENT AND CONTROL

C. OFFICERS

1. **Election:** Officers are generally elected by the board of directors and hold office at its pleasure. Some statutes permit election of officers by shareholders · ....

2. **Authority of Corporate Officers—Liability of Corporation to Outsiders:** Only authorized officers can bind the corporation. Authority may be: *actual* (expressed in bylaws or by valid board resolution), *apparent* (corporation gives third parties reason to believe authority exists), or *power of position* (inherent to position). If *ratified* by the board, even unauthorized acts may bind the corporation ....

    a. **Authority of president:** Three different views are applicable to the authority inherent to the president's position. One view is that the president has only those *powers of a director* except for presiding at meetings—this is probably not good law today. The "New York" rule gives the president prima facie *power to do any act* the board could authorize or ratify (unclear whether this still is followed). The majority rule is that the president has power to bind the corporation in transactions arising in *regular course of business* ....

3. **Duty of Corporate Officers:** The duty of care owed by an officer is similar to that owed by directors (and sometimes higher) ....

D. CONFLICTS OF INTEREST IN CORPORATE TRANSACTIONS

1. **Duty of Loyalty:** Because of their fiduciary relationship with the corporation, officers and directors have the duty to promote the interests of the corporation without regard for personal gain ....

2. **Business Dealings with Corporations:** Conflict of interest issues arise when a corporation transacts business with one of its officers or directors, or with a company in which an officer or director is financially interested ....

    a. **Effect of self-interest on right to participate in meeting:** At common law, interested directors could not be counted toward a quorum or for a majority vote approving a transaction; many state statutes now allow them to be counted toward a quorum and some statutes for majority approval

    b. **Voidability because of director's self-interest:** Today, such transactions are voidable only if *unfair* to the corporation. Note that a director's failure to *fully disclose* material facts may be per se unfair ......

        (1) **Unanimous shareholder ratification:** If, after *full disclosure*, shareholder ratification is unanimous, the corporation will be *estopped* from challenging the transaction with the interested director (except as to creditors) ....

            (a) **Less-than-unanimous ratification:** If there is less-than-unanimous ratification, courts will look at whether the majority shares were owned or controlled by the interested director. Courts are more likely to uphold ratification by a disinterested majority so as to preclude the transaction from being attacked by the corporation or by a shareholder in a derivative suit ....

        (2) **Statutes:** Most statutes provide that such transactions are *not* voidable if approved, after *full disclosure*, by a *disinterested board majority or by a majority of shareholders*, or, if the transaction is *fair* to the corporation. The transaction must be fair notwithstanding disclosure ....

    c. **Remedies:** The corporation may rescind, or affirm and sue for damages

3. **Interlocking Directorates:** Generally, transactions between corporations with common directors are subject to the same rules of interested director transactions. There is no conflict of interest if one corporation is the wholly-

if: (i) the plaintiff bears *substantially equal responsibility* for the violations, and (ii) preclusion of the suit would not significantly interfere with the enforcement of securities laws .... [349]

17. **Remedies**

    a. **Out-of-pocket damages:** This is the difference between the price paid for stock and its actual value .... [352]

        (1) **Compare—benefit-of-the-bargain damages:** These are measured by the value of the stock as it really is and the value it would have had if a misrepresentation had been true .... [353]

        (2) **Standard measure of conventional damages:** Out-of-pocket damages is the standard measure in private actions under rule 10b-5; benefit-of-the-bargain damages are generally not granted .... [354]

    b. **Restitutionary relief:** This may be sought instead of conventional damages .... [355]

        (1) **Rescission:** The most common form of restitutionary relief is rescission, which returns the parties to their status quo before the transaction, *e.g.,* seller returns purchase price and gets back stock she sold .... [356]

        (2) **Rescissionary or restitutionary damages:** These damages are another form of restitutionary relief. They are measured by the difference between the value of what plaintiff gave up and the value of what the defendant received .... [357]

        (3) **Difference between conventional damages and restitutionary relief:** Out-of-pocket damages are based on the plaintiff's loss while restitutionary relief is based on the defendant's wrongful gain .... [358]

            (a) **Comment:** Rescission or rescissionary damages may be attractive remedies when the value of the stock changed radically after the transaction.

    c. **Remedies available to the government:** Although the SEC cannot sue for damages, it can pursue several remedies including special monetary remedies .... [376]

        (1) **Injunctive relief:** The SEC often seeks injunctive relief accompanied with a request for disgorgement of profits or other payments that can be used as a fund for injured private parties................................. [377]

        (2) **Other remedies:** A person who violates rule 10b-5 can be subject to *criminal sanctions* (fines and jail sentences) and *civil penalties* (up to three times the profit gained or loss avoided) .... [378]

E. **SECTION 16 OF THE 1934 ACT**
Section 16 concerns purchases followed by sales, or sales followed by purchases, by certain insiders, within a six-month period; *i.e.,* "short-swing trading" .... [380]

    1. **Securities Affected Under Section 16:** Section 16 applies to those securities that must be registered under section 12 of the 1934 Act .... [381]

        a. **Note:** Trading in *all* of a corporation's equity securities is subject to section 16 if *any class* of its securities is registered under section 12.

    2. **Disclosure Requirement:** Section 16(a) requires every *beneficial owner* of more than 10% of registered stock and directors and officers of the issuing corporation to file periodic reports with the SEC showing their holdings and any changes in their holdings .... [382]

    3. **Liability:** To prevent the unfair use of information, section 16(b) allows a corporation to recover profits made by an officer, director, or more-than-10% beneficial owner on the purchase and sale *or* sale and purchase of its securities within a *six-month period* .... [385]

        a. **Coverage:** Section 16(b) does not cover all insider trading and is not limited to trades based on inside information. The critical element is short-swing trading by officers, directors, and more-than-10% beneficial owners......... [386]

   b. **Calculation of short-swing profit:** The profit recoverable is the difference between the price of the stock sold and the price of the stock purchased within six months *before or after* the sale...................................... [387]

    (1) **Multiple transactions:** If there is more than one purchase or sale transaction within the six-month period, the transactions are paired by matching the highest sale price with the lowest purchase price, the next highest sale price with the next lowest purchase price, etc. A court can look six months forward or backward from any sale (to find a purchase) or from any purchase (to find a sale). *Any pair* of transactions within that period must be accounted for..................... [388]

   c. **Who may recover:** The profit belongs to the corporation alone. Although not a typical derivative action, if the corporation fails to sue after a demand by a shareholder, the shareholder may sue on the corporation's behalf. Note that there is no posting of security requirement, and no contemporaneous shareholder requirement...................................... [390]

   d. **"Insiders":** Insiders are officers (named officers and those persons who function as officers), directors (actually serving or who authorized deputization of another), and beneficial owners of more than 10% of the shares. Insider status for officers and directors is determined at the time they made a purchase *or* sale (they need not have held office at both times); liability is imposed on a beneficial owner only if she owned more than 10% of the shares at the time of *both* the purchase and sale......... [392]

   e. **"Purchase or sale":** This includes any garden-variety purchase or sale of stock (*e.g.,* exchange of stock for cash). Unorthodox transactions that result in the acquisition or disposition of stock (*e.g.,* merger for stock, redemption of stock) are also purchases and sales............................ [407]

F. SECTION 16(b) COMPARED TO RULE 10b-5

  1. **Covered Securities:** Section 16(b) applies to securities *registered* under the 1934 Act; rule 10b-5 applies to *all* securities.. [412]

  2. **Inside Information:** Section 16(b) allows recovery for short-swing profits *regardless* of whether they are attributable to misrepresentations or inside information; rule 10b-5 recovery is available *only* where there was a misrepresentation or a trade based on inside information.............................. [413]

  3. **Plaintiff:** Recovery under section 16(b) belongs to the corporation, while rule 10b-5 recovery belongs to the injured purchaser or seller........................... [414]

  4. **Overlapping Liability:** It is possible that insiders who make short-swing profits by use of inside information could be liable under both section 16(b) and rule 10b-5 to the injured purchaser or seller... [415]

  5. **Common Law Liability for Insider Trading:** Insider trading constitutes a breach of fiduciary duties owed to the corporation, so the *corporation* can recover profits made from insider trading... [416]

   a. **Common law liability compared to section 16(b) liability:** Both common law and section 16(b) liability run against insiders and in favor of the corporation. However, unlike section 16(b), the common law theory applies to *all* corporations (not just those with registered securities), recovery can be had against *any* corporate insider, the purchase and sale is not limited by a six-month period, and the transaction *must* be based on inside information... [417]

   b. **Common law liability compared to rule 10b-5 liability:** The theories of recovery are similar except that under the common law recovery runs to the corporation (not the injured purchaser or seller), there is no purchaser

I. STATUTES REGULATING ISSUANCE OF SHARES

IX. DISTRIBUTIONS TO SHAREHOLDERS

A. DIVIDENDS

B. REDEMPTION AND REPURCHASE OF SHARES

4. **Dissolution Under Shareholder Agreement:** Agreements among shareholders (usually of a close corporation) to dissolve upon the occurrence of a specified event are valid even if not statutorily authorized .... [1060]

5. **Action by State:** The state may bring an action in *quo warranto* where the corporation has abused its authority or when a particular requirement in which the state has an important interest is not met .... [1062]

6. **Liquidation:** After dissolution, the corporate business continues only to wind up its affairs, *e.g.,* pay debts, distribute assets, etc. The winding up period must be reasonable or the directors may be personally liable for corporate debts...... [1063]

    a. **Rights of shareholders:** If only one class of shares is outstanding, each shareholder receives a pro rata share of the assets after the creditors are satisfied. If there are several classes, preferred shareholders are paid off before a pro rata distribution among common stock .... [1065]

    b. **Rights of creditors:** A corporation remains liable on its debts after dissolution. Statutes govern the manner in which creditors must be given notice of the dissolution and the time within which they must file their claims [1068]

I. LIMITATIONS ON POWER OF CONTROLLING SHAREHOLDERS TO EFFECT FUNDAMENTAL CHANGES IN CORPORATE STRUCTURE

1. **Fiduciary Duty to Minority:** The fiduciary duty owed by controlling shareholders to the minority exists when any fundamental change in which the controlling shareholder is interested occurs .... [1072]

2. **Freezeouts**

    a. **Sale of substantially all assets:** A controlling shareholder normally may not freeze out the minority by a sale of substantially all the corporation's assets to a corporation that he controls .... [1075]

    b. **Merger:** In a freezeout merger (stock for stock, or cash for stock), it must normally be shown that the transaction has efficiency implications and not simply that the controlling shareholders want more of the pie .... [1076]

    c. **Reverse stock splits:** Most statutes allow the corporation to eliminate fractional (less than one full share) shares .... [1077]

    d. **When permissible:** A freezeout may be permissible *if* effected for a legitimate business purpose, *e.g.,* operating efficiency. This requirement does not apply in Delaware, but Delaware does require "entire fairness"... [1079]

3. **Effect of Securities Acts:** In addition to rights under state law (*e.g.,* appraisal rights), a shareholder dissenting to a fundamental change may sue under rule 10b-5 or the federal proxy rules if the controlling shareholders engaged in deceptive conduct .... [1084]

4. **Self-Tender:** A corporation may make a tender offer for its minority shares. This is *not* technically a freezeout since shareholders are not legally required to accept the offer, although it may be the only economically feasible alternative [1085]

5. **Going-Private Transactions:** Transactions eliminating public ownership are governed by rule 13e-3 of the Securities Exchange Act, which defines such transactions to include: (i) *a purchase* of any equity security by the issuer; (ii) *a tender offer* for any equity security by the issuer; and (iii) *a solicitation of proxies* in connection with a fundamental corporate change under defined circumstances that tend to devalue the remaining securities .... [1086]

    a. **Other factors:** In going-private actions, the issuer is required to file and disseminate certain information. The transaction is also subject to an anti-fraud rule similar to that of rule 10b-5 (minus the "purchase and sale" requirement) .... [1088]

6. **Effect of Appraisal Rights:** Even under statutes making appraisal an exclusive remedy, usually a dissenting shareholder can attack the transaction on the basis of lack of authorization, improper procedures, and fraudulent

XI. CONFLICT OF LAWS PRINCIPLES

As a general rule, all questions concerning the organization or internal affairs of a corporation are decided according to the law of the state in which it was incorporated. A few states have statutes subjecting foreign corporations having substantial local contacts to local regulations intended to protect shareholders and creditors. Corporations listed on a national securities exchange may be exempt from the statutes .... [1137]

TEXT CORRELATION CHART

Gilbert Law Summary Corporations	Cary, Eisenberg Corporations 1988 (6th ed.—Unabridged)	Conard, Knauss, Siegel Enterprise Organization 1987 (4th ed.)	Choper, Coffee, Morris Corporations 1989 (3rd ed.)	Hamilton Corporations 1986 (3rd ed.)	Henn Corporations 1986 (2nd ed.)	Jennings, Buxbaum Corporations 1979 (5th ed.)	Vagts Corporations 1989 (3rd ed.)
I. CHARACTERISTICS OF THE CORPORATION							
A. Principal Characteristics	91-95	4-5	1-4	1-21	24-26	70-71	1-18
B. Corporations Distinguished from Partnerships	25-90	1-10, 17-64	39-121	21-127	49-80	1-69	18-34
C. Disregard of Corporate Entity	151-191	54-58	140-165	219-250	38-48, 176-227	141-152, 976-1008	82-98
II. ORGANIZING THE CORPORATION							
A. General Corporation Laws	97-102	518-539	6-22	128-155	1-23	70-93	1-17
B. Formalities in Organizing Corporation	102-108	43-53, 539-547	123-130	156-172	137-154	93-96	76-78
C. Defects in Formation Process—"De Jure" and "De Facto" Corporations	140-151	44-47	130-140	200-218	155-175	96-101	78-87
III. PROMOTERS							
A. Introduction	130-131		180-182	182-183	118-121	101-109	98-100
B. Contracts Made by Promoters on Corporation's Behalf	131-140	265-267	182-193	183-200	121-136	817-836	
IV. POWERS OF A CORPORATION							
A. Corporate Powers	108-115	487-518	216-225	164-166	143-146, 275-279	116-135	101-130
B. Ultra Vires Transactions	108-115	516-518	216-225	172-182	278-279, 386-387, 399	116-135	104-130, 435-438
V. MANAGEMENT AND CONTROL							
A. Allocation of Powers Between Directors and Shareholders	197-206, 329-430	646-649	195-197, 697-711, 725-757	378-419, 528-543	265-274	200-246, 334-367	385-403
B. Directors	206-228, 471-555, 603-632	670-741	197-199, 225-268, 289-314, 605-608	472-479, 543-570, 633-709	332-365, 384-442, 521-541	171-230, 261-262, 275-287, 290-295, 962-977	196-224, 362-403
C. Officers	206-211, 228-241	212-219, 712-717, 721-741	199-216, 289-314, 608-609	479-492	366-442, 521-541	136-141	287-361

TEXT CORRELATION CHART (continued)

Gilbert Law Summary Corporations	Cary, Eisenberg Corporations 1988 (6th ed.—Unabridged)	Conard, Knauss, Siegel Enterprise Organization 1987 (4th ed.)	Choper, Coffee, Morris Corporations 1989 (3rd ed.)	Hamilton Corporations 1986 (3rd ed.)	Henn Corporations 1986 (2nd ed.)	Jennings, Buxbaum Corporations 1979 (5th ed.)	Vagts Corporations 1989 (3rd ed.)
D. Conflicts of Interest in Corporate Transactions	556-655	356-371, 674-676	225-289, 314-332	710-775	442-520	441-514	224-276
VI. INSIDER TRADING	720-927	892-943	459-539	859-1073	464-471, 681-698, 713-719	549-598	543-616
VII. RIGHTS OF SHAREHOLDERS							
A. Voting Rights	241-248, 270-328, 339-378, 415-430	649-664, 791-797	541-682, 697-784	528-543, 571-622	285-321, 610-625, 698-713	262-333, 387-417	362-443, 757-776
B. Restrictions on Transfer of Shares		766-778	687-697	461-472	632-649	367-386	753, 777-787
C. Shareholders' Right to Inspect Corporate Records	249-266	664-670	613-626	623-632	321-330	247-260	405, 480
D. Fiduciary Obligations of Controlling Shareholders	690-719	741-778	742-749	1031-1073	471-508	535-543, 598-617	443-454, 616-636, 739-747
E. Shareholder Suits	928-1087	555-584	785-901	1074-1128	974-1138	618-767	455-535
VIII. CAPITALIZATION OF THE CORPORATION							
A. Shares—In General	1478-1484	585-594	903-906	251-252	236-245	668-777, 1016-1022	131-136
B. Classes of Shares—Preferences	1443-1444	585-594	128, 988-990	252-259	236-240, 774-779, 799-808	268-271	131-136, 652-656, 748-749
C. Authorization and Issuance of Shares	1440	594-597	128, 903-934	259-265	236-245	769-785	131-167
D. Stock Subscriptions	1399-1404		909-934	259	125-126, 263-264	778-785	135-136
E. Consideration Required to Be Paid for Shares	1419-1437	595-596	909-925	265-268	245-251	795-816	135-169
F. Fiduciary Duty of Promoters	1404-1411		925-934	183-188	118-136	817-846	40-54
G. Preemptive Rights	1445-1466	634-642	934-951	317-329	561-567	869-892	643-652
H. Underwriting	1468-1475		335-347	296, 303-304	672-674	789-795	167, 176-187, 561-562
I. Statutes Regulating Issuance of Shares	1467-1601	597-645	333-459	294-307	671-743	786-795	167-195

TEXT CORRELATION CHART (continued)

Gilbert Law Summary Corporations	Cary, Eisenberg Corporations 1988 (6th ed.—Unabridged)	Conard, Knauss, Siegel Enterprise Organization 1987 (4th ed.)	Choper, Coffee, Morris Corporations 1989 (3rd ed.)	Hamilton Corporations 1986 (3rd ed.)	Henn Corporations 1986 (2nd ed.)	Jennings, Buxbaum Corporations 1979 (5th ed.)	Vagts Corporations 1989 (3rd ed.)
IX. DISTRIBUTIONS TO SHAREHOLDERS							
A. Dividends	1294-1375	982-1017, 1020-1024	951-1006	329-351, 370-377	744-793, 806-828	893-939	665-676
B. Redemption and Repurchase of Shares	1375-1398	982-985, 1017-1024, 1162-1169	1006-1050	351-370	793-799, 823-825	939-962	446-454, 676-683
X. FUNDAMENTAL CHANGES IN CORPORATE STRUCTURE							
A. Introduction	1088-1090	1025-1029			830-844	1009-1016	684-687
B. Appraisal Rights of Shareholders	1094-1117	1091-1099	1167-1187	747, 1139-1147	892-911	1066-1090	688-693, 743-748
C. Statutory Mergers	1118-1120, 1147-1150	1030-1034, 1045-1054	1223, 1245-1281	1129-1139	852-873	1042-1066	697-701, 718-749
D. De Facto Mergers	1125-1147	1043-1054	1249-1256, 1264-1266	1139-1147	896-898	1051-1059	688-697
E. Triangular Mergers	1150-1157	1033, 1054-1057	1247-1249,				
F. Sale of Substantially All Assets	1090-1094	1030-1031, 1043-1054	1258-1260	1139-1147	874-892	1009-1042	385-389, 443-446, 688-697
G. Amendment of Articles	1279-1283, 1290-1293	1030-1034	1187-1214	1129-1139	844-852	1016-1041	684-685, 748-749
H. Dissolution and Liquidation	444-459, 1126-1138	779-791	764-784, 1214-1215	495-504, 508-514	654-670, 799-806, 911-919	427-440	698-699, 786-793, 796
I. Limitations on Power of Controlling Shareholders to Effect Fundamental Changes in Corporate Structure	431-470, 1168-1203	1030-1031, 1043-1054	1214-1243	732-747, 1031-1073, 1129-1139	471-508, 862-871	1066-1155	717-718, 725-750
J. Tender Offers	1204-1268	1099-1162	1051-1166	785-858	924-973	1145-1156	704-717
XI. CONFLICT OF LAW PRINCIPLES	1065-1070	518-539, 547-549	123-126	156-158, 623-629	81-117, 975-980	78-89, 684-696	76-79

Corporations problems may require a determination either of the rights and liabilities of parties within the corporate structure (shareholders, officers, directors); parties outside the corporate structure (creditors, underwriters, promoters, etc.); and/or of the corporation itself.

Such rights and liabilities may arise under three separate bodies of law: First, the traditional **common law** rules governing corporations; second, **state statutes**, as most states today have enacted comprehensive codes that have altered or displaced the common law rules; and third, **federal securities laws** which, in various areas, have engrafted totally new doctrines into the law of corporations.

Analysis of corporations problems may be facilitated by considering the following factors:

A. HAS ENTITY INVOLVED ATTAINED STATUS OF A CORPORATION?

1. Has it been organized in **sufficient compliance** with statutory requirements governing the formation of a corporation?

2. If not, should the case be decided **as if** a corporation has been validly formed?

   a. Has the entity attained at least a "**de facto**" status?

   b. Or, are the facts such that a particular party may be **estopped** from challenging the corporate status?

3. If still no basis for treating as a corporation, what are the **liabilities of the members**? Are members **individually liable** for the debts incurred in the entity name?

4. Assuming that a corporation has been formed, are the circumstances such that the **corporate entity should be disregarded**? That is, should the case be decided **as if there were no corporation**?

5. Is there any issue as to **consequence of the corporate status**? The fact that a valid corporation has been formed may in itself be determinative of various issues involved (_e.g._, the corporation's right to hold title to property, or to sue in the corporate name). More frequently, however, the fact that the entity has attained corporate status is merely a stepping-stone to determination of some issue as to the validity of a corporate act or the rights and liabilities of individuals involved with the corporation.

B. ANY ISSUE AS TO VALIDITY OF CORPORATE ACT?

Examine each act undertaken by the corporation, and each act for which the corporation is sought to be held liable (_e.g._, each contract, conveyance, distribution to shareholders, etc.), with the following in mind:

1. Was the act within the **express or implied powers** of the corporation?

a. ***Source of power***? Remember that a corporation, by its very nature, has only the powers conferred upon it by its articles, bylaws, or applicable statutes or case law.

b. ***Any limitations or prohibitions*** applicable?

    (1) Consider whether the act would violate any ***statutory or certificate restriction***—*e.g.,* unlawful dividend; unlawful redemption or purchase of shares.

    (2) Of at least equal importance, would the act violate any ***equitable limitation*** on corporate powers—limitations implied by courts for the protection of minority shareholders, creditors, or the public—*e.g.,* "interested director" transactions; "inadequate" capitalization, etc.

2. Was there a ***valid exercise*** of such power by the corporation?

a. If the corporation is sought to be held liable for the act of some ***individual*** (promoter, officer, director, etc.), the issue is basically one of authority—was the individual the authorized agent of the corporation with respect to the particular act?

b. As to corporate resolutions, or other direct acts by the entity, the issue is whether the necessary "***internal procedures***" specified in the articles, bylaws, statutes, etc., have been complied with:

    (1) Valid ***adoption or ratification by the board*** of directors?

    (2) Was ***shareholder approval*** required; and if so, was it obtained?

    (3) Did ***personal interest*** of directors or shareholders disqualify their vote?

3. ***Who may challenge*** the validity of the corporate act?

a. Are the parties to the transaction (including corporation) ***estopped*** to challenge it?

b. Will a shareholders' ***derivative suit*** lie?

c. What about ***quo warranto*** proceedings by the state?

C. WHAT ARE RIGHTS AND LIABILITIES OF INDIVIDUALS INVOLVED?

1. **Characterization:** The first step in analyzing the rights and liabilities of the various individuals involved in a corporations problem is to determine their status—*e.g.,* shareholders, officers, directors, creditors, contracting parties, etc.

a. This may require a determination of the ***validity of some prior corporate act or other event*** (*supra*) upon which their status depends: *e.g.,* as to a claimed shareholder, were the shares validly issued in the first place? Were the shares validly transferred to this individual? What is the effect of any restriction on the transfer of the shares? Of failure to deliver the certificate to the transferee, etc.?

(1) In characterizing corporate acts or events, remember that ***de facto doctrines*** may be employed to avoid injustice (*e.g.,* a sale of corporate assets that has the effect of a merger may be treated as such, with appropriate requirements for shareholder approval, etc.).

b. It may not be enough merely to categorize an individual as "shareholder," "creditor," etc. ***Distinctions*** may have to be drawn between the rights and liabilities of ***persons in the same category***. For example, as a shareholder (controlling vs. minority); as a creditor (prior vs. subsequent); as a director (dissenting vs. approving, present vs. absent, "interested" vs. "noninterested").

c. Keep in mind that ***the same person may play multiple roles*** in the problem—may be both a director and a shareholder, or both an officer and creditor of the corporation, etc. In such cases, consider whether that person owes any duties to the corporation in one capacity (*e.g.,* as officer or director) that might impair or limit her rights in the other capacity (*e.g.,* as creditor or shareholder).

2. **Rights:** Once the status of each individual is ascertained, the next step is to determine the nature and extent of his or her rights with respect to whatever issues are raised in the problem. For example, as to shareholder, the problem may require analysis of the "right" to dividends; voting rights; the right to protection against majority action; etc.

3. **Liabilities:** The determination of liability usually flows from the determination of status; *e.g.,* a person who is shown to be a promoter, director, or controlling shareholder may owe various duties to the corporation, to the shareholders, to creditors, or to others.

a. Consider first what duties are prescribed by the ***articles or bylaws*** of the corporation itself.

b. Next consider what duties are prescribed by statute—with attention both to state corporations statutes and ***federal securities laws***.

c. If no statutory duties, consider whether any ***common law fiduciary duty*** is owed by such person ***to the corporation*** (*e.g.,* full disclosure as to transactions in which she has an interest; right of first refusal as to corporation opportunities; etc.); and/ or to ***any other aggrieved party*** (minority shareholders, creditors, etc.).

d. The rules may vary somewhat where ***close corporations*** are involved. By statute or case law, less formalities are required in the corporate structure, but stricter fiduciary duties are usually imposed among the shareholders.

4. **Remedies:** Consider what remedies should be made available to each possible plaintiff (including corporation), as against each possible defendant (including corporation):

a. **Form of action:** Federal or state court? Law or equity? Individual suit or class action? Suit by corporation or derivative action by shareholder?

b. **Form of relief:** Appraisal, injunction, rescission, constructive trust, specific performance, or damages? What is the measure of damages (secret profits measure; penalty measure; restitutionary measure)?

I. CHARACTERISTICS OF THE CORPORATION

chapter approach

This chapter describes the principal characteristics of corporations and compares them with those of partnerships. You may find a question on your exam asking you to determine which form of business organization would best meet particular clients' needs. In such a case, you would need to consider the advantages and disadvantages of the corporate and partnership forms. For example, you should weigh a corporation's limited liability versus a partnership's greater management and control.

A fairly common exam question involves the disregard of the corporate entity (*i.e.*, piercing the corporate veil). For suits seeking to impose liability on **shareholders**, determine whether the corporation was merely the "alter ego" of the shareholders or whether other elements, such as undercapitalization or commingling of funds, were present. In suits to pierce the wall between **affiliated corporations**, determine whether each affiliated corporation is a free-standing enterprise. Remember too that the corporate entity may also be disregarded where it is used to evade statutory or contractual obligations. Finally, in questions involving an insolvent corporation, keep in mind that a shareholder-creditor's claim may be subordinated to all other claims based on equitable grounds.

A. PRINCIPAL CHARACTERISTICS

1. **Entity Status:** [§1]   A corporation is a legal entity, separate from its shareholders, created under the authority of the legislature.

2. **Limited Liability:** [§2]   As a legal entity, a corporation is responsible for its own debts. A corporation's shareholders normally are not responsible for its debts. Their liability—or more accurately, their risk—is **limited** to the amount of their investment.

3. **Free Transferability of Interests:** [§3]   Ownership interests in a corporation are represented by shares, which are freely transferable.

4. **Centralized Management and Control:** [§4]   The management and control of a corporation's affairs are centralized in a board of directors and officers acting under the board's authority. Although the shareholders elect the board, they cannot directly control its activities. Shareholders, as such, have no power to either participate in management or determine questions within the scope of the corporation's business. These matters are for the board. [Charlestown Boot & Shoe Co. v. Dunsmore, 60 N.H. 85 (1880)] Correspondingly, shareholders, as such, have no authority to act on the corporation's behalf.

5. **Continuity of Existence:** [§5]   As a legal entity, the corporation's existence continues notwithstanding the death or incapacity of its shareholders or a transfer of its shares. Therefore, a corporation is capable of perpetual existence.

B. CORPORATIONS DISTINGUISHED FROM PARTNERSHIPS [§6]

At one time, the corporation was only one of a number of forms of organization employed for the conduct of business. Other forms included partnerships, joint stock companies, and business trusts. Today, where more than one owner is involved the only significant alternative form of business organization is a partnership.

1. **General Partnership:** [§7]   In most states, general partnerships (or "partnerships") are governed by the Uniform Partnership Act ("U.P.A."). Under the U.P.A., a partnership has the following characteristics:

   a. **Association status:** [§8]   In contrast to a corporation, a partnership is not a legal entity. Rather, it is an **association** of two or more persons who are engaged in business as co-owners. [U.P.A. §6] If strictly pursued, the theory that a partnership is not an entity would lead to highly impracticable results. For example, the partnership could not hold property in its own name. In practice, therefore, certain rules of partnership law treat a partnership **as if** it were a legal entity. For example, a partnership can hold and convey title to property in its own name. [U.P.A. §8]

   b. **Unlimited liability:** [§9]   Every partner of a general partnership is subject to unlimited personal liability for all debts of the partnership, whereas the liability of corporate shareholders is limited to the amount of their investment.

   c. **Transferability of interests:** [§10]   Unless otherwise agreed, a partner cannot transfer his partnership interest in such a way as to make the transferee a member of the partnership, except with the consent of all the remaining partners. [U.P.A. §18(q)] However, a partner can assign his **interest** in the partnership. Such an assignment does not entitle the assignee, during the continuance of the partnership, to interfere in the management or administration of the partnership business or affairs, require any information or account of partnership transactions, or inspect the partnership books. It merely entitles the assignee to receive, in accordance with his contract, the profits to which the assigning partner would otherwise be entitled. In case of a dissolution of the partnership, the assignee is entitled to receive his assignor's interest. [U.P.A. §27; Rapoport v. 55 Perry Co., 50 A.D.2d 54 (1975)]

   d. **Duration:** [§11]   Unlike a corporation, a partnership is not capable of perpetual existence. A number of circumstances will result in dissolution.

      (1) **Rightful dissolution:** [§12]   A partnership is terminable at will unless a definite term is specified or can be implied. [U.P.A. §31(1)(a); Page v. Page, 55 Cal. 2d 192 (1961)] Furthermore, because a partnership is not an entity, but only an association of the individual partners, normally it is dissolved—even before the expiration of any stated term—by the death, incapacity, or withdrawal of any partner.

      (2) **Wrongful dissolution:** [§13]   Dissolution can also be caused, **in contravention of the agreement between the partners**, by the express will of any partner at any time, or by a court, where a partner has (i) been guilty of conduct

that tends to prejudicially affect the carrying on of the business, (ii) willfully or persistently committed a breach of the partnership agreement, or (iii) otherwise so conducted himself, in matters relating to the partnership business, that it is not reasonably practicable to carry on the business in partnership with him. [U.P.A. §§31, 32]

(a) **Consequences of wrongful dissolution:** [§14] When dissolution is caused in contravention of the partnership agreement, each partner who has not wrongfully caused the dissolution has the right to damages, for breach of the agreement, from the partner who wrongfully caused the dissolution. The partners who have not wrongfully caused the dissolution, if they all desire to continue the business in the same name, may do so during the agreed term for the partnership, provided they pay to the partner who has wrongfully caused the dissolution the value of his interest in the partnership at the dissolution, less any damages, or give a bond for such payment. However, in ascertaining the value of that interest, the value of the goodwill of the business is not considered. [U.P.A. §38]

e. **Management and control:** [§15] Unlike corporate shareholders, partners have a right to participate in the management of the business. Unless otherwise provided in the partnership agreement:

(i) Every partner has a *right to participate* in the management of the partnership business.

(ii) Any difference arising as to ordinary matters connected with the partnership business may be *decided by a majority* of the partners, with each partner having one vote regardless of the relative amount of his capital contribution.

(iii) Extraordinary matters require approval by *all* the partners.

[U.P.A. §18; Summers v. Dooley, 481 P.2d 318 (Idaho 1971)]

(1) **Comment:** The right of a partner to participate in the management of the partnership's business is one reason that partners have unlimited liability. In contrast, the fact that a shareholder has no right to participate in the management of a corporation's business is one reason that shareholders have limited liability.

f. **Authority:** [§16] Unlike a corporate shareholder, every partner is an agent of the partnership for the purpose of its business. Accordingly, the act of every partner for apparently carrying on, in the usual way, the business of the partnership binds the partnership, unless the partner so acting in fact has no actual authority to act for the partnership in the particular matter, and the person with whom he is dealing knows that he has no such authority. However, an act of a partner that is *not* apparently for the carrying on of the business of the partnership in the usual way does not bind the partnership, unless the act is actually authorized by the other partners. [U.P.A. §9; Owens v. Palos Verdes Monaco, 142 Cal. App. 3d 855 (1983)]

g.   **Ownership of assets:** [§17] A partnership can hold and convey title to property in its own name. [U.P.A. §8] But even though *title* to assets may be held in the name of the partnership, the assets are said to be "owned" by the partners, in a unique form of ownership known as "tenancy in partnership." [U.P.A. §25(1)] However, the partners' "ownership" interest in partnership assets is largely theoretical, because U.P.A. section 25(2) strips away from the partners all the usual incidents of ownership, such as the right to assign and the right to bequeath.

h.   **Party to lawsuit:** [§18] Because a partnership is not an entity, in theory, a partnership cannot sue or be sued in its own name. Rather, suit on a partnership obligation must be brought by or against the individual partners. Furthermore, the partners are liable jointly, rather than jointly and severally, for nontortious partnership obligations. [U.P.A. §15] Since at common law all joint obligees must be joined as parties in an action on a joint obligation, in theory all the partners must sue or be sued in an action on a nontortious partnership obligation. This is obviously impractical. In many states, therefore, "common name" statutes provide that a partnership may sue or be sued in the partnership name. [*See, e.g.,* Cal. Corp. Code §338] Also, many states vary U.P.A. section 15, by making all partnership liabilities joint and several, or by adopting joint debtor statutes, which provide that a suit against joint obligors can proceed even if some of the joint obligors are not joined as parties. [Cal. Civ. Proc. Code §410.70]

2.   **Joint Venture:** [§19] A joint venture is essentially a species of partnership, except that a joint venture is formed for some ***limited investment or operation***, such as the construction of a single building, while a partnership is generally formed as a continuing business enterprise. There is a split of authority on the extent to which joint ventures are governed by partnership law. Some commentators argue that joint ventures are governed by all the rules applicable to partnerships, while other commentators argue that joint ventures are not entirely subject to partnership rules. The same split is found in the cases. Even under the concept that joint ventures are not subject to all the rules of partnership law, however, it is clear that they are subject to most of those rules.

3.   **Limited Partnership:** [§20] In a limited partnership, the partners are divided into two classes: ***general partners***, who have the rights and obligations incident to partnership status in an ordinary partnership, and ***limited partners***, who do not participate in the management of the partnership's business and are subject to only limited liability.

a.   **General partners:** [§21] A limited partnership must have one or more general partners. The general partners have unlimited liability for partnership obligations, as in an ordinary partnership. (However, a corporation can be a general partner. If a corporation is the sole general partner, as a practical matter no individual will have unlimited liability.)

b.   **Limited partners:** [§22] Generally, the liability of a limited partner for partnership debts is limited to the capital she contributes to the partnership. Under certain circumstances, however, a limited partner may have the liability of a general partner.

There have been three versions of the Uniform Limited Partnership Act ("U.L.P.A."). Each version has a different provision concerning the liability of limited partners to third parties, and each version is in force in at least some states.

(1) **Uniform Limited Partnership Act (1916):** [§23] Under the original U.L.P.A., a limited partner is generally not liable as a general partner unless, in addition to the exercise of her rights and powers as a limited partner, she takes part in the control of the business. [Holzman v. de Escamilla, 86 Cal. App. 2d 858 (1948)]

(2) **Revised Uniform Limited Partnership Act (1976):** [§24] Under the first Revised Uniform Limited Partnership Act ("R.U.L.P.A."), a limited partner is not liable for the obligations of a limited partnership unless she is also a general partner or, in addition to the exercise of her rights and powers as a limited partner, she takes part in the control of the business. However, if the limited partner's participation in the control of the business is not **substantially the same as the exercise of the powers of a general partner,** she is liable only to persons who transact business with the limited partnership with actual knowledge of the limited partner's participation in control.

(3) **Revised Uniform Limited Partnership Act (1985):** [§25] Under the most current version of the R.U.L.P.A., a limited partner is not liable for the obligations of a limited partnership unless, in addition to the exercise of her rights and powers as a limited partner, she participates in the control of the business. However, if the limited partner participates in the control of the business, she is liable only to persons who transact business with the limited partnership **reasonably believing,** based upon the limited partner's conduct, **that the limited partner is a general partner.** [R.U.L.P.A. §303]

C. DISREGARD OF CORPORATE ENTITY

1. **In General:** [§26] Since a corporation is a legal entity distinct from its shareholders, the rights and obligations of a corporation are normally separate from those of the shareholders. In certain cases, however, the corporate entity will be disregarded.

2. **Suits by Corporate Creditors Against Shareholders:** [§27] The most important class of case in which the corporate entity is disregarded involves suit by corporate creditors to impose liability on the shareholders for corporate obligations. In such cases, it is said, the creditors try to "pierce the corporate veil." The tests for when the corporate veil will be pierced are generally vague. Generally, a corporation will be considered a legal entity until sufficient reason to the contrary appears. However, when the concept of legal entity is used to "defeat public convenience, justify wrong, protect fraud, or defend crime, the law will regard the corporation as an association of persons." [United States v. Milwaukee Refrigerated Transit Co., 142 F. 247 (E.D. Wis. 1905)] Often, courts put the issue in terms of whether the corporation was the "alter ego" or "instrumentality" of its shareholders. A particularly important issue is whether the corporation was undercapitalized.

a. **"Alter ego":** [§28] This theory is applied where the corporation has been used by its shareholders so that, ***in reality, no separate entity has been maintained.*** The following are the major factors upon which courts focus in determining whether the corporation is the "alter ego" or "instrumentality" of its shareholders, so as to hold shareholders liable for corporate obligations:

(1) **Domination and control by shareholder:** [§29] Courts will pierce the corporate veil when another individual or corporation, owning all or most of the corporation's stock, so completely dominates not only the finances but the policy and business practice of the corporation with respect to the transaction attacked that the corporate entity had at the time of the transaction no separate mind, will, or existence of its own. Such control by these shareholders must have been used to commit fraud or wrong, perpetuate the violation of a statutory or other positive legal duty, or commit a dishonest or unjust act in contravention of the creditor's legal right. [Zaist v. Olson, 227 A.2d 552 (Conn. 1967)]

(2) **Commingling of assets:** [§30] An important factor in determining whether the corporate veil should be pierced is whether there has been a commingling of the corporation's assets and the shareholders' personal assets—*i.e.,* whether the shareholders have dealt with the assets of the corporation as if those assets were their own, as by using corporate funds to pay private debts or using other corporate assets for other private purposes.

(3) **Lack of corporate formalities:** [§31] Also relevant to piercing the corporate veil is whether basic corporate formalities were followed (*e.g.,* whether stock was issued, corporate records maintained, directors or officers elected, regular meetings of directors or shareholders held, etc.).

(a) **Statutory close corporations:** [§32] Many states today have special provisions for "statutory close corporations," which among other things permit less formal management of these corporations' affairs. (*See infra,* §§119-136.) Some of these statutes provide that the failure to hold formal meetings of the board of directors or shareholders, pursuant to shareholder agreement, is not to be considered a factor in determining whether the shareholders of a statutory close corporation should be held liable for the corporation's debts. [*See, e.g.,* Cal. Corp. Code §300(e)]

b. **Undercapitalization:** [§33] An extremely important factor in deciding whether the corporate veil should be pierced is whether the corporation was organized with sufficient resources to meet the obligations that reasonably could be expected to arise in that business. [Minton v. Cavaney, 56 Cal. 2d 576 (1961)] The issue here is not whether the shareholders have respected and maintained the corporation as a separate entity; rather, the issue is whether the shareholders should reasonably have anticipated that the corporation would be unable to pay the debts it was incurring. Undercapitalization is always a major element to be considered in determining whether to pierce the corporate veil. The rationale is that the legislature, in conferring limited liability, assumed that shareholders would in good faith put at the risk of the business unencumbered capital reasonably adequate for its prospective liabilities, or insurance for that purpose.

c. **Application:** [§34]   Cases in which the courts pierce the corporate veil to impose personal liability on shareholders are usually limited to corporations with only a small number of shareholders (including corporations that are wholly owned subsidiaries of other corporations).

3. **Piercing Corporate Wall Between Affiliated Corporations:** [§35]   A related but somewhat different problem arises where a plaintiff with a claim against one corporation seeks to satisfy the claim against the assets of an *affiliated* corporation under common ownership. Here the plaintiff is not seeking to impose individual liability on the *shareholders*, but to *aggregate* brother-sister corporations as if they were one corporation. [38 A.L.R. 3d 1102]

a. **Enterprise liability:** Some opinions suggest that this kind of aggregation may be permitted where each affiliated corporate entity is not a free-standing enterprise, but only a fragment of an enterprise that is composed of all the affiliated corporations. [Walkovszky v. Carlton, 18 N.Y.2d 414 (1966)]

b. **Rationale:** In permitting incorporation and limited liability, the legislature contemplated the incorporation of business enterprises. The separate incorporation of enterprise fragments was not within the legislative intent in granting limited liability. [Berle, The Theory of Enterprise Entity, 47 Colum. L. Rev. 343 (1947); Landers, A Unified Approach to Parent, Subsidiary and Affiliate Questions in Bankruptcy, 42 U. Chi. L. Rev. 589 (1975)]

c. **Example:** Where a parent corporation operated through three wholly owned subsidiaries, each of which actively implemented the activities of the other as part of a single business enterprise, tort liabilities incurred by any one of the subsidiaries could be imposed upon any of the other subsidiaries. [Sisco-Hamilton Co. v. Lennon, 240 F.2d 68 (7th Cir. 1957)]

4. **Use of Corporate Form to Evade Statutory or Contract Obligations:** [§36]   To prevent fraud or injustice, the courts may ignore the corporate form where it is used to evade a statutory or contractual obligation. Typically, the question in these cases is not whether the shareholders are personally liable for the debts of the corporation. Rather, the question is whether a statute or contract, which nominally applies only to the corporation, was intended to also apply to its shareholders.

a. **Example:** A statute prohibiting railroads from giving rebates to shippers was held to apply to a corporation that was not itself a shipper, but had been formed by a shipper's officers and principal shareholders for the purpose of obtaining what were, in substance, rebates. [United States v. Milwaukee Refrigerated Transit Co., *supra*, §27]

b. **Example:** A consent decree was entered against S Corporation, a subsidiary of P Corporation, which was controlled by a single family. The decree prohibited S from violating the Fair Labor Standards Act. Later, S was merged into T, another subsidiary of P. T had the same officers as S and few assets. The court held that the consent decree was binding on T, and applied not only to the employees at S's old operation but also to a new operation T began after the merger. [*Wirtz v. Ocala Gas Co.,* 336 F.2d 236 (5th Cir. 1964)]

5. **Disregard of Corporate Entity in Favor of Corporation or Its Shareholders:** [§37]   Only *third parties,* and not the corporation or its shareholders, are generally allowed to disregard the corporate entity. So, for example, a corporate defendant cannot assert an obligation running to its shareholders as a set-off in an action on a claim against the corporation.

D. SUBORDINATION OF SHAREHOLDER DEBTS—"DEEP ROCK" DOCTRINE [§38]

If a corporation becomes insolvent, debts owed by the corporation to a shareholder may be subordinated to the claims of other creditors. This means that the shareholder's debt claims against the corporation are not paid until and unless all other corporate creditors are paid—even where the shareholder's claims are secured and all other creditor claims are unsecured. [*Taylor v. Standard Gas & Electric Co.,* 306 U.S. 307 (1939)]

1. **Effect of Subordination:** [§39]   Where a shareholder's claims are subordinated, "loans" from the shareholder to the corporation are treated as if they were *invested capital* (stock), at least vis-a-vis the claims of creditors who are not shareholders.

   a. **Compare to piercing:** [§40]   Subordination differs in a crucial way from piercing the corporate veil. When the corporate veil is pierced, the shareholder is ordered to *pay* the corporation's debts. In subordination, the shareholder's claims merely get placed in line behind the claims of nonshareholder debtors.

2. **Grounds:** [§41]   The doctrine of equitable subordination is often referred to as the "Deep Rock" doctrine, named after a subsidiary corporation in the seminal case of *Taylor v. Standard Gas & Electric Co.,* 306 U.S. 307 (1939). Under the Deep Rock doctrine, when a corporation is in bankruptcy, the claim of a controlling shareholder (which can be either an individual or a parent of a bankrupt subsidiary) may, on equitable grounds, be subordinated to other claims, including the claims of preferred shareholders. [*Costello v. Fazio,* 256 F.2d 903 (9th Cir. 1958)] The major factors in determining whether to order subordination are:

   (i) *Fraud* or other wrongdoing;

   (ii) *Mismanagement* in excess of simple negligence;

   (iii) *Undercapitalization;*

   (iv) *Commingling of funds and properties;*

(v) ***Failure to develop the corporation*** into an independently profitable business, an overdependence of the corporation's business upon that of the shareholder, or both;

(vi) ***Excessive control,*** indicated by a failure to observe the formalities of separate corporations; and

(vii) Whether or not, under all the circumstances, the transaction that gave rise to the shareholder's debt claim carries the earmarks of an ***arm's length bargain.***

[Arnold v. Phillips, 117 F.2d 497 (5th Cir. 1941)]

II. ORGANIZING THE CORPORATION

chapter approach

This chapter details the creation of a corporation. If you see a question concerning the incorporation of a business, keep in mind that: (i) *articles of incorporation* must be filed by the incorporators; and (ii) to complete the organization's structure, an *organizational meeting* of either the incorporators or initial directors must be held.

Most exam questions in this area will probably concern defects in the formation process that may subject the would-be shareholders to personal liability. In analyzing such a question, ask yourself the following:

1. Was there *substantial compliance* with statutory requirements? If so, it may be a *de jure* corporation, which cannot be attacked by anyone.

2. Was there a *good faith and colorable attempt* to incorporate *and good faith actual use* of the corporate existence? If so, and if the statutory compliance was insufficient to constitute a de jure corporation vis-a-vis the state but sufficient to be treated as a corporation with respect to dealings with third parties, it is a *de facto* corporation. Remember to determine whether any statutes in the jurisdiction have abrogated the de facto doctrine.

3. Do the circumstances suggest a *corporation by estoppel*? Those who have claimed corporate status in previous transactions are generally estopped to deny that status when a suit is brought against the corporation. Likewise, a party who has dealt with the entity is estopped from claiming as a defense that the entity lacks corporate status (making it unable to sue). Here, again, as with the de facto doctrine, you should determine whether there are any statutes that affect the estoppel doctrine.

4. If there is no de jure, de facto, or estoppel corporation, who may be held liable? Under the traditional view, all would-be owners of the corporation are subject to liability. However, the modern trend is to impose liability upon only those owners who *participated* in management. Moreover, under modern statutes, liability may be limited to persons who *knew* the corporation had not been properly organized.

A. GENERAL CORPORATION LAWS [§42]

Under early English and American law, corporations were created by a "special charter" granted by the King or the legislature. Today, with only a few exceptions, corporations are created by compliance with a "general corporation law" or "business corporation law" of the state in which formation is sought.

B. FORMALITIES IN ORGANIZING CORPORATION

1. **Articles (Certificate) of Incorporation:** [§43] Typically, a corporation is organized by the *execution and filing* of articles of incorporation. The articles are executed by one

or more "incorporators." What must and what may go into the articles of incorporation depends on state law. The Revised Model Business Corporation Act ("Model Act") is fairly typical.

a. **Required provisions:** [§44]   Under section 2.02(a) of the Model Act, the articles of incorporation **must** set forth: the **corporate name,** *the* **number of shares** the corporation is authorized to issue, the street **address** of the corporation's initial registered office and the name of its initial registered agent at that office, and the name and address of **each incorporator.**

b. **Optional provisions:** [§45]   In addition, the articles of incorporation **may** set forth the names and addresses of the individuals who are to serve as the initial directors, and provisions not inconsistent with law regarding:

   (i)   **The purpose** or purposes for which the corporation is organized;

   (ii)   **Managing the business and regulating the powers** of the corporation, its board of directors, and shareholders;

   (iii)   **The definition, limitation, and regulation of the powers** of the corporation, its board of directors, and shareholders;

   (iv)   **A par value** for authorized shares or classes of shares;

   (v)   **The imposition of personal liability** on shareholders for the debts of the corporation to a specified extent and upon specified conditions; and

   (vi)   **Any provision that is required or permitted** to be set forth in the bylaws.

   [Revised Model Business Corp. Act ("RMBCA") §2.02(b) (1984)]

c. **Purpose clause:** [§46]   Before the adoption of modern statutes, the clauses in the articles of incorporation that stated the purpose for which the corporation was formed tended to be extremely elaborate, to avoid the problem of ultra vires (*see infra,* §98). Under modern statutes, elaborate purpose clauses are no longer necessary. For example, under the Model Act, every corporation has "the purpose of engaging in any lawful business unless a more limited purpose is set forth in the articles of incorporation." [RMBCA §3.01(a)] Similarly, under the Delaware statute, it is sufficient to state, either alone or with other business purposes, that the purpose of the corporation is to engage in any lawful activity for which corporations may be organized. All lawful acts and activities are thus within the purposes of the corporation, except for express limitations, if any. [Del. Gen. Corp. Law §102(e)]

2. **Organizational Meeting:** [§47]   Filing the articles in proper form creates the corporation. However, several steps are required to complete a corporation's structure. These steps are taken at organizational meetings of either the incorporators or the initial board of directors named in the articles, if the statute provides for naming the initial board this way. [*See, e.g.,* Del. Gen. Corp. Law §§107, 108]

a. **Matters determined at organizational meeting of incorporators:** [§48]   If initial directors are not named in the articles of incorporation, the incorporators, at their organizational meeting, will typically adopt bylaws, fix the number of directors, and elect directors to serve until the first shareholders' meeting. The directors, at their first meeting, would then adopt a corporate seal and form of stock certificate, authorize the issuance of stock, elect officers, and designate the corporation's bank.

b. **Matters determined at organizational meeting of initial directors:** [§49]   If initial directors are named in the certificate of incorporation, at the organizational meeting the initial directors will typically adopt bylaws, elect officers, adopt a form of corporate seal and a form of stock certificate, authorize the issuance of shares to designated persons at designated prices, and designate the corporation's bank.

C. DEFECTS IN FORMATION PROCESS—"DE JURE" AND "DE FACTO" CORPORATIONS

1. **In General:** [§50]   Sometimes there is a defect or irregularity in the process of forming a corporation; *e.g.,* one of the named incorporators may not have signed the certificate of incorporation, the certificate may fail to include a required provision in proper form, or the certificate may not have been properly filed. The issue then arises of the effect of such a defect on corporate status. This issue is usually put in terms of whether the corporation exists "de jure," "de facto," "by estoppel," or not at all.

   a. **Liability actions:** [§51]   This issue arises most commonly (but not exclusively) in cases in which a third party seeks to impose personal liability on would-be shareholders on the ground that corporate status was not attained and, therefore, neither was limited liability.

   b. **Quo warranto actions:** [§52]   Another method for testing corporate status is through a "quo warranto" proceeding brought by the state. Most states provide by statute for proceedings in the nature of quo warranto, often without using that name. [*See, e.g.,* N.Y. Bus. Corp. Law §109; Cal. Corp. Code §180(a)]

2. **De Jure Corporation:** [§53]   A de jure corporation is a corporation organized in compliance with the requirements of the state of incorporation. Its status as a corporation cannot be attacked by anyone, not even by the state in a quo warranto proceeding. [People v. Ford, 128 N.E. 479 (Ill. 1920)]

   a. **"Substantial compliance" sufficient:** [§54]   Most courts hold that perfect compliance with statutory requirements is not required for de jure status; instead, "substantial compliance" will suffice. Therefore, an enterprise that fails to meet all the requirements for incorporation may nevertheless be a corporation "de jure" if the noncompliance is extremely insubstantial. What constitutes substantial compliance is determined on a case-by-case basis, according to the nature of the unsatisfied requirement and the extent to which compliance has been attempted. [People v. Montecito Water Co., 97 Cal. 276 (1893)]

(1) **Example:** If the articles were properly filed except that the address for the corporation's principal place of business inadvertently states the wrong street number, there would undoubtedly be "substantial compliance."

b. **Distinction between "mandatory" and "directory" requirements:** [§55] Some courts hold that for a corporation to attain de jure status, there must be exact compliance with all "mandatory" statutory requirements, but that failure to comply with statutory requirements that are only "directory" will not preclude de jure status. [J.W. Butler Paper Co. v. Cleveland, 77 N.E. 99 (Ill. 1906)] Whether a particular requirement is "mandatory" or "directory" is a matter of statutory interpretation. Factors to be considered include the wording of the statute (*e.g.,* "must," "shall," or "may") and the relative importance of the provision.

(1) **Example:** The attorney general filed an information in the nature of a quo warranto against three incorporators who had failed to comply with a statutory requirement that the statement of incorporation be sealed. The incorporators had filed on the secretary of state's forms, which neither contained nor mentioned a seal. The court concluded that a de jure status had been attained: The provision for a seal was only directory, because the purpose of the statute was to make a public record, and a seal did not further that purpose. [People v. Ford, *supra,* §53]

3. **De Facto Corporation:** [§56] A de facto corporation is said to exist where there was insufficient compliance to constitute a de jure corporation vis-a-vis the **state**, but the steps taken toward formation were sufficient to treat the enterprise as a corporation with respect to its **dealings with third parties.** In such cases, the corporate status can be invalidated by the state, but not by creditors or other persons who have had dealings with the enterprise.

a. **Requirements:** [§57] A de facto corporation requires a good faith and colorable attempt to incorporate, and good faith actual use of the corporate existence (*e.g.,* contracting in the corporate name).

(1) **Example:** On November 21, the corporate name of Sunshine Greenery, Inc. was reserved for B by the secretary of state. On December 3, B and C executed a certificate of incorporation for that corporation. The certificate was sent by mail to the secretary of state on that same date, with a check for the filing fee, but for some unexplained reason the certificate was not officially filed until December 18, two days after the execution of a lease by the corporation. The corporation was a de facto corporation, and therefore B and C were not personally liable to the lessor. [Cantor v. Sunshine Greenery, Inc., 398 A.2d 571 (N.J. 1979)]

b. **Quo warranto:** [§58] A quo warranto proceeding can be maintained even against a de facto corporation, because the de facto theory is a defense only against a collateral attack on corporate status—in effect, only against a challenge raised by private parties—not against a challenge by the state itself.

4. **Corporation by Estoppel:** [§59]   In appropriate cases, a party may be estopped from challenging the corporate status of an enterprise—even though the enterprise has not achieved de jure or de facto status—on the ground of "estoppel." The estoppel principle is not a single theory, but a cluster of different rules.

   a. **Shareholders estopped to deny corporate status:** [§60]   The shareholders of a nominal corporation, having claimed corporate status in an earlier transaction with a third party, are estopped to deny that status in a suit brought by the third party against the corporation.

   b. **Technical defenses:** [§61]   Sometimes the question of corporate status is raised in a technical procedural context. For example, in a suit brought against a third party by a nominal corporation, the third party may seek to raise the defense that the nominal corporation is not really a corporation and, therefore, cannot sue in a corporate name. The courts tend to regard such a defense as nonmeritorious and hold that the third party is estopped from raising the defense, on the ground that the defense is technical and would defeat the interests of justice.

   c. **Personal liability of would-be shareholders:** [§62]   A third party who has dealt with an enterprise as a corporation may seek to impose personal liability on would-be shareholders, who in turn raise estoppel as a defense. Here the issue is whether, as a matter of equity, the third party, having dealt with the enterprise as if it were a corporation, should be prevented (*i.e.*, estopped) from treating it as anything else. Less in the way of corporateness must be shown to establish a corporation by estoppel than to establish a de facto corporation.

      (1) **Example:** Where a business is not a corporation because, without the knowledge of the would-be shareholders, their attorney negligently failed to file the certificate of incorporation before the business entered into a transaction with a third party, the third party who dealt with the business as if it were a corporation is estopped from suing the would-be shareholders. [Cranson v. IBM Corp., 200 A.2d 33 (Md. 1964)]

      (2) **Tort claims:** [§63]   The basis of the estoppel theory in liability cases is that the third party has dealt with the business as if it were a corporation. Therefore, the theory does not apply to tort claimants or other involuntary creditors.

5. **Who May Be Held Liable:** [§64]   Where a would-be corporation is neither a de jure or a de facto corporation nor a corporation by estoppel, the courts have split on whether *all* of the would-be "shareholders" may be held personally liable for debts incurred in the corporation's name.

   a. **Traditional view:** [§65]   Older decisions imposed personal liability against all owners of the would-be corporation, on the theory that if the enterprise is not a corporation, it is a partnership, and therefore the would-be shareholders are general partners. [Harrill v. Davis, 168 F. 187 (8th Cir. 1909)]

b. **Modern trend:** [§66] The modern trend, however, imposes personal liability against only those owners who *actively participated* in the management of the enterprise. Those owners are held personally liable as if they were partners, but passive investors are not. [Baker v. Bates-Street Shirt Co., 6 F.2d 854 (1st Cir. 1925)]

6. **Effect of Statutes:** [§67] A number of statutes directly or indirectly address the de facto and estoppel doctrines.

   a. **Effect of statutes on de facto doctrine:** [§68] The prior version of the Model Act provided that persons who act as a corporation without the authority of a properly issued certificate of incorporation are jointly and severally liable for all debts and liabilities incurred as a result of that action. [Model Business Corp. Act §146 (1979)] The comment to this section stated that the section was designed "to prohibit the application of any theory of de facto incorporation." [Model Business Corp. Act §146, comment (1979)] Accordingly, in those states with statutes based on this provision, the de facto doctrine was abolished. [Timberline Equipment Co. v. Davenport, 514 P.2d 1109 (Or. 1973); Robertson v. Levy, 197 A.2d 443 (D.C. 1964); *but see* Vincent Drug Co. v. Utah State Tax Commission, 407 P.2d 683 (Utah 1965)]

      (1) **Revised Model Business Corporation Act:** [§69] The Revised Model Business Corporation Act, approved in 1984, makes a significant change in the prior Model Act language. Under the Revised Model Act, only persons acting as or on behalf of a corporation who *know* there was no incorporation are jointly and severally liable for all liabilities created while so acting. [RMBCA §2.04] The requirement that a defendant *knew* there was no incorporation protects would-be shareholders of defectively formed corporations against liability under a variety of circumstances. For example, the requirement affords protection in cases where the defendant honestly and reasonably but erroneously believes the articles were filed [Cranson v. IBM Corp., *supra*, §62], or where the defendant mails the certificate of incorporation to be filed, but either the letter is delayed or the secretary of state's office does not file the certificate after receiving it, and meanwhile a contract is entered into [Cantor v. Sunshine Greenery, Inc., *supra*, §57].

   b. **Effect of statutes on estoppel doctrine:** [§70] The effect of section 146 of the prior Model Act and section 2.04 of the Revised Model Act on the estoppel doctrine is an unsettled point. [*See* Robertson v. Levy, *supra;* Thompson & Green Machinery Co. v. Music City Lumber Co., 683 S.W.2d 340 (Tenn. 1984)—section 146 abrogates the estoppel doctrine; *but see* Namerdy v. Generalcar, 217 A.2d 109 (D.C. 1966)—contra; Timberline Equipment Co. v. Davenport, *supra*, §68—raises but does not resolve the issue]

   c. **Effect of statutes on the issue of liability of passive investors:** [§71] Section 146 of the prior version of the Model Act, which imposes liability on all persons who act as a corporation without a properly issued certificate of incorporation, has been held not to include persons whose only connection with the enterprise is as an investor. Instead, the provision is interpreted to reach only those persons who not only have an investment in the enterprise, but also exercise control or actively participate in policy and operational decisions. [Timberline Equipment Co. v. Davenport, *supra*; Flanagan v. Jackson Wholesale Building Supply Co., 461 So. 2d 761 (Miss. 1984)] Presumably, section 2.04 of the Revised Model Act will be interpreted in much the same way.

III.   PROMOTERS

chapter approach

Promoters participate in the formation of the corporation. Most exam questions about promoters concern the rights and liabilities of the promoter and the corporation with respect to contracts entered into by the promoter on the corporation's behalf prior to formation of the corporation. Your approach to this type of question should be as follows:

1.   The first issue to consider is whether the corporation is liable pursuant to the ***American rule***. Under the American rule, the corporation is liable if it ***ratifies or adopts*** the contract.

2.   The second issue to consider is the ***rights and liabilities of the promoter.*** Recall that a promoter is not personally liable on these contracts if he has made it explicit that he is contracting solely on behalf of the proposed corporation. But if this is not explicit, the promoter is liable. If the corporation is never formed, the promoter may be permitted to enforce the contract himself; but if a corporation is formed and it adopts or ratifies the contract, only the corporation may enforce it.

A.   INTRODUCTION

1.   **Definition:** [§72]   A promoter is one who participates in the formation of a corporation. The promoter usually arranges compliance with the legal requirements to form a corporation, secures initial capitalization, and enters into necessary contracts on behalf of the corporation before it is formed. Often the promoter remains active in the corporation after it comes into existence.

2.   **Fiduciary Duties to Each Other:** [§73]   Prior to formation of the corporation, the promoters are regarded as joint venturers (similar to partners) and for that reason owe to each other a duty of ***full disclosure*** and ***fair dealing*** as to all matters pertaining to the corporation.

B.   CONTRACTS MADE BY PROMOTERS ON CORPORATION'S BEHALF [§74]

Litigation frequently arises from contracts entered into by promoters on the corporation's behalf prior to formation of the corporation. For example, the promoter negotiates a lease in the name of the proposed corporation on property to be used as its principal office. What are the rights and liabilities of the corporation and the promoters on this lease?

1.   **Rights and Liabilities of Corporation**

   a.   **English rule:** [§75]   Under the English rule, the corporation cannot be held liable on contracts made on its behalf prior to incorporation—even where the corporation has adopted or ratified the contract. The corporation may only become a party by entering into a new contract or by formal novation.

(1) **Rationale:** Under agency law, the promoter cannot be said to be acting as agent of the corporation, because the corporation was not yet in existence and therefore could not have authorized the acts. Nor can a subsequent ratification by the corporation make it a party to the contract, since ratification relates back to the time the contract was made and the corporation was not then in existence. [Kelner v. Baxter, 2 L.R.-C.P. 174 (1866)]

(2) **Quasi-contractual liability:** [§76] However, courts following this view recognize recovery in quasi-contract against the corporation for the value of any goods or services that it chose to accept after it came into being. If the corporation had a choice to accept or reject the services offered under a contract negotiated by the promoters, and chose to accept them, it would constitute unjust enrichment if the corporation were not required to pay the reasonable value thereof.

(3) **Massachusetts rule:** [§77] Massachusetts has been thought to follow the English rule [Abbott v. Hapgood, 22 N.E. 907 (Mass. 1899)], but a more recent decision suggests that the corporation can be held liable on a promoter's contract if the other party performs and the corporation knowingly accepts the benefits of the contract [Framingham Savings Bank v. Szabo, 617 F.2d 897 (1st Cir. 1980)].

b. **American rule:** [§78] Under the American rule, a corporation can be held liable on contracts negotiated on its behalf by its promoters prior to incorporation, but only if the corporation *ratifies or adopts* the contract. The ratification may be express or may be implied.

(1) **Rationale:** Some courts treat the promoter's contract as a continuing offer to the corporation, which it is free to accept or reject. Basically, however, the courts have developed a rule in response to commercial needs surrounding the formation of corporations.

(2) **What constitutes ratification or adoption by corporation:** [§79] Corporations may *expressly* ratify or adopt promoters' contracts by a resolution by the board of directors. The more difficult problem is to determine the sufficiency of the acts constituting implied ratification or adoption of promoters' contracts. Usually, some affirmative act by the corporation is required, *e.g.,* accepting benefits or making use of services or materials obtained under the contract with knowledge of the contract. [D.A. McArthur v. Times Printing Co., 51 N.W. 216 (Minn. 1892)]

(a) **Example:** The corporation is clearly charged with knowledge of the promoters' contracts if the board of directors is wholly composed of promoters with such knowledge. And it *may* be deemed to have knowledge if the promoter who made the contract has become a director of the corporation or is a controlling shareholder. [Chartrand v. Barney's Club, Inc., 380 F.2d 97 (9th Cir. 1967)]

    (b) **Note:** There is a split of authority on whether mere use of the corporate charter is sufficient "acceptance" of benefits to hold the corporation liable on pre-incorporation contracts for the services essential to its formation (attorneys' fees to incorporate, etc.). [Kridelbaugh v. Aldrehn Theatres Co., 191 N.W. 503 (Iowa 1923)]

  (3) **Quasi-contractual liability:** [§80] Even where the corporation expressly disavows its promoters' contracts, it cannot with impunity keep the benefits obtained thereby. Quasi-contractual liability can be imposed to the extent of the fair value of the services or materials obtained, although some courts do not impose quasi-contractual liability for pre-incorporation services that it had no real option to reject (*e.g.*, attorneys' fees, filing costs, etc.). [David v. Southern Import Wine Co., 171 So. 180 (La. 1936)]

 c. **Corporation's right to enforce contract:** [§81] Under both the English and American rules, the corporation may enforce the contract against the party with whom the promoter contracted, if it chooses to do so.

  (1) *Under the English rule* (no contract with corporation), the corporation must sue as *assignee* of the promoters.

  (2) *Under the American rule*, the corporation's adoption of the contract makes it a party thereto so that it can maintain the action directly. [Builders' Duntile Co. v. W.E. Dunn Manufacturing, 17 S.W.2d 715 (Ky. 1929)]

2. Rights and Liabilities of Promoters

 a. **Liability on pre-incorporation contract:** [§82] Where the corporation never comes into existence, rejects the pre-formation contracts negotiated for it by its promoters, or ratifies the contract but never performs or pays as agreed, the other party to the contract frequently attempts to hold the promoters personally liable.

  (1) **No liability:** [§83] If the contracting party *clearly intended* to contract with the proposed corporation and *not* with the promoters individually, it must rely solely on the credit of the proposed corporation and has no claim against the promoters individually. [Quaker Hill, Inc. v. Parr, 364 P.2d 1056 (Colo. 1961)]

    (a) **Rationale:** Where this is so, there really is *no contract* at all prior to the corporation's becoming a party thereto—only a continuing offer to be communicated to the corporation after its formation, which it can then accept (expressly or impliedly) or reject.

(2) **Liability:** [§84] However, where the promoters have *not* made it explicit that they are contracting solely on behalf of the proposed corporation, courts tend to hold the promoters *personally liable* on pre-formation contracts. This is particularly true where such contracts require the other party to render *performance prior* to formation of the corporation. [Stanley J. How & Associates v. Boss, 222 F. Supp. 936 (S.D. Iowa 1963)]

    (a) **Rationale:** Various theories for holding promoters liable have been advanced. Some courts talk about the promoters having impliedly warranted their authority, or having impliedly warranted that the corporation would be formed and, once formed, would adopt the pre-formation contract. Other courts talk about the promoters remaining personally liable as surety or guarantor of the corporation's performance.

    (b) **Note:** Where the promoters have been held personally liable on pre-formation contracts, they have a right to be *reimbursed* or indemnified by the corporation for their expenses or losses, at least to the extent of any *benefits* received by the corporation under the contracts.

b. **Right to enforce against other party:** [§85] Only a few cases have dealt with an attempt by a promoter to enforce a contract made by him for a corporation to be formed. At least where the corporation was *never formed*, the promoter may be permitted to enforce the contract on the theory that since the promoter could have been held liable in event of breach (*see* above), there was sufficient "mutuality" to allow him to enforce it against the other party. Unless the contract was expressly limited to the proposed corporation, the failure to incorporate is not deemed an essential condition to the other party's duty to perform. [Erskine v. Chevrolet Motors Co., 117 S.E. 706 (N.C. 1923)]

(1) **Compare:** On the other hand, if the corporation is formed and adopts or ratifies the contract, it alone has the right to enforce the contract; thus, the promoter cannot sue. [Speedway Realty Co. v. Grasshoff Realty Corp., 216 N.E.2d 845 (Ind. 1966)]

IV.   POWERS OF THE CORPORATION

chapter approach

Generally, corporations have those powers expressly set forth in their articles of incorporation and conferred by statute, and those implied powers necessary to carry out the express powers. Transactions beyond the purposes and powers of the corporation are ultra vires.

Although exam questions often raise the issue of ultra vires transactions, it is not usually a viable plea. It is no defense to tort or criminal actions. In contract actions, there are only three common situations where ultra vires may be allowed:

(1) At common law, if a contract is **purely executory**, either party can raise ultra vires as a defense. _But note:_ Most states have **statutes** that prohibit the use of ultra vires as a defense.

(2) Most statutes allow the corporation to **sue directors or officers** for damages for their ultra vires acts.

(3) Most statutes also allow shareholders to **enjoin performance** of an ultra vires contract.

A.   CORPORATE POWERS

1. **Express and Implied Powers:** [§86]   At one time, a corporation's powers were generally limited to those powers set forth in the corporation's articles of incorporation ("express powers") and those powers reasonably necessary to accomplish the purposes set forth in its articles of incorporation ("implied powers"). This approach gave rise to various ultra vires issues and verbose articles of incorporation.

2. **Modern Statutes:** [§87]   Modern statutes avoid these problems by setting out a long list of powers conferred on every corporation, whether or not stated in the articles of incorporation. Under the Delaware statute, which is typical, a corporation is granted the following express powers, among others:

   (i)   To have **perpetual succession** (_i.e.,_ perpetual existence);

   (ii)   To **sue and be sued**;

   (iii) To have a **corporate seal**;

   (iv)   To **acquire, hold, and dispose of personal and real property**;

   (v)   To **appoint officers**;

   (vi)   To **adopt and amend bylaws**;

(vii) To **conduct business** inside and outside the state;

(viii) To establish **pension and other incentive and compensation plans**;

(ix) To **acquire, hold, vote, and dispose of securities** in other corporations;

(x) To make **contracts of guaranty and suretyship**;

(xi) To **participate with others in any corporation, partnership, or other association** of any kind that it would have power to conduct by itself, whether or not such participation involves sharing or delegating control with others; and

(xii) To **make donations** for the public welfare or for charitable, scientific, or educational purposes, and in time of war or other national emergency, in aid thereof.

[Del. Gen. Corp. Law §122]

3. **Traditional Problem Areas:** [§88] The last three powers are the most significant, in the sense that the existence of these powers was deemed questionable under the older statutes, which did not specifically confer them.

   a. **Guaranties:** [§89] The older statutes typically did not explicitly confer upon corporations the power to guarantee the debts of others. Cases under these statutes held that the exercise of such a power was normally ultra vires. Modern statutes explicitly permit a corporation to make contracts of guaranty and suretyship. Like other corporate powers, however, this power can be exercised only in furtherance of the corporate business (*e.g.*, by guaranteeing a loan to a customer to enable the customer to buy the corporation's product).

   b. **Participation in a partnership:** [§90] The older statutes did not explicitly confer upon corporations the power to be a partner. Cases under these statutes held that a corporation had no implied power to enter into a partnership (although a corporation could enter into a joint venture, which is usually temporary in nature and for a limited purpose). The rationale was that in a partnership the corporation would be bound by the acts of its partners, who are not its duly appointed agents and officers, and that such responsibility cannot be delegated by the board. [60 A.L.R.2d 920] Modern statutes make these cases moot by explicitly conferring upon corporations the power to be a partner.

   c. **Donations:** [§91] The law concerning donations and other uses of the corporation's resources for public welfare, charitable, educational, or like purposes, in the absence of an explicit statutory power, has never been completely well-defined, partly because it is in a process of continual growth.

      (1) **General rule:** [§92] The general rule is that the objective of the business corporation is to conduct business activity with a view to corporate profit and shareholder gain. [Dodge v. Ford Motor Co., 170 N.W. 668 (Mich. 1919)]

(2) **Traditional view:** [§93]   Some cases, mostly arising at or before the turn of the century, built either on that rule or on a strict notion of ultra vires (or on both) to preclude use of corporate resources, by donation or otherwise, for humanitarian, educational, philanthropic, or other public activities. [*See, e.g.,* Brinson Railway v. Exchange Bank, 85 S.E. 634 (Ga. 1915); McCrory v. Chambers, 48 Ill. App. 445 (1892)] Normally, however, use of corporate resources for public welfare, humanitarian, philanthropic, or educational purposes can be justified on traditional profit grounds (*e.g.,* on the ground that it increases good will). Accordingly, this strict position was modified by cases holding that a corporation *could* use its resources for such purposes if the use was likely to produce a *direct benefit* to the corporation. [Whetstone v. Ottawa University, 10 Kan. 240 (1874); Corning Glass Works v. Lucase, 37 F.2d 798 (D.C. Cir. 1929), *cert. denied,* 281 U.S. 742 (1930)]

(3) **Modern view:** [§94]   Modern cases have in effect dropped this direct-benefit test, and permit the use of corporate resources for public welfare, humanitarian, educational, or philanthropic purposes without requiring a showing that a direct benefit is likely. Some cases reach this result by treating such uses as *profit-maximizing* even where the evidence looks the other way. [Shlensky v. Wrigley, 237 N.E.2d 776 (Ill. 1968); Union Pacific Railroad v. Trustees, Inc., 329 P.2d 398 (Utah 1958); Kelly v. Bell, 266 A.2d 878 (Del. 1970)] Other cases take the more direct approach that the use of corporate resources for such purposes is a *legitimate end* in itself, on the ground that (i) activity that maintains a healthy social system necessarily serves a long-run corporate purpose; or (ii) there is an independent social policy to maintain diversified centers of charitable, educational, etc., activity, and full effectuation of that policy depends upon, and therefore justifies, corporate support. [*See, e.g.,* A.P. Smith Manufacturing Co. v. Barlow, 98 A.2d 581 (N.J. 1953); Union Pacific Railroad v. Trustees, Inc., *supra*]

  (a) **Limitation—reasonableness test:** [§95]   Generally, though, the corporation's ability to make donations is not unlimited. The modern cases have invoked a limit of *reasonableness* on the use of corporate resources for public welfare, humanitarian, educational, or philanthropic purposes.

(4) **Statutes:** [§96]   Many statutes, like Delaware's, explicitly confer upon corporations the power to make donations for charitable (etc.) purposes. Like all corporate powers, this power is also subject to an implied limit of reasonableness. Thus, it would still be improper to convert a business corporation into a charitable institution.

(5) **Restatement view:** [§97]   According to the American Law Institute's Principles of Corporate Governance, the "objective of the business corporation is to conduct business activities with a view to corporate profit and shareholder gain, except that, even if corporate profit and shareholder gain are not thereby enhanced, the corporation, in the conduct of its business . . . may devote resources, within reasonable limits, to public welfare, humanitarian, educational, and philanthropic purposes." [A.L.I. Principles of Corporate Governance §2.01 (Tent. Draft No. 2)]

B. ULTRA VIRES TRANSACTIONS

1. **In General:** [§98]   An "ultra vires" transaction is one that is ***beyond the purposes and powers*** of the corporation.

   a. **Implied powers:** [§99]   It was established even in early cases that corporate powers could be implied as well as explicit. [*See* Sutton's Hospital Case, 10 Coke 23a (1613)] The courts eventually became very liberal in finding implied powers, including implied powers to enter into business activities not specified in the articles. Thus, in *Jacksonville, Mayport, Pablo Railway & Navigation Co. v. Hooper,* 160 U.S. 514 (1896), the Supreme Court held that a Florida company whose purpose was to run a railroad could also engage in leasing and running a resort hotel, on the ground that the latter activity was auxiliary or incidental to the former.

   b. **Effect of shareholder ratification:** [§100]   Even where an ultra vires defense would otherwise be allowed, under American common law a corporation was not permitted to assert the defense if all shareholders had given their consent to or acquiesced in the contract.

2. **Tort Actions:** [§101]   Under the modern rule, ultra vires is ***no defense*** to tort liability. A corporation cannot escape civil damages by claiming that it had no legal power to commit the wrongful act. [Nims v. Mt. Herman Boys' School, 35 N.E. 776 (Mass. 1893)]

   a. **Rationale:** The fact that a wrongful act exceeded the powers conferred upon the corporation by statute or its articles should not result in the loss falling on the innocent injured party, assuming the act was one for which the corporation would otherwise be civilly liable.

3. **Criminal Actions:** [§102]   Similarly, it is ***no defense*** to criminal liability that a corporate act was beyond the corporation's authorized powers.

4. **Contract Actions—Common Law:** [§103]   The most substantial questions at common law arose where a corporation entered into a contract that was not authorized under its articles of incorporation or the relevant statute. The extent to which a plea of ultra vires was allowed in contract actions depended largely on the extent to which the contract had been performed.

   a. **Contract purely executory:** [§104]   Where there had been no performance on either side, the defense of ultra vires could be raised by the corporation or by the party with whom it had contracted. The rationale was that since the contract was beyond the corporation's powers, it was unenforceable ***against*** the corporation; and under the doctrine of mutuality of obligation, the contract was therefore unenforceable ***by*** the corporation. [Ashbury Railway Carriage & Iron Co. v. Riche, 7 L.R.-E. & I. App. 653 (1875)]

   b. **Contract fully performed on both sides:** [§105]   If the contract was fully performed by both parties, neither party could rescind on the ground that the contract had been ultra vires. The courts left the parties where they were. [Long v. Georgia Pacific Railway, 8 So. 706 (Ala. 1891)]

    c. **Contract partly performed:** [§106] The difficult case occurred where the contract had been fully or partly performed on one side, and the nonperforming party then sought to assert ultra vires as a defense to enforcement of its side of the contract.

        (1) **Majority view—no defense:** [§107] The majority view held that the nonperforming party, having received a benefit, was estopped to assert a defense of ultra vires. [Joseph Schlitz Brewing Co. v. Missouri Poultry & Game Co., 229 S.W. 813 (Mo. 1921)]

        (2) **Minority view (federal rule):** [§108] Some cases held that the nonperforming party could assert ultra vires, on the ground that the contract was void ab initio and could not be enforced. However, even cases that adopted this minority rule recognized that the party who had received a benefit from the part performance would be liable in *quasi-contract* for the value of the benefit. [Central Transportation Co. v. Pullman's Palace Car Co., 139 U.S. 24 (1891)]

5. **Statutes:** [§109] Most states now have statutes that severely curtail the doctrine of ultra vires. The most common type of statute precludes the *parties* to an unauthorized contract from raising ultra vires as a defense, but permits ultra vires to be raised by a *shareholder* in a suit to *enjoin* performance of the contract. [RMBCA §3.04; Del. Gen. Corp. Law §124]

    a. **Corporation and third party:** [§110] Under this type of statute, neither the corporation nor the third party with whom it contracts can assert ultra vires as a *defense* to the other's suit to enforce the contract; and this is true regardless of whether the contract is still executory or has been performed in whole or in part.

    b. **Suit against officers or directors:** [§111] However, if the contract has been performed and has resulted in a loss to the corporation, the corporation can sue the officers or directors for damages for exceeding their authority. And, if the corporation refuses to sue, a shareholder may bring a derivative suit (*see infra,* §592).

    c. **Suit by the state:** [§112] These statutes do not prohibit the state from suing to enjoin the corporation from transacting unauthorized business.

    d. **Suit by shareholders:** [§113] These statutes permit a shareholder of the corporation to sue to *enjoin performance* of an ultra vires contract, provided all parties to the contract are made parties to the action and the court finds that injunctive relief would be equitable.

        (1) **Damages:** [§114] If an injunction is granted, the court may allow compensation to the injured party for any damages resulting from noncompletion of the contract, *exclusive of lost profits.*

(2) **Interpretation:** [§115]   These statutes do not provide that the court *must* enjoin an ultra vires contract upon the suit of a shareholder, but only that the court may do so if an injunction would be equitable. A shareholder who actively participated in authorizing an ultra vires contract, or who purchased a corporation knowing it had made such a contract, would probably be unable to enjoin performance of the contract, since an injunction in favor of such a shareholder would normally be inequitable. [Goodman v. Ladd Estate Co., 427 P.2d 102 (Or. 1967)]

V.   MANAGEMENT AND CONTROL

___chapter approach___

This chapter covers a great deal of material, so to help you study, the most likely topics for exam questions are discussed below.

1. **Allocation of Powers Between Directors and Shareholders:** Remember that generally the power to manage the business of the corporation belongs to the board of directors, not the shareholders. However, in exam questions, look for indications of a *close corporation* (*e.g.,* small number of shareholders, no general market for stock, limitations on admission of shareholders, etc.), which may mean that shareholder participation in management is acceptable.

2. **Directors:** A likely topic for an exam question concerning directors is whether the directors have acted properly and effectively. Ask yourself the following questions: Was there proper *notice* of the meeting? Was a *quorum* present? Was the action *approved by the necessary majority*? If there was an *agreement* affecting board decisions, was it valid?

    A question concerning directors may also test your knowledge of the rights, duties, and liabilities of directors. Keep in mind that although directors owe the corporation the duty to exercise the care of *ordinarily prudent and diligent persons* in like positions under similar circumstances, they are *not* liable for mere bad business judgment. If a director fails to exercise the proper measure of care, he is personally liable for the losses resulting from the breach. A director is not liable for the wrongful acts of other directors or officers, unless he participated in the act, was negligent in discovering the misconduct, or was negligent in appointing the wrongdoer.

3. **Officers:** Any question concerning officers (other than one dealing with a conflict or "insider" status, *see* below) will probably center on the officer's authority to act on behalf of the corporation. Note that an officer may have *actual or apparent authority*. Even an unauthorized act may bind the corporation, if the act is *ratified* by the board. Remember that officers owe a duty of care and loyalty to the corporation similar to that owed by directors.

4. **Conflicts of Interest in Corporate Transactions:** This is a popular exam topic. Consider the five basic conflicts of interest situations:

    a. **Business dealings with corporations:** Whenever you see a question where a corporation contracts either directly with a director or officer, or with a company in which the director or officer is financially interested, you should analyze it as follows:

        (1) May the director *participate* in the meeting authorizing the transaction? Most statutes permit an interested director to be counted in a quorum and vote.

        (2) Was there *full disclosure* to an *independent* board, *and* is the transaction *fair*? Most courts hold that an interested director transaction is voidable by the corporation only if it is unfair. For the transaction to be fair, the director must make a full disclosure to an independent board, and the transaction must be fair in price, terms, or other conditions. The burden of proof is on the interested director.

       (3)   Was there *shareholder ratification*, and if so, by how many? Unanimous shareholder ratification after full disclosure estops the corporation from challenging the transaction. Ratification by a majority of shareholders carries less weight, particularly when the interested director owns most of the shares.

       (4)   What is the appropriate *remedy*? If the interested director did not act in bad faith or profit personally, rescission may be the corporation's only remedy. Otherwise, the corporation may seek damages from the director.

   b.   **Interlocking directorates:** If the question concerns a contract between corporations having common directors, remember that most jurisdictions permit these transactions, subject to the same general requirements as *interested director transactions*.

   c.   **Corporate opportunity doctrine:** A director's fiduciary duty of loyalty bars her from personally taking any business opportunity that properly belongs to the corporation. To determine whether an opportunity properly belongs to the corporation, ask: Does the corporation have a *specific need* for it? Has the corporation *actively considered* acquiring it? Did the director discover the opportunity *while acting as a director*, and were any *corporate funds involved* in the discovery? Remember, if the director fully informs the board, and an independent board declines the opportunity, the director may usually pursue it. Similarly, if the corporation is financially unable to take advantage of the opportunity, or if doing so would be an ultra vires act, some courts allow the director to take advantage of it. However, if a director usurps a corporate opportunity, the corporation may seek a constructive trust of the property and profits, or if the property has been resold, damages in the amount of the director's profit.

   d.   **Competing with corporation:** Recall too that if a director or officer obtains an interest in a *business that competes* with the corporation, it is a conflict of interest and a possible breach of her fiduciary duty.

   e.   **Compensation for services to corporation:** Excessive compensation for services as a director, officer, or employee may be challenged as a waste of corporate assets and thus a breach of the directors' duty of care. If this issue arises, discuss the following major issues: Was the compensation *duly authorized* by the board? Does the compensation bear a *reasonable relationship* to the value of services rendered?

A.   ALLOCATION OF POWERS BETWEEN DIRECTORS AND SHAREHOLDERS

   1.   **Shareholder Approval of Organic Changes:** [§116]   Shareholder approval is required for certain fundamental changes in the corporation—in particular, amendment of the articles of incorporation, merger, sale of substantially all assets, and dissolution. (*See infra*, §§968 *et seq.*)

   2.   **Bylaws:** [§117]   Shareholders also normally have the power to adopt and amend bylaws. Under some statutes, however, the board may have concurrent power to adopt and amend bylaws.

3. **Management of Corporation's Business:** [§118] Virtually all the corporate statutes provide that the business of a corporation shall be managed by or under the direction of a board of directors. Accordingly, except as provided by a valid agreement in a close corporation, the power to manage the business of the corporation is vested in its *board of directors*, not in the shareholders. At least in publicly held corporations, therefore, the shareholders have no power over the management of corporate affairs and cannot order the board of directors to take a particular course of action in managing the corporation's business. [Charlestown Boot & Shoe Co. v. Dunsmore, 60 N.H. 85 (1880)]

4. **Close Corporations:** [§119] Special problems are raised where shareholders of a close corporation attempt to vary the normal rule that the power to manage the corporation's business is vested exclusively in the directors.

   a. **Definition:** [§120] A "close corporation" is generally regarded as having these attributes:

      (1) *Ownership by a small number of shareholders*, most or all of whom are active in management of the corporation;

      (2) *No general market* for the corporation's stock; and, often,

      (3) *Some limitation upon the transferability* of stock.

   b. **Traditional view—shareholder agreements invalid:** [§121] In the past, close corporations often were treated the same as any other corporation. Thus, courts tended to invalidate agreements among the shareholders of a close corporation that curtailed the powers of the board. [Long Park, Inc. v. Trenton-New Brunswick Theatres Co., 297 N.Y. 174 (1948); McQuade v. Stoneham & McGraw, 263 N.Y. 323 (1934)] However, agreements among *all* the shareholders of a close corporation that involved only a *slight* impingement on the statutory norm were generally upheld. [Clark v. Dodge, 269 N.Y. 410 (1936)]

   c. **Modern trend—special governance rules allowed:** [§122] More recently, the courts have increasingly accommodated the needs and structure of the close corporation. In most respects, a close corporation is similar to a partnership, and it is therefore appropriate to permit the shareholders to adopt special governance rules. [Galler v. Galler, 203 N.E.2d 577 (Ill. 1964)] Also, many states now have statutory provisions that allow direct shareholder control of management in close corporations. For example, in New York, if a corporation's stock is not publicly traded, a certificate provision otherwise prohibited by law as improperly restrictive of the board's discretion is valid if authorized by all shareholders. [N.Y. Bus. Corp. Law §620] Other statutes go further and create a class of "statutory" close corporations.

5. **Statutory Close Corporation Status**

   a. **Definition:** [§123] Typically, these statutes require that in order to qualify as a "statutory close corporation," the corporation must: (i) identify itself as such in its articles of incorporation (and also, under some statutes, in its share certificates); and (ii) include certain limitations in its articles of incorporation as to number of shareholders, transferability of shares, or both. However, the precise requirements vary considerably in different jurisdictions.

(1) **Delaware statute:** [§124] The Delaware statute defines a statutory close corporation as one whose articles of incorporation contain:

    (i) A provision that all of the stock shall be held by *not more than 30 persons*;

    (ii) A provision making all of the stock *subject to a restriction on transferability*;

    (iii) A provision that the corporation shall make *no public offering* of its stock; and

    (iv) A *statement* that the corporation is a close corporation.

[Del. Gen. Corp. Law §§342, 343] There must also be "conspicuous notice" on the share certificate as to any qualifications of the persons entitled to be the holders of its shares or any provision in the articles of incorporation that confers management powers on the shareholders rather than the directors (*see* below). [Del. Gen. Corp. Law §351]

(2) **Model Statutory Close Corporation Supplement:** [§125] The Model Statutory Close Corporation Supplement ("MSCCS") avoids defining a statutory close corporation in terms of shareholdings or other characteristics. Rather, the MSCCS is applicable to: (i) any corporation whose original articles of incorporation contain a statement that the corporation is a statutory close corporation; or (ii) any corporation with 50 or fewer shareholders whose articles are amended by a two-thirds vote to include such a statement. (In the latter case, dissenting shareholders are entitled to elect to be paid the fair value of their shares.)

(3) **California statute:** [§126] The California statute defines a statutory close corporation as one whose articles provide that its stock shall not be held by more than 35 record shareholders and contain an express statement that "this corporation is a close corporation." [Cal. Corp. Code §158(a)] Share certificates for the corporation must also contain a conspicuous legend to the following effect: "This corporation is a close corporation. The number of holders of record cannot exceed _____ [a number not in excess of 35]. Any attempted voluntary inter vivos transfer that would violate this requirement is void. Refer to the articles, bylaws, and shareholder agreements on file with the secretary of the corporation for further restrictions." [Cal. Corp. Code §418(c)] If such a statement is *not* placed on the share certificate and there is a transfer resulting in the corporation having more than the maximum number of shareholders specified in its articles of incorporation, its status as a close corporation automatically terminates. [Cal. Corp. Code §158(e)]

b. **Functioning as a close corporation:** [§127] Once a corporation qualifies as a statutory close corporation, it is given great flexibility concerning management.

(1) **Shareholder agreements concerning management:** [§128] An agreement among the shareholders of a statutory close corporation relating to any phase of the corporation's affairs (*e.g.,* election of officers, payment of salaries, or distribution of dividends) is not subject to attack on the grounds that it interferes with the discretion of the directors or treats the corporation as if it were a partnership. [Del. Gen. Corp. Law §§350, 354; MSCCS §20; Cal. Corp. Code §§186, 300(b)] Some statutes provide that such agreements are valid only if entered into by *all* shareholders. [MSCCS §20; Cal. Corp. Code §§186, 300(b)] Others appear to permit a majority of the shareholders to enter into such agreements. [Del. Gen. Corp. Law §350]

(2) **Management by shareholders:** [§129] Under some statutes, the business of a statutory close corporation may be managed directly by the shareholders, rather than by directors. [MSCCS §20; Del. Gen. Corp. Law §351]

(a) **Liabilities for management:** [§130] To the extent that the shareholders of a statutory close corporation are authorized to and do manage the affairs of the corporation, they become personally liable for managerial acts or omissions for which directors would be liable. [MSCCS §§20, 21; Del. Gen. Corp. Law §350; Cal. Corp. Code §300(d)] Thus, while shareholders in a statutory close corporation may run the enterprise as a partnership, their potential liability increases as they assume more management responsibility.

(3) **Rights and liabilities of transferees:** [§131] As noted above, close corporation statutes frequently provide that the share certificates of a statutory close corporation must contain a conspicuous notation of the corporation's status and the existence of shareholder agreements imposing special rules for the management of the corporation or other matters. The statutes address the problem of transfers to ineligible or unknowing transferees in a variety of ways.

(a) **Delaware statute:** [§132] Under Delaware law, whenever any transferee has actual notice, or is conclusively presumed to have notice, that (i) he is ineligible to be a shareholder of the corporation, (ii) the transfer would cause the corporation's stock to be held by more than the number of persons permitted by its articles of incorporation, or (iii) the transfer is in violation of a valid restriction on transfer, the corporation may refuse to register the transfer. [Del. Gen. Corp. Law §347]

1) **Transferee not entitled to be a holder:** [§133] Under the Delaware statute, if stock of a statutory close corporation is issued or transferred to any person who is not entitled, under any valid provision of the articles of incorporation, to be a holder of the corporation's stock, and if the stock certificate conspicuously notes the qualifications of the persons entitled to be holders of the corporation's stock, the

transferee is *conclusively presumed* to have notice of his ineligibility to be a stockholder.

2) **Transfer will cause holders to exceed permitted number:** [§134] If the articles of incorporation of a Delaware statutory close corporation state the number of persons (not in excess of 30) who are entitled to be holders of record of its stock, the stock certificate conspicuously states that number, and the issuance or transfer of stock to any person would cause the corporation's stock to be held by more than that number of persons, the transferee is *conclusively presumed* to have notice of this fact.

3) **Transfer violates valid restriction:** [§135] Similarly, if the stock certificate of a Delaware statutory close corporation conspicuously notes a valid restriction on transfer of stock of the corporation, a transferee who acquires stock in violation of the restriction is *conclusively presumed* to have notice of that fact.

(b) **Model Statutory Close Corporation Supplement:** [§136] Under the MSCCS, the following statement must appear conspicuously on each share certificate issued by a statutory close corporation: "The rights of shareholders in a statutory close corporation may differ materially from the rights of shareholders in other corporations. Copies of the articles of incorporation and bylaws, shareholders' agreements, and other documents, any of which may restrict transfers and affect voting and other rights, may be obtained by a shareholder on written request to the corporation." [MSCCS §10] A transferee of shares of a statutory close corporation that has complied with the notice requirement is bound by the documents referred to in the notice. A transferee of shares of a statutory close corporation that has not complied with the notice requirement is bound by any documents of which he has knowledge or notice.

B. DIRECTORS

1. **Appointment of Directors:** [§137] The initial directors of the corporation are either designated in the articles of incorporation or elected at a meeting of the incorporators. Thereafter, the board is elected by the shareholders at their annual meetings, except that the board members themselves may fill vacancies on the board that occur between shareholders' meetings.

   a. **Number:** [§138] The number of directors is usually prescribed in the articles or the bylaws. At one time, the statutes required a minimum of three directors, but that is now less common. For example, both Delaware and the Model Act require only that the board consist of one or more members. [Del. Gen. Corp. Law §141; RMBCA §8.03]

   b. **Qualifications:** [§139] Unless otherwise provided in the articles of incorporation or bylaws, persons may be elected or appointed as directors even though they are not shareholders of the corporation or residents of the state of incorporation.

(1) **De facto directors:** [§140] Where there are qualifications for directors, the election of an unqualified person is merely voidable, not void, if the person holds title pursuant to color of office and assumes the duties of the office. Such a person may be ousted by appropriate legal proceedings, but until that time, her acts as director are effective. The unqualified person is regarded as a "de facto director" and is held to the same fiduciary standards as other directors (*see infra,* §175).

(a) **Limitation:** [§141] While a de facto director normally has the same powers as a de jure director, she does **not** have the power to appoint others as de jure directors to fill vacancies on the board. Directors appointed by de facto directors are themselves de facto.

c. **Vacancies:** [§142] The statutes vary somewhat in their treatment of vacancies. For example, in Delaware, any vacancy occurring in any office by reason of death, resignation, removal, or otherwise, is filled as the bylaws provide. In the absence of such a provision, the vacancy is filled by the board of directors or other governing body. [Del. Gen. Corp. Law §142] Under the Model Act, unless the articles of incorporation provide otherwise, if a vacancy occurs on a board of directors, including a vacancy resulting from an increase in the number of directors: (i) the shareholders may fill the vacancy; (ii) the board of directors may fill the vacancy; or (iii) if the directors remaining in office constitute fewer than a quorum of the board, they may fill the vacancy by the affirmative vote of a majority of all the directors remaining in office. [RMBCA §8.10]

(1) **Compare—removal of directors:** [§143] Under some statutes, vacancies on the board caused by **removal** of a director (*see* below) must be filled by the **shareholders,** unless the articles or bylaws give the directors that authority. [Cal. Corp. Code §305(a)]

2. Tenure of Office

a. **Term of appointment:** [§144] Statutes generally provide that directors of a corporation hold office until the next annual meeting, unless the board is "classified."

(1) **"Classified" boards:** [§145] A number of statutes permit the board to be divided into some maximum number of classes, usually three to five. [*See, e.g.,* Del. Gen. Corp. Law §141 *and* RMBCA §8.06—up to three classes] The directors in each class are then elected for a multiyear term whose length corresponds to the number of classes into which the board is divided. For example, in a board consisting of nine directors divided into three classes, three new directors will be elected each year for three-year terms.

(2) **Term:** [§146] Directors hold office until their successors are elected and accept their appointment.

(3) **Effect of resignation:** [§147] A director may resign at any time, and the resignation is effective as of the date indicated. Acceptance of a resignation by the board is not necessary. [Cal. Corp. Code §305(d)]

b. **Power to bind corporation beyond term:** [§148]   Unless limited by the articles of incorporation, the board has power to make contracts that bind the corporation beyond the directors' terms of office.

c. **Removal of director during term**

(1) **Removal by shareholders:** [§149]   Under the common law, the shareholders can remove a director during his term of office only for *cause* (*e.g.,* fraud, incompetence, dishonesty). The power to remove for cause is known as "amotion." Under the common law, shareholders cannot remove a director without cause unless there is specific authority in the articles of incorporation or bylaws. [Frank v. Anthony, 107 So. 2d 136 (Fla. 1958)] However, an article or bylaw provision can permit the removal, without cause, of directors elected after the provision has been adopted. [Everett v. Transnation Development Corp., 267 A.2d 627 (Del. 1970)]

(a) **Hearing:** [§150]   Where a director is to be removed for cause, he is entitled to a hearing by the shareholders before a vote to remove. [Auer v. Dressel, 306 N.Y. 427 (1954); Campbell v. Loew's, Inc., 134 A.2d 852 (Del. 1957)]

(b) **Compare—statutes:** [§151]   In contrast to the common law, a number of statutes permit the shareholders to remove a director without cause, unless otherwise provided in the articles of incorporation. [RMBCA §8.08]

(2) **Removal by board:** [§152]   Under common law, the board cannot remove a director, with or without cause. [Bruch v. National Guarantee Credit Corp., 116 A. 738 (Del. 1922)] However, some statutes permit the board to remove a director for cause [Mass. Gen. L. ch. 156B, §51(c)] or for specified reasons, such as conviction of a felony [Calif. Corp. Code §302].

(3) **Removal by court:** [§153]   The cases are split on whether a court can remove directors for cause. [Webber v. Webber Oil Co., 495 A.2d 1215 (Me. 1985)— courts do not have power to remove directors; Brown v. North Ventura Road Development Co., 216 Cal. App. 227 (1963)—courts have power to remove directors, at least for fraud or the like]

(a) **Statutes:** [§154]   Some statutes permit the courts to remove a director for specified reasons, such as fraudulent or dishonest acts. These statutes usually provide that a petition for such removal can be brought only by a designated percentage of the shareholders (most commonly 10%), by the attorney general, or in some cases, by either. [Calif. Corp. Code §304; N.Y. Bus. Corp. Law §706(d); RMBCA §8.09]

3. **Functioning of Board**

a. **Meetings:** [§155]   Absent a statute, directors can act only at a duly convened meeting at which a quorum is present. However, most statutes provide that a meeting of the board can be conducted by conference telephone or any other means of communication through which all participating directors can simultaneously hear each other. Most statutes also permit the board to act by unanimous written consent, without a meeting of any kind. [RMBCA §8.21]

(1) **Notice:** [§156] Formal notice is not required for a regular board meeting. In the case of a special meeting, however, notice of date, time, and place must be given to every director. The notice need not state the purpose of a meeting unless the articles of incorporation or the bylaws otherwise provide. Most statutes provide that notice can be waived in writing before or after a meeting, and that attendance at a meeting constitutes a waiver unless the director attends only to protest the holding of the meeting.

(2) **Quorum:** [§157] A quorum consists of a majority of the ***authorized number of directors***—not a majority of the directors then in office. Many statutes permit the articles of incorporation or bylaws to require a greater number for a quorum than a majority of the full board. A substantial minority of the statutes, including the Delaware statute and the Model Act, permit the articles or bylaws to set a lower number, but usually no less than one-third of the full board.

(3) **Voting:** [§158] Assuming that a quorum is present when a vote is taken, the affirmative vote of a ***majority of those present*** (not simply a majority of those voting) is required. Most statutes provide that the articles or bylaws can require a greater-than-majority vote for board action.

b. **Consequences of noncompliance with formalities**

(1) **Unanimous but informal approval:** [§159] Some cases hold that informal approval by directors is ineffective even if the approval is explicit and unanimous. [Baldwin v. Canfield, 1 N.W. 261 (Minn. 1879)] However, most modern courts would hold that informal but explicit approval by all the directors is effective, particularly where all the shareholders are directors or have acquiesced in the transaction or in a past practice of informal board action. [Gerard v. Empire Square Realty Co., 195 A.D. 244, 187 N.Y.S. 306 (1921); Anderson v. K.G. Moore, Inc., 376 N.E.2d 1238 (Mass. 1978), *cert. denied,* 439 U.S. 1116 (1979)]

(2) **Unanimous acquiescence:** [§160] Most modern courts will also treat as effective the explicit approval by a majority of the directors, without a meeting, together with acquiescence by the remaining directors. [Winchell v. Plywood Corp., 85 N.E.2d 313 (Mass. 1949)]

(3) **Majority acquiescence:** [§161] Where a majority of the directors approve a transaction explicitly or by acquiescence, without a meeting, but the remaining directors lack knowledge of the transaction, some courts hold the corporation is not liable [Hurley v. Ornsteen, 42 N.E.2d 273 (Mass. 1942)], while other courts hold it is liable, at least if the ***shareholders*** acquiesced in the transaction, or the shareholders or the remaining directors acquiesced in a practice of informal action by the directors [Holy Cross Gold Mining & Milling Co. v. Goodwin, 223 P. 58 (Colo. 1924)].

c. **Delegation of authority:** [§162]   It is within the power of the board, and is in fact a common practice, to appoint committees of its own members to act for the board either in particular kinds of matters (*e.g.,* a compensation committee) or to handle day-to-day management in the intervals between board meetings. [Ford v. Magee, 160 F.2d 457 (2d Cir. 1947)]

(1) **Executive committees:** [§163]   Statutes in many states authorize the board to appoint a committee of its members (frequently called "executive committees") to exercise the authority of the board within certain limits. [Del. Gen. Corp. Law §141]

(a) **Limitations:** [§164]   Typically, the statutes carve out certain powers that **cannot** be delegated to a board committee. For example, the Delaware statute prohibits delegating to a committee the power or authority to:

(i) *Amend the articles of incorporation*;

(ii) *Adopt an agreement of merger*;

(iii) *Recommend* to the shareholders the *sale, lease, or exchange* of all or substantially all of the corporation's property and assets;

(iv) *Recommend* to the shareholders a *dissolution* of the corporation;

(v) *Recommend* to the shareholders an *amendment of the bylaws*; or

(vi) *Declare a dividend or authorize the issuance of stock*, unless a board resolution, the bylaws, or the articles of incorporation expressly so provide.

[Del. Gen. Corp. Law §141]

d. **Provisional directors:** [§165]   Some statutes provide that where the board is deadlocked and the business of the corporation is endangered, a court may appoint an impartial person as "provisional director," to prevent impairment of business resulting from the deadlock. Such a provisional director serves with all the rights and powers of a director until the deadlock is broken, or until she is removed from office by court order or by vote or written consent of a majority of the shareholders. [Cal. Corp. Code §308]

e. **Voting agreements among directors:** [§166]   Although the laws allow shareholders to make binding agreements as to how they will vote their shares (*see infra,* §§491-499), traditionally, an agreement in advance among shareholder-directors as to how they will vote *as directors* was void as contrary to public policy. [McQuade v. Stoneham & McGraw, *supra,* §121] *Rationale:* Directors are fiduciaries of the corporation and must have unfettered discretion in voting on corporate affairs. However, courts have become more liberal in permitting special rules of governance in close corporations, and thus, modern courts might permit such an agreement, at least if all of the shareholders agreed, particularly if the agreement covered only certain matters. Some statutes specifically validate such agreements in the case of statutory close corporations. For example, the Delaware statute provides that a written agreement among a majority of stockholders of a statutory close corporation is not invalid on the ground that it restricts or interferes with the discretion or powers of the board of directors. [Del. Gen. Corp. Law §350]

4. **Compensation**

   a. **Compensation for services as director:** [§167]   The traditional rule is that a director is **not** entitled to compensation for services **as director**, unless the services are extraordinary (*see* below) or compensation is provided for in the articles or by a resolution of the board passed **before** the services are rendered.

      (1) **Extraordinary services:** [§168]   Where the services rendered are **beyond the scope** of normal duties of a director, and where properly authorized corporate officials either request the services or accept the benefits for the corporation, recovery in quasi-contract may be allowed for their reasonable value even without a specific agreement (*e.g.,* a member of the board travels cross-country to investigate possible corporate business opportunity).

   b. **Compensation for services as officer or employee:** [§169]   A director who also serves as an officer or employee of the corporation is entitled to compensation for such services—even where the rate of compensation is **not** set in advance.

      (1) **Limitation—conflict of interest problem:** [§170]   A director-officer has a conflict of interest in connection with any action by the board adopting or approving a contract fixing compensation for his services as an officer or employee of the corporation. (As to the effect of such conflict of interest on his right to participate in the board action, *see* discussion *infra*, §§259-278.)

      (2) **Limitation—waste:** [§171]   Executive compensation is also subject to the test of waste. Even where approved by a disinterested board, an agreement to pay executive compensation that is unreasonable or excessive may be held unenforceable against the corporation (*see infra*, §§267-278).

5. **Directors' Rights, Duties, and Liabilities**

   a. **Right to inspect corporate records:** [§172]   A director is ordinarily entitled to inspect corporate records or properties firsthand to enable him to discharge his fiduciary duties.

      (1) **Limitation:** [§173]   This right of inspection is often said to "absolute." [Cohen v. Cocoline Products, Inc., 309 N.Y. 119 (1955)] However, some cases have held that the inspection must be in **good faith** and for some purpose related to corporation affairs. Thus, a court might not order the corporation to permit inspection if it appeared that the director was attempting to obtain information for a purpose that would hurt the corporation (*e.g.,* to obtain lists of its customers

to hand over to a competitor). [State *ex rel.* Farber v. Sieberling Rubber Co., 168 A.2d 310 (Del. 1961)]

(2) **Basis of right:** [§174] The director's right to inspect corporate records is usually governed by common law principles. However, a few states have **statutes** recognizing such right. Where the statute provides that the director's right is "absolute" [*e.g.,* Cal. Corp. Code §1602], courts may be less inclined to read in any exceptions.

b. **Duty of care:** [§175] Directors occupy a fiduciary relationship to the corporation and must exercise the care of **ordinarily prudent and diligent persons** in like positions under similar circumstances. [Francis v. United Jersey Bank, 432 A.2d 814 (N.J. 1981)] In many states this duty is codified by statute. For example, California requires that a director perform his duties "in good faith, in a manner such director believes to be in the best interests of the corporation, and with such care, including reasonable inquiry, as an ordinarily prudent person in a like position would use under similar circumstances." [Cal. Corp. Code §309(a); N.Y. Bus. Corp. Law §717]

(1) **Amount of care required:** [§176] The standard of "reasonable care and prudence" is often difficult to apply to the judgmental decisions on "business risks," which directors are often called upon to make. Courts recognize that (i) since potential profit often corresponds to the potential risk, shareholders often assume the risk of bad business judgment; (ii) after-the-fact judgment is a most imperfect device to evaluate business decisions; and (iii) if liability were imposed too readily, it might deter many persons from serving as directors. [Joy v. North, 692 F.2d 880 (2d Cir. 1982)]

(a) **"Business judgment rule":** [§177] For these reasons, some courts have adopted the rule that where the act or omission involves no fraud, illegality, or conflict of interest but is a question of policy or business judgment, a director who acts in good faith is not personally liable for mere errors of judgment or want of prudence, short of **clear and gross negligence**. [Shlensky v. Wrigley, 237 N.E.2d 776 (Ill. 1968)]

1) **Majority view:** [§178] Most courts conclude that a director cannot invoke the business judgment rule if he has not been **"reasonably diligent,"** as where he knew or should have known that he did not have sufficient facts to make a judgment, yet failed to make reasonable efforts to inform himself. [Francis v. United Jersey Bank, *supra*] Some courts have stated that "**gross** negligence is the standard for determining whether a business judgment reached by the board of directors was an informed one." [Smith v. Van Gorkom, 488 A.2d 858 (Del. 1985)]

2) **Illegality:** [§179] A director cannot invoke the business judgment rule if he causes the corporation to engage in acts that are illegal or contrary to public policy. A director is liable for any loss sustained by the corporation because of such acts, even if undertaken for the

benefit of the corporation. [Miller v. American Telephone & Telegraph Co., 507 F.2d 759 (3d Cir. 1974)]

(b) **Directors of banks and other financial institutions:** [§180]   Many early cases impose a higher duty of care on directors of banks and other financial institutions, particularly in overseeing the activities of officers and management. Such directors may be found negligent for deviation from generally accepted banking principles. *Rationale:* Public interest in safety of banks requires a higher fiduciary duty of care by bank directors. [Bates v. Dresser, 251 U.S. 524 (1920)]

(2) Extent of liability

(a) **Injury and causation:** [§181]   Even where a director has not exercised the proper measure of care, he will be held personally liable only for corporate losses suffered as the ***direct and proximate result*** of his breach of duty—*i.e.,* injury to the corporation and causation must still be shown. [Barnes v. Andrews, 298 F. 614 (S.D.N.Y. 1924)]

(b) **Acts of others:** [§182]   A director is liable for the wrongful acts of other officers and directors only if he ***participated*** therein, was ***negligent in failing to discover*** the misconduct (general standard of care above), ***or*** was ***negligent in appointing*** the wrongdoer. [Graham v. Allis-Chalmers Manufacturing Co., 188 A.2d 125 (Del. 1963)]

1) **Note:** A director may seek to avoid being held liable for acts of the board by recording his ***dissent.*** However, in some circumstances, he may have to pursue other means such as threatening suit. [Francis v. United Jersey Bank, *supra,* §175]

(c) **Abolishing liability:** [§183]   Many state statutes permit the articles of incorporation to ***limit or eliminate*** the directors' liability for breach of the duty of care—apart from action in bad faith, intentional misconduct, or knowing violation of law. [*See, e.g.,* Del. Gen. Corp. Law §102(b)(7)] A few statutes have directly modified the standard of liability. [*See, e.g.,* Va. Code Ann. §13.1-690A—"good faith business judgment of the best interests of the corporation"]

(3) Defenses to liability

(a) **Nominal directors:** [§184]   It is usually no defense that the director was serving gratuitously or merely as a figurehead. [Francis v. United Jersey Bank, *supra,* §175; *but see* Harman v. Willbern, 520 F.2d 1333 (10th Cir. 1975)—contra]

(b) **Disabilities:** [§185]   Ill health, old age, and lack of experience have been held not to constitute defenses, on the theory that a person subject to one of these disabilities should not have accepted (or should have resigned from) the directorship. [McDonell v. American Leduc Petroleums, Ltd., 491 F.2d 380 (2d Cir. 1974)] But some courts have considered these factors in determining whether a director has met the standard of care required of a director. [Briggs v. Spaulding, 141 U.S. 132 (1891)]

(c) **Reliance on reports of management:** [§186] Directors are not required to make firsthand investigations of every detail of corporate business, at least in the absence of suspicious circumstances. As long as the director acts in good faith, he is entitled to rely on statements and reports made to him by corporate officers or employees and on reports by any committee of the board of which he is not a member, as to matters within their authority that appear to merit confidence. [Cal. Corp. Code §309(b); RMBCA §8.30(b)]

1) **Compare:** This may not be a defense to a federal securities act violation (*see infra,* §§865-867).

(d) **Reliance on expert opinion:** [§187] A director is also entitled to rely on the advice given by attorneys, accountants, or other persons as to matters the director reasonably believes to be within that person's expertise. As long as the director's reliance was reasonable and in good faith, it is a defense to liability even if the opinion proves to be erroneous. [Cal. Corp. Code §309(b); RMBCA §8.30(b)]

(e) **Shareholder ratification of directors' failure to exercise due care:** [§188] This issue is discussed *infra,* §§614-622.

c. **Duty of loyalty:** [§189] Directors have a duty of loyalty in all dealings with the corporation. (*See infra,* §§207 *et seq.*)

d. **Statutory duties and liabilities regarding management:** [§190] In addition to the general duty of care (above), various duties and liabilities are imposed on directors by federal and state statutes. These provisions seek to protect a broad range of public interests in addition to those of corporate shareholders and creditors.

(1) **Securities Act of 1933:** [§191] This statute makes directors liable for misstatements or omissions of material fact in a registration statement, unless they exercise *due diligence*. (*See infra,* §§855-872.)

(2) **Rule 10b-5:** [§192] Directors are liable for fraudulent misstatements or omissions of material fact by the corporation if they *participated* in or had *knowledge* of the fraud, or if their lack of knowledge resulted from *willful or reckless disregard of the truth*. (*See infra,* §§285 *et seq.*)

(3) **Illegal dividends:** [§193] Directors who participate in declaring a dividend from an unlawful source, or under other circumstances making a dividend illegal, are jointly and severally liable to the extent of the injury to creditors and preferred shareholders. (*See infra,* §§929-933.)

(4) **Criminal liability:** [§194]   A wide variety of state and federal statutes impose criminal liability on corporate managers for unlawful corporate action. This liability may arise if the managers personally engage in or cause the unlawful act [*see, e.g.,* N.Y. Penal Law §20.25], or if they have control over the corporate employees who commit the unlawful act [United States v. Park, 421 U.S. 658 (1975)—president of national retail food chain criminally liable for violation of Federal Food, Drug, and Cosmetic Act because of unsanitary conditions in a corporate warehouse].

C.   OFFICERS

1.   **Election:** [§195]   Under most statutes, the major officers of a corporation (normally, the president, vice president, secretary, and treasurer) are elected by the board, although some statutes permit election of officers by shareholders. Officers hold their office at the pleasure of the board. Even if they have contracts, they can be discharged, subject to their right to damages for breach of contract. Minor officers (assistant treasurer, assistant secretary, etc.) may be appointed by the board or by the chief executive officer.

2.   **Authority of Corporate Officers—Liability of Corporation to Outsiders**

a.   **Types of authority:** [§196]   A corporate officer may have any of the following types of authority:

(1) **Actual authority:** [§197]   Actual authority is the authority that a reasonable person in the officer's position would reasonably believe had been conferred upon him by the corporation. Actual authority may be *expressly* conferred on the officer by the bylaws, valid resolutions of the board of directors, a valid delegation from a superior, or acquiescence by the board or superior officers in a past pattern of conduct. An officer also has *implied* actual authority to do what can reasonably be implied from a grant of express authority.

(2) **Apparent authority:** [§198]   Apparent authority is authority that the corporation allows third parties to reasonably believe an officer possesses. Apparent authority can arise from intentional or negligent representations by the corporation to the third party or through permitting an officer or employee to assume certain powers and functions on a continuing basis with the third party's knowledge.

(3) **Power of position:** [§199]   This is a special type of apparent authority, which arises by reason of holding a particular position in the corporation that normally carries certain authority. For example, a vice president for sales would probably have power of position to hire a salesperson.

(4) **Ratification:** [§200]   Even an unauthorized act by a corporate officer may bind the corporation, if the officer purports to act on the corporation's behalf and the act is later ratified by the board.

b.   **Authority of president:** [§201]   A common issue is the scope of authority possessed by the president by virtue of that title. There are three competing views:

    (1)   **Only the power of a director:** [§202]   Under one view, the president has only those powers possessed by any other director, except for the power of presiding at corporate meetings. This is obviously unrealistic and probably not good law today.

    (2)   **Broad power to act:** [§203]   A second view, known as the "New York rule" (although it is not clear whether New York courts or any other courts still subscribe to it), holds that the president has presumptive or prima facie power to do any act that the board could authorize or ratify. [Schwartz v. United Merchants & Manufacturers, Inc., 72 F.2d 256 (2d Cir. 1934)]

    (3)   **Power to bind corporation in regular course of business:** [§204]   A third view, which is the law in virtually all jurisdictions today, is that the president has the power to bind the corporation in transactions arising in the "usual and regular course of business," but not in "extraordinary" transactions. [Joseph Greenspon's Sons Iron & Steel Co. v. Pecos Valley Gas Co., 156 A. 350 (Del. 1931)]

        (a)   **Compare:** A variant of this rule is that the president has such power if—but only if—he is the "general manager" of the corporation by title or in fact. [Memorial Hospital Association v. Pacific Grape Products Co., 45 Cal. 2d 634 (1955)]

        (b)   **"Ordinary and regular course of business":** [§205]   Modern courts following this approach generally take an expansive view of what constitutes the ordinary and regular course of business. [Lee v. Jenkins Bros., 268 F.2d 357 (2d Cir. 1959)] However, even under an expansive view, presidential authority would not extend to all corporate actions. It would not, for example, cover the sale of a major part of the corporate assets without the consent of the board. Such a transaction is clearly outside the usual and regular course of business of the corporation.

3.   **Duties of Corporate Officers:** [§206]   Officers owe a duty of care to the corporation similar to that owed by directors (*supra*, §175). Indeed, since the officers may have more intimate knowledge of the corporate affairs than nonofficer directors, they may be held to a higher standard of care. Officers, like directors, also owe a duty of loyalty in their dealings with the corporation (*see* below).

D.   CONFLICTS OF INTEREST IN CORPORATE TRANSACTIONS

1.   **Duty of Loyalty:** [§207]   As a further consequence of their fiduciary relationship with the corporation, officers and directors are held to a duty of *loyalty* in all dealings with the corporation—*i.e.*, the duty to promote the interests of the corporation without regard for personal gain.

2. **Business Dealings with Corporations:** [§208] Conflict of interest issues arise whenever a corporation contracts directly with one of its officers or directors, or with a company in which the officer or director is financially interested. For example, if Corporation contracts to purchase property in which Director has a financial interest, or to sell corporate assets to an entity in which Director has a financial interest, does Director's adverse interest disqualify her from voting on the contract? Does it render the contract voidable by the corporation, even where her adverse interest was disclosed at the meeting?

    a. **Effect of director's self-interest on right to participate in meeting authorizing transaction**

        (1) **Common law:** [§209] At common law, directors who had interests adverse to the corporation could not be counted for purposes of making up a quorum, or for purposes of making up a majority vote at the meeting in which the transaction was approved. [Weiss Medical Complex, Ltd. v. Kim, 408 N.E.2d 959 (Ill. 1980)]

        (2) **Statutes:** [§210] Today, many statutes permit an "interested" director to be counted in determining the presence of a quorum, and further provide that interested director transactions are *not automatically voidable* by the corporation simply because the interested director's vote was necessary for approval. [Cal. Corp. Code §310(a); N.Y. Bus. Corp. Law §713; Del. Gen. Corp. Law §144] Under these statutes, such transactions may still be valid if other conditions are met. (*See infra,* §228.)

    b. **Effect of director's self-interest in rendering transaction voidable by corporation**

        (1) **Strict view:** [§211] The historic common law rule was that any contract in which a director is financially interested is *voidable* at the option of the corporation—without regard to fairness or whether the director's adverse interest was disclosed in advance to the directors who then approved the transaction.

        (2) **Modern view:** [§212] Most courts today adopt the more liberal position that contracts and dealings in which a director has a financial interest are voidable by the corporation only where the contract is found to be *unfair* to the corporation considering all the relevant circumstances.

            (a) **Disclosure requirement:** [§213] Following this view, it has been held that failure of an interested director to make *full disclosure* to an *independent* board respecting the transaction is in itself "unfair" to the corporation. [State *ex rel.* Hayes Oyster Co. v. Keypoint Oyster Co., 391 P.2d 979 (Wash. 1964)]

                1) **"Full disclosure":** [§214] "Full disclosure" requires that the director inform the board as to all matters affecting the *value* of the property involved and perhaps also the *amount of the director's profit.*

2) **"Independent board":** [§215] An "independent board" means that a majority of the directors are not under the control of the interested director (directly or indirectly).

(b) **Fairness requirement:** [§216] Even if there has been a full disclosure to an independent board, courts following the modern view generally hold that the transaction is still voidable by the corporation (*e.g.,* where the board later changes it mind, new directors take office and reevaluate the transaction, a trustee in bankruptcy takes over, or a shareholder brings a derivative suit challenging the transaction) if it is unfair to the corporation in price, terms, or other conditions. [Globe Woolen Co. v. Utica Gas & Electric Co., 224 N.Y. 483 (1918)—sale of valuable corporate asset to director who is otherwise insolvent, for a token down payment, with balance of purchase price payable over many years and without adequate security is voidable by corporation]

1) **Burden of proof:** [§217] The burden of establishing the fairness of the transaction is usually placed on the interested director. In effect, there is a *presumption of unfairness* that must be rebutted. [Pepper v. Litton, 308 U.S. 295 (1939); *but see* Durfee v. Durfee & Canning, Inc., 80 N.E.2d 522 (Mass. 1948)—"Massachusetts rule"]

2) **Fairness where no ability to disclose:** [§218] Where disclosure to an independent board is not possible (as where the interested director controls a majority of the board), dealings between the corporation and an interested director will be upheld as long as the interested director proves that the transaction was fair and reasonable to the corporation. [Shlensky v. South Parkway Building Corp., 159 N.E.2d 31 (Ill. 1959)]

(c) **Effect of shareholder ratification**

1) **Unanimous ratification:** [§219] If after *full disclosure* the shareholders *unanimously* ratify the corporation's dealings with the interested director, the corporation will be estopped from later challenging the transaction (and so will any shareholder bringing a derivative suit).

a) **But note:** No such estoppel is invoked unless there was *full* disclosure. [Rivoli Theatre Co. v. Allison, 152 A.2d 449 (Pa. 1959)]

b) **Compare:** And although unanimous shareholder ratification will bar suits by or on behalf of the corporation, it may not preclude *creditors' suits* if the effect of the transaction was to deplete corporate assets and thereby render the corporation *insolvent* and unable to pay its debts—at least where the ratifying shareholders are also interested in the transaction.

2) **Less-than-unanimous ratification:** [§220] The effect of a *majority* (but less than all) of the shareholders voting to ratify dealings with an interested director usually turns on whether the majority shares were also *owned or controlled* by the interested director.

    a) **Ratification by "disinterested" majority:** [§221] If the majority shareholders approving the transaction have full disclosure and have no financial interest in the transaction, some courts hold that the transaction cannot be attacked by the corporation (or by a shareholder bringing a derivative suit). Other courts hold that such ratification *shifts the burden of proving "unfairness"* to the corporation (or derivative suit plaintiff) challenging the transaction. [Eliasberg v. Standard Oil Co., 92 A.2d 862 (N.J. 1952)]

        1/ **Waste:** [§222] Even if a disinterested majority of the shareholders ratifies the transaction, if the interested director is charged with "waste," it has been held that the court itself must examine the facts to determine whether they fall within the realm of business judgment. [Michelson v. Duncan, 407 A.2d 211 (Del. 1979)]

    b) **Ratification by "interested" majority:** [§223] Less weight is generally given to shareholder ratification where the majority shares are owned or controlled (directly or indirectly) by the interested director.

        1/ **Corporation can later rescind:** [§224] Some courts hold an interested majority's ratification makes no difference even when most of the *disinterested* shareholders also approved the transaction. If even a single shareholder disapproved, the corporation (or derivative suit plaintiff) can later sue to rescind for unfairness, and the burden of proving fairness remains on the interested director. [Pappas v. Moss, 393 F.2d 865 (3d Cir. 1968)]

        2/ **Subsequent attack precluded or burden shifted:** [§225] Other courts, however, are more lenient in holding that ratification by a majority of the disinterested shareholders (even though they are a minority in the corporation) precludes subsequent attack by the corporation, or at least shifts the burden of proving "unfairness" to the corporation (or derivative suit plaintiff).

        3/ **Older cases—corporation estopped even without disinterested majority:** [§226] Some older cases go further and estop the corporation even where the shares of the interested director(s) were necessary to make up the majority shareholder vote ratifying the transaction. [Kirwan v. Parkway Distillery, Inc., 148 S.W.2d 720 (Ky. 1941)]

c) **Estoppel against shareholder:** [§227] In any event, a shareholder who received full disclosure and voted to approve the corporation's dealings with the interested director(s) would probably be estopped from later bringing a derivative suit charging "unfairness."

(3) **Statutes:** [§228] Most states have adopted statutes regulating interested director transactions. The Delaware law is illustrative. It provides that such transactions are not voidable by the corporation for conflict of interest if (i) the material facts as to the director's interest and the transaction were disclosed or known to the board and the transaction was nonetheless approved in good faith by a disinterested majority of the board; (ii) the same information was disclosed or known to the shareholders, and a *majority of the shareholders* approves; or (iii) the transaction is fair to the corporation. [Del. Gen. Corp. Law §144]

(a) **Fairness required notwithstanding disclosure:** [§229] Although "fairness" and "approval after disclosure" seem to be alternatives under these statutes, courts have interpreted the statutes as requiring fairness in any event. Thus, an interested director transaction may be set aside if unfair to the corporation, notwithstanding that there was full disclosure to and approval by the majority of the directors or shareholders. [Remillard Brick Co. v. Remillard-Dandini Co., 109 Cal. App. 2d 405 (1952); Flieger v. Lawrence, 361 A.2d 218 (Del. 1976)] Indeed, this is now expressly required under the California statute. Transactions between a corporation and one of its directors must be "just and reasonable as to the corporation" notwithstanding full disclosure and approval by the directors. [Cal. Corp. Code §310(a)(2)] This provision is *not applicable,* however, where there has been disclosure to and approval by *shareholders*. [Cal. Corp. Code §310(a)(1)]

(b) **Shareholder approval:** [§230] Some statutes provide that the requisite shareholder approval must occur *without* counting the shares owned by interested directors. [Cal. Corp. Code §310(a)(1)] Others are less clear on whether such shares may be counted. [*See* Del. Gen. Corp. Law §144; N.Y. Bus. Corp. Law §713]

(c) **Burden of proof:** [§231] Some statutes are silent on whether the interested director has the burden of proving compliance with the statute. [Del. Gen. Corp. Law §144] Other statutes provide that if an interested director transaction is defended on grounds of "fairness," the interested director has the burden of proof. [N.Y. Bus. Corp. Law §713(b); Cal. Corp. Code §310(a)(3)]

c. **Remedy:** [§232] If the transaction is voidable under any of the views above, the corporation is entitled to *rescind* (unwind the transaction). Alternatively, it may affirm the contract and hold the interested director for damages.

(1) **Measure of damage:** [§233] Where damages are granted, the usual measure is the amount of the *unfair profit* made on the transaction, *i.e.,* the difference between fair value and the price at which the transaction was consummated. Thus, where the interested director sold personal assets to the corporation at an inflated value, the corporation can recover the excess over the fair value. Or where the interested director purchased corporate assets at an inadequate price, the corporation can recover the *additional amounts* it should have received. [Shlensky v. South Parkway Building Corp., *supra* §218]

   (a) **Loss of salary:** [§234] In addition to damages, some courts have held that the interested director must repay any salary earned during the period of fiduciary breach. [American Timber & Trading Co. v. Niedermeyer, 558 P.2d 1211 (Or. 1976)]

   (b) **Punitive damages:** [§235] Some courts have awarded punitive damages against directors who have breached their fiduciary duty. [Rowen v. LeMars Mutual Insurance Co. of Iowa, 282 N.W.2d 639 (Iowa 1979)]

(2) **Alternate measure:** [§236] Alternatively (particularly in cases of *trickery* or *fraud,* or where the director acquired assets for the purpose of reselling to the corporation at an excessive price), some courts penalize the director by awarding damages based on the difference between the price paid by the corporation and the interested director's acquisition cost. This effectively *deprives the director of the profit* she could have made on a sale of such assets to any third party.

   (a) **Example:** Director buys assets for $5,000 for the purpose of resale to Corporation at $20,000, although fair value is only $12,000. Under the normal measure, Corporation could recover $8,000. Under this "penal" measure it can recover $15,000. Director is thus deprived of the $7,000 she could have made had she sold to a third party.

(3) **Rescission as sole remedy:** [§237] If the interested director did not act in *bad faith* or *profit personally* from the transaction (as where her corporation sells property to another corporation in which she is a director but owns no shares; *see* below), courts may decide not to hold her personally liable for damages. In such cases, the corporation's *only remedy is to rescind.* [Chelrob, Inc. v. Barrett, 293 N.Y. 442 (1944)]

   (a) **Note:** Some older decisions have held that damages should not be awarded against an interested director in *any* transaction unless rescission is impracticable. [New York Trust Co. v. American Realty Co., 244 N.Y. 209 (1926)]

3. **Interlocking Directorates:** [§238]   Conflicts of interest may also arise where the same individual sits as a director of two corporations that contract with each other. The conflict stems from the fact that the director owes each corporation the duty to make the best possible deal for it. The problem is even more acute when the boards of both corporations are composed entirely of the same individuals (which is frequently the case with parent and subsidiary corporations).

   a. **Strict view:** [§239]   The historic common law rule held that contracts between corporations having common directors may be avoided by either corporation because of the conflict of interest—regardless of the fairness of the transaction.

   b. **Modern view:** [§240]   However, the clear weight of authority today permits such intercorporate transactions subject to the same general requirements as for interested director transactions (*i.e.,* full disclosure and fairness).

      (1) **Statutes:** [§241]   Some statutes suggest that intercorporate dealings are not voidable for conflict of interest if the director who sits on both boards of the contracting corporations owns stock in neither. For example, the California statute provides that "a mere common directorship does not constitute a material financial interest" that should be disclosed. [Cal. Corp. Code §310(a)(3)]

      (2) **Parent-subsidiary transactions:** [§242]   There is no conflict of interest where one corporation is a wholly owned subsidiary of another. But conflicts frequently arise where the parent owns only a majority of the subsidiary's shares, and there are other (minority) shareholders who may be affected by parent-subsidiary dealings. The basic question in each case is whether the transaction was *fair* to the subsidiary.

         (a) **Burden of proof on parent:** [§243]   As in interested director cases generally, the burden of proof is usually on the parent corporation to demonstrate that it has taken no unfair advantage of the subsidiary through control of its board. [Sterling v. Mayflower Hotel Corp., 93 A.2d 107 (Del. 1952)]

         (b) **Limitation:** [§244]   However, some courts place this burden on the parent only where, by virtue of its domination, it has received something from the subsidiary to the *exclusion* of the minority shareholders of the subsidiary. For example, it has been held that minority shareholders of a subsidiary corporation cannot complain that the majority shareholder (parent) caused the subsidiary to pay "excessive" dividends (draining too much capital out of the subsidiary and injuring its operations) because the minority shareholders had received their proportionate share of the dividends. [Sinclair Oil Corp. v. Levien, 280 A.2d 717 (Del. 1971)]

4. **Corporate Opportunity Doctrine:** [§245]   The fiduciary duty of loyalty, discussed above, bars a director from taking for herself any advantage or business opportunity that properly belongs to the corporation. As to any such opportunity, a director owes the corporation

at least a *right of first refusal*, *i.e.,* the right to acquire it on the same terms offered to her.

a. **What constitutes a corporate opportunity:** [§246]   There is no clear-cut definition of what constitutes a corporate opportunity. Rather, it depends upon whether, under all the circumstances, it would be *unfair* for the director to exploit the opportunity. [Johnston v. Greene, 121 A.2d 919 (Del. 1956)] The following factors are those most frequently relied upon by courts in holding that an opportunity is "corporate" and hence may not legitimately be taken advantage of by the directors personally:

  (1) **Corporate plans and expectations:** [§247]   If the corporation has a present interest or "tangible expectancy" in the opportunity in the sense that it has a specific need for it, has resolved to acquire it, or has *actively considered* its acquisition, it may not be taken advantage of by a director.

    (a) **Note—"useful" not enough:** [§248]   The mere fact that the property or opportunity would be "useful" to the corporation is ordinarily not enough to render it a corporate opportunity. [Burg v. Horn, 380 F.2d 897 (2d Cir. 1967)]

  (2) **Director's capacity in dealing:** [§249]   If the opportunity was discovered by the director in her *capacity as director* of the corporation (*e.g.,* offer delivered to the director intended for the corporation), it is a corporate opportunity. [*See* Johnston v. Green, *supra*]

    (a) **Note:** The fact that an opportunity relates to the corporation's "line of business" does *not* necessarily mean that the director must deal with it on behalf of the corporation—particularly where it also falls within the director's personal business interests that are outside the capacity of director of the corporation. [Burg v. Horn, *supra*]

  (3) **Funds used:** [§250]   If the corporation's funds were involved in the director's discovering or acquiring the opportunity, or if the corporation's *facilities or employees* were used in developing it, the opportunity may not be personally taken advantage of by a director. [Guth v. Loft, Inc., 5 A.2d 503 (Del. 1939)]

b. **Where corporation unable to take advantage:** [§251]   Although much depends on the particular facts of the case, it is frequently stated that directors *may* take advantage of corporate business opportunities of which the corporation is unable to take advantage. Thus, if the corporation is *insolvent or financially unable* to make the investment required, it has been held that the director is free to do so. [Miller v. Miller, 222 N.W.2d 71 (Minn. 1974)]

  (1) **Disclosure:** [§252]   Some courts have held that the director must promptly disclose all known material facts to the disinterested directors (or, if there are none, to the disinterested shareholders). The rationale is that if the investment is sufficiently attractive, the corporation might itself be able to raise the necessary funds. After full disclosure, the director may take advantage of the business

opportunity if it is rejected by the corporation, or if the director proves that the corporation unreasonably failed to reject it and it would be otherwise fair for the director to personally take the opportunity. [Klinicki v. Lundgren, 695 P.2d 906 (Or. 1985)]

   (a) **Compare:** Other courts have held that the director's fiduciary duty *precludes* her taking advantage of such opportunities, reasoning that to permit her to do so might discourage her making her best efforts *to obtain* the needed money for the corporation. [Irving Trust Co. v. Deutsch, 73 F.2d 121 (2d Cir. 1934)]

   (2) **Ultra vires transaction:** [§253] If the acquisition would be ultra vires by the corporation, a number of cases hold that the director may make use of the opportunity. *But note:* There is a strong contrary argument on the rationale that the corporation should at least have the right to consider the investment. It might be so advantageous that it would justify amending the articles to make the acquisition *intra vires.*

c. **Where corporation unwilling to take advantage:** [§254] If the director *fully* informs the board of the opportunity, and an independent board declines to take it, the director generally may pursue it for herself. [*See* Kerrigan v. Unity Savings Association, 317 N.E.2d 39 (Ill. 1974)]

d. **Remedies:** [§255] If a director usurps a corporate opportunity, the corporation may invoke any of the following remedies:

   (1) **Constructive trust:** [§256] Courts may declare that the director holds the opportunity as constructive trustee for the corporation, forcing a *conveyance* of the property to the corporation at the cost to the director and an accounting to the corporation for any *rents, income, or profits derived* through ownership thereof. [Irving Trust Co. v. Deutsch, *supra*]

   (2) **Damages:** [§257] If the director has already *resold* the property, a suit will lie for damages for breach of fiduciary duty—forcing the director to disgorge all profits made on the transaction.

5. **Competing with Corporation:** [§258] A director (or officer) who obtains a financial interest in a business that competes with that of the corporation puts herself in a conflict of interest situation—even where the competing business is *not* a corporate opportunity. Depending on all the circumstances, competition by a director or officer may be held a breach of fiduciary duty, in which event she may be barred from such competition or held liable for damages. [Lincoln Stores, Inc. v. Grant, 34 N.E.2d 704 (Mass. 1941)]

a. **Example:** A breach of fiduciary duty will most likely be found where the director has used corporate funds, facilities, or employees (or corporate secrets) in starting up or acquiring the competing business. [Guth v. Loft, Inc., *supra*, §250]

b. **Compare:** However, the mere fact that an officer or director makes ***preparations*** to compete with the corporation before resigning from office does not in itself establish a breach of fiduciary duty; nor does the failure to disclose to the board any plans to compete. [Maryland Metals, Inc. v. Metzner, 382 A.2d 564 (Md. 1978)] But if there are added circumstances (*e.g.*, concealment of material facts, use of corporate facilities or assets, or "raids" on key corporate personnel), this clearly constitutes a breach of fiduciary duty. [Duane Jones Co. v. Burke, 306 N.Y. 172 (1954)]

6. **Compensation for Services to Corporation:** [§259]   Finally, a conflict of interest issue arises in dealings between the corporation and one of its directors relative to compensation for services as director, officer, or employee of the corporation. Such compensation may take various forms—*e.g.*, salary, bonuses, profit-sharing and pension plans, stock options, expense accounts, etc. Usually, the conflict of interest issue is raised by a dissident minority shareholder in a derivative suit charging excessive compensation to the director and resultant unfairness to the corporation.

a. **Authorization:** [§260]   The first question is whether the compensation arrangement has been ***duly authorized*** by the board. This often turns on whether the interested director is entitled to participate in the meeting and to vote on her own compensation.

(1) **Issues:** [§261]   Since this is simply another form of interested director transaction, the various common law and statutory rules (*supra*, §§208-237) govern (i) whether the director may be counted in determining the presence of a quorum at the meeting, (ii) whether her vote may be counted on her own compensation, and (iii) the effect of shareholder ratification and the like.

(2) **Statutory resolution:** [§262]   Statutes in some states resolve the problem by expressly authorizing members of the board to establish reasonable compensation for directors notwithstanding their personal interest in such matters (provided there are no contrary provisions in the articles or bylaws). [*See* Ill. Bus. Corp. Act §8.05]

b. **"Reasonableness":** [§263]   Assuming the compensation plan is duly authorized and adopted by the board, the next question is whether the terms of the plan are ***reasonable***. If not, it may be challenged as a waste of corporate assets by the directors, and hence a violation of their duty of care to the corporation.

(1) **Disinterested directors protected by business judgment rule:** [§264]   Good faith and the business judgment rule (*supra*, §177) will ***ordinarily*** protect disinterested directors from liability to the corporation for approving executive compensation plans to other directors, officers, or employees of the corporation. Courts are reluctant to second guess the directors' business decisions on the value of an employee's services.

(a) **Recipients also protected:** [§265]   And where the compensation was authorized by disinterested directors, recipients of the compensation will usually be protected against a suit by the corporation (or a shareholder's derivative suit) for rescission or return of allegedly excessive compensation.

(b) **Caution—"mutual back scratching":** [§266]   Directors who vote for each other's compensation plans or for trade-offs in some other capacity (*e.g.,* retainer fee as attorney for the corporation) are ***not*** considered disinterested.

(2) **Limitation—doctrine of waste:** [§267]   Even disinterested directors have no power to "give away" or "waste" corporate assets, absent unanimous shareholder approval. Nor may a mere majority of the shareholders condone a waste or gift of the corporate assets to the prejudice of the minority. Consequently, courts have placed limitations on executive compensation plans ***notwithstanding approval*** by disinterested directors and/or a majority of the disinterested shareholders.

(a) **Legally sufficient consideration to corporation:** [§268]   Courts have held that it must appear that the compensation is paid for services that constituted legally sufficient consideration to the corporation for such payment.

1) **Expressly or impliedly authorized:** [§269]   It must appear that the services rendered by the officer or director were expressly or impliedly authorized by the corporation. Normally, the fact that the services are reasonably related to the corporation's business is sufficient.

2) **Compensation for past services:** [§270]   Courts have generally ***invalidated*** agreements by the corporation to pay an officer or director (or the widows of an officer and director) for past services (or to increase compensation retroactively), on the rationale that there is no legal consideration for the agreement. [Adams v. Smith, 153 So. 2d 221 (Ala. 1963)]

a) **Future consulting fees:** [§271]   One way to avoid this rule is for the corporation to grant compensation to a departing employee in exchange for a promise to be available to "advise" or "consult" with the corporation in the ***future*** or for a promise not to compete with the corporation. [Osborne v. Locke Steel Chain Co., 218 A.2d 526 (Conn. 1966)]

b) **Bonuses:** [§272]   Some courts hold that reasonable bonuses (or the like) may be paid to officers and employees for recent past services, if approved by a majority of the shareholders. [Chambers v. Beaver-Advance Corp., 140 A.2d 808 (Pa. 1958)]

c) **Retirement benefits:** [§273]   And some statutes now specifically authorize the board to provide pensions and retirement benefits in recognition of past services. [*See* Pa. Bus. Corp. Law §316]

3) **Compensation for future services:** [§274] Compensation for services to be rendered in the future may be held improper if there is no reasonable assurance that the corporation will ultimately receive the benefit of the services for which it is paying.

    a) **Stock options:** [§275] Some courts have invalidated the grant of stock options exercisable by officers and employees in future years when the options were ***not conditioned*** on the recipient's remaining in the corporation's employ for any designated period of time and when the option would be exercised even after the recipient left the corporation's employ. [Kerbs v. California Eastern Airways, 90 A.2d 652 (Del. 1952)] Other courts have upheld such plans (when adopted by a disinterested board) as an exercise of "reasonable business judgment." [Beard v. Elster, 160 A.2d 731 (Del. 1960)]

(b) **Value of services rendered:** [§276] There must be some ***reasonable relationship*** between the amount paid by the corporation and the value of the services rendered. [Rogers v. Hill, 289 U.S. 582 (1933)]

    1) **"Reasonable":** [§277] What constitutes "reasonable" (as opposed to "excessive" or "wasteful") compensation is determined by all the facts and circumstances, *e.g.*: the recipient's qualifications; time spent and responsibilities assumed; the size and complexity of the corporation's business; the amount of its income; and amounts paid to comparable persons performing similar services for other corporations. [Ruetz v. Topping, 453 S.W.2d 624 (Mo. 1970)]

    2) **Percentage of profits:** [§278] The mere fact that the officer or employee is to receive a percentage of corporate profits is ***not*** ordinarily enough by itself to show the compensation "excessive," even though another individual could be found to do the same work on a straight salary basis. [*Compare* Rogers v. Hill, *supra*—bonus percentage, valid when established 18 years earlier, might amount to waste due to enormous increase in corporate profits]

VI.   INSIDER TRADING

chapter approach

This chapter considers securities trading by corporate insiders, such as officers, directors, and controlling shareholders. Most exam questions in this area concern the **_federal_** securities laws that regulate insider trading; thus, that is the primary focus of this chapter.

1. **Rule 10b-5:** Whenever you have a question involving trading by insiders or persons to whom they have given inside information (tippees), consider applying rule 10b-5. Analyze the 10b-5 issues as follows:

   a. Look for a **_material misrepresentation or omission_** in connection with the sale or purchase of **_any_** security. **_Causation_** (of loss), **_reliance,_** and **_scienter_** are also crucial factors.

   b. It is a violation for an **_insider_** to trade on material nonpublic information; so be careful to determine whether the trader is an insider (_i.e.,_ whether he has a fiduciary duty to the corporation).

   c. Analyze a **_tippee's_** liability by determining whether: (i) the insider-tipper breached his **_fiduciary duty_**, (ii) the insider-tipper communicated the information **_for his own advantage_**, and (iii) the **_tippee knew of the breach_**.

   d. If the facts of your question do not involve a traditional insider or tippee, consider whether the person trading on the material, nonpublic information obtained the information wrongfully. For example, did he obtain the information through a breach of duty to **_his_** employer?

   e. Remember that a suit can be brought under rule 10b-5 by either a private plaintiff who is a **_purchaser or seller_** or the **_SEC_**. Keep in mind that even nontrading parties (_e.g.,_ a corporation that makes a material misrepresentation) may be liable under rule 10b-5.

   f. Consider the **_defenses_** to a 10b-5 action—**_due diligence_** or **_in pari delicto_**—and determine whether either applies to the facts in question.

   g. Finally, discuss the **_remedies_**. Potential **_remedies_** for private plaintiffs are: out-of-pocket damages, rescission, and restitutionary damages. Remedies available to the government include injunctive relief, criminal sanctions, and civil penalties.

2. **Section 16(b):** Whenever you encounter a question concerning the trading by corporate "insiders" in a corporation that has securities that are required to be **_registered_** under section 12 of the 1934 Act, consider applying section 16(b). Under this section, a corporation can recover any profit made by an insider from any **_purchase and sale_** (or sale and purchase) of its securities made within a **_six-month period_**. Remember that, for this purpose, **_officers, directors, and beneficial owners of more than 10% of the shares_** are considered insiders and must periodically disclose changes in their holdings.

When analyzing a question under section 16(b), first determine whether the trader is a statutory insider and, if so, at what time he became an insider. Then, try to pair up purchase and sale transactions within a six-month period during which the trader was an insider, and calculate the short-swing profits.

3. **Common Law:** Remember that some courts now impose liability on insiders in favor of the corporation as a matter of common law.

A. INTRODUCTION [§279]

The purchase and sale of a corporation's stock by a director, officer, or other insider raises important and complex issues of fiduciary responsibility. The basic problem is the possibility that an insider has an unfair advantage because he knows facts about the corporation that are not known to those with whom he deals, and he knows those facts only because of his fiduciary position, not because he has exercised skill or diligence.

B. COMMON LAW

1. **Duty to Shareholders:** [§280]   It was clear at common law that a director or officer could not make misrepresentations, or even state half-truths, in connection with the purchase or sale of stock. However, the courts were split concerning the duty of officers and directors to make ***affirmative disclosure.***

    a. **Majority rule:** [§281]   The majority rule was that there was no duty of disclosure to shareholders regarding any inside information that might affect the value of the shares, because officers and directors owed fiduciary duties only to the corporation, not to individual shareholders. [Goodwin v. Aggasiz, 186 N.E. 659 (Mass. 1933)]

        (1) **"Special facts" exception:** [§282]   A number of jurisdictions that followed the majority rule nevertheless imposed a duty of disclosure if there were "special facts" that made nondisclosure unfair to the shareholder. [Strong v. Repide, 213 U.S. 419 (1909)] This exception was most typically applied where the parties dealt face-to-face, rather than over a stock exchange. "Special facts" were found in so many cases that the exception tended to overshadow the rule. [Taylor v. Wright, 69 Cal. App. 2d 371 (1945)]

    b. **Minority rule:** [§283]   Under a minority rule, an insider was considered a fiduciary for the shareholders as well as the corporation and was required to disclose any material information he had obtained as an insider that might affect the value of the shares. [King Manufacturing Co. v. Clay, 118 S.E.2d 581 (Ga. 1961)]

C. SECURITIES EXCHANGE ACT OF 1934—IN GENERAL [§284]

The common law rules governing insider trading have been largely superseded by the Securities Exchange Act of 1934. [15 U.S.C. §§78a *et seq.*] The principal focus of the 1934 Act is the regulation of trading in securities after their initial issuance. Most, but not all, of the Act's provisions are keyed to whether securities are required to be registered with the Securities Exchange

Commission ("SEC") under section 12 of the Act. Broadly speaking, section 12 and the rules thereunder require registration of (i) any security that is ***traded on a national securities exchange,*** and (ii) any equity security that is issued by a corporation that has ***total assets*** (not net worth) ***exceeding $5 million*** and is held by ***500 or more persons.*** [15 U.S.C. §78l] One provision that is ***not*** keyed to whether securities are required to be registered is section 10(b) of the Act.

D. SECTION 10(b) AND RULE 10b-5 [§285]

Section 10(b) of the 1934 Act makes it unlawful "to use or employ . . . any manipulative or deceptive device" in contravention of SEC rules in connection with the purchase or sale of any security. [16 U.S.C. §78j] To implement section 10(b), the SEC promulgated rule 10b-5. Under rule 10b-5, it is unlawful, in connection with the purchase or sale of any security, by use of the mails or any means of interstate commerce, to:

(i)   Employ any ***device, scheme, or artifice to defraud***;

(ii) Make any ***untrue statement of a material fact*** or ***omit a material fact*** necessary to make the statements made not misleading; or

(iii) Engage in any ***act, practice, or course of business that operates as fraud or deceit*** upon any person.

[Rule 10b-5]

1. **Nondisclosure:** [§286]   It is clear that rule 10b-5 applies to ***nondisclosure*** by directors or officers, as well as to misrepresentations. [*In re* Cady, Roberts & Co., 40 S.E.C. 907 (1961)] Rule 10b-5 is often referred to as an insider-trading rule because its major significance is to prohibit insider trading. In fact, however, rule 10b-5 extends well beyond insider trading. For example, ***any person*** who makes a misrepresentation in connection with the purchase or sale of stock may be liable under rule 10b-5, whether or not he is an insider.

2. **Covered Securities:** [§287]   Rule 10b-5 applies to the purchase or sale of ***any security***, whether or not required to be registered under section 12. The rule applies whether the corporation is large or small, and whether its shares are widely or closely held. [Hooper v. Mountain States Securities Corp., 282 F.2d 195 (5th Cir. 1960); Kardon v. National Gypsum Co., 83 F. Supp. 613 (E.D. Pa. 1947)] The only limitation is jurisdictional: The violation must involve the use of some ***instrumentality of interstate commerce***. However, this limitation is seldom a problem, since use of the telephone, telegraph, or mail satisfies the interstate commerce requirement.

3. **Jurisdiction, Venue, and Service of Process**

    a. **Jurisdiction:** [§288]   Suits under rule 10b-5 are based on the 1934 Act. Under section 27 of that Act, the federal district courts have exclusive federal question jurisdiction of violations of the Act and the rules promulgated thereunder.

(1) **Pendent jurisdiction of state claims:** [§289] Under the doctrine of "pendent jurisdiction," the plaintiff may join, with a rule 10b-5 claim, any claim he has under state law relating to the same transaction (*e.g.,* for fraud, breach of a common law duty of disclosure, or violation of a state securities statute).

b. **Venue and service:** [§290] Actions under rule 10b-5 are governed by the liberal venue provisions of the 1934 Act. Under those provisions, an action under rule 10b-5 can be filed wherever *any* act or transaction constituting a violation occurred, or in the district where the defendant is found or transacts business. Service of process is also governed by a liberal provision: Process can be served in any district where the defendant can be found, or of which defendant is an inhabitant (whether or not it is the district in which the action was brought). [15 U.S.C. §78aa]

4. **Statute of Limitations:** [§291] No statute of limitations is provided in the 1934 Act. Some courts apply the local period of limitations governing fraud actions. [Newman v. Prior, 518 F.2d 97 (4th Cir. 1975)] Others apply the local period governing state blue sky law actions. [Newman v. Prior, *supra*]

5. **Materiality:** [§292] Rule 10b-5 is applicable to misrepresentations and nondisclosures only if the misrepresented or omitted fact is ***material***. An "omitted fact is material if there is a substantial likelihood that a reasonable shareholder would consider it important in deciding" whether to buy or sell. There "must be a substantial likelihood that the disclosure of the omitted fact would have been viewed by the reasonable investor as having significantly altered the 'total mix' of information made available." [Basic, Inc. v. Levinson, 108 S. Ct. 978 (1988)—quoting TSC Industries v. Northway, 426 U.S. 438 (1976)] Materiality depends "at any given time upon a balancing of both the indicated probability that the event will occur and the anticipated magnitude of the event in light of the totality of the company activity." [Basic, Inc. v. Levinson, *supra*—quoting SEC v. Texas Gulf Sulphur Co., 401 F.2d 833 (2d Cir. 1968)]

a. **Example:** Where insiders knew that the corporation had done exploratory drilling that gave a promise of a gigantic mineral strike, this knowledge was deemed material even though it was possible that after thorough exploration it would turn out that the company did not have a mineable body of ore. Knowledge of the possibility of a gigantic mine could affect the price of stock. If it turned out there was no mineable body of ore, the market price of the stock would not fall, assuming the information about the exploratory holes was neither leaked nor acted upon by insiders. If it turned out there was a mineable body of ore, the market price would rise substantially when that news was disclosed. [SEC v. Texas Gulf Sulphur Co., *supra*]

6. **Fault Required—Scienter:** [§293] A material misrepresentation or omission will not violate rule 10b-5 if the defendant was without fault or merely negligent. Liability can be imposed under rule 10b-5 only if the defendant had scienter. [Ernst & Ernst v. Hochfelder, 425 U.S. 185 (1976)]

a. **Definition of scienter—recklessness:** [§294] Under tort law, scienter is satisfied by an intent to deceive, to mislead, or to convey a false impression. Decisions since *Ernst & Ernst* have unanimously held that recklessness also satisfies the scienter requirement. [Rolf v. Blyth, Eastman Dillon & Co., 570 F.2d 38 (2d Cir. 1976), *cert. denied,* 439 U.S. 1039 (1978)] Many courts have adopted a definition of recklessness as highly unreasonable conduct, "involving not merely simple or even inexcusable negligence, but an extreme departure from the standards of ordinary care, and which presents a danger of misleading buyers or sellers that is either known to the defendant or is so obvious that the actor must have been aware of it." [Sundstrand Corp. v. Sun Chemical Corp., 553 F.2d 1033 (7th Cir. 1977), *cert. denied,* 434 U.S. 875 (1977)]

b. **Injunctive relief:** [§295]   Scienter is also a requirement in an injunctive action under rule 10b-5. [Aaron v. SEC, 446 U.S. 680 (1980)]

7. **Causation and Reliance:** [§296]   The plaintiff in a rule 10b-5 case must prove that the rule 10b-5 violation caused her a loss. In theory, this means that the plaintiff must prove that she relied on the defendant's wrongful statement or omission. In practice, however, the reliance requirement has been greatly attenuated.

a. **Omissions:** [§297]   In omissions cases, "positive proof of reliance is not a prerequisite to recovery. All that is necessary is that the facts withheld be material in the sense that a reasonable investor might have considered them important" in the making of her decision. [Affiliated Ute Citizens of Utah v. United States, 406 U.S. 128 (1972)]

(1) **Presumption of reliance:** [§298]   Subsequent court of appeals cases have held that *Ute* "merely established a presumption that made it possible for the plaintiffs to meet their burden." [Shores v. Sklar, 647 F.2d 462 (5th Cir. 1981) (en banc), *cert. denied,* 459 U.S. 1102 (1983)] The defendant can rebut this presumption by showing that the plaintiff would have followed the same course of conduct even with full disclosure. For example, the defendant might show that the plaintiff learned the omitted fact from an independent source before making her investment; thus, the investment could not have been caused by the defendant's nondisclosure.

b. **Face-to-face misrepresentations:** [§299]   In an action based on a face-to-face misrepresentation, the plaintiff has the burden of showing reliance. [REA Express, Inc. v. Interway Corp., 538 F.2d 953 (2d Cir. 1976); Holdsworth v. Strong, 545 F.2d 687 (10th Cir. 1976)] However, the plaintiff can normally satisfy this burden by showing that the representation was material, testifying that she relied on it, and showing that she traded soon after the misrepresentation. [Robinson v. Cupples Container Co., 513 F.2d 1274 (9th Cir. 1975)] The burden will then shift to the defendant to show that the plaintiff did not rely on the misrepresentation. For example, the defendant might be able to show that the plaintiff knew from other sources that the misrepresentation was false.

c. **"Fraud on the market":** [§300]   Where securities are sold in a well-developed market, a plaintiff may be able to prove reliance on a misrepresentation by alleging that she relied on the integrity of the market. This is known as the "fraud on the market" theory. [Basic, Inc. v. Levinson, *supra*]

(1) **Rationale:** In an open and well-developed securities market, material misrepresentations (or the withholding of material information) generally affects the price of the stock. Since purchasers rely on the price of the stock as a reflection of its value, they may be defrauded even if they do not directly rely on the misstatements. [Basic, Inc. v. Levinson, *supra*]

(2) **Effect:** The effect of the fraud on the market theory is to create a ***presumption*** of reliance. The defendant can rebut the presumption by showing, for example, that a misrepresentation in fact did not lead to a distortion of price, or that an individual plaintiff traded or would have traded despite knowing the statement was false, or that before the plaintiff traded, the correct information credibly entered the market.

8. **When Nondisclosure Constitutes a Violation:** [§301]   Assuming that materiality and scienter are established, rule 10b-5 is clearly violated when a person makes a misrepresentation or states a half-truth in connection with the purchase or sale of stock. Most such cases would constitute common law fraud as well as a violation of rule 10b-5. The primary advantages of rule 10b-5 in such cases is the ability to bring suit in federal court, the liberal venue and service-of-process provisions of the 1934 Act, and a relatively expansive view of what constitutes a misrepresentation or half-truth. More difficult issues are presented, however, where the defendant is claimed to have violated rule 10b-5 not by a misrepresentation or half-truth, but by failure to make disclosure.

a. **Mere possession of material information:** [§302]   Broadly speaking, nondisclosure of material nonpublic information violates rule 10b-5 ***only*** when there is a duty, ***independent of rule 10b-5,*** to disclose. A duty to disclose under rule 10b-5 does not arise from the mere possession of nonpublic information. [Chiarella v. United States, 445 U.S. 222 (1980); Dirks v. SEC, 463 U.S. 646 (1983)] So, for example, a person who acquires material nonpublic information merely by skill and diligence in searching out information, without using any wrongful methods, does not violate rule 10b-5 if he trades on the basis of that information. Similarly, a person who innocently overhears material nonpublic information can make use of it in trading without violating rule 10b-5.

b. **Trading by insiders:** [§303]   At the other end, it is clear that insiders—directors, officers, controlling shareholders, and corporate employees—violate rule 10b-5 if they trade on the basis of material nonpublic information that they obtained through their positions ("inside information"). The duty of such persons to disclose before trading rests on the existence of a relationship giving them access to information intended to be available only for a corporate purpose and the unfairness of allowing a corporate insider to take advantage of that information by trading without disclosure. [*In re* Cady, Roberts & Co., *supra*, §286; Chiarella v. United States, *supra*] Trading by insiders on the basis of inside information is commonly referred to as "insider trading."

c. **Misappropriation:** [§304]   Between the extremes of skillfully or innocently acquired nonpublic information on the one hand, and inside information on the other, is information that a noninsider wrongfully acquires, *i.e.,* "misappropriates." Whether a person who trades on the basis of such information is liable under rule 10b-5, and if so, the extent of that liability, are questions that are not completely settled. However, the misappropriation theory is most useful where the defendant had no independent fiduciary duty to the party with whom he actually traded.

(1) **Trading on improperly obtained information could be a violation:** [§305] In *Chiarella v. United States, supra,* Chiarella worked in the composing room of a financial printer and learned of prospective takeover bids before they were made public. Then, in violation of his employer's rules, Chiarella traded in the target's stock before the tender offer was made and sold the target's stock at a profit after the tender offer was made. Chiarella was indicted for violation of section 10(b) and rule 10b-5. The trial court instructed the jury that Chiarella should be found guilty if he used material nonpublic information at a time when he knew that other people trading in the securities market did not have access to the same information. The jury convicted Chiarella. The United States Supreme Court reversed, holding that the trial court's instruction imposed too broad a duty. However, the Court reserved decision on whether Chiarella could have been convicted on the theory that he breached a duty to the acquiring corporation when he acted upon information that he obtained by virtue of his position as an employee of a printer employed by that corporation. Furthermore, at least four Justices explicitly embraced the misappropriation theory, that trading on the basis of improperly obtained nonpublic information violated rule 10b-5.

(a) **Misappropriation theory applied:** [§306] In *SEC v. Materia,* 745 F.2d 197 (2d Cir. 1984), *cert. denied,* 471 U.S. 1053 (1985), Materia (like Chiarella) was employed by a financial printer and used confidential information obtained in that capacity to trade in the stock of target corporations. The court held that Materia had criminally violated rule 10b-5 under the misappropriation theory. *Chiarella* was distinguished on the ground that the instruction to the jury in that case had been much broader than the misappropriation theory.

(2) **Violation of duty to employer:** [§307] In *United States v. Newman,* 664 F.2d 12 (2d Cir. 1981), *cert. denied,* 464 U.S. 863 (1983), Courtois was employed in the mergers and acquisitions department of Morgan Stanley, an investment banking firm. Warner-Lambert Corporation retained Morgan Stanley to assess the desirability of making a tender offer for Deseret Pharmaceutical Corporation. Courtois learned of Warner's plan, and, acting with and through others, purchased Deseret stock at $28 per share. When Warner publicly announced the tender offer, the Deseret stock jumped to $38. The Second Circuit held that Courtois had criminally violated rule 10b-5, based on the misappropriation theory.

(a) **Does not apply to private actions:** [§308] In a private, rather than criminal, action based on the same facts as *Newman, supra,* the Second Circuit held that although Newman and his associates had criminally violated rule 10b-5 by trading on the basis of information they used in violation of Newman's fiduciary duty to his employer, they were not liable under private actions by those persons with whom they actually traded. An employee's duty to "abstain or disclose" with respect to his employer does not stretch to encompass a duty to disclose to the general public. [Moss v. Morgan Stanley, Inc., 719 F.2d 5 (2d Cir. 1983), *cert. denied*, 465 U.S. 1025 (1984)]

(b) **Insider Trading and Securities Fraud Enforcement Act:** [§309] The Insider Trading and Securities Fraud Enforcement Act of 1988 is intended in part to overrule the result in *Moss v. Morgan Stanley*. Under one section of that Act, any person who violates rule 10b-5 by purchasing or selling a security while in the possession of material nonpublic information is expressly made liable to ***any person*** who, contemporaneously with the purchase or sale, purchased or sold (as the case may be) securities of the same class. Liability under this provision is limited to the profit the defendant gained or the loss he avoided.

(3) **Mail and wire fraud:** [§310] A federal criminal statute concerning mail and wire fraud [18 U.S.C. §§1341, 1343] may render the misappropriation theory less important. In *United States v. Carpenter,* 791 F.2d 1024, *aff'd,* 108 S. Ct. 316 (1987), a *Wall Street Journal* reporter who wrote a widely read and influential column, participated, in violation of the *Journal's* rules, in a scheme in which he provided two stockbrokers with securities-related information that was scheduled to appear in his column. Based on this advance information, the two brokers would buy or sell the securities before the column appeared, and sell or buy immediately thereafter. The reporter was found guilty of criminally violating rule 10b-5, based on the misappropriation theory, and was also found guilty of mail and wire fraud, since the *Wall Street Journal* was distributed by mail. The rule 10b-5 violation was affirmed by an equally divided United States Supreme Court, without an opinion. Therefore, the Supreme Court's view of the misappropriation theory is still not clear. The mail and wire fraud conviction, however, was unanimously affirmed. The Court held that the interest of the *Journal's* owner in the confidentiality of the *Journal's* contents was a property right, and that by using the information for his own purposes, the reporter had obtained "money or property" from the *Journal* by fraud.

(a) **Comment:** As a practical matter, the status of the misappropriation theory under rule 10b-5 has been rendered somewhat less important by the Court's adoption of a comparable theory in the interpretation of the mail and wire fraud statute. Most persons who misappropriate and then trade on information will now be guilty of the crime of mail and wire fraud, whether or not they are guilty of criminally violating rule 10b-5. The mail and wire fraud statute, however, unlike rule 10b-5, may not give rise to private actions.

d. **"Disclose or abstain":** [§311] Where a person has a duty to disclose material nonpublic information in his possession before he trades, the applicable rule is often expressed as "disclose or abstain." That is, nondisclosure ***in itself*** normally does not violate rule 10b-5. Nondisclosure by a person with a duty to disclose violates rule 10b-5 *only* if the person trades. Such a person has a choice: disclose and trade, or do not disclose and do not trade.

9. **Who Can Bring Suit Under Rule 10b-5**

a. **Suit by SEC:** [§312]   A suit for violation of rule 10b-5 may be brought by the SEC. [SEC v. Texas Gulf Sulphur Co., *supra,* §292]

b. **Suit by private plaintiff:** [§313]   It is also well-established that section 10(b) and rule 10b-5 create an "implied" or private right of action in favor of an injured private party. [Superintendent of Insurance v. Bankers Life & Casualty Co., 404 U.S. 6 (1971); Kardon v. National Gypsum Co., *supra,* §287]

c. *Blue Chip* **rule—private plaintiff must be purchaser or seller:** [§314]   A private cause of action can be maintained only by a person who actually purchased or sold the securities to which the violation of rule 10b-5 relates. It is not enough that the violation caused the plaintiff *not* to buy or *not* to sell. [Blue Chip Stamps v. Manor Drug Stores, 421 U.S. 723 (1975)]

(1) **Rationale:** The *Blue Chip* rule is based largely on considerations of administrability. The Supreme Court was concerned that it would be too easy for a person to bring a contrived suit under rule 10b-5, based on the allegation, which would be supported by the plaintiff's oral testimony and difficult to disprove, that he failed to buy or sell because of defendant's misrepresentation or omission. In contrast, when a plaintiff has actually bought or sold, there is an objective and documented action, not merely a claim of subjective response.

(2) **Meaning of "sale":** [§315]   Although *Blue Chip* allows private actions to be brought only by persons who have actually purchased or sold, the term "sale" has an expansive meaning under the securities acts.

(a) **Stock for assets:** [§316]   An exchange of stock for assets, property, or other stock is a "sale" within the meaning of rule 10b-5.

(b) **Mergers and liquidations:** [§317]   A merger can be a sale under rule 10b-5. [Vine v. Beneficial Finance Co., 374 F.2d 627 (2d Cir. 1967)]

(c) **Contracts to sell stock:** [§318]   An executory contract to sell stock is a sale under rule 10b-5. [A.T. Brod & Co. v. Perlow, 375 F.2d 393 (2d Cir. 1967)]

(d) **Pledges:** [§319]   A pledge can be a sale under rule 10b-5. [Rubin v. United States, 449 U.S. 424 (1981); Chemical Bank v. Arthur Andersen & Co., 726 F.2d 930 (2d Cir. 1984)]

(3) **Standing of SEC:** [§320]   The *Blue Chip* rule bars only a *private action* based on rule 10b-5 by a private person who has neither purchased nor sold

the securities. The *SEC* can bring an action against a violator of rule 10b-5 even though the SEC neither purchased nor sold the securities. By its nature, the SEC is never a purchaser or a seller. Furthermore, the SEC is unlikely to bring contrived suits.

10. **Fiduciary Violations by Directors, Officers, or Controlling Shareholders Involving Purchase or Sale of Stock**

   a. **"Ordinary mismanagement" without misrepresentation, nondisclosure, or manipulation—the *Santa Fe* rule:** [§321] A breach of fiduciary duty by a corporate manager that does not involve a misrepresentation, nondisclosure, or manipulation does not violate rule 10b-5 even if it involves the purchase or sale of stock. [Santa Fe Industries, Inc. v. Green, 430 U.S. 462 (1977)] This kind of 10b-5 case is often referred to as an "ordinary mismanagement" case.

   (1) **Example:** A Corp. and B Corp. are both incorporated in State X. A owns 90% of B. Under the law of State X, a short-form merger can be used to cash out minority shareholders if the parent owns at least 90% of the subsidiary. A minority shareholder who is dissatisfied with the price offered for his shares may demand appraisal, but this is his only remedy. A Corp. proposes to merge B Corp. into itself by a short-form merger for a cash price that is wholly inadequate, but A Corp. discloses all the relevant facts concerning the value of B Corp., from which the inadequacy of the price could be determined. B Corp.'s minority shareholders have no cause of action against A Corp. under rule 10b-5. [Santa Fe Industries, Inc. v. Green, *supra*]

   (2) **Example:** Similarly, there apparently would be no liability under rule 10b-5 where a transaction with a controlling shareholder involves a purchase or sale of stock at an unfair price, but the transaction requires shareholder approval under state law, and such approval is given after complete disclosure. [Popkin v. Bishop, 464 F.2d 714 (2d Cir. 1972)] The minority shareholders are not powerless, however. They may be able to sue under state law to enjoin the transaction, if it constitutes unfair self-dealing.

   b. **Purchase or sale of stock by fiduciary on the basis of misrepresentation or nondisclosure:** [§322] Notwithstanding *Santa Fe*, if a director or officer purchases stock from or sells stock to the corporation on the basis of a misrepresentation or nondisclosure, the corporation can sue the fiduciary under rule 10b-5, even though it can *also* sue her for breach of fiduciary duty.

   (1) **Derivative suits:** [§323] If the corporation does not sue in such a case, a minority shareholder can maintain a derivative suit on the corporation's behalf (*see infra*, §592). The *Blue Chip* rule would not be a barrier to such an action, because the corporation is a purchaser or seller, and the action is maintained on its behalf.

   c. **Purchase or sale of stock by controlling shareholder with approval of majority of directors:** [§324] Suppose that a controlling shareholder causes a corporation to issue stock to him, or buy stock from him, at an unfair price, and the material facts are not disclosed to the minority shareholders. A derivative action can be brought against the controlling shareholder under rule 10b-5 in such a case *if* the nondisclosure *caused a loss* to the minority shareholders. [Goldberg v. Meridor, 567 F.2d 209 (2d Cir. 1977), *cert. denied,* 434 U.S. 1069 (1978)]

(1) **Causation:** [§325]   To show that the nondisclosure caused a loss to the minority shareholders, the plaintiff must establish that **an effective state remedy was forgone** as a result of the nondisclosure to the minority shareholders. The plaintiff usually attempts to satisfy this requirement by arguing that if disclosure had been made to the minority shareholders, they could have sued for injunctive relief against the proposed transaction under state law. The courts are divided concerning what the plaintiff must show concerning the likelihood that the suit would have been successful.

   (a) **Actual success:** [§326]   Some courts hold that the plaintiff must show that the shareholders would actually have succeeded if they had brought the forgone suit. [Kidwell *ex rel.* Penfield v. Meikle, 597 F.2d 1273 (9th Cir. 1979)]

   (b) **Reasonable probability of success:** [§327]   Other courts hold that the plaintiff must show "there was a reasonable probability of ultimate success." [Healey v. Catalyst Recovery, 616 F.2d 641 (3d Cir. 1980)]

   (c) **Prima facie case for relief:** [§328]   Still other courts have adopted a requirement "that the facts shown make out a prima facie case for relief." [Alabama Farm Bureau Mutual Casualty Co. v. American Fidelity Life Insurance Co., 606 F.2d 602 (5th Cir. 1979), *cert. denied,* 449 U.S. 820 (1980)]

11. **Liability of Nontrading Persons for Misrepresentations:** [§329]   Normally, a rule 10b-5 action is brought against a person who traded in stock. However, even persons who do not trade may be liable under rule 10b-5 in certain types of cases. [Basic, Inc. v. Levinson, *supra,* §300] A corporation or other person who makes a misrepresentation of a sort that would cause reasonable investors to rely thereon in the purchase or sale of securities would be liable under rule 10b-5. So, for example, a nontrading corporation may be liable under rule 10b-5 if it issues a misleading press release that would be likely to affect investment decisions. [SEC v. Texas Gulf Sulphur Co., *supra,* §312]

   a. **Scienter required:** [§330]   A nontrading corporation or other person, like any other defendant, will be liable under rule 10b-5 only if it had scienter. [Ernst & Ernst v. Hochfelder, *supra,* §293] A misrepresentation that is without fault, or that results only from negligence, will not result in rule 10b-5 liability.

12. **Liability of Corporation for Nondisclosure:** [§331]   The basic principle of rule 10b-5, as to nondisclosure, is disclose or abstain. Accordingly, a **nontrading** corporation is unlikely to be liable under rule 10b-5 for **nondisclosure** of material facts even though

persons who do trade would have deemed the information material and made different investment decisions if they had known the undisclosed information. The timing of disclosure of material facts is "a matter for the business judgment of the corporate officers entrusted with the management of the corporation within the affirmative disclosure requirements promulgated by the exchanges and by the SEC." [*SEC v. Texas Gulf Sulphur Co., supra;* *Financial Industrial Fund, Inc. v. McDonnell Douglas Corp.,* 474 F.2d 514 (10th Cir.), *cert. denied,* 414 U.S. 874 (1973)]

13. **Tippee and Tipper Liability:** [§332]   A tippee is a person who is not an insider, but who trades on information she has received from an insider. The basic principles of tippee liability were laid down by the Supreme Court in *Dirks v. SEC* (*supra,* §302).

   a.   **Broad rule rejected:** [§333]   The Court in *Dirks* rejected the broad rule that a person would be liable, as a tippee, solely because she knowingly received material nonpublic information from an insider and traded on it. Such a broad rule would conflict with the conclusion in *Chiarella* (*supra,* §§302-304) that only some persons, under some circumstances, will be barred by rule 10b-5 from trading while in the possession of material nonpublic information. The Court was also concerned that a broad rule would inhibit the role of market analysts, who often, as part of their research into particular stocks, interview corporate executives and acquire information that may not have theretofore been public. However, the Court identified several kinds of cases in which tippees would be liable.

   b.   **Tippee liability based on fiduciary obligations of tipper:** [§334]   A person who receives information from an insider and trades on it is liable if—but only if— she receives the information improperly because the insider breached a fiduciary duty in communicating the information, and the tippee knows or should know of the breach. The primary test for determining whether the communication of information by an insider constitutes a breach of fiduciary duty is whether the insider communicated the information to realize a gain or advantage. [*Dirks v. SEC, supra*] Not only are insiders forbidden by their fiduciary relationship from personally using undisclosed corporate information for the purpose of reaping personal gain or advantage, but they may not give such information to others for that purpose. An insider who tips for that purpose breaches his fiduciary duty to the corporation. A tippee who knows or should know that the tipper, in disclosing inside information to the tippee, has breached his fiduciary duty to the corporation by using corporate information for his own gain or advantage, will be liable as a knowing participant in a breach of fiduciary duty. On the surface, this test seems narrow. However, the Court defined gain or advantage, in this connection, so broadly as to include most tipping activity.

      (1)   **Tips to friends or relatives:** [§335]   There is a gain or advantage to the insider when he makes a gift of confidential information to a trading relative or friend. The tip to the relative or friend, followed by a trade by the tippee, is like a trade by the insider followed by a gift of his profits from the trade. [*Dirks v. SEC, supra*]

      (2)   **Quid pro quo for past or future benefits:** [§336]   Even if the tippee is not a friend or a relative, the insider breaches his fiduciary duty, and the tippee

is therefore liable, if there is a relationship between the insider and the tippee that suggests that the tip is a quid pro quo for a past or future benefit from the tippee. [Dirks v. SEC, *supra*]

    (3) **Tippers:** [§337]   Under *Dirks*, if a tippee will be liable, so will the tipper.

    (4) **Outsiders in special confidential relationships:** [§338]   Outsiders who receive information from the corporation as a result of a special confidential relationship could be liable, under a separate principle (*see* below). [Dirks v. SEC, *supra*]

14. **"Temporary Insiders":** [§339]   Where corporate information is legitimately revealed to an underwriter, accountant, lawyer, or other professional or consultant working for the corporation, that person may become a fiduciary of the corporation's shareholders regarding that information. [Dirks v. SEC, *supra*] The theory is that the person has entered into a special confidential relationship with the corporation and is given access to the information solely for corporate purposes. If such a person trades on the information, he will be just as liable as an ordinary insider (and he will be liable as a tipper if he improperly tips the information). Persons who acquire information in this way are sometimes referred to as "temporary insiders."

15. **Aiders and Abettors:** [§340]   An aider and abettor is a person who aids or abets someone who improperly trades. For example, an accountant or lawyer may aid or abet a client's wrongful trading, or a banker may finance such trading. A person who aids or abets a violation of rule 10b-5 may be liable, along with the person he aids and abets. [Woods v. Barnett Bank of Fort Lauderdale, 765 F.2d 1004 (11th Cir. 1985); Metge v. Baehler, 762 F.2d 621 (8th Cir. 1985); IIT v. Cornfeld, 619 F.2d 909 (2d Cir. 1980)]

    a. **Test of aiding and abetting liability:** [§341]   There is a three-part test for imposing aiding and abetting liability under Rule 10b-5:

        (i) A *person other than the aider and abettor* must have violated rule 10b-5 (the violation by this person is sometimes referred to as the "primary violation," in contrast to the secondary violation of the aider and abettor).

        (ii) There must be some degree of *knowledge* by the aider and abettor that his role furthered an improper activity.

        (iii) The aider and abettor's role must reach some *designated level of significance* in furthering the primary activity.

    [SEC v. Coffey, 493 F.2d 1304 (6th Cir. 1974), *cert. denied,* 420 U.S. 908 (1975)] A more colloquial statement than this three-part test is that to be held as an aider and abettor, a person must in some sort associate himself with the venture, participate in it as something that he wishes to bring about, and seek by his action to make it succeed. [United States v. Peoni, 100 F.2d 401 (2d Cir. 1938)]

    b. **Aiding and abetting by silence or inaction:** [§342]   Silence or inaction may constitute aiding and abetting if the defendant had a *duty* to speak or to act [Woods

v. Barnett Bank of Fort Lauderdale, *supra;* IIT v. Cornfeld, *supra*], or if the defendant consciously **intended** to assist in the commission of a wrongful act [Monsen v. Consolidated Dressed Beef Co., 579 F.2d 793 (3d Cir. 1978), *cert. denied,* 439 U.S. 930 (1979)].

c. **Scienter requirement—recklessness:** [§343] Scienter is a requirement of aiding and abetting liability, just as of all other liability under rule 10b-5. The courts have taken several different approaches to the question of whether **recklessness** suffices to impose liability for aiding and abetting.

   (1) **Same as for primary violations:** [§344] Under one approach, recklessness is applied to aiding and abetting in the same manner as it is applied to primary violations. [Herm v. Stafford, 663 F.2d 669 (6th Cir. 1981)]

   (2) **Independent duty:** [§345] Under a second approach, aiding and abetting liability can be based on recklessness only where the defendant violated an independent duty—in particular, a duty to disclose the primary violation. [Cleary v. Perfectune, Inc., 700 F.2d 774 (1st Cir. 1983)]

   (3) **Degrees of scienter and assistance:** [§346] Under a third approach, aiding and abetting liability can be based on recklessness even if there is no independent duty, but an inverse relationship is drawn between the degree of scienter and the degree of assistance: the less substantial the assistance, the more demanding is the requirement of scienter. [Metge v. Baehler, 762 F.2d 621 (8th Cir. 1985)] A related approach is that a greater degree of scienter—"high conscious intent," or "something closer to an actual intent to aid in the fraud"—must be shown where the aider and abettor is not under an independent duty of disclosure. [Woodward v. Metro Bank of Dallas, 552 F.2d 84 (5th Cir. 1975); Edwards & Hanley v. Wells Fargo Securities Clearance Corp., 602 F.2d 478 (2d Cir. 1979), *cert. denied,* 444 U.S. 1045 (1980)]

16. **Defenses:** [§347] Two important defenses to a rule 10b-5 claim are the "due diligence" and "in pari delicto" defenses.

    a. **Due diligence:** [§348] If the plaintiff is at fault in relying on the defendant's misrepresentation or in failing to learn an omitted fact, in the sense that if the plaintiff had used due diligence he would not have been misled, that fault may bar recovery. Mere **negligence** by the plaintiff will not constitute a lack of due diligence for rule 10b-5 purposes. Since a **defendant** is not liable for negligence under rule 10b-5 (*see supra,* §330), it would be anomalous to hold the **plaintiff** to a higher standard. [Dupuy v. Dupuy, 551 F.2d 1005 (5th Cir.), *cert. denied,* 434 U.S. 911 (1977); *and see, e.g.,* Holdsworth v. Strong, *supra,* §299] The plaintiff will, however, be barred from recovery by his own intentional misconduct, and will be barred by his own recklessness if the defendant was merely reckless. It is not yet clear whether the plaintiff will be barred by his own recklessness if the defendant was guilty of intentional misconduct.

(1) **Example:** Seller recklessly makes oral statements to Buyer, a sophisticated businessperson, about C stock. These statements are incorrect. Subsequently, however, and before Buyer agrees to purchase C stock, Seller furnishes Buyer with documents that correctly state the facts about C. Buyer does not read the documents. In a suit by Buyer against Seller under rule 10b-5, Seller may prevail under the due diligence defense. [Zobrist v. Coal-X, Inc., 708 F.2d 1511 (10th Cir. 1983)]

b. **In pari delicto:** [§349] "In pari delicto" is a Latin phrase that means that in a case of equal fault, the position of the defendant is better. In a rule 10b-5 context, the doctrine refers to the fault of a plaintiff who has *himself* violated rule 10b-5. (The doctrine is most commonly raised in suits by a tippee against a tipper for misrepresentation of alleged inside information. The tipper replies that the tippee was in pari delicto because he violated rule 10b-5 by trading on the tipped information.) A private action for damages under the securities laws may be barred on the grounds of the plaintiff's culpability, but only where (i) as a direct result of his own actions the plaintiff bears at least *substantially equal responsibility* for the violations he seeks to redress, and (ii) preclusion of suit would not *significantly interfere* with the effective enforcement of the securities laws and protection of the investing public. Note that an investor who engages in insider trading as a tippee is not necessarily as blameworthy as a corporate insider who discloses the information for personal gain. [Bateman Eichler, Hill Richards, Inc. v. Berner, 472 U.S. 299 (1985)]

(1) **Effect:** Although *Bateman Eichler* severely limited the in pari delicto defense in rule 10b-5 cases, it did not foreclose that defense in situations "in which the relative culpabilities of the tippee and his insider source merit a different mix of deterrent incentives." [Rothberg v. Rosenbloom, 808 F.2d 252 (3d Cir. 1986)]

17. **Remedies:** [§350] A great variety of remedies are available for violations of rule 10b-5.

a. **Potential remedies:** [§351] Before examining exactly which remedies are available in which kinds of cases, it is helpful to understand the meaning of various remedies.

(1) **Out-of-pocket damages:** [§352] Out-of-pocket damages are the difference between the price paid for stock and its actual value. This measure is designed to put the injured person back in the same financial position he was in before the transaction occurred, but not to give him the benefit of the bargain.

(a) **Compare—benefit-of-the-bargain damages:** [§353] Benefit-of-the-bargain damages are measured by the difference between the value of stock as it really is and the value the stock would have had if a misrepresentation had been true. The difference between out-of-pocket and benefit-of-the-bargain damages can be illustrated as follows: Buyer paid $20,000 for O Oil Company stock, based on Seller's representation that O had just struck a new well. O stock would have been worth $22,000 if the representation had been true. In fact, O had not just struck a new well, and the stock was worth only $19,000. Benefit-of-the-bargain damages would be $3,000—the difference between the actual value of the O stock ($19,000) and the value it would have had if it had struck a new well ($22,000). Out-of-pocket damages, however, are only $1,000—the difference between the amount Buyer paid ($20,000) and the value of the stock ($19,000).

(b) **Standard measure of conventional damages in rule 10b-5 cases:** [§354]   In private actions under rule 10b-5 in which the plaintiff seeks conventional damages, *out-of-pocket damages* is the standard measure; benefit-of-the-bargain damages are generally not granted. [Estate Counseling Service, Inc. v. Merrill Lynch, Pierce, Fenner & Smith, Inc., 303 F.2d 527 (10th Cir. 1962); Green v. Occidental Petroleum Co., 541 F.2d 1335 (9th Cir. 1976)]

(2) **Restitutionary relief:** [§355]   A plaintiff may seek restitutionary relief rather than conventional damages.

   (a) **Rescission:** [§356]   The most common form of restitutionary relief is rescission. If a seller sues for rescission and succeeds, she returns the purchase price and gets back the stock she sold. If a buyer sues for rescission and succeeds, he returns the stock and gets back his purchase price.

   (b) **Rescissionary or restitutionary damages:** [§357]   Another form of restitutionary relief is rescissionary or restitutionary damages. Such damages are the money equivalent of rescission. They are measured by the difference between the value of what plaintiff gave up and the value of what the defendant received.

   (c) **Difference between conventional damages and restitutionary relief:** [§358]   The major difference between conventional damages and restitutionary relief (whether rescission or rescissionary damages) is that out-of-pocket damages are based on the *plaintiff's loss*, while restitutionary relief is based on the *defendant's wrongful gain*.

      1) **Comment:** Rescission or rescissionary damages may be especially attractive remedies to a plaintiff when the value of the stock in question changed radically after the transaction. For example, suppose the facts of the oil company hypothetical (above, §353) are reversed: O Oil Company *has* struck a new well, but Buyer tells Seller that it has not. As a result, Seller sells Buyer O stock for $20,000, when it was really worth $22,000. By the time of the trial, however, the O stock is worth $40,000. Under the conventional out-of-pocket damages measure, Seller would be entitled to $2,000, the difference between the value of what she gave up (stock worth $22,000) and the value of what she got ($20,000 in cash). Seller is much better off if she can either get back the stock itself (which will give her $40,000 worth of O stock in return for repaying only $20,000 in

cash) or rescissional damages (which will be $20,000—the value of the stock minus the value of what she received for it).

b. **Application of remedy provisions:** [§359] The next several sections show how these potential remedies are actually used to remedy violations of rule 10b-5. Which remedies are available in which cases depends to a considerable extent on whether the stock is closely or publicly held, and, if publicly held, whether the injured party sold to or purchased from the person who violated rule 10b-5.

(1) **Remedies for 10b-5 violations in connection with stock of closely held corporations:** [§360] Suppose that Seller owns stock in C, a closely held corporation. Buyer makes a material representation to Seller concerning C. If the representation were true, it would have a negative impact on the value of C stock. In fact, it is false. In reliance on the misrepresentation, Seller sells his C stock to Buyer. Later, Seller learns that he was deceived.

(a) **Out-of-pocket damages:** [§361] Seller can sue for conventional damages under rule 10b-5. In that case, his recovery will normally be based on the out-of-pocket measure; thus, he will be awarded the difference between the price he received for his stock and its actual higher value. (Similarly, a buyer can sue for out-of-pocket damages based on a misrepresentation by a seller; and either a seller or a buyer can sue for out-of-pocket damages based on failure to disclose a material fact, where disclosure is required.)

(b) **Restitutionary relief:** [§362] Alternatively, a seller or buyer who acted on the basis of a misrepresentation or a wrongful nondisclosure may sue for rescissionary relief.

1) **When plaintiff is a seller:** [§363] If the plaintiff is a seller, and sues for rescission, he would return the purchase price to the buyer and recover the stock. Suppose that Buyer has already resold the stock. In that case, Seller may be able to recover Buyer's profit, *i.e.,* the difference between the price at which Seller sold the stock to Buyer, and the price at which Buyer resold the stock. The theory of such a recovery is that Buyer holds the profit in constructive trust for Seller. In effect, the money Buyer received when he resold the stock replaced the stock, to which Seller was entitled. Seller should get the equivalent of rescission by recovering the difference between the price at which he sold to Buyer and the proceeds of Buyer's resale. [Janigan v. Taylor, 344 F.2d 781 (1st Cir.), *cert. denied,* 382 U.S. 879 (1965); Affiliated Ute Citizens of Utah v. United States, *supra,* §297; Harris v. American Investment Co., 523 F.2d 220 (8th Cir. 1975), *cert. denied,* 423 U.S. 1054 (1976)] This is a form of rescissionary damages.

2) **When plaintiff is a buyer:** [§364] Similarly, if the injured party is a buyer, she may return the stock and recover the purchase price. If she resold the stock at a lower price before she discovered the

violation of rule 10b-5, she should be able to recover the difference between the price she paid and the resale price. [Chasins v. Smith, Barney & Co., 438 F.2d 1167 (2d Cir. 1970), *aff'g* 306 F. Supp. 177 (S.D.N.Y. 1969); Randall v. Loftsgaarden, 478 U.S. 647 (1986)]

(2) **Remedies for 10b-5 violations in connection with stock in publicly held corporations:** [§365]   Where a rule 10b-5 case involves stock in a publicly held corporation, the situation is much different. To keep the discussion as simple as possible, the focus will be on cases where the injured party is a seller. The same principles generally apply where the injured party is a buyer.

(a) **Plaintiff deals directly with defendant:** [§366]   Suppose that Seller owns stock in P, a publicly held corporation. Buyer publicly makes a material misrepresentation concerning P, which has a negative impact on the value of P stock. In reliance on the misrepresentation, Seller sells his stock to Buyer.

1) **Damages:** [§367]   Assume first that Seller sues Buyer for conventional damages. Under the out-of-pocket measure, Seller would recover the difference between the price at which he sold stock in P and the actual value of the stock. There is a good reason, however, for measuring the actual value of the stock, not by its price *at the time of the wrong,* but by its price *at the time of disclosure of the correct information.* The market price of P stock at the time of the wrong is *not* a good indicator of the actual value of the stock at that time, because the market will have been affected by Buyer's misrepresentation. In contrast, the market price of P stock after the misrepresentation is corrected normally is a good indicator of the actual value of the stock at the time of the wrong, because that price will reflect the market's valuation of P stock in light of the new, correct information. [Harris v. American Investment Co., *supra,* §363] The use of market price at the time of disclosure to determine the actual value of the stock at the time of the wrong is sometimes referred to as the "modified" out-of-pocket measure.

a) **Conversion measure:** [§368]   Some cases put a slight twist on this rule, and allow the seller to measure damages by the highest price within a reasonable time after disclosure. The theory is that if Buyer had not caused Seller to sell his P stock at an unfairly low price, Seller might have sold the stock at the highest price available in the market during a reasonable time after he learned the true facts. Of course, we cannot know exactly what price Seller would have obtained—he might have sold at less than the highest price—but the wrongdoer should bear the burden of this uncertainty, since she created it. [Mitchell v. Texas Gulf Sulphur Co., 446 F.2d 90 (10th Cir.), *cert. denied,* 404 U.S. 1004 (1971)] This is sometimes known as the "conversion" measure.

2) **Restitutionary relief:** [§369] Restitutionary relief (rescission and rescissional damages) is usually **_unavailable_** in the case of publicly held stock, because such relief is unnecessary to compensate the seller or prevent unjust enrichment of the buyer. Where publicly held stock is involved, once the misrepresentation is corrected, the seller can replace himself by purchasing the stock on the market.

a) **Example:** On January 10, Seller sells P stock to Buyer, who makes a material misrepresentation that P is badly off, when in fact it is not. The price is $30. On February 20, disclosure is made, and P stock goes up to $35, where it hovers until March 20. A year later, at the time of trial, P stock is at $60. Seller's failure to realize a gain from the further increase in the value of P stock from $35 to $60 after February 20 does not derive from Buyer's misrepresentation, but from Seller's fully informed decision not to buy P stock at $35. Similarly, Buyer's gain after February 20 reflects not her fraud, but her decision to retain the P stock, which she could have purchased at $35 on February 20 even without having made the misrepresentation. [SEC v. MacDonald, 699 F.2d 47 (1st Cir. 1983)]

b) **Compare—close corporations:** [§370] The rule that restitutionary relief is generally not available under rule 10b-5 in the case of stock in publicly held corporations is not inconsistent with the rule that restitutionary relief generally **_is_** available under rule 10b-5 in the case of close corporation stock. Where a close corporation is involved, disclosure normally does not put the plaintiff and defendant on an equal footing: Since stock in a close corporation cannot be purchased and sold on the market, the injured seller cannot replace himself by buying shares of the stock on the market after disclosure is made.

(b) **Plaintiff does not deal directly with defendant:** [§371] Suppose that, although Buyer violates rule 10b-5 by a misrepresentation or wrongful omission, she does not deal directly with Seller. In other words, Seller did sell, and would not have sold but for the misrepresentation or omission, but Buyer did not buy from Seller.

1) **Misrepresentation:** [§372] If the defendant made a public misrepresentation that had the foreseeable effect of causing members of the public to buy or sell the stock, she will probably be liable for all the resulting damages. [Mitchell v. Texas Gulf Sulphur Co., *supra*, §368; Blackie v. Barrack, 524 F.2d 891 (9th Cir. 1975), *cert. denied*, 429 U.S. 816 (1976)]

2) **Omission:** [§373] Suppose the defendant did not make a public misrepresentation, but traded on the basis of inside information without having made disclosure.

a) **Case law:** [§374] Two leading cases in the Second Circuit, *Shapiro v. Merrill Lynch, Pierce, Fenner & Smith, Inc.,* 495 F.2d 228 (2d Cir. 1974) and *Elkind v. Liggett & Myers, Inc.,* 635 F.2d 156 (2d Cir. 1980), imposed liability in such cases. However, *Elkind* limited damages to a "disgorgement" measure, in which the defendant is obliged only to surrender profits, not to compensate everyone who traded at the same time for the difference between the price they realized and the value of the stock. A Sixth Circuit case, *Fridrich v. Bradford,* 542 F.2d 307 (6th Cir. 1976) (decided after *Shapiro* but before *Elkind*), refused to impose liability, partly out of concern that to do so would "unduly" extend liability under rule 10b-5—a problem that is cured by using the disgorgement measure to limit damages.

b) **Insider Trading Act of 1988:** [§375] Under the Insider Trading and Securities Fraud Enforcement Act of 1988, any person who violates rule 10b-5 by purchasing or selling a security while in the possession of material nonpublic information is expressly made liable to any other person who, contemporaneously with the purchase or sale, sold or purchased securities of the same class. Liability under this provision is limited to the profit the defendant gained, or the loss avoided. The Act therefore seems to adopt the approach taken in *Elkind.* (The statute also provides that it shall not be construed to limit the right of any person to bring an implied private right of action. The committee report adds that the "Committee recognizes that where the plaintiff demonstrates that he was defrauded by the defendant's insider trading and suffered actual damages proximately caused by the defendant's behavior, a cap of profit gained or loss avoided by the defendant, which is applicable for actions by contemporaneous traders, is not appropriate. Rather, in such an implied private cause of action, the plaintiff should be able to recover the full extent of those actual damages.")

(3) **Remedies available to the government:** [§376] The SEC, as a government agency, rather than a buyer or a seller, cannot sue for damages in the normal sense. However, the SEC can seek several different remedies for violation of rule 10b-5, including special monetary remedies.

(a) **Injunctive relief:** [§377] The SEC can, and commonly does, seek injunctive relief. In seeking injunctive relief, the SEC often seeks ancillary monetary relief in the form of disgorgement of profits, or other payments, that can be used as a fund for private parties injured by the violation. [SEC v. Texas Gulf Sulphur, *supra*, §292—insiders ordered to pay their profits to corporation; corporation ordered to hold profits in escrow for five years for claimants—at the end of the five-year period, balance to become property of corporation]

(b) **Criminal sanctions:** [§378]   Violation of rule 10b-5 is a criminal act. The Justice Department often seeks fines and sometimes jail sentences for such violations.

(c) **Civil penalties:** [§379]   Under the Insider Trading Sanctions Act, a person who purchases or sells securities while in the possession of material nonpublic information may be ordered, in an action by the SEC or the Attorney General, to pay a civil penalty to the Treasury of up to three times the profit gained or loss avoided as a result of the purchase or sale. [15 U.S.C. §§78c, 78o, 78t, 78u, 78ff]

E.   SECTION 16 OF THE 1934 ACT [§380]

A second major provision of the 1934 Act governing insider trading is section 16, which relates to purchases followed by sales, or sales followed by purchases, by certain types of insiders, within a six-month period. Such trading is known as "short-swing trading." [15 U.S.C. §78p]

1. **Securities Affected Under Section 16:** [§381]   Section 16 applies only to trading in equity securities of those corporations that have a class of equity securities that must be registered under section 12 of the 1934 Act. Basically, this means a class of equity securities (i) *traded on a national securities exchange,* or (ii) held by at least *500 shareholders* and issued by a corporation having *total assets exceeding $5 million.* (*See supra*, §284.)

   a. **Note:** It is enough to trigger section 16 that *any class* of the corporation's equity securities is registered under section 12. If so, trading in *all* of the corporation's equity securities is subject to section 16. For example, if the corporation has outstanding an issue of common stock registered under section 12, trading in the preferred stock is subject to section 16, even though that stock is not required to be registered (because, for example, it is held by less than 500 persons).

2. **Disclosure Requirement—Section 16(a):** [§382]   Section 16(a) requires that every person who is directly or indirectly the *beneficial owner of more than 10%* of any class of equity securities registered under section 12, or who is a *director or officer* of a corporation that has issued such a class of securities, must file periodic reports showing the amount of the corporation's securities that he beneficially owns and any changes in those holdings.

   a. **Place of filing:** [§383]   These reports must be filed with the SEC and with any national securities exchange on which the stock is traded.

b. **Time of filing:** [§384] The initial report must be filed within 10 days after the person has become a more-than-10% beneficial owner, an officer, or director. Subsequent reports must be filed within 10 days after the end of any calendar month in which there have been any changes in the beneficial ownership of the securities.

3. **Liability—Section 16(b):** [§385] To prevent the unfair use of information that may have been obtained by a more-than-10% beneficial owner, a director, or officer by reason of his relationship to the issuer, a corporation can recover any profit realized by such a person from a *purchase and sale* (or *sale and purchase*), within *less than six months,* of equity securities of a corporation that has a class of equity securities registered under section 12.

   a. **Coverage of section 16(b):** [§386] Although section 16(b) is popularly referred to as an insider-trading provision, it does not actually use the term "insider," does not cover all insider trading, and is not limited to trades based on inside information. On the one hand, section 16(b) covers short-swing trading by directors, officers, and more-than-10% beneficial owners even if the trading is not based on inside information. On the other hand, a person who is not a director, officer, or more-than-10% beneficial owner normally does not fall within section 16(b) even if he does trade on the basis of inside information.

   b. **Calculation of short-swing profit:** [§387] The profit recoverable under section 16(b) is calculated by subtracting, from the price of stock sold, the price of an equal amount of stock purchased within six months *before or after* the sale.

      (1) **Example:** On January 2, D, a director of C Corp. (whose common stock is registered under section 12 of the 1934 Act), sells 500 shares of C common stock at $40 per share. Four months later, on May 1, D purchases 400 shares of C common stock at $30 per share. D has realized a $4,000 profit within the meaning of section 16(b), *i.e.,* the excess of the $40 sale price over the $30 purchase price, multiplied by 400 shares.

      (2) **Multiple transactions:** [§388] If there is more than one purchase or sale transaction within the six-month period, the court pairs off transactions by matching the highest sale price with the lowest purchase price, the next highest sale price with the next lowest purchase price, and so on. [Gratz v. Claughton, 187 F.2d 46 (2d Cir. 1951)] Of course, once any two transactions have been paired off with each other, neither can be paired off with a third transaction.

         (a) **Rationale:** The purpose is to squeeze all possible profits out of short-swing trading by insiders.

         (b) **Example:** As a result of this formula, what looks to the untrained eye like a series of losses may be turned into a profit for purposes of section

16(b). For example, assume the following trading by Director D in C Corp.'s common stock:

Date	Purchases or Sells	Number of Shares	Price
6/1	Purchases	1,000	$60
7/1	Sells	1,000	$55
8/1	Purchases	1,000	$50
9/1	Sells	1,000	$45

D may believe that she has lost $10,000 on her trading ($60 - $55 $\times$ 1,000; and $50 - $45 $\times$ 1,000). However, for purposes of section 16(b), D has a $5,000 profit, since the purchase at $50 on August 1 can be matched with the sale at $55 on July 1.

(3) **Time computation:** [§389] The court can look six months forward or backward from any sale to find a purchase, or from any purchase to find a sale. If there is *any pair* of transactions within that period in which the sale price is higher than the purchase price, the officer, director, or more-than-10% beneficial owner must account for it (even though there were other transactions involving losses).

c. **Who is entitled to recover:** [§390] The profit derived by the officer, director, or more-than-10% beneficial owner belongs to the corporation (rather than the shareholders with whom the insider dealt), and the corporation alone is entitled to recover that profit.

(1) **Shareholder action on corporation's behalf:** [§391] If the corporation fails to sue within 60 days after demand by a shareholder, the shareholder may bring an action on the corporation's behalf. However, this is not a typical derivative suit (*see infra,* §627). The cause of action is federal. Therefore, state security-for-expenses provisions (*see infra,* §§648-660) do not apply. Moreover, the "contemporaneous shareholder" requirement normally applicable to derivative suits (*see infra,* §625) does not apply; thus, the shareholder maintaining the action need not have been a holder at the time of the transactions in question. [Dottenheim v. Murchison, 227 F.2d 737 (5th Cir. 1955)]

d. **"Insiders" under section 16(b):** [§392] As mentioned, section 16(b) covers persons who are officers or directors at the time of either the purchase or the sale, and persons who are more-than-10% beneficial owners at the time of both the purchase and the sale. (*See infra,* §§402-406.)

(1) **"Officer":** [§393] "Officer" means a president, vice president, secretary, treasurer or principal financial officer, comptroller or principal accounting officer, and any person routinely performing corresponding functions. [Rule 3b-2]

(a) **"Assistants" are not "officers":** [§394] The term "officer" does not include a person with the title "assistant treasurer," "assistant secretary," or "assistant comptroller," etc., unless the chief is so inactive that the burden of office is thrust upon the assistant. [Lockheed Aircraft Corp. v. Campbell, 110 F. Supp. 282 (S.D. Cal. 1953)]

(b) **Title:** [§395] Under rule 3b-2, to impose liability under section 16(b), it is enough that a person has a relevant title. Several courts have held or suggested that despite rule 3b-2, persons with a relevant title (*e.g.,* a vice president) who have no policy-making functions or access to inside information are not officers for purposes of section 16(b). However, the Ninth Circuit has endorsed the concept of liability based on title, with a very limited exception applicable only where the title is essentially honorary or ceremonial. [National Medical Enterprises, Inc. v. Small, 680 F.2d 83 (9th Cir. 1982)]

(c) **Function:** [§396] Although liability under section 16(b) may be based on an officer's title, rule 3b-2 is not *limited* to liability based on title. It also picks up "any other persons routinely performing corresponding functions" to those performed by the officers named in the first part of the rule.

(2) **"Director":** [§397] The term "director" clearly covers persons actually named as directors. In addition, it covers anyone who has *deputized* another to act as director for him. The person making such a deputization will himself be deemed a director.

(a) **Example:** C Corp. deputizes one of its officers, D, to sit as its representative on the board of X Corp., in which C holds less than 10% of the stock. D is a director of X Corp. for purposes of section 16(b), and so is C Corp.

(b) **What constitutes "deputization":** [§398] Suppose C Corp. holds stock in X Corp. and that D is both an officer of C Corp. and a director of X Corp. Deputization will be found if it was agreed that in serving as a director of X, D would represent C's interests. Deputization will also be found if D regularly passes on inside information to C Corp., even in the absence of any agreement to do so. Short of these two situations, however, what constitutes "deputization" is still unsettled.

1) **Example:** D was a partner in L Bros., a large investment-banking partnership. D was also a director of Oil Co. L Bros. traded in Oil Co. stock. Although D had succeeded another L Bros. partner on the Oil Co. board, L Bros. was found *not* to have deputized D to represent its interests in Oil Co. because (i) there was no express understanding that D was to represent L Bros.' interests; (ii) D had never discussed the operating details of Oil Co.'s affairs with any member of L Bros.; and (iii) L Bros.' purchase and sale of Oil Co.

securities did not result from receipt of inside information from D. Thus, L Bros. was not a director of Oil Co. within the meaning of section 16(b). [Blau v. Lehman, 368 U.S. 403 (1962)]

    2)   **Compare:** Martin Marietta owned Sperry Rand stock, and Martin Marietta's president, P, sat on Sperry Rand's board. Although there was no express understanding that P was to represent Martin Marietta's interests, and P had not passed on any inside information to Martin Marietta, a number of facts showed deputization for section 16(b) purposes: P was ultimately responsible for the total operation of Martin Marietta, and personally approved all of its financial investments—in particular, its purchase of the Sperry stock. P's control over Martin Marietta, coupled with his membership on Sperry's board, placed him in a position in which he could acquire inside information concerning Sperry and could use such information for Martin. Furthermore, P admitted discussing Sperry's affairs with two officials at Martin Marietta and participating in sessions when Martin Marietta's investment in Sperry was reviewed, and P's ultimate letter of resignation stated that "When I became a member of the [Sperry] board . . . it appeared to your associates that the Martin Marietta ownership of a substantial number of shares of Sperry Rand should have representation on your Board." [Feder v. Martin Marietta Corp., 406 F.2d 260 (2d Cir. 1969), *cert. denied*, 396 U.S. 1036 (1970)]

(3)   **"Beneficial ownership" under section 16(b):** [§399] What constitutes beneficial ownership under section 16(b) is important in determining (i) whether a particular person is a more-than-10% beneficial owner, and (ii) whether a purchase or sale of stock by someone related to or associated with a section 16(b) insider can be ***attributed*** to the insider.

    (a)   **Ownership by relatives:** [§400] Generally a person will be regarded as the beneficial owner of securities held in the name of the person's spouse and minor children. Such relationships ordinarily result in the person obtaining benefits substantially equivalent to ownership, such as application of the income derived from the securities to maintain a common home or to meet expenses that the person would otherwise meet from other sources. [Securities Exchange Act Release No. 7824]

        1)   **Example:** A husband is the "beneficial owner" of his wife's shares even though he neither furnished the funds to buy the shares nor controlled her investments, where the wife's dividend income was used for the couple's living expenses and they managed their assets jointly. [Whiting v. Dow Chemical Co., 523 F.2d 680 (2d Cir. 1975)]

    (b)   **Other relationships:** [§401] A person is also regarded as the beneficial owner of securities held in the name of another, for purposes of section 16(b), if by reason of a contract, understanding, relationship, agreement, or other arrangement, that person obtains, from the other person's holding, benefits substantially equivalent to those of ownership. [Securities Exchange Act Release No. 7824, *supra*] Thus, such a person may be deemed the beneficial owner of securities that are owned by a corporation, partnership, or trust in which the person has a controlling influence. For example, a partner with a half interest in a partnership that owns securities may be deemed the beneficial owner of one-half of those securities.

(4) **Time at which insider status of officers and directors determined**

(a) **Office held at one end of swing:** [§402]   A purchase and sale by a director or officer falls within section 16(b) if she was such at the time of *either* the purchase *or* the sale, even though she did not hold office at *both* times.

1) **Example:** D, a director, purchases stock in her corporation, resigns her position, and makes a sale within six months of the purchase. D is liable under section 16(b). D would also be liable if she sells stock while a director, resigns, and then makes a purchase within six months of the sale. [Feder v. Martin Marietta Corp., *supra*, §398]

2) **Example:** E purchases stock while neither a director nor an officer, then accepts appointment as a director, and sells within six months of her purchase. E is liable under section 16(b). The same result follows where E sells stock while neither a director nor an officer, becomes a director, and then makes a purchase within six months of the sale. [Adler v. Klawans, 267 F.2d 840 (2d Cir. 1959)]

(b) **Office not held at either end of swing:** [§403]   Section 16(b) does not apply unless at least *one* end of the short-swing transaction occurred while the defendant was an officer or director. [Lewis v. Varnes, 505 F.2d 785 (2d Cir. 1974); Lewis v. Mellon Bank, 513 F.2d 921 (3d Cir. 1975)]

1) **Example:** D is a director and officer of C Corp. On January 2, D purchases 5,000 shares of C stock. On February 1, D retires. On March 1, D purchases an additional 5,000 shares. On July 6, D sells 5,000 shares. D is not liable under section 16(b). Although the July 6 sale occurred within six months of the March 1 purchase, both ends of that purchase and sale occurred while she was no longer an officer or director. The July 6 sale cannot be matched with the January 2 purchase, because more than six months separated these two transactions.

(5) **Time at which insider status of more-than-ten-percent beneficial owner determined:** [§404]   Unlike the case of an officer or director, liability for short-swing profits is imposed on a beneficial owner of more than 10% of the stock only if the person owned more than 10% of the shares at the time of *both* the purchase and the sale.

(a) **Purchase by stages:** [§405]   Section 16(b) does not cover any transaction where a more-than-10% beneficial owner was not such "both at the time of the purchase and sale, or the sale and purchase, of the security involved." [15 U.S.C. §78p] In *Foremost-McKesson, Inc. v. Provident Securities Co.,* 423 U.S. 232 (1976), the Supreme Court held that in the case of a purchase-sale sequence, a beneficial owner is not liable unless he was a more-than-10% owner **before** he made the purchase in question. To put this differently, the purchase that first lifts a beneficial owner above 10% cannot be matched with a subsequent sale under section 16(b).

1) **Example:** D purchases 6% of the outstanding shares of C Corp. on January 2, an additional 6% on February 1, and another 6% on March 1. D sells all of these shares at a substantial profit on April 1. The profit on the January 2 and February 1 purchases is not subject to section 16(b), because D was not a more-than-10% beneficial owner at the time he made either purchase. The profits on the March 1 purchase are subject to section 16(b), because D held a 12% interest at that time.

2) **Sale followed by purchase:** [§406]   The *Foremost* case involved a purchase followed by a sale. However, a sale by a more-than-10% beneficial owner reducing his interest to less than 10%, followed by a purchase within six months, presents greater potential for abuse. In such a case, the defendant would presumptively have had access to inside information prior to the first leg of the swing, and such information might well carry over to the second leg. Thus, the opinion in *Foremost* left open the question whether a sale-purchase sequence by a person who was a more-than-10% beneficial owner at the time of the sale might result in liability under section 16(b).

e. **"Purchase" or "sale" under section 16(b)**

(1) **Garden-variety transactions:** [§407]   Any "garden-variety" purchase or sale of stock—in particular, an exchange of shares for cash—is a purchase or sale. This is true regardless of motive, *i.e.,* whether or not the purchase or sale was based on inside information.

(2) **Unorthodox transactions:** [§408]   The terms "purchase" and "sale" in section 16(b) are not limited to garden-variety purchases and sales. Rather, these terms potentially encompass **any** acquisition or disposition of stock. Acquisitions or dispositions other than garden-variety purchases or sales are sometimes referred to as "unorthodox transactions."

(a) **Examples:** A merger in which stock in C Corp. is exchanged for stock in D Corp. may be treated as a purchase or sale under section 16(b). Likewise, a conversion or redemption of stock, or the exercise of a stock option, may be treated as a purchase or sale under section 16(b).

(b) **Application of section 16(b)—theories of interpretation:** [§409]   Courts have relied on two conflicting theories in interpreting section 16(b) in cases involving unorthodox transactions.

    1) **"Objective" theory:** [§410]   Some decisions follow the theory that section 16(b) should be applied broadly to every transaction it can be read to reach, regardless of whether the result is necessary to effectuate the stated purpose of section 16(b) (to prevent the unfair use of inside information). [*See* Smolowe v. Delendo Corp., 136 F.2d 231 (2d Cir.), *cert. denied,* 320 U.S. 751 (1943)] This is known as the objective theory.

    2) **"Subjective" or "pragmatic" theory:** [§411]   Under a second approach, known as the "subjective" or "pragmatic" theory, section 16(b) is applied only to those transactions that give rise to a potential for abuse. Assuming that an unorthodox transaction *may* be deemed a purchase or sale, whether it *will be* deemed a purchase or sale under this theory depends in large part on whether the transaction is of *a type that has a potential for insider abuse*.

        a) **Example:** Occidental Petroleum acquired more than 10% of the stock of Kern County Land as the result of a tender offer. To avoid a takeover by Occidental, Kern County entered into a merger with a subsidiary of Tenneco Corporation. The merger was consummated less than six months after the tender offer, and liability was sought against Occidental under section 16(b), on the theory that the share exchange pursuant to the merger constituted a sale by Occidental of its Kern stock. The Supreme Court held for Occidental on the ground that while a merger *could* constitute a sale of stock for purposes of section 16(b), under the circumstances of this case—the merger was involuntarily thrust upon Occidental by an antagonistic corporation—there was no real potential for speculative abuse by Occidental of the kind section 16(b) was designed to prevent. [Kern County Land Co. v. Occidental Petroleum Corp., 411 U.S. 582 (1973)]

F.   SECTION 16(b) COMPARED TO RULE 10b-5

1. **Covered Securities:** [§412]   Section 16(b) applies only to securities of corporations that have a class of securities required to be registered under the 1934 Act. Rule 10b-5 applies to all securities.

2. **Inside Information:** [§413]   Short-swing profits are recoverable under section 16(b) whether or not they are attributable to misrepresentations, inside information, or misappropriation. Recovery is available under rule 10b-5 only where the defendant has made a misrepresentation or has traded on the basis of inside (or perhaps misappropriated) information.

3. **Plaintiff:** [§414]   Recovery under section 16(b) belongs to the corporation. Recovery under rule 10b-5 belongs to the injured purchaser or seller.

4. **Overlapping Liability:** [§415]   It is conceivable that insiders who make short-swing profits by the use of inside information could end up subject to both a claim by the

corporation suing under section 16(b) and a claim by the injured seller or buyer under rule 10b-5. However, section 16(b) provides for recovery of the "profits realized" by the defendant, and damages that a defendant must pay because of a rule 10b-5 claim arising out of the same transaction would probably reduce the "profits realized" within the meaning of section 16(b).

5. **Common Law Liability for Insider Trading:** [§416]   As discussed at the very beginning of this topic, the majority rule at common law was that shareholders could not recover against directors or officers who traded with them without disclosing inside information, partly on the theory that directors and officers owed a fiduciary duty only to the corporation, not to shareholders (*see supra,* §281). Several modern cases have held that as a matter of common law, insider trading does constitute a breach of fiduciary duties owed to the *corporation*—specifically, a breach of the duty not to use corporate assets (inside information) for other than corporate purposes. Under this approach, the *corporation* can recover profits made by insider trading. [Diamond v. Oreamuno, 24 N.Y.2d 494 (1969); Brophy v. Cities Service Co., 70 A.2d 5 (Del. 1949); *but see* Schein v. Chasen, 313 So. 2d 73 (Fla. 1975); Freeman v. Decio, 584 F.2d 186 (7th Cir. 1978)—contra]

    a. **Common law liability compared to liability under section 16(b):** [§417]   Like liability under section 16(b), common law liability runs against insiders and in favor of the corporation. In other respects, however, common law liability differs from liability under section 16(b):

        (1) **Scope:** [§418]   The common law theory applies to all corporations. Section 16(b) applies only to corporations with a class of equity securities required to be registered under section 12 of the 1934 Act.

        (2) **Defendants:** [§419]   Under the common law theory, recovery can be had against any corporate insider. Recovery under section 16(b) is allowed only against officers, directors, or more-than-10% beneficial owners.

        (3) **Short-swing requirement:** [§420]   The common law theory is available even though the purchase and sale did not occur within a six-month period. Section 16(b) is applicable only to a purchase and sale that occurs within a six-month period.

        (4) **Informational requirement:** [§421]   The common law theory applies only if an insider uses inside information. Section 16(b) applies whether or not inside information is used.

    b. **Common law liability compared to liability under rule 10b-5:** [§422]   Liability under the common law differs from rule 10b-5 liability, in that it runs to the corporation rather than to the injured purchaser or seller. In other respects, the two kinds of liability are highly comparable. However, they do differ in some ways.

        (1) **No purchaser or seller requirement:** [§423]   Under rule 10b-5, the plaintiff must be either a purchaser or a seller. The common law theory permits recovery even where the corporation is neither a purchaser or a seller.

        (2) **Tippees, etc.:** [§424]   Common law liability has so far been imposed only against corporate insiders. It is still unclear whether courts would allow recovery under the common law theory against noninsiders (such as tippees or aiders and abettors), which may be allowed under rule 10b-5 under certain conditions (*see supra,* §§332-338, 340-346).

VII. RIGHTS OF SHAREHOLDERS

chapter approach

This chapter details shareholders' rights with respect to voting, transferring shares, inspecting corporate records, and bringing direct and derivative actions. It also considers the fiduciary obligations of controlling shareholders. A great deal of important information is covered in this chapter. Some key things to remember for exam purposes are discussed below.

1. **Voting Rights:** Generally shareholders may vote (i) for the election and removal of directors, (ii) to amend the articles or bylaws, and (iii) on "fundamental" corporate changes. Besides that rule, the things you should know about voting rights are:

    a. **Straight voting:** Remember that except for the election of directors, or if the articles otherwise provide, shareholders are generally entitled to *one vote per share*.

    b. **Cumulative voting:** Most states permit cumulative voting for directors, which means that each share is given *one vote for each director to be elected*. The purpose is to give minority shareholders a voice on the board. You may have to memorize the formula for electing directors by cumulative voting so that you can calculate the ability of particular shareholders to elect directors. Keep in mind that the majority shareholders may wish to employ devices such as staggering directors' terms, removing directors elected by the minority, and reducing the size of the board, to avoid the effects of cumulative voting.

    c. **Voting by proxy:** A proxy is a power granted by a shareholder to exercise his voting rights. If you see a proxy question on your exam, make sure that the proxy is in writing and is being exercised during its statutory effective period. Remember too that, unless coupled with an interest, a proxy is *revocable* at any time.

    (1) **Proxy solicitation:** This is a likely source of exam questions. In publicly held corporations, nearly all shareholders vote by proxy. Management solicits proxies for reelection of directors and approval of corporate actions. Occasionally, insurgent groups try to take control of the corporation through a proxy solicitation. Most exam questions will want you to apply the *federal proxy rules* to these situations. These rules forbid misstatements or omissions of *material* facts in proxy materials. In addition, the rules contain detailed *disclosure requirements*, particularly with respect to director-nominees and committees. Generally, shareholder proposals must be included in corporate proxy materials. If this issue comes up on your exam, however, be aware of the lengthy list of exceptions.

    (a) **Remedies:** The SEC may institute a suit for a violation of section 14(a) or the proxy rules. The proxy rules also provide for a *private cause of action* for material misstatements or omissions with respect to proxy solicitations. For these private actions, the crucial elements are: materiality, causation, (although this is satisfied by a showing of materiality), standing, and fault. Remember that fairness is no defense. Rescission and damages are the remedies available under this private action.

(b) **Expenses:** An important possible exam issue is whether corporate funds may be used to reimburse the expenses of a proxy fight. Remember that *management's expenses* may be reimbursed for (i) soliciting proxies to obtain a quorum, and (ii) a proxy fight involving corporate policy, not personnel. *Insurgents* never have a *right* to reimbursement of their proxy expenses, but the corporation may voluntarily reimburse the expenses of insurgents who win a contest involving policy.

d. **Combining votes for control—close corporations:** If your exam question involves a *close corporation,* the shareholders may be able to control corporate policy through the following voting devices: shareholder voting agreements, agreements requiring greater-than-majority approval, shareholder agreements binding votes as directors, and voting trusts.

2. **Restrictions on Transfer of Shares:** Transfer restrictions are often used by close corporations to limit the number of shareholders, prevent entry of unwanted shareholders, or avoid a shift of control. (These restrictions are also used on certain classes of shares by large corporations.) If this comes up in an exam question, remember that, to be valid, the restriction must be *reasonable* and *noted conspicuously* on the certificate. Also, recall that restrictions are not favored and will be strictly construed.

3. **Shareholders' Right to Inspect Corporate Records:** Generally, a shareholder acting for a *proper purpose* has a right to inspect corporate books and records at reasonable times. At common law, the shareholder has the burden of proving a proper purpose. Most statutes, however, shift the burden to the corporation to prove improper purpose. To determine whether a purpose is proper, ask yourself whether the shareholder is seeking inspection *primarily to protect his interest as a shareholder,* rather than as a potential business rival or litigant.

4. **Fiduciary Obligations of Controlling Shareholders:** A controlling shareholder owes a fiduciary duty to minority shareholders to act *with good faith and inherent fairness* toward them. The obligation is even greater in close corporations. Thus, when a question arises concerning a controlling shareholder's business dealings with the corporation, ask whether the transactions are fair. The burden of proof is on the controlling shareholder. Likewise, if a controlling shareholder causes a fundamental corporate change, ask whether it promotes his own self-interest at the expense of the minority. Be sure that when the controlling shareholder deals with the minority, he makes a *full disclosure*.

Although a controlling shareholder may sell his control stock at a *premium,* the following transactions are forbidden: a bare sale of directorships or corporate offices is invalid. Similarly, under the theory of corporate action, transactions where controlling shareholders are considered to have usurped a corporate opportunity are breaches of the fiduciary duty, as are sales where the controlling shareholder persuades the minority to sell on less favorable terms than he receives. It is also a breach for a controlling shareholder to sell control to a transferee whom he knows will deal unfairly with the corporation.

5. **Shareholder Suits:** Direct suits by shareholders, which concern the breach of duties *owed to shareholders as individuals,* are rare exam topics. In contrast, derivative suits, which concern the breach of duties *owed to corporations,* are exam favorites. Whenever a breach of a duty owed to the corporation arises, consider whether a shareholder derivative suit is appropriate.

Ask yourself: Have the *corporate remedies* been exhausted (*e.g.,* has a demand for suit been made on directors and, if required, shareholders)? Is the plaintiff now *a shareholder,* and was he a shareholder at the time of the wrong? Does the plaintiff *fairly and adequately represent* the interests of the other shareholders? Note that any defense that would have been available if the corporation had brought the suit is available in a derivative suit.

Since the cause of action belongs to the corporation, so does any *recovery or settlement.* At this point, you will want to consider whether the plaintiff-shareholder is entitled to *reimbursement* for expenses and whether officers and directors are entitled to *indemnification.* Many courts order reimbursement of a victorious plaintiff's expenses if the suit has resulted in a substantial benefit to the corporation. Every state permits the corporation to reimburse the expenses of officers or directors who win on the merits. However, where a director or officer settles or loses a suit, he may be reimbursed for litigation expenses only, indemnified for the settlement, or denied protection altogether depending upon (i) the state statute and (ii) whether he acted in good faith, with reasonable care, and believed he was acting in the best interests of the corporation.

A. VOTING RIGHTS

1. **Right to Vote—In General:** [§425]   Subject to certain exceptions for close corporations (*supra,* §§119-136), shareholders generally have no right to exercise direct management or control over ordinary corporate affairs. However, they may control the corporation *indirectly* to some extent through their voting rights. Shareholders generally have the right to vote (i) for the *election and removal of directors;* (ii) to *amend the articles or bylaws;* and (iii) on *"major corporate action"* or *"fundamental changes"* (*e.g.,* sale of all the assets, merger, consolidation, and dissolution).

   a. **Who may vote:** [§426]   The right to vote is held by the shareholders of record (of shares having voting rights) as of the date of the notice of the shareholders' meeting, unless the articles or bylaws require (as they frequently do) that shareholders be "of record" on some designated date prior to the meeting in order to vote. [Del. Gen. Corp. Law §213(a)—"record date" cannot be more than 60 days, nor less than 10 days, prior to shareholders' meeting]

      (1) **Sale of shares after record date:** [§427]   The corporation must permit the owner of the shares as of the record date to vote, even if he no longer owns the shares at the time of the shareholders' meeting. But the new owner can protect himself by requiring the record owner to give him a *proxy* (*see infra,* §452). In any event, a record owner who votes in a way that injures the new owner may be liable to the new owner for damages. [*In re* Giant Portland Cement Co., 21 A.2d 697 (Del. 1941)]

   b. **Restrictions on right:** [§428]   Voting rights are not "inherent" in any class of stock. Generally, shares may be either voting or nonvoting, or may have multiple votes per share. [Del. Gen. Corp. Law §151(a)] A few statutes have been interpreted to preclude nonvoting stock. [C.A. Davendes Sociedad Financiera v. Florida National Banks, 565 F. Supp. 254 (M.D. Fla. 1982)]

    (1) **Maximum votes per shareholder:** [§429] A limit on the number of votes that any shareholder may have, regardless of the number of shares he owns, has been upheld. [Providence & Worcester Co. v. Baker, 378 A.2d 121 (Del. 1977)]

    (2) **Publicly issued common stock:** [§430] A number of state regulatory agencies prohibit the issuance of common stock without voting rights or with unequal voting rights.

2. **Shareholders' Meetings:** [§431] Whereas some informality is accepted as to actions by directors (*see supra,* §159), this is not generally true as to actions by the shareholders. In most states, shareholders can act only at meetings duly called and noticed, at which a quorum (usually a majority unless otherwise provided in the articles) is present, by resolution passed by a specified percentage of those present (usually a majority, but a greater percentage may be required for certain shareholder resolutions).

    a. **Timing of meeting:** [§432] Statutes usually require an ***annual meeting*** of the shareholders for the election of directors. In addition, ***special meetings*** are authorized whenever called by a designated corporate officer, by the holders of some designated percentage of the voting shares (*e.g.,* 10%), or by "such other persons as may be provided in the articles or bylaws." [Del. Gen. Corp. Law §211]

    b. **Notice:** [§433] Written notice must generally be given some period in advance—*e.g.,* not less than 10 nor more than 60 days before the shareholder meeting. The notice must specify the place, date, and hour of the meeting, and the general nature of the business to be transacted. [Del. Gen. Corp. Law §222]

        (1) **Waiver of notice:** [§434] The required notice may be waived by a shareholder who signs a written waiver of notice either before or after the meeting, or who attends the meeting without objecting to the lack of notice. [Del. Gen. Corp. Law §229]

    c. **Withdrawal of quorum:** [§435] Courts are divided on the question of whether a shareholder meeting that begins with a quorum present may validly continue to transact business after shareholders withdraw, leaving less than a quorum remaining. [*Compare* Levisa Oil Corp. v. Quigley, 234 S.E.2d 257 (Va. 1977)—meeting may not continue when majority shareholders withdraw to protect their interests; *with* Duffy v. Loft, Inc., 151 A. 223 (Del. 1930)—meeting may continue despite withdrawal of person holding proxies for shares necessary for a quorum]

        (1) **Statutory view:** [§436] Some statutes provide that the meeting may continue notwithstanding the withdrawal of shareholders necessary for a quorum. [Cal. Corp. Code §602(b)]

d. **Informal action:** [§437]   Statutes permit shareholder action to be taken without a meeting, upon the unanimous ***written consent*** of all shareholders entitled to vote; or simply upon the written consent of the number of shareholders (*e.g.,* majority) required to take the action. But in the case of nonunanimous consents, prompt notice must be given to ***all*** shareholders of whatever action was approved. [*See* Del. Gen. Corp. Law §228]

3. **Shareholder Voting**

a. **Straight voting:** [§438]   Unless the articles otherwise provide, in all matters other than the election of directors, a shareholder who is entitled to vote has ***one vote*** for each share held. The shareholder vote is determined by counting the number of votes for or against each proposition. Anything over 50% of the votes thus controls in the absence of some greater requirement in the articles. (*See infra,* §502.)

   (1) **Compare—statutory provisions:** [§439]   However, to effect certain fundamental changes in the corporate structure (*e.g.,* dissolution, merger, certain amendments of articles), statutes frequently require a higher percentage of shareholder approval. (*See infra,* §§993, 1026, 1034, 1051.)

b. **Cumulative voting for directors:** [§440]   Straight voting allows the holders of a bare majority of the shares complete control over the minority (except where statutes require a higher percentage of shareholder approval). To assure some representation on the board for a minority holding some significant percentage of the shares, shareholders may be granted the right to vote ***cumulatively*** for directors. [Cal. Corp. Code §708]

   (1) **Mechanics:** [§441]   Each share is given one vote for each director to be elected. Thus, if a shareholder owns 10 voting shares, and there are five directors to be elected, the shareholder has 10 votes for each director, or a total of 50 votes. She may than "cumulate" her votes—meaning that she can cast them all for one director, some for one and some for another, or any other way she chooses.

      (a) **Effect:** Where five directors are to be elected, a shareholder holding approximately 17% of the shares can insure the election (and prevent the removal) of one director on the board by casting all her votes for a single director.

      (b) **Formula:** The number of shares needed to assure representation on the board varies with the number of shares outstanding and the number of directors to be elected. The following formula can be used:

$$X \text{ (no. of shares needed)} = \frac{Y \text{ (no. of directors wanted)} \times Z \text{ (no. of shares voting)}}{1 + T \text{ (total no. of directors being elected)}} + 1$$

(c) **Example:** If a minority shareholder wishes to assure election of two members on a five-person board, and there are 600 shares outstanding, she needs at least—

$$X = \frac{2 \times 600}{1 + 5} + 1 \qquad X = 201 \text{ shares}$$

(2) **Right to cumulative voting**

(a) **Mandatory:** [§442] Cumulative voting is mandatory in some states; *i.e.,* it exists whether or not provided for in the articles, it cannot be refused in any election, and any provision to the contrary in the articles or bylaws is void. [Cal. Corp. Code §708]

(b) **Permissive:** [§443] In most states, however, cumulative voting is only permissive; *i.e.,* the statutes allow, ***but do not require,*** cumulative voting for directors. Some of these statutes provide that cumulative voting exists in all corporations except where specifically denied in the articles. [*See* Pa. Bus. Corp. Law §1505] Most, however, provide that it exists only if expressly granted in the articles. [Del. Gen. Corp. Law §214]

1) **Note:** If cumulative voting exists only where provided for in the articles (or bylaws), it can always be eliminated by whatever percentage vote is required to amend the articles (or bylaws)—often a simple majority of shareholders. [Maddock v. Vorclone Corp., 147 A. 255 (Del. 1929)]

(3) **Devices to avoid cumulative voting:** [§444] The majority may attempt to curtail the minority's right to representation on the board in a number of ways, only some of which are valid.

(a) **Staggering terms of directors:** [§445] The fewer directors being elected at any one time, the greater the number of shares needed to assure representation (*see* formula above). Consequently, the majority may seek to amend the articles or bylaws to stagger the terms of directors (*e.g.,* only three members of nine-person board elected each year for three-year term), in order to cut down the impact of the minority's cumulative voting rights.

1) **Statutory prohibition:** [§446] To prevent this, staggering of elections is prohibited by statute in some states where cumulative voting is mandatory. All directors must be elected each year. [Cal. Corp. Code §301]

2) **Compare—case law:** [§447] Absent such statutes, the cases are split. [Bohannan v. Corporation Commission, 313 P.2d 379 (Ariz. 1957); Humphrey v. Winous Co., 133 N.E.2d 780 (Ohio 1956)—permitting staggered terms; Wolfson v. Avery, 126 N.E.2d 701 (Ill. 1955)—statute authorizing staggered terms violated state constitutional requirement of cumulative voting]

(b) **Removal of directors elected by minority:** [§448] If the majority shareholders could remove the directors elected by the minority, the benefits of cumulative voting would be eliminated.

1) **Statutory limitation:** [§449] To prevent this, many statutes provide that the majority shareholders may remove the entire board, but that no individual director can be removed during his term if the votes against his removal would be sufficient to elect him through cumulative voting. [N.Y. Bus. Corp. Law §706(c)]

a) **Compare:** Some such statutes provide that this limitation on the shareholders' power to remove a director applies only to removing an individual director *without cause.* [Del. Gen. Corp. Law §141(k)]

2) **Removal for cause:** [§450] In any event, some states provide that individual directors can be *removed by court action for cause* (*e.g.,* breach of fiduciary duty to the corporation), regardless of shareholder votes for retention. Some statutes authorize such action on motion of a state official or a designated percentage of the shareholders. [N.Y. Bus. Corp. Law §706(d)]

(c) **Reducing size of the board:** [§451] Reducing the number of board members may decrease minority representation. As the above formula indicates, the fewer directors being elected, the more shares will be needed by the minority to assure a seat on the board. For example, if there are five directors, the shareholder holding 17% of the outstanding shares may obtain representation. However, if the number of directors is reduced to three, that shareholder has no assurance of representation (since this would take more than 25%).

4. Voting by Proxy

a. **Definition:** [§452] A "proxy" is a power granted by a shareholder to another person to exercise the shareholder's voting rights. The term "proxy" is also sometimes applied to the person to whom the power is given, but such a person will be referred to herein as a "proxy holder." The proxy holder is normally an agent of the shareholder, although in some cases the proxy holder has an independent and property-like or contractual interest in the subject matter of the proxy. (*See infra,* §456.)

b. **Formalities:** [§453] A proxy normally must be in writing. Typically, the effective period of a proxy is limited by statute [*see, e.g.,* Del. Gen. Corp. Law §212—three years; RMBCA §7.22—11 months], unless the proxy is validly irrevocable (*see infra,* §456).

c. **Revocability:** [§454] Like most other agency powers, a proxy is normally revocable at any time by the shareholder. A shareholder may revoke the proxy by notifying the proxy holder, by giving a new proxy to someone else, or by personally attending the meeting and voting the shares.

(1) **Shareholder's death or incapacity:** [§455] The death or incapacity of a shareholder ordinarily does not revoke a proxy, unless written notice is given to the corporation before the vote is counted. [RMBCA §7.22; Cal. Corp. Code §705(c)]

(2) **Irrevocable proxies:** [§456] A proxy may be made irrevocable if but only if it *expressly* so states and it is *"coupled with an interest"*—*i.e.,* the proxy holder has an independent interest in the subject matter of the proxy.

(a) **Interest in shares themselves:** [§457] The general common law rule is that the interest required to make a proxy irrevocable must be an interest in the *shares* themselves, not in the corporation. [*In re* Chilson, 168 A. 82 (Del. 1933); *but see* Deibler v. Chas. H. Elliott Co., 81 A.2d 557 (Pa. 1951)]

1) **Example:** Shareholder S borrows money from L. S pledges her shares to L as security for repayment, and gives L an irrevocable proxy to vote her shares until the loan is repaid. [150 A.L.R. 308] The interest of L in the shares qualifies to make the proxy irrevocable.

2) **Example:** Shareholder S agrees to sell her shares to P. S gives P an irrevocable proxy to vote her shares, pending a transfer of the shares on the corporation's books. The interest of P in the shares qualifies to make the proxy irrevocable.

(b) **Interest in corporation:** [§458] Statutes in many states provide that certain types of interest in the corporation can support an irrevocable proxy. These include the interests of: persons who have extended credit to the corporation partly in consideration of the proxy, persons who have agreed to serve as corporate employees on condition that they receive a proxy, and parties to shareholder voting agreements. [RMBCA §7.23]

(c) **Termination of interest:** [§459] Even when a proxy is irrevocable, because coupled with an interest, it becomes revocable when the interest supporting the proxy terminates (*e.g.,* when the loan is repaid). [RMBCA §7.23]

d. **Proxy solicitation:** [§460] In publicly held corporations, almost all shareholders vote by proxy. Typically, the management of a publicly held corporation solicits proxies from the shareholders, both for reelection of directors and to approve various types of actions that require shareholder approval. Occasionally, insurgent groups attempt to obtain control of the corporation through a proxy solicitation.

(1) **State regulation:** [§461] Prior to the 1930s, state courts sometimes invalidated proxy solicitations, and set aside corporate elections pursuant thereto, when

the solicitations misrepresented material facts or were found grossly inadequate in disclosing relevant information. Generally, however, state regulation of proxy solicitation was inadequate. This led to federal regulation, in the form of section 14(a) of the Securities Exchange Act of 1934 and the federal proxy rules (*see* below). Recently, state law has also improved in this area. The Delaware courts, for example, now hold that in self-interested transactions involving a controlling shareholder, the controlling shareholder has a duty of "complete candor." [Lynch v. Vickers Energy Corp., 383 A.2d 278 (Del. 1977); Weinberger v. UOP, Inc., 457 A.2d 701 (Del. 1983)]

(2) **Federal proxy rules:** [§462]   Section 14(a) of the 1934 Act provides that it is unlawful for any person, in contravention of SEC rules and regulations, to solicit any proxy with respect to any security registered under section 12 of the 1934 Act. Acting under section 14(a), the SEC has adopted the proxy rules, which regulate the solicitation of proxies. [Rules 14a-1 *et seq.*]

   (a) **Securities covered:** [§463]   The federal proxy rules apply to any solicitation of proxies, oral or written, in connection with any security registered under section 12 of the 1934 Act. Section 12 requires registration of securities traded on national securities exchanges or equity securities that are held by at least 500 persons and issued by a corporation having total assets in excess of $5 million. (*See supra,* §284.)

      1) **Exception:** [§464]   The proxy rules do not apply to a solicitation of 10 or fewer shareholders made on behalf of persons other than management.

   (b) **What constitutes "solicitation":** [§465]   The terms "solicit" and "solicitation" have a very broad sweep under the proxy rules and go well beyond a formal request for a proxy. For example, they encompass any writing that is "part of a continuous plan" leading to a formal solicitation or preparing the way for it. [Studebaker Corp. v. Gittlin, 360 F.2d 692 (2d Cir. 1966); SEC v. Okin, 132 F.2d 784 (2d Cir. 1943)—letter that did not request authorization was subject to proxy rules if part of "a continuous plan" intended to end in solicitation and to prepare way for success]

   (c) **Requirement of full disclosure:** [§466]   The proxy rules are very complex, and require disclosure of a great deal of information. They set forth detailed requirements concerning the "form of proxy" (the written authorization to vote) and the "proxy statement" (the pamphlet that must accompany a solicitation). The form of proxy and proxy statement, taken together, comprise the "proxy materials." Among other things, the rules:

      (i) ***Forbid misstatements or omissions of material facts*** in proxy solicitations [Rule 14a-9];

      (ii) ***Require all persons soliciting proxies***—management or insurgents— to set forth, fully and completely, in the proxy statement, ***all pertinent*** *facts* regarding the matters to be voted upon and the *identity of all participants* in a proxy contest;

(iii) *Require disclosure* in the proxy statement of the *compensation* paid to the five highest paid officers, compensation paid to officers and directors as a group, and *conflict-of-interest transactions* involving more than $60,000; and

(iv) *Require that solicitations by management* contain or be preceded by an *annual report,* if directors are to be elected at the meeting.

1) **Requirements regarding director nominees:** [§467] Proxy statements sent in connection with the election of directors must disclose whether each nominee for director:

(i) Has during the past five years had a *principal occupation with the corporation* or an affiliate;

(ii) Is *related to an executive officer* of the corporation or an affiliate;

(iii) Has been associated with a company that has recently done or plans to do *substantial business with the corporation* or its subsidiaries; and

(iv) Has been associated with a law firm or an investment banking firm that recently has performed or plans to perform *services for the corporation.*

2) **Disclosure concerning committees:** [§468] The proxy statement must also disclose whether the corporation has audit, nominating, and compensation committees, and, if so, the number of meetings each committee held during the last fiscal year, and the functions each committee performs.

(d) **Form of proxy:** [§469] Under rule 14a-4, a form of proxy providing for the election of directors must set forth the names of persons nominated for directors. The form of proxy must also clearly provide the means for a shareholder to withhold authority to vote for each nominee. A proxy executed by the shareholder in such a way as not to withhold authority to vote for the election of any nominee will be deemed to grant such authority, provided that the proxy so states in boldface type.

(e) **Shareholder proposals:** [§470] Under rule 14a-8, the corporation must include shareholder proposals in the corporate proxy materials, provided certain conditions are met. To be eligible under rule 14a-8, the proponent must be a record or beneficial owner of *at least 1% or $1,000 in market value* of securities entitled to be voted on the proposal. The proposal and its supporting statement may not exceed 500 words.

1) **Exceptions:** [§471] The corporation is *not* required to include a shareholder proposal *if:*

a) Under the laws of the state in which the corporation is incorporated, the proposal is *not a proper subject for action by shareholders.* Whether a proposal is a proper subject for action by shareholders will depend on the applicable state law. A proposal that mandates certain action by the board of directors may not be a proper subject matter for shareholder action, while a proposal recommending or requesting such action of the board may be a proper subject.

b) The proposal would require the corporation to *violate state or federal law* or the law of a foreign jurisdiction to which the corporation is subject.

c) The proposal or supporting statement is *false or misleading.*

d) The proposal concerns the *redress of a personal claim* or grievance against the corporation or any other person, or is designed to result in a benefit to the shareholder or to further a personal interest that is not shared with the other shareholders at large.

e) The proposal relates to operations that account for *less than 5% of the corporation's total assets and less than 5% of its net earnings and gross sales,* and is not otherwise *significantly related to the registrant's business. Note:* In adopting the 5% standard, the SEC stated that shareholder proposals must be included in the proxy statement, notwithstanding their failure to reach the 5% thresholds, "if a significant relationship to the issuer's business is demonstrated on the face of the resolution or supporting statement." [Exchange Act Release No. 19, 135 (1982)] Thus, the meaning of "significantly related" is not limited to economic significance.

1/ *Example:* A shareholder submitted a proposal calling on the board to appoint a committee to report to the shareholders on whether the production methods of a supplier of pate de foie gras caused undue distress, pain, or suffering to the animals involved and, if so, whether further distribution of the product should be discontinued until a more humane production method was developed. The corporation had annual revenues of $141 million, annual profits of $6 million, and assets of $78 million. Its sales of pate de foie gras were $79,000, gave rise to a net loss of $3,121, and the corporation had only $34,000 in assets related to pate. Thus, none of the company's net earnings, and less than .05% of its assets, were implicated by the shareholder proposal. The court held, however, that in light of the ethical and social significance of the shareholder proposal, and the fact that it implicated significant levels of sales, the shareholder had shown a likelihood of prevailing on the merits with regard to the issue of whether the proposal was "otherwise significantly related" to the corporation's business. [Lovenheim v. Iroquois Brands, Inc., 618 F. Supp. 554 (D.D.C. 1985); *see also* Medical Committee for Human Rights v. SEC, 432 F.2d 659 (D.C. Cir. 1970)]

f) The proposal deals with a matter *beyond the registrant's power* to effectuate.

g) The proposal deals with a matter relating to the conduct of *ordinary business operations.*

h) The proposal relates to an *election* to office.

i) The proposal is *counter* to a proposal to be submitted by the corporation at the same meeting.

j) The proposal has been rendered *moot.*

k) The proposal is substantially *duplicative* of a proposal submitted to the corporation by another shareholder, which will be included in the corporation's proxy material for the meeting.

l) The proposal deals with substantially the *same subject matter as a prior proposal* that was submitted within the previous five prior years, if the proposal was last submitted within three years, and: (i) the proposal was submitted at only one meeting during the five years and received less than 3% of the votes; or (ii) the proposal was submitted at two meetings during the preceding five years and received at the time of its second submission less than 6% of votes; or (iii) the proposal was submitted at three or more meetings during the previous five years and received at the time of its last submission less than 10% of votes.

m) The proposal relates to *specific amounts of cash or stock dividends.*

(f) **Providing shareholder lists or mailing communications:** [§472] A shareholder who wishes to communicate with the other shareholders is entitled either to be supplied with a list of shareholders or to have his communication included with the corporate proxy materials, if the shareholder pays the cost. [Rule 14a-7]

(g) **Remedies for violation of proxy rules:** [§473] Various remedies can be granted to prevent violation of proxy rules.

1) **Administrative remedies:** [§474] The SEC may institute suit for violation of section 14(a) or the proxy rules (*e.g.,* to enjoin the solicitation, to bar a party from voting improperly obtained proxies, or to order a new election).

2) **Private suits:** [§475] The proxy rules also create an implied private right of action in the individual investor. [J.I. Case Co. v. Borak, 377 U.S. 426 (1964)] Typically, such actions are brought under rule 14a-9, which provides that no solicitation shall be made by means of any proxy statement, form of proxy, notice of meeting, or other communication, written or oral, containing any statement that is false or misleading with respect to any material fact, or which omits to state any material fact necessary to make the statements therein not false or misleading.

a) **Materiality:** [§476] To establish materiality for purposes of a rule 14a-9 action, there must be "a showing of a substantial likelihood that, under all the circumstances, the omitted fact would have assumed actual significance in the deliberations of the reasonable shareholder"—or, to put it differently, a showing of "a substantial likelihood that the disclosure of the omitted fact would have been viewed by the reasonable investor as having significantly altered the 'total mix' of information made available." [TSC Industries, v. Northway, Inc., *supra,* §292]

1/ **Note:** It is not enough simply to show that the information "might" have been considered important by a reasonable shareholder, because such a standard could force management to disclose so much trivial data that the real issues in the proxy solicitation could be obscured. [TSC Industries, Inc. v. Northway, Inc., *supra*]

2/ **Example:** The board of C Corp. solicits proxies from C's shareholders for approval of a proposed merger with D Corp. The fact that C's directors, who were recommending approval of the merger, were nominees of D, would be material, because reasonable shareholders would likely take such fact into consideration in deciding whether to follow the directors' recommendation. [Mills v. Electric Auto-Lite Co., 396 U.S. 375 (1970)]

3/ **Compare:** Where full disclosure has been made concerning the extent of a parent corporation's voting control over a subsidiary, mere failure to disclose that officers of the parent are also serving as officers of the subsidiary is not necessarily material, since in light of the disclosures made as to the parent's voting control, the officers' status is not necessarily a matter that a reasonable shareholder would have considered important in voting on the proposed merger. [TSC Industries, Inc. v. Northway, Inc., *supra*]

4/ **Qualitative information:** [§477] "Qualitative information" is information that relates to the integrity and quality of management, and whose financial significance cannot readily be quantified. Qualitative information concerning *self-dealing* by directors who are candidates for reelection to the board is material, and failure to disclose such information violates rule 14a-9 even if the information does not fall within one of the categories that are specifically required to be disclosed under the proxy rules. [Maldonado v. Flynn, 597 F.2d 789 (2d Cir. 1979); Weisberg v. Coastal States Gas Corp., 609 F.2d 650 (2d Cir. 1979), *cert. denied,* 445 U.S. 951 (1980)] However, qualitative information concerning only alleged *mismanagement* (sometimes called "simple mismanagement") normally would not have to be disclosed in the proxy statement. [Gaines v. Haughton, 645 F.2d 761 (9th Cir. 1981), *cert. denied,* 454 U.S. 1145 (1982)]

b) **Causation:** [§478] A false or misleading statement will not give rise to a private action under rule 14a-9 unless it is the cause of a shareholder vote that the proxy statement solicits. However, a showing of *materiality* satisfies the causation requirement. Accordingly, where a shareholder seeks to set aside or enjoin a transaction on the ground that shareholder approval was solicited by a proxy statement that involved misstatements or omissions, she need do nothing more to prove causation than to prove materiality. [Mills v. Electric Auto-Lite Co., *supra*, §476; Gaines v. Haughton, *supra*, §477]

1/ **Where management or parent controls majority of stock:** [§479] It is an open question whether a private action can be brought for violation of the proxy rules where the management or a parent owns or controls a majority of the stock, so that it can cause shareholder approval of the relevant transaction without any votes from the minority (and omissions or misstatements in the proxy materials would not affect the outcome). However, the trend of decisions is in favor of permitting private actions in such cases. [Schlick v. Penn-Dixie Cement Corp., 507 F.2d 374 (2d Cir. 1974), *cert. denied,* 421 U.S. 976 (1975)]

c) **Standing:** [§480] Even a shareholder who did not grant a proxy on the basis of a misleading solicitation has standing to challenge the solicitation. The injury a shareholder suffers from corporate action pursuant to a deceptive proxy solicitation flows from the damage done to the corporation, rather than from the damage inflicted directly upon the shareholder. The damage suffered results not from the deceit practiced on the shareholder alone, but rather from the deceit practiced on the shareholders as a group. [J.I. Case Co. v. Borak, *supra,* §475; *but see* Gaines v. Haughton, *supra*]

d) **Fault required:** [§481] Scienter is required to establish a violation of *rule 10b-5.* [Ernst & Ernst v. Hochfelder, *supra,* §293] It is unclear, however, whether mere negligence is sufficient to impose liability in an action for violation of the *proxy rules.* The Third Circuit has held that negligence is sufficient, on the ground that the language of section 14(a) of the 1934 Act does *not* suggest a scienter requirement. [Gould v. American-Hawaiian Steamship Co., 535 F.2d 761 (3d Cir. 1976)] The Second Circuit has intimated in dicta that a scienter standard should probably apply under rule 14a-9 to *outside directors and accountants.* [Gerstle v. Gamble-Skogmo, Inc., 478 F.2d 1281 (2d Cir. 1973)] The Sixth Circuit has held that scienter must be established in a suit against accountants under rule 14a-9, and strongly intimated that it would apply a scienter requirement in *all* rule 14a-9 suits. [Adams v. Standard Knitting Mills, Inc., 623 F.2d 422 (6th Cir. 1980)]

e) **Fairness no defense:** [§482] A materially misleading solicitation entitles the complainant to relief regardless of whether the matter acted upon was fair to the corporation and its shareholders. Otherwise, a judicial finding of fairness could be used to bypass the shareholders' right to make an informed choice after full disclosure. [Mills v. Electric Auto-Lite Co., *supra,* §478]

f) **Nature of relief available:** [§483] The federal courts are empowered to award whatever relief will effectuate the purposes of the statute, which may include both prospective and retroactive remedies. [J.I. Case Co. v. Borak, *supra,* §480]

1/ **Rescission:** [§484] If necessary and otherwise equitable, a court may rescind an action that was approved by the shareholders as a result of a misleading proxy solicitation (*e.g.*, by setting aside a corporate merger). [J.I. Case Co. v. Borak, *supra*]

2/ **Monetary damages:** [§485] Monetary damages are also recoverable, if they can be shown. [Mills v. Electric Auto-Lite Co., *supra*]

(h) **Jurisdiction:** [§486] Federal courts have exclusive jurisdiction in any suit for violation of the proxy rules. Any related claim for violation of state law may be joined with the federal claim under the doctrine of pendent jurisdiction.

e. **Expenses incurred in proxy contest:** [§487] Since the expenses involved in a large-scale proxy fight may be enormous, the question of whether corporate funds may be used to reimburse those expenses is extremely important.

(1) **Reimbursement of management's expenses:** [§488] The corporation may properly pay the normal expense of preparing and soliciting proxies to obtain a quorum for the annual meeting. In the event of a proxy contest, the corporation may also properly reimburse reasonable amounts expended by management, as long as the matter in controversy is one of corporate policy, rather than one of personnel (*i.e.*, one in which management seeks simply to retain its office). [Steinberg v. Adams, 90 F. Supp. 604 (S.D.N.Y. 1950)] Management may use corporate funds to fully inform the shareholders concerning the relevant issues and to protect the corporation against a "raid" by wealthy insurgents. [Rosenfeld v. Fairchild Engine & Airplane Corp., 309 N.Y. 168 (1955); 51 A.L.R.2d 860]

(2) **Insurgents' expenses:** [§489] Unlike management, insurgents do not have a right to reimbursement of their proxy expenses, even if they win. However, the corporation can voluntarily reimburse the reasonable expenses of insurgents who win a proxy contest involving policy (rather than personnel), on the ground that they have conferred a benefit on the corporation, at least if the body of shareholders ratify the reimbursement. [Rosenfeld v. Fairchild Engine & Airplane Corp., *supra*]

5. **Other Methods to Combine Votes for Control—Close Corporations:** [§490] Various voting devices may be used by shareholders (particularly in close corporations) to assure control of corporate policies.

a. **Shareholder voting agreements:** [§491] Shareholders (often those owning a majority of the stock) may agree with other shareholders to vote in a specified way for a specified period of time. They may agree for a variety of reasons—*e.g.*, as a condition of the other shareholders investing in the corporation. Such agreements usually concern voting for the election of certain directors, but may also cover other matters subject to shareholder vote (amendment of the articles, dissolution, etc.).

(1) **Pooling agreements:** [§492] A "pooling agreement" is a particular kind of voting agreement whereby shareholders (none of whom usually owns a majority

of the stock) agree to vote their shares together in a specified way (or as the majority of them decides) for a specified period.

(2) **Validity:** [§493] Early cases often refused to enforce shareholder voting agreements (particularly if all the shareholders were not parties thereto), on the ground that shareholders could not irrevocably separate their voting rights from their ownership rights. However, shareholder voting agreements are generally upheld today, as long as they are made for a proper purpose and work no fraud upon creditors or other stockholders. [E.K. Buck Retail Stores v. Harkert, 62 N.W.2d 288 (Neb. 1954)]

    (a) **Purpose of agreement:** [§494] Shareholders generally may vote their shares as they please, and are permitted to combine their votes to serve certain of their own purposes, *e.g.,* to elect themselves as directors.

    (b) **Consideration:** [§495] Pooling agreements have sometimes been challenged for lack of consideration. [Roberts v. Whitson, 188 S.W.2d 875 (Tex. 1945)] Most courts, however, find sufficient consideration in the shareholders' exchange of mutual promises to vote their shares in a specified way.

        1) **Compare:** Alternatively, pooling agreements have been upheld on the theory that the combining of votes for control gives each shareholder a sufficient "interest" in the shares of the other that their agreement is enforceable as a grant of an *irrevocable proxy* (*supra,* §§456-459). [Abercrombie v. Davies, 130 A.2d 338 (Del. 1957)]

    (c) **Statutory authority:** [§496] Statutes today frequently authorize shareholders to enter into agreements respecting the voting of their shares. [Cal. Corp. Code §706(a)—applicable to close corporations only; N.Y. Bus. Corp. Law §620(a)] Some statutes limit the duration of such agreements. [Del. Gen. Corp. Law §218(c)—10 years, unless renewed]

    (d) **Agreements limited to shareholder action:** [§497] The agreements under discussion concern only shareholder action (*e.g.,* voting for directors, amendment of articles, etc.). The validity of shareholder agreements insofar as they seek to bind the parties in voting as directors is considered below (*see infra,* §§504-509).

(3) **Self-executing agreements:** [§498] Sometimes, the parties to a pooling agreement may attempt to make it "self-executing" by requiring each shareholder to execute and deposit a *proxy* with an agent to vote the shares.

    (a) **But note:** This self-executing plan may not work if any of the shareholders decides to revoke her proxy. Even though she may have expressly agreed not to revoke, her proxy may be held revocable because it is not coupled with "an interest." (Some courts have not regarded a pooling agreement as creating a sufficient "interest" in each other's shares to render the proxy irrevocable [*In re* Chilson, *supra,* §457], but this approach has been modified by statute in a number of states (*see supra,* §458). Consequently, the other shareholders will have to sue for enforcement of the pooling agreement; they cannot rely on the proxy.

(b) **And note:** Even where the proxies are held irrevocable, the self-executing arrangement may be viewed as a *voting trust,* in which event it must comply with special requirements (below). [Abercrombie v. Davies, *supra,* §495] Statutes in some states will prevent this result. [*See, e.g.,* Cal. Corp. Code §706(c)—shareholders' voting agreements shall not constitute voting trusts]

(4) **Remedy for breach:** [§499]   If the voting agreement is enforceable, the remedy usually sought in the event of breach is *specific performance, i.e.,* a court order compelling the shareholder to vote her shares as agreed. Equitable relief would appear to be justified on the ground that the legal remedy (damages) is usually inadequate.

  (a) **Statutes:** [§500]   Some statutes expressly authorize specific performance of shareholder voting agreements. [*See, e.g.,* Cal. Corp. Code §706(a)]

  (b) **When fewer than all shareholders participate:** [§501]   Absent statutory authorization, however, some courts have refrained from granting specific performance of pooling agreements to which *fewer than all* of the shareholders were parties. [Ringling Bros.-Barnum & Bailey Combined Shows, Inc. v. Ringling, 53 A.2d 441 (Del. 1947); *but see* Weil v. Berseth, 220 A.2d 456 (Conn. 1966)—contra]

b. **Agreements requiring greater-than-majority approval:** [§502]   Minority shareholders in a close corporation may seek to achieve a certain degree of control (or, more precisely, a veto power) by obtaining the agreement of the other shareholders (in a contract, or through a charter or bylaw provision) that no shareholder action may be taken without a unanimous (or some percentage greater than majority) vote.

(1) **Modern trend:** [§503]   The modern trend of judicial decisions permits such devices. [*See, e.g.,* Katcher v. Ohsman, 97 A.2d 180 (N.J. 1953)] Many statutes now expressly authorize greater-than-majority voting requirements if provided for in the articles of incorporation. [N.Y. Bus. Corp. Law §616; RMBCA §7.27]

c. **Shareholder agreements binding votes as directors:** [§504]   In addition to agreeing how they will vote as shareholders, the shareholders of a close corporation may seek to control more detailed matters of corporate policy, *e.g.,* who will be the corporate officers, what will be the salaries, how much will be paid in dividends. These are "management" questions, traditionally committed to the board of directors (*supra,* §118).

(1) **Fewer-than-unanimous agreements:** [§505]   When fewer than all the shareholders are parties to agreements seeking to bind the directors, most courts have held them *unenforceable,* reasoning that corporate directors are charged

with fiduciary duties to the corporation and any agreement that seeks to restrict or limit their actions as directors is therefore void. It is contrary to public policy to have a "passive board." [McQuade v. Stoneham & McGraw, *supra*, §121]

    (a) **But note:** Some recent decisions, recognizing the special nature and needs of close corporations, have upheld such nonunanimous agreements—at least where no nonparty shareholder claimed prejudice to herself as a result. [Galler v. Galler, *supra*, §122; Glazer v. Glazer, 374 F.2d 390 (5th Cir. 1967)]

    (2) **Unanimous agreements:** [§506]   When all the shareholders are parties to such agreements, courts have been quicker to uphold them—at least when no damage to creditors or the public has been shown. [Clark v. Dodge, *supra*, §121] But even unanimous agreements have been held unenforceable if they involve "substantial impingements" on the discretion of the board. [Long Park, Inc. v. Trenton-New Brunswick Theatres Co., *supra*, §121]

    (3) **Statutes:** [§507]   In recent years, a number of special statutes applicable to close corporations have validated shareholder agreements that bind the discretion of directors. Some require that such agreements be unanimous [N.Y. Bus. Corp. Law §620(b)], while others do not [Del. Gen. Corp. Law §§350, 354].

        (a) **Notice:** [§508]   A number of these statutes require that these agreements be included in a provision of the articles of incorporation. [*See, e.g.,* N.Y. Bus. Corp. Law §620(b)] Some go further and require that the provision be noted conspicuously on all share certificates. [N.Y. Bus. Corp. Law §620(g)]

            1) **Estoppel:** [§509]   It has been held that a shareholder who promised, but failed, to fulfill these statutory requirements is estopped from denying the validity of a shareholder agreement to which he was a party. [Zion v. Kurtz, 50 N.Y.2d 92 (1980)]

d. **Voting trusts:** [§510]   A voting trust is another device employed by shareholders to assure control. Each shareholder transfers *legal title* of her shares to a trustee, in return for a transferable "voting trust certificate" that evidences her equitable ownership of the shares involved and carries the right to dividends and other distributions of assets. Since the right to vote follows legal title, the trustee has the voting right for the shares involved for the life of the trust.

    (1) **Formalities:** [§511]   Statutes in most states require such trust agreements to be in writing, filed with the corporation, and open to inspection by all shareholders and owners of voting trust certificates. [Del. Gen. Corp. Law §218(a)]

        (a) **Failure to comply with statutory requirements:** [§512]   Although some courts have invalidated voting trusts that do not comply with the statute, others have nonetheless enforced voting trust agreements when the policy of the voting trust statute has been fulfilled. [Oceanic Exploration Co.

v. Grynberg, 428 A.2d 1 (Del. 1980)—all shareholders had notice of voting trust agreement even though it was not filed with corporation]

(2) **Revocability:** [§513]   Voting trusts are usually deemed irrevocable for their designated life—unless termination is agreed to by all certificate holders and there is no prejudice to creditors, etc. [Thomas v. Kliesen, 201 P.2d 663 (Kan. 1949)]

(3) **Duration:** [§514]   Statutes generally limit the period for which such trusts may be created (the usual term being 10 years). However, voting trusts set up for a longer term are valid for whatever period is authorized by the statute. [Del. Gen. Corp. Law §218(a)]

    (a) **Extensions:** [§515]   Some statutes permit a voting trust to be extended for additional terms—usually on condition that only the assenting shareholders shall be so bound. [Del. Gen. Corp. Law §218(b)]

(4) **Authority of voting trustees:** [§516]   The scope of the trustees' authority to vote depends on the terms of the voting trust agreement. This almost always extends to voting for the election of directors. But absent explicit authority in the voting trust agreement, most courts hesitate to allow the trustees to vote on such extraordinary matters as sale of all the corporation's assets, dissolution of the corporation, or termination or extension of the voting trust. [Brown v. McLanahan, 148 F.2d 703 (4th Cir. 1945); *compare* Clarke Memorial College v. Monaghan Land Co., 257 A.2d 234 (Del. 1969)]

    (a) **Note:** [§517]   Some statutes are contra, stating that unless otherwise provided in the voting trust agreement, the trustees have authority to vote on such matters. [S.C. Bus. Corp. Act §11-160(g)]

    (b) **Fiduciary duty:** [§518]   In any event, voting trustees are held to a fiduciary duty to the beneficiaries of the trust in exercising their authority. [Brown v. McLanahan, *supra*, §516]

(5) **Rights of holder of voting trust certificate:** [§519]   Other than voting, the shareholder's rights generally remain intact. The shareholder is still entitled to receive dividends, inspect corporate records, etc., and even bring a representative suit (*infra*).

B.   RESTRICTIONS ON TRANSFER OF SHARES

1. **Restrictions Imposed by Articles, Bylaws, or Shareholder Agreement:** [§520]   Stock transfer restrictions are frequently used in close corporations to limit the total number of shareholders (often to enable the corporation to retain statutory benefits as a "close corporation"; *see supra*, §§122-126), to prevent the entry of unwanted shareholders, or to avoid a major shift in control. Larger corporations on occasion may also limit the transferability of a certain class of shares—*e.g.*, to restrict ownership to a certain group, such as employees. Usually, stock transfer restrictions will be in the corporation's articles

or bylaws. Sometimes, however, they are contained in a separate agreement among the shareholders.

a. **Types of restrictions:** [§521]   The two most common types of restrictions on transferability of shares are the right of first refusal and the mandatory buy-sell provision.

    (1) **Right of first refusal:** [§522]   A right of first refusal is a provision giving the corporation or the other shareholders (or both) a first option to buy the stock before any shareholder may sell or otherwise transfer shares to a third party.

    (2) **Mandatory buy-sell:** [§523]   A mandatory buy-sell provision stipulates that on the occurrence of a designated event (*e.g.,* death of the shareholder), the corporation or surviving shareholders *must* buy the stock, and the shareholder (or the shareholder's estate) *must* sell to the corporation or other shareholders.

b. **Validity of restrictions**

    (1) **Common law—reasonableness requirement:** [§524]   The right to transfer is deemed an inherent right of property ownership, and at common law total restraints or effective prohibitions on the transferability of shares were usually held invalid. To be valid at common law, a restriction on transfer must be "reasonable" in view of the needs of the particular corporation and shareholders involved. [Allen v. Biltmore Tissue Corp., 2 N.Y.2d 534 (1957)]

        (a) **"Consent" restrictions:** [§525]   Thus, at common law, a provision that "these shares are nontransferable," or "nontransferable without the consent of each other shareholder," was usually held invalid as unreasonable restraints on alienation. [Rafe v. Hindin, 29 A.D.2d 481 (1968)]

            1) **Special circumstances:** [§526]   Provisions requiring the consent of other shareholders or directors may be upheld under special circumstances. [Penthouse Properties, Inc. v. 1158 Fifth Ave., Inc., 256 A.D. 685 (1939)—corporation owned cooperative apartment house in which shareholders were tenants; restriction requiring shareholders' consent to stock transfer upheld because right of occupancy went with it]

            2) **Modern decisions:** [§527]   Some recent decisions have shown a greater tolerance for consent restrictions and upheld them when not an unreasonable method of limiting corporate control to particular individuals. [Gray v. Harris Land & Cattle Co., 737 P.2d 475 (Mont. 1987)]

        (b) **Restrictions as to whom shares may be transferred:** [§528]   Restrictions limiting the type of persons to whom the shares may be transferred will be upheld if the restriction is reasonable under the circumstances (*e.g.,* provisions against selling shares to persons engaged in business that competes with the corporation).

(c) **Right of first refusal:** [§529]   A right of first refusal (option) for a limited period of time in favor of the corporation or other shareholders (or both) will almost always be upheld as a reasonable restraint. (*Example:* "No sale of these shares to a nonshareholder shall be made until the holder first offers them to the corporation on the same terms and conditions as offered to the nonshareholder; and the corporation shall have 30 days thereafter within which to purchase same on such terms.")

(d) **Options to purchase:** [§530]   Similarly, provisions giving the corporation an option to purchase the shares in question at a fixed price or book value are usually upheld—even where the shares are now worth much more than the price. More than a large disparity between the option price and current market value must be shown to render an option agreement unreasonable. [*In re* Mather's Estate, 189 A.2d 586 (Pa. 1963)]

(2) **Statutes:** [§531]   Today, a large number of states have statutes dealing with the validity of stock transfer restrictions.

(a) **"Reasonable" restrictions:** [§532]   Some statutes simply codify the common law, authorizing "reasonable" restrictions on the transfer of shares. [Cal. Corp. Code §204(b)]

(b) **Detailed restrictions:** [§533]   Others deal with such restrictions in more detail. For example, the Delaware statute authorizes the following types of stock transfer restrictions, which may appear in the articles, bylaws, or separate shareholder agreements: (i) provisions giving the corporation or other shareholders a right of first refusal for a reasonable time; (ii) provisions giving the corporation or other shareholders the right to consent to a proposed transfer; (iii) mandatory buy-sell provisions; (iv) restrictions on transfer to designated classes of persons "unless manifestly unreasonable"; and (v) "any other lawful restriction on transfer." [Del. Gen. Corp. Law §202]

1) **And note:** Even if the stock transfer restriction is held not to be authorized by statute, the corporation nevertheless is given the *option* to acquire whenever shares are sought to be transferred at a "fair price" to be determined by agreement of the parties or by the court. [Del. Gen. Corp. Law §349]

(3) **Limitation—proper fund available for repurchase:** [§534]   Even if the stock transfer restriction is otherwise valid, where the corporation seeks to repurchase its own shares pursuant to such restriction, most states require that the corporation have available funds from a proper source (*e.g.,* surplus) with which to make the repurchase. (*See infra,* §§950-954.) [Van Kampen v. Detroit Bank & Trust Co., 199 N.W.2d 470 (Mich. 1972); *but see* Lewis v. Powell, 203 So. 2d 504 (Fla. 1967)—contra]

c. **Shares subject to restriction**

(1) **Common law:** [§535]   Courts at common law have split on whether stock transfer restrictions can be enforced with respect to shares *already issued* at the time the restrictions were adopted. Some hold that the corporation has the power, through amendment of its articles or bylaws (*see infra*, §§1033 *et seq.*), to alter existing shareholder rights—even where the shareholder neither knew nor consented to the restriction. [Tu-Vu Drive-In Corp. v. Ashkins, 61 Cal. 2d 283 (1964); *but see* B&H Warehouse, Inc. v. Atlas Van Lines, Inc., 490 F.2d 818 (5th Cir. 1974)—contra]

(a) **Removal of restriction:** [§536]   There is a similar split on whether stock transfer restrictions can be removed over the objection of dissenting stockholders. [Silva v. Coastal Plywood & Timber Co., 124 Cal. App. 2d 276 (1954)—upholding bylaw retroactively removing stock transfer restrictions; *but see* Bechtold v. Coleman Realty Co., 79 A.2d 661 (Pa. 1951)—contra]

(2) **Statutes:** [§537]   Some modern statutes provide that stock transfer restrictions can be enforced only against shares issued *subsequent* to adoption of the restriction. Such restrictions cannot be enforced against the transfer of shares already issued, unless the owner consents. [Cal. Corp. Code §204(b); Del. Gen. Corp. Law §202(b)]

d. **Transactions subject to restriction:** [§538]   Since restrictions on alienation of property are disfavored as a matter of public policy, stock transfer restrictions may be *strictly construed.* Provisions that contain only general restraints (*e.g.,* covering "all sales or transfers") are often interpreted as applying only to *voluntary* sales. Therefore, in the absence of specific language, the restriction may be held inapplicable to transfers on death, to a sale of shares in bankruptcy, or to pledges of shares as security for loan (no transfer of title).

e. **Notice requirement:** [§539]   Unless "noted conspicuously" on the *certificate itself,* a lawful stock transfer restriction is of no effect against a person who otherwise had no knowledge of the restriction at the time of transfer. [U.C.C. §8-204]

(1) **Actual knowledge:** [§540]   This applies, of course, only to "innocent" persons. One who has *actual* knowledge of a stock transfer restriction is bound by it, even if it is not "conspicuously noted" on the face of the certificate. [U.C.C. §8-204]

(2) **"Noted conspicuously":** [§541]   The requirement that the restriction be "noted conspicuously" on the certificate means only that it reasonably appear from the face of the certificate that the shares are subject to some sort of transfer restriction. The restriction itself need not be set forth in full text. [Ling & Co. v. Trinity Savings & Loan Association, 482 S.W.2d 841 (Tex. 1972)]

(3) **"Innocent" transferee:** [§542] Without such notice, an innocent transferee of the certificate (whether a donee or purchaser) is entitled to have the shares transferred into his name on the books of the corporation and thereafter to receive dividends, vote the shares, etc. Moreover, he takes free and clear of the stock transfer restriction—so he can thereafter resell his shares to another without regard to the restriction.

C. SHAREHOLDERS' RIGHT TO INSPECT CORPORATE RECORDS

1. **Types of Books and Records:** [§543] The books and records of a corporation fall into four basic categories: (i) shareholder lists; (ii) minutes of board meetings, shareholders' meetings, board committees, and officer committees; (iii) financial records, such as books of account and monthly, quarterly, and annual period summaries; and (iv) business documents, such as contracts, correspondence, and office memoranda.

2. **Common Law:** [§544] At common law, a shareholder acting *for a proper purpose* has a right to "inspect" (examine) the corporate books and records at reasonable times. The shareholder has the burden of alleging and proving proper purpose. [Albee v. Lamson & Hubbard Corp., 69 N.E.2d 811 (Mass. 1946)]

3. **Statutes:** [§545] In most states today, shareholder inspection rights are affected by statutes. Many of these statutes apply only to certain kinds of shareholders, such as those who are record holders of at least 5% of the corporation's stock, or who have been record holders for at least six months. [N.Y. Bus. Corp. Law §624] The statutes are normally interpreted to preserve the proper purpose test, but to place on the corporation the burden of proving that the shareholder's purpose is improper. [Crane Co. v. Anaconda Co., 39 N.Y.2d 14 (1976)] Those statutes that are limited to only certain shareholders, or only certain books and records, are usually interpreted to supplement the common law, so that a suit for inspection that does not fall within the statute can still be brought under the common law. [Tucson Gas & Electric Co. v. Schantz, 428 P.2d 686 (Ariz. 1967); *but see* Caspary v. Louisiana Land & Exploration Co., 707 F.2d 785 (4th Cir. 1983)]

a. **Kind of record sought:** [§546] The burden of proof under a statute may be affected by the *kind* of corporate record sought. For example, the Delaware statute provides that where inspection is sought of shareholder lists, the burden is on the corporation to prove that the information is being sought for an improper purpose; for other corporate records, the burden is on the shareholder to prove proper purpose. [Del. Gen. Corp. Law §220(c)]

4. **Proper vs. Improper Purposes:** [§547] In determining what constitutes a proper or improper purpose, the basic test is whether the shareholder is seeking inspection *to protect his interest* as a shareholder, or is acting primarily for another purpose, such as furthering his interest as a potential business rival or as a litigant. [Rosentool v. Bonanza Oil & Mine Corp., 352 P.2d 138 (Or. 1960)]

a. **Multiple purposes:** [§548]   As long as the ***primary*** purpose is a proper one, the fact that the shareholder has an improper secondary purpose usually will not defeat the claim. [General Time Corp. v. Talley Industries, 240 A.2d 755 (Del. 1968)]

b. **Proxy fights:** [§549]   Inspection of a shareholders list to enable a shareholder to make a takeover bid or engage in a proxy contest with management is normally considered a proper purpose, since it is reasonably related to the interest of the shareholder.

c. **Other purposes:** [§550]   Among other purposes the courts have recognized as proper for exercising the inspection right are the following: (i) to determine whether the corporation is being ***properly managed*** or whether there has been managerial misconduct, at least if the shareholder alleges some specific concerns [Skouras v. Admiralty Enterprises, Inc., 386 A.2d 674 (Del. 1978)]; (ii) to determine the corporation's ***financial condition*** [Riser v. Genuine Parts Co., 258 S.E.2d 184 (Ga. 1979)]; and (iii) to determine the ***value*** of the shareholder's stock [Friedman v. Altoona Pipe & Steel Supply Co., 460 F.2d 1212 (3d Cir. 1972)].

d. **Social or political interests:** [§551]   Several cases have held that a shareholder is not entitled to inspect corporate records solely for the purpose of advancing political or social views, as contrasted with economic or financial interests in the corporation. [50 A.L.R.3d 1056]

(1) **Example:** Shareholder bought 100 shares in H Corp., a Delaware corporation, for the sole purpose of giving himself a voice in H's affairs so that he could persuade H to cease producing munitions. Shareholder then demanded access to the shareholder list and all corporate records dealing with weapons and munitions manufacture, for the purpose of communicating with other shareholders to elect a new board of directors who would represent his viewpoint. The Minnesota court denied inspection. It construed the Delaware statute to require a proper purpose germane to the applicant's interest as a shareholder and held that inspection that is sought solely to persuade the company to adopt a shareholder's social and political concerns, irrespective of any economic benefit to the shareholder or the corporation, did not meet this standard. [State *ex rel.* Pillsbury v. Honeywell, Inc., 191 N.W.2d 406 (Minn. 1971)]

(2) **But note:** A subsequent Delaware case held that the desire to solicit proxies for a slate of directors in opposition to management is a purpose reasonably related to the shareholder's interest as a shareholder; that any further or secondary purpose in seeking the list is irrelevant; and that insofar as *Pillsbury* is inconsistent with these rules, it is inconsistent with the Delaware statute as properly applied. [Credit Bureau Reports, Inc. v. Credit Bureau of St. Paul, Inc., 290 A.2d 691 (Del. 1972)] It is not clear, however, whether these rules are applicable to more than the shareholder list.

5. **Compare—Mandatory Disclosure of Information:** [§552]   In contrast to the law governing the shareholder's inspection right, which puts the initiative on the individual

shareholder, various federal and state statutes require corporations to make affirmative disclosure of certain information.

a. **Securities Exchange Act of 1934:** [§553]   Extensive disclosure requirements are imposed on corporations whose stock is registered under section 12 of the Securities Exchange Act of 1934.

  (1) **Annual and periodic reports:** [§554]   Such corporations must file with the SEC, and any securities exchange on which the stock is listed, periodic reports disclosing their financial condition and certain types of material events. These reports are open to inspection by the public.

  (2) **Proxy rules:** [§555]   Under the proxy rules (*supra* §§462-486), corporations whose stock is registered under section 12 must annually disclose certain information to shareholders, such as the compensation of the five highest paid officers, the compensation of officers and directors as a group, details on the operation of stock option and pension plans, and transactions with insiders during the previous year involving amounts in excess of $60,000.

b. **State statutes:** [§556]   State laws vary greatly as to the amount of information that must be provided by corporations incorporated in the jurisdiction.

  (1) **Report to state:** [§557]   Most states require corporations incorporated in the jurisdiction to file an annual report with an appropriate state officer, such as the secretary of state, providing at least certain minimal information—*e.g.,* the names and addresses of its directors and officers, the address of its principal business office, its principal business activity, and the name and address of its agent for the service of process upon the corporation. [RMBCA §16.22]

  (2) **Report to shareholders:** [§558]   In addition, some states require corporations to send an annual report to shareholders containing financial statements. For example, under the Model Act, a corporation must furnish its shareholders with annual financial statements that include a balance sheet, an income statement, and a statement of changes in shareholders' equity. If financial statements are prepared for the corporation on the basis of generally accepted accounting principles, the annual financial statements furnished to the shareholders must also be prepared on that basis. If the annual financial statements are reported upon by a public accountant, the accountant's report must accompany them. If not, the statements must be accompanied by a statement of the president or the person responsible for the corporation's accounting records: (i) stating his reasonable belief whether the statements were prepared on the basis of generally accepted accounting principles and, if not, describing the basis of preparation; and (ii) describing any respects in which the statements were not prepared on the basis of accounting consistent with the statements prepared for the preceding year.

D. FIDUCIARY OBLIGATIONS OF CONTROLLING SHAREHOLDERS

1. **Introduction:** [§559] Where a controlling shareholder serves as a director or officer, he owes fiduciary obligations to the corporation in those capacities. Even where a controlling shareholder does not serve as a director or officer, he may owe fiduciary obligations to the minority shareholders in exercising his control. A controlling shareholder must refrain from using his control to obtain a special advantage, or to cause the corporation to take an action that unfairly prejudices the minority shareholders. [Pepper v. Litton, *supra*, §217]

    a. **Business dealings with corporation:** [§560] Although a controlling majority shareholder may validly contract with the corporation, he cannot exploit the corporation at the expense of the minority. Thus, if the contract is unfair—as where the price terms are not those that would be set in an arm's-length bargain—the controlling shareholder has breached his fiduciary obligation to the minority. [Sinclair Oil Corp. v. Levien, *supra*, §244]

        (1) **Parent-subsidiary dealings:** [§561] The most common cases in which there are dealings between a controlling shareholder and a corporation are those in which the controlling shareholder is a parent and the corporation is a subsidiary with minority ownership. [Sinclair Oil Co. v. Levien, *supra*]

        (2) **Burden of proof:** [§562] When a transaction between a corporation and its controlling shareholder is challenged, as in a derivative suit by minority shareholders, the burden is on the controlling shareholder to prove its fairness. [Sinclair Oil Corp. v. Levien, *supra*]

    b. **Fundamental changes:** [§563] A controlling shareholder also owes a duty of fairness in causing fundamental changes, such as mergers or amendments of the articles of incorporation, that may promote his own self-interest at the expense of the minority. (*See infra*, §§1072-1094.)

2. **Actions Entirely in Shareholder Capacity—No Corporate Action:** [§564] The fiduciary obligations owed by a controlling shareholder may apply, even where he does not cause the *corporation* to do anything, where an act he takes in his shareholder capacity benefits himself unduly at the expense of the minority shareholders. [Jones v. H.F. Ahmanson & Co., 1 Cal. 3d 93 (1969)]

    a. **Standard:** In any transaction in which control of the corporation is material, the controlling shareholders must act with "good faith and inherent fairness" toward the minority. [Jones v. H.F. Ahmanson & Co., *supra*]

    b. **Example:** There were relatively few shares of X Corp. outstanding, and they had a very high value; thus, their marketability was highly impaired. The dominant shareholders transferred their shares to Holding Co., which they had formed. Holding Co. then "went public," which allowed the controlling shareholders to cash out part of their investment and greatly increased the value and marketability of the remainder, while the minority shareholders in X were stuck with shares that were even less marketable than before. The controlling shareholders of X Corp. violated their fiduciary duties by engaging in a transaction that, with no business justification, increased the marketability of their own shares and decreased the marketability of the minority's shares, without affording the minority an opportunity to participate. [Jones v. H.F. Ahmanson & Co., *supra*]

3. **Obligations of Shareholders in Close Corporations:** [§565] Shareholders in a close corporation owe each other an even stricter duty than controlling shareholders in publicly held corporations. It has been said that such shareholders owe each other the same duty of utmost good faith and loyalty that is owed by partners to each other. This duty is owed by all shareholders, majority and minority. [Donahue v. Rodd Electrotype Co., 328 N.E.2d 505 (Mass. 1975); Helms v. Duckworth, 249 F.2d 482 (D.C. Cir. 1957)]

   a. **Selling shares to corporation:** [§566] In the *Donahue* case, *supra,* the court held that controlling shareholders of a close corporation who cause the corporation to acquire some of their shares must see that minority stockholders have an equal opportunity to sell a proportionate number of shares to the corporation at an identical price.

   b. **Legitimate business purpose:** [§567] The majority shareholders of a close corporation cannot sever a minority shareholder from the corporate payroll, or refuse to reelect him as a salaried officer and director, without a legitimate business purpose. [Wilkes v. Springside Nursing Home, Inc., 353 N.E.2d 657 (Mass. 1976)]

   c. **Obligation of minority shareholders:** [§568] A *minority* shareholder in a close corporation cannot use a veto power *unreasonably,* as by refusing to vote for dividends when the accumulation of undistributed earnings will lead to a foreseeable tax penalty to the corporation. [Smith v. Atlantic Properties, Inc., 422 N.E.2d 798 (Mass. 1981)]

4. **Disclosure:** [§569] A controlling shareholder must make full disclosure when dealing with the minority shareholders, as by making a tender offer for their shares [Lynch v. Vickers Energy Corp., *supra,* §461], or when causing *the corporation* to deal with minority shareholders, as by calling redeemable stock [Zahn v. Transamerica Corp., 162 F.2d 36 (3d Cir. 1947)].

   a. **Duty of "complete candor":** [§570] The Delaware courts have expressed this principle by holding that a controlling shareholder has a duty of "complete candor" to disclose all material facts when dealing with the minority. [Lynch v. Vickers Energy Corp., *supra;* Weinberger v. UOP, Inc., *supra,* §461]

5. **Sale of Control:** [§571] Controlling shareholders may also owe fiduciary duties to other shareholders in transactions involving sale of controlling stock at a premium or the transfer of control in connection with the sale of their stock.

   a. **General rule:** [§572] The general rule is that a controlling shareholder has the right to sell his controlling stock at a premium, *i.e.,* for a price that is not available to other shareholders. [Zetlin v. Hanson Holdings, Inc., 48 N.Y.2d 684 (1979); Clagett

v. Hutchison, 583 F.2d 1259 (4th Cir. 1978)] So, for example, a controlling shareholder can sell his stock at a premium over market, even though other shareholders are only able to sell at the market price.

(1) **Rationale:** This rule reflects the experiential proposition that controlling stock normally sells at a higher price than noncontrolling stock, and serves a policy purpose by facilitating the transfer of control from less efficient to more efficient hands.

(2) **Equal opportunity doctrine:** [§573]   Some commentators have urged that where a purchaser offers to purchase control of a corporation at a premium, the controlling shareholders owe a fiduciary duty to provide **all** shareholders with an equal opportunity to participate; *i.e.,* the controlling shareholder must arrange that the offer be made to all shareholders on a pro rata basis. [78 Harv. L. Rev. 505]

    (a) **Example:** Suppose S owns 51% of C Corp.'s stock. Under the equal opportunity doctrine, if a purchaser offers to buy S's 51% of C Corp.'s stock at a premium above market price, S could not sell his shares alone, but instead would be required to ask the minority shareholders if they wanted to participate in the 51% offer on a pro rata basis.

    (b) **Comment:** There is little case support for this doctrine, and it has been specifically rejected in various cases.

    (c) **Impact of *Jones v. H.F. Ahmanson & Co.*:** [§574]   In *Jones v. H.F. Ahmanson & Co., supra,* §564, the California Supreme Court held that controlling shareholders were under a duty to act toward minority shareholders with "good faith and inherent fairness . . . in any transaction in which control of the corporation is material." Although that case did **not** involve a sale of control, the theory on which it was decided **could** be extended to a sale of control. If so, it would be the equivalent of the equal opportunity doctrine. As of now, however, the doctrine has found little judicial acceptance in straight sale-of-control-stock cases.

b. **Exceptions:** [§575]   The general rule, that control can be sold at a premium, is subject to a number of exceptions in cases where there is something **more** than a straight sale of control stock at a premium.

(1) **Bare sale of office:** [§576]   While a sale of control stock at a premium is permissible, a bare sale of directorships or other corporate offices is invalid. Thus, a controlling shareholder cannot transfer control of the board for consideration where the transfer of control is not simply incidental to a transfer of an amount of stock that is sufficient in itself to carry control. Accordingly, if a person (i) controls the board although he owns only a relatively small amount of stock, and (ii) transfers control of the board in connection with a sale of his stock at a premium, by seriatim resignations and simultaneous appointment of the purchaser's nominees, the appointment of the purchaser's

nominees is voidable at the suit of a shareholder, and the seller must account for the premium. [Caplan v. Lionel Corp., 20 A.D.2d 301 (1969), *aff'd*, 14 N.Y.2d 679 (1964)—transfer of control of board in connection with sale of only 3% of outstanding shares held a wrongful "sale of office"]

(a) **Damages:** [§577]   In case of a bare sale of office, the amount that the controlling shareholders receive for "control" belongs to the ***corporation.***

(b) **Exception:** [§578]   However, it is not improper for a selling shareholder to arrange for the resignations of existing officers and directors and the appointment of a new board chosen by the purchaser, as part of a sale of controlling stock, *if* the block of shares sold constitutes either a majority of the outstanding stock or an amount sufficiently large to carry control "as a practical certainty" (so that the purchaser could have forced the changes of office herself, even if the seller had not facilitated the change of office). [Essex Universal Corp. v. Yates, 305 F.2d 572 (2d Cir. 1962); 13 A.L.R.3d 361]

   1) **Test:** [§579]   What constitutes control "as a practical certainty" is a question of fact. In a publicly held corporation, less than 51% will usually suffice; *i.e.,* large blocks of shares may carry voting control even though short of a majority. [*See* Essex Universal Corp. v. Yates, *supra*—indicating that 28% of outstanding shares of publicly held corporation may be sufficient]

(2) **Theory of corporate action:** [§580]   Suppose a prospective purchaser, P, wants to acquire complete control of the assets and business of a corporation, C, and proposes to make an offer to C to ***buy C's assets,*** or have C ***merge*** with a corporation that P controls. If C's controlling shareholders instead convince P to purchase just their stock, at a premium, the minority shareholders may assert that the controlling shareholders have diverted a corporate opportunity from C to themselves. This is the theory of "corporate action." It has been successfully employed by minority shareholders in several cases. [Commonwealth Title Insurance & Trust Co. v. Seltzer, 76 A. 77 (Pa. 1910); Dunnett v. Arn, 71 F.2d 912 (10th Cir. 1934); Roby v. Dunnett, 88 F.2d 68 (10th Cir.), *cert. denied,* 301 U.S. 706 (1937)]

   (a) **Comment:** The problem with this theory is that a controlling shareholder cannot be compelled to sell his shares at a price he does not accept. A knowledgeable controlling shareholder therefore can probably avoid the application of this theory by (i) allowing P to make an offer to C, (ii) voting to reject the offer to C, and (iii) then waiting for an offer from P to purchase his controlling shares.

(3) **Sales involving fraud or nondisclosure:** [§581]   A controlling shareholder violates his fiduciary duty to the remaining shareholders if, as part of the sale of stock at a premium, he ***deals with minority shareholders*** without disclosing the terms of his premium sale.

(a) **Example:** In some cases, especially where the buyer wants more stock than the controlling shareholder owns, the premium paid to the controlling shareholder may depend upon the controlling shareholder convincing minority shareholders who are ignorant of the premium to sell their stock to the buyer at a price lower than that paid to the controlling shareholder.

(4) **Sale of control to transferee who plans to deal unfairly with corporation:** [§582] Controlling shareholders breach their fiduciary duties to the minority shareholders if they transfer their controlling shares to a person or group whom they know or have reason to know will deal unfairly with the corporation.

(a) **Looting:** [§583] The principal type of case in this category is a sale of controlling shares to a purchaser whom the controlling shareholder *knows or has reason to know* intends to loot the corporation. [Gerdes v. Reynolds, 28 N.Y.S.2d 622 (1941); Insuranshares Corp. v. Northern Fiscal Corp., 35 F. Supp. 22 (E.D. Pa. 1940)]

1) **Knowledge of purchaser's intent:** [§584] Usually in such cases there is no question, by the time of the trial, that the purchaser did loot. The main problem is whether the controlling shareholder knew or had reason to know of the purchaser's intent at the time of the sale.

a) **Terms of sale may put controlling shareholder on inquiry:** [§585] Typically, these cases concern a corporation whose assets are highly liquid (*e.g.,* investment companies whose assets consist of readily marketable securities). Since the value of the stock in such a corporation can be determined with a high degree of precision (because liquid assets are easy to value, and there is normally no goodwill attached to the business), payment of a premium significantly above the fair value of the shares may be enough to put the controlling shareholder on notice that the purchaser intends to recover the premium by looting the corporation's assets. [Gerdes v. Reynolds, *supra*, §583]

1/ **Example:** Bank held controlling shares in C Corp. Bank sold its shares to a purchaser whom Bank knew had a long history of business failures, outstanding fraud judgments, and no apparent assets with which to pay for the shares. Under such circumstances, it was reasonably foreseeable that the purchaser would be likely to loot C Corp., which he did. Bank's sale to such a purchaser was a breach of duty to C and the minority shareholders. [De Baun v. First Western Bank & Trust Co., 46 Cal. App. 3d 686 (1975)]

2) **No duty to investigate:** [§586]   In the absence of some ground for suspicion, however, a seller of control stock generally does **not** have an affirmative obligation to investigate the purchaser's plans to determine whether looting or fraud is intended or likely. [Swinney v. Keebler Co., 480 F.2d 573 (4th Cir. 1973); Levy v. American Beverage Corp., 265 A.D. 208 (1942)]

3) **Damages:** [§587]   Where the controlling shareholder knows or has reason to know that the purchaser plans to deal unfairly with the corporation, he is accountable to the minority shareholders for the premium he received (*i.e.*, the amount by which the purchase price exceeded the fair value of his stock) and for any damage caused to the corporation by the purchasers. [Gerdes v. Reynolds, *supra*, §583]

4) **Plans to deprive corporation of profits:** [§588]   Even if the controlling shareholder has no reason to expect looting, he is accountable where he knows or has reason to know that the purchaser intends to use control to prevent the corporation from realizing profits it otherwise would have obtained.

a) **Example:** In *Perlman v. Feldmann*, 219 F.2d 173 (2d Cir. 1955), the controlling shareholder of a steel company sold his controlling shares to a group of steel consumers. Steel was in short supply, and the purchasers paid a premium for the control of stock in order to obtain the steel company's output at artificially low prices. The steel company was thereby deprived of the profits that it otherwise could have made on sale of its products on the open market. The court held that the controlling shareholder had breached his fiduciary duties to the minority shareholders, and ordered him to account for that portion of the price that exceeded the fair value of his stock.

E.   SHAREHOLDER SUITS

1. **Introduction:** [§589]   Actions brought by shareholders fall into two categories: (i) a **direct action** on the shareholder's own behalf (or on behalf of a class of shareholders to which he belongs) for injury to his interest **as a shareholder;** or (ii) a **derivative suit** filed on **behalf of the corporation** for injury done to the corporation for which it has failed to sue.

2. **Direct (Individual) Suits:** [§590]   Where management has abridged a contractual or statutory duty owed directly **to the shareholder** as an individual (*e.g.*, directors refuse to permit shareholder inspection of corporate records), the shareholder may bring a suit on **his own behalf**—*i.e.*, a direct (or individual) suit.

a. **Class action:** [§591]   If the alleged misconduct affects the rights of a number of shareholders, the suit may be maintained as a class action in which case the individual shareholder sues as the **representative** of the class of shares that has been damaged.

(*Example:* Management denies all shareholders preemptive rights in new stock issuance; or corporate insider fails to disclose material information when purchasing shares from a number of existing shareholders.)

3. **Derivative Suits:** [§592]   If management (or a third party) has abridged a duty *owed to the corporation* (*e.g.,* officers loot the corporate treasury, or customer fails to pay for goods purchased from corporation), and the corporation fails to enforce its cause of action, a shareholder may bring a suit on behalf of the corporation—*i.e.,* a derivative suit.

    a. **Nature of action:** [§593]   The derivative suit is a creature of equity. It was conceived to permit a shareholder to redress injuries done directly to the corporation (injuring the shareholder only indirectly or derivatively), where management has refused to enforce the corporate cause of action, usually because recovery is sought against management for breach of fiduciary duty.

        (1) **Who benefits:** [§594]   A derivative suit enforces the corporation's cause of action, and any recovery usually belongs to *the corporation* rather than the plaintiff-shareholder. (But the plaintiff-shareholder may be entitled to reimbursement for expenses in obtaining such recovery; *see infra,* §674.)

        (2) **Distinguishing direct suits from derivative suits:** [§595]   It must be determined initially whether the shareholder's action is properly direct or derivative in nature. (This is significant because derivative suits are subject to certain prerequisites and security-for-expenses statutes (*infra,* §648) that do not apply to direct suits.) While borderline cases may be difficult to classify, the basic test is which party has the cause of action—*i.e.,* whether the injury was suffered by the corporation or directly by the shareholder—and to whom the defendant's *duty* ran.

            (a) **Direct actions:** [§596]   The following kinds of shareholder actions have been held *direct* (individual) rather than derivative in nature, because the immediate injury is to the shareholder rather than the corporation.

                1) **Example:** Directors of XYZ Corp. refuse to declare a dividend, in order to depress the value of the shares. Shareholder action to compel payment of dividend is a direct action (injury to the shareholder), and a class action in such a case would be proper. [Knapp v. Bankers Securities Corp., 230 F.2d 717 (3d Cir. 1956)]

                2) **Example:** Shareholder complains of reorganization allegedly diluting his voting influence in the corporation. This is a direct suit (again a class action may be proper). [Eisenberg v. Flying Tiger Line, Inc., 451 F.2d 267 (2d Cir. 1971)]

            (b) **"Special duty" cases—still direct actions:** [§597]   Cases occasionally arise in which the corporation has sustained immediate injury, but the action is nevertheless deemed direct because of some "special duty" owed to the plaintiff-shareholder.

1) **Example:** A suit by a shareholder/pledgor against a director/pledgee for dissipating the corporation's assets has been held to be a direct action. Even though the injury was to the corporation, thus giving rise to a derivative action as well, there was a "special duty" owed arising out of the pledge arrangement. [Citibank, N.A. v. Data Lease Financial Corp., 828 F.2d 686 (11th Cir. 1987)]

2) **Example:** A suit by a corporation-shareholder against one of its directors for looting the assets of the corporation's subsidiary has been held to be a direct action. Even though the injury was to the subsidiary corporation, there was a special fiduciary duty owed by the director to the corporation-shareholder. [General Rubber Co. v. Benedict, 215 N.Y. 18 (1915)]

(c) **Securities acts violations—derivative action:** [§598]   A derivative action will lie for violations of the federal securities acts where the violation constitutes a breach of management's duties to the corporation.

1) **Example:** Where a violation of rule 10b-5 results in injury to the corporation (as distinct from its shareholders), a derivative action will lie if the corporation fails to sue. (*See supra,* §592.)

2) **Example:** Under section 16(b), recovery of "short swing profits" by insiders belongs to the corporation. If it fails to sue, the statute authorizes a minority shareholder to sue on its behalf (*supra,* §391). (*Note:* This is a statutory action, rather than a true derivative suit, and as a consequence, it is not subject to the same procedural limitations, *see infra,* §§627, 645, 658.)

b. **Prerequisite to suit—exhaustion of corporate remedies:** [§599]   Since a derivative suit seeks to enforce a corporate cause of action, the plaintiff must first show that he has exhausted his remedies within the corporate structure. This is an essential element of the plaintiff's cause of action and must be specifically ***pleaded and proven.*** [Fed. R. Civ. P. 23.1; Cal. Corp. Code §800(b)(2)]

(1) **Demand on directors:** [§600]   Since only the board of directors is authorized to bring suit on behalf of the corporation, a shareholder, before proceeding with a derivative suit, must make a sincere effort to induce the directors to remedy the wrong complained of. His complaint must "allege with particularity the efforts, if any, made by the plaintiff to obtain the action he desires from the directors or comparable authority . . . and the reasons for his failure to obtain the action or for not making the effort." [Fed. R. Civ. P. 23.1]

(a) **When excused:** [§601]   Demand on the directors is excused when the shareholder demonstrates that it would be "futile," *i.e.,* when all or a majority of the directors are themselves the alleged wrongdoers or under their control, or have failed to exercise reasonable care to prevent the wrong. [Barr v. Wackman, 36 N.Y.2d 371 (1975)]

1) **Note—majority approval does not excuse demand:** [§602]   In the absence of negligence, self-interest, or other indication of bias, the fact that a majority of the directors merely *approved* the transaction under attack does not itself excuse the demand; *i.e.,* it does *not* follow that these directors will refuse to remedy the error of their business judgment when it is brought to their attention. [Aronson v. Lewis, 473 A.2d 805 (Del. 1984); Lewis v. Graves, 701 F.2d 245 (2d Cir. 1983)]

(b) **Effect of directors' rejection of demand:** [§603]   If a derivative suit alleges wrongdoing by a majority of the directors (or by persons who control them), the board's decision not to sue will not prevent the derivative suit. [Lewis v. Curtis, 671 F.2d 779 (3d Cir. 1982)]

1) **Note:** Even if a demand is required because a majority of the directors "merely approved" the challenged transaction (*see supra*), some courts have held that it does not necessarily follow that their decision not to sue will end the matter. [Galef v. Alexander, 615 F.2d 51 (2d Cir. 1980)—participation insufficient to excuse a demand may nonetheless disqualify directors from barring derivative suit]

(c) **"Business judgment, honestly exercised":** [§604]   Where the matter complained of does not involve any claim of wrongdoing by the directors or by persons who control them (*e.g.,* where plaintiff-shareholder complains that a third party has breached a contract with the corporation, and wants the corporation to bring suit for damages), the board's good faith refusal to sue may *bar* the action. If the directors reasonably conclude that there is no likelihood of recovery, or that the costs of suit would outweigh any recovery, courts may refuse to allow a derivative suit. *Rationale:* A court will not interfere with a good faith exercise of discretion by the board elected to make business judgments for the corporation. [United Copper Securities Co. v. Amalgamated Copper Co., 244 U.S. 261 (1917)]

1) **Reasonable diligence:** [§605]   But the court may review the directors' judgment to determine whether they used reasonable diligence in deciding not to sue.

(d) **Derivative suit against directors:** [§606]   Where the derivative suit alleges wrongdoing by a minority of the directors, the suit may be barred if the disinterested director majority makes a good faith business judgment that the suit is not in the corporation's best interests. [Untermeyer v. Fidelity Daily Income Trust, 580 F.2d 22 (1st Cir. 1978)]

1) **Special litigation committee in suits alleging wrongdoing by a majority of directors:** [§607]   A board of directors (a majority of which may be interested) may appoint a special committee of disinterested directors, which may be advised by special counsel, to determine whether the suit would be in the corporation's best interest.

Most courts have held that the good faith decision of such committee to terminate the suit is similarly governed by the business judgment rule. [Auerbach v. Bennett, 47 N.Y.2d 619 (1979)]

a) **Limited judicial review:** [§608] The court will determine whether the special committee was truly disinterested and whether its procedures and methodology of investigation were sufficient. [Auerbach v. Bennett, *supra*]

  1/ **Note:** Some courts have explicitly placed the burden of proving independence, good faith, reasonableness of investigation, and reasonable bases for the special committee's conclusions on the corporation seeking to dismiss the derivative suit. [Zapata Corp. v. Maldonado, 430 A.2d 779 (Del. 1981)]

b) **Compare—court's independent judgment:** [§609] Some decisions further provide that the court *may* also apply its *own* independent business judgment (as well as consider matters of public policy) as to whether termination of the derivative suit is in the corporation's best interest. [Zapata Corp. v. Maldonado, *supra;* Kaplan v. Wyatt, 499 A.2d 1184 (Del. 1985)—emphasizing that this step is within court's discretion]

  1/ **Burden of proof:** [§610] It has been held in cases where a majority of the directors are charged with self-dealing that the court must determine whether the defendant-directors will be able to show that the transaction complained of was fair and reasonable to the corporation (*see supra,* §218). [Alford v. Shaw, 358 S.E.2d 323 (N.C. 1987)]

c) **Minority view:** [§611] At least one court has held that directors charged with misconduct have no power to select a special litigation committee. Rather, if the derivative suit alleges wrongdoing by a majority of the board, the corporation may request the court to appoint a "special panel" to act in place of the board of directors. [Miller v. Register & Tribune Syndicate, Inc., 336 N.W.2d 709 (Iowa 1983)]

d) **Violations of federal law:** [§612] If the derivative suit charges a violation of federal law, the question of whether a special litigation committee may terminate the suit by deciding that it is not in the corporation's best interest depends on (i) whether the relevant state law allows the board to delegate such decisions to a committee of disinterested directors, and (ii) whether it would be consistent with the federal law allegedly violated. [Burks v. Lasker, 441 U.S. 471 (1979)]

1/ **Section 10(b):** [§613]   Neither the policies underlying rule 10b-5 nor the disclosure requirements of the federal proxy rules are offended by permitting a special litigation committee to terminate a derivative suit alleging a violation of section 10(b) or of section 14(a) of the Securities Exchange Act of 1934. [Lewis v. Anderson, 615 F.2d 778 (9th Cir. 1979)]

(2) **Demand on shareholders:** [§614]   In most states, the plaintiff in a derivative suit must also make a demand on the shareholders—although this is often qualified by some phrase such as "if necessary." [Fed. R. Civ. P. 23.1] (California and New York require only that demand be made on the directors. [Cal. Corp. Code §800(b)(2); N.Y. Bus. Corp. Law §626; *and see* RMBCA §7.40])

(a) **When excused:** [§615]   Demand on the shareholders is usually excused if the alleged wrongdoing is beyond the power of the shareholders to "ratify." [Continental Securities Co. v. Belmont, 206 N.Y. 7 (1912)]

1) **Fraud:** [§616]   Courts are split on whether a majority of the disinterested shareholders may "ratify" an alleged fraud on the corporation by its directors. [Claman v. Robertson, 128 N.E.2d 429 (Ohio 1955)—fraud ratifiable; Mayer v. Adams, 141 A.2d 458 (Del. 1958)—contra]

2) **Illegal acts:** [§617]   It has been held that shareholders have no power to ratify illegal acts by the directors that cause injury to the corporation (*e.g.,* antitrust violations), and hence no demand need be made prior to a derivative suit. [Rogers v. American Can Co., 305 F.2d 297 (3d Cir. 1962)]

3) **Negligence, unreasonable business judgment:** [§618]   Shareholders do have power to ratify alleged negligence or unreasonable business judgment by the directors. Hence the demand is not excused. [Smith v. Brown-Borhek Co., 200 A.2d 398 (Pa. 1964)]

4) **Lack of prior authorization:** [§619]   Similarly, shareholders may ratify actions by the board that are voidable due to lack of prior authorization (*e.g.,* no shareholder approval). [Continental Securities Co. v. Belmont, *supra,* §615]

5) **Nonratifiable wrongs:** [§620]   Even if the wrongdoing is not ratifiable, some courts still require a demand on shareholders so as to inform them and give them an opportunity to take appropriate action—such as removing the directors, electing new ones who will cause the corporation to sue, or determining that the suit is not in the corporation's best interest. [Bell v. Arnold, 487 P.2d 545 (Colo. 1971)]

6) **Cost of demand as excuse:** [§621]   Courts are split on the question of whether a shareholder demand should be excused when the shareholders are so numerous and widespread as to make the cost of such demand extremely expensive. [Levitt v. Johnson, 334 F.2d 815 (1st Cir. 1964)—demand excused; Saigh v. Busch, 403 S.W.2d 559 (Mo. 1966)—contra]

(b) **Effect of shareholders' refusal to sue:** [§622]   If a demand on the shareholders is required (*i.e.*, if the alleged wrongdoing is subject to ratification by the shareholders, or if the jurisdiction requires that the shareholders be informed of the suit) and the majority of disinterested shareholders make a good faith decision not to sue, the derivative suit ordinarily may not be maintained. [S. Solomont & Sons Trust, Inc. v. New England Theatres Operating Corp., 93 N.E.2d 241 (Mass. 1950)]

1) **Rationale:** The shareholder body has power to determine what is in the best interests of the corporation.

2) **Limitation:** [§623]   Of course, the ratification or refusal to sue must be by a *disinterested* majority—not by shareholders who were the direct or indirect wrongdoers or beneficiaries of the allegedly wrongful transaction.

c. **Qualifications of plaintiff**

(1) **Shareholder status:** [§624]   A few states require that the plaintiff be a "registered" shareholder or shareholder "of record" in order to bring a derivative suit. [Wash. Bus. Corp. Act §23A.08.460] However, most also permit suit to be initiated by a "beneficial" or "equitable" owner of shares—*e.g.*, the holder of a voting trust certificate, or the purchaser of shares who has not yet been recorded on the corporation's books. [Theodora Holding Corp. v. Henderson, 257 A.2d 398 (Del. 1969); Cal. Corp. Code §800(b)(1)]

(2) **Contemporaneous ownership:** [§625]   Most states require that plaintiff must have been a shareholder at the time of the alleged wrongdoing. Shareholders cannot complain of wrongs that occurred *before* they purchased their shares. [Fed. R. Civ. P. 23.1; Cal. Corp. Code §800(b)(1)]

(a) **Rationale:** One historic purpose is to prevent so-called "strike suits"—actions stirred up by persons who search out corporate irregularities, buy a few shares, and file suit to secure a private settlement, rather than to obtain recovery for the corporation. (The current rule, however, requires that any amount received in settlement be paid over to the corporation; *see infra,* §667.) Another reason for the rule is that one not a shareholder at the time of the alleged wrongdoing suffers no injury and thus should not be permitted to sue. [Home Fire Insurance Co. v. Barber, 93 N.W. 1024 (Neb. 1903)]

(b) **Exceptions**

1) **"Operation of law":** [§626] The contemporaneous ownership requirement generally does not apply if the plaintiff acquires her shares "by operation of law from a holder who was a holder at the time of the transaction" complained of (*e.g.,* by inheritance). [Cal. Corp. Code §800(b)(1)]

2) **Securities Exchange Act section 16(b):** [§627] The contemporaneous ownership requirement is expressly inapplicable to shareholder suits for short-swing profits under section 16(b), which really are not true derivative suits. [Dottenheim v. Murchison, *supra,* §391]

3) **Injustice:** [§628] A few state statutes also waive the rule of contemporaneous ownership if it is shown "that there is a strong prima facie case in favor of the claim asserted on behalf of the corporation" and that without such suit serious injustice will result. [Pa. Bus. Corp. Law §516; Cal. Corp. Code §800(b)(1)]

4) **Continuing wrongs:** [§629] Where the wrong is continuing in nature, plaintiff need not have owned the shares at the inception thereof. [Palmer v. Morris, 316 F.2d 649 (5th Cir. 1963)—corporation sold assets to defendant at unduly low price before plaintiff became shareholder but received payments therefor after plaintiff was shareholder]

(c) **Corporation may be barred where controlling shareholder disqualified—"piercing corporate veil":** [§630] Where the controlling shareholder acquired the shares *after* the alleged wrongdoing, the shareholder is clearly barred by the contemporaneous shareholder requirement from maintaining a derivative suit against the former management. And in such cases, equitable considerations may require that the *corporation itself* also be barred. [Bangor Punta Operations, Inc. v. Bangor & Aristook Railroad, 417 U.S. 703 (1974)]

1) **Example:** A purchases 99% of the stock of XYZ Corp. from B for a fair price. A cannot maintain a derivative suit charging B with mismanagement during the time B owned the controlling shares. Nor will A be permitted to cause XYZ Corp. to file a suit against B under these circumstances.

2) **Rationale:** Equity will not permit a controlling shareholder to use the corporate veil to obtain indirectly that which he could not recover directly. Since he bargained for and received the controlling shares for a fair price, the seller's prior acts of corporate mismanagement caused the purchaser no injury. To allow the corporation to recover would in effect allow the purchaser to recoup what he voluntarily

paid for the shares. [Bangor Punta Operations, Inc. v. Bangor & Aristook Railroad, *supra*]

(3) **Motive in bringing suit:** [§631]   At least under the Federal Rules [Fed. R. Civ. P. 23.1], it must appear that the plaintiff-shareholder "fairly and adequately" represents the interests of the shareholders generally in enforcing the rights of the corporation. [Hornreich v. Plant Industries, Inc., 535 F.2d 550 (9th Cir. 1976)—action dismissed where it appeared motive of plaintiff-shareholder was to force corporation to settle direct suit by plaintiff against it]

(4) **Compare—action by former shareholders:** [§632]   One who is no longer a shareholder normally cannot maintain either a direct or a derivative suit. However, where he sold his shares *without knowledge* of management's wrongdoing, and the wrong would otherwise go *unremedied,* a former shareholder may be allowed a *direct* action against the wrongdoers to compensate for the loss in value of the shares sold. [Watson v. Button, 235 F.2d 235 (9th Cir. 1956)]

    (a) **Example:** A and B were the sole shareholders of XYZ Corp. A looted the corporate treasury, unbeknownst to B. Then, A and B sold their shares to C. Later, B discovered A's wrongdoing, and realized that she received less for her shares because of it.

        1) **No derivative action possible:** B cannot maintain a derivative suit on behalf of XYZ because she is no longer a shareholder of record. Nor can C maintain such an action, because of the contemporaneous ownership requirement. Furthermore, because the sole shareholder, C, is barred from suing on behalf of the corporation, the corporation itself is also barred. [Kirk v. First National Bank, 439 F. Supp. 1141 (M.D. Ga. 1977)]

        2) **Direct action permitted:** Under these circumstances, the courts permit the innocent former shareholder (B) to bring a direct action against the wrongdoer (A) for the amount by which the fraud or mismanagement reduced the value of the shares sold because the wrong would otherwise go unremedied. [Watson v. Button, *supra*]

  d. **Procedural issues in derivative suits**

(1) **Pleadings:** [§633]   Under most statutes, the plaintiff-shareholder's complaint must specifically allege a qualification to sue (contemporaneous share ownership), exhaustion of corporate remedies (demand on directors and shareholders, if necessary), and the wrong or injury to the corporation. [Fed. R. Civ. P. 23.1]

    (a) **Verify pleadings:** Although plaintiff is required, under the Federal Rules, to verify the pleadings, he need not personally understand the allegations. He may properly rely on the judgment of another person (*i.e.,* his attorney). [Surowitz v. Hilton Hotels Corp., 383 U.S. 363 (1966)]

(2) **Parties:** [§634] The plaintiff-shareholder sues in his own name although he is suing on behalf of the corporation. The alleged wrongdoers are named as defendants.

    (a) **Joinder of corporation:** [§635] The corporation is an indispensable party to the action, and therefore must be joined and served. It is normally joined as a party-defendant (for the reason that it refused to prosecute the action as plaintiff). [Smith v. Sperling, 354 U.S. 91 (1957)]

(3) **Legal representation—conflict of interest problem:** [§636] Although the corporation is joined as a defendant, the action is still brought on its behalf; its interests are ordinarily adverse to the other defendants (especially where its officers and directors are charged with wrongdoing). Thus, most courts hold that it is improper for the corporation attorney, or any other lawyer, to represent **both** the corporation and the real defendants. They must retain separate counsel. [Cannon v. U.S. Acoustics Corp., 398 F. Supp. 209 (N.D. Ill. 1975); *and see* Legal Ethics Summary]

    (a) **Attorney-client privilege:** [§637] The corporation is a "client" of its attorney; thus, communications between the corporation's lawyer and either the corporation's control group of managers or its lower level executives are privileged. [Upjohn Co. v. United States, 449 U.S. 383 (1981)]

(4) **Personal jurisdiction:** [§638] All parties-defendant (including the corporation) must be subject to the personal jurisdiction of the court in which the action is brought. This may pose serious problems for the plaintiff when the officers or directors charged with wrongdoing reside in several states—problems that are further complicated if the corporation is a resident of yet a different state.

    (a) **State statutes:** [§639] The problem has been alleviated in some states by statutes that provide the following solutions:

        1) **Secretary of state as agent:** [§640] Some statutes deem nonresident directors of domestic corporations to have "appointed" the local secretary of state to receive service of process in actions relating to the corporation. [10 Del. Code §3114] Such statutes have been held to satisfy due process. [Armstrong v. Pomerance, 423 A.2d 174 (Del. 1980)]

        2) **Long arm statutes:** [§641] Other statutes subject nonresident directors (and other defendants) to personal jurisdiction under long arm statutes (but usually only when they have committed some act within the state; *see* Conflict of Laws Summary).

        3) **Attachment of shares:** [§642] Still other statutes subject nonresident shareholders of domestic corporations to quasi in rem jurisdiction by permitting attachment of their shares.

a) **Procedure:** [§643]   U.C.C. section 8-317 permits attachment of shares only when they are actually *seized,* but some states permit attachment on the books of the corporation. [Del. Gen. Corp. Law §324]

b) **Due process:** [§644]   In any event, such quasi in rem jurisdiction will satisfy due process only if the claim in the derivative suit is actually related to the attached shares or the defendant (apart from owning shares in the corporation) has adequate contacts with the state. [Shaffer v. Heitner, 433 U.S. 186 (1977)]

(b) **Where suit based on securities violations:** [645]   The Securities Exchange Act of 1934, section 27, authorizes nationwide service of process in any derivative suit based on violations of the Act. Since this solves most jurisdiction problems for plaintiff-shareholders, it is to the shareholders' distinct advantage to allege a cause of action for violation of some provision of the Act (usually the anti-fraud provisions of section 10(b); *supra,* §285).

(5) **Right to jury trial**

(a) **General rule:** [§646]   Since a derivative suit is an equitable action, a jury trial often is *not* available in state courts. [Rankin v. Frebank Co., 47 Cal. App. 3d 75 (1975)] But some states do provide a right to a jury trial. [Finance, Investment & Rediscount Co. v. Wells, 409 So. 2d 1341 (Ala. 1981)]

(b) **Federal actions:** [§647]   In federal actions, however, the seventh amendment right to a jury trial has been held to apply to those issues upon which the *corporation* would have had a right to a jury trial had it brought the action. Thus, for example, where the issue is the corporation's right to recover damages for fraud, plaintiff is entitled to a jury trial. [Ross v. Bernhard, 396 U.S. 531 (1970)—decision applicable to federal litigation only, as seventh amendment is not binding on states]

e. **Security for expenses:** [§648]   To discourage "strike suits" (*supra,* §625), a number of states have statutes that require the plaintiff-shareholder in a derivative suit, under certain circumstances, to *post a bond* or other security to indemnify the corporation against certain of its litigation expenses in the event the plaintiff loses the suit.

(1) **When plaintiff must post security:** [§649]   Statutes vary considerably as to when security is required.

(a) **Mandatory posting of security:** [§650]   Under some statutes, the plaintiff is required to post security if he owns less than a specified percentage of outstanding shares (*e.g.,* 5%); or less than a specified dollar amount of the corporation's stock (*e.g.,* $25,000 or $50,000). [N.Y. Bus. Corp. Law §627]

1) **May aggregate holdings:** [§651] In these states, if several shareholders join in bringing the action (or join after the action is filed), their holdings may be aggregated to avoid the security requirement. [Baker v. MacFadden Publications, Inc., 300 N.Y. 325 (1950)]

2) **Acquiring shares after action is filed:** [§652] It is unclear whether a plaintiff may avoid the security requirement by acquiring the specified percentage or dollar amount after suit is filed. [Haberman v. Tobin, 626 F.2d 1101 (2d Cir. 1980)—suit dismissed, but plaintiff repeatedly disregarded judge's orders]

(b) **Discretionary posting of security:** [§653] Other statutes make the posting of security discretionary with the court. For example, they may provide that the trial judge is authorized to order the plaintiff to deposit security if it appears "that there is no reasonable possibility that the action will benefit the corporation or its shareholders." [Cal. Corp. Code §800(c)]

1) **Compare:** One statute authorizes the court to deny a request for security if plaintiff can show that it would "impose undue hardship . . . and serious injustice would result." [Pa. Bus. Corp. Law §516]

(2) **Who is entitled to security:** [§654] Under most statutes, only the *corporation* is entitled to move for the posting of security; and the bond or other security posted runs only in its favor. [N.Y. Bus. Corp. Law §627]

(a) **But note:** A few statutes also permit officers or directors who are defendants in the action to demand security. [Cal. Corp. Code §800(c)]

(3) **Expenses to be covered:** [§655] Most statutes require the security to cover all expenses reasonably incurred by the corporation as the result of the derivative suit, including *attorneys' fees*—plus whatever litigation expenses the corporation may be legally or contractually required to pay by way of *indemnification* to its officers or directors as defendants therein (*infra*, §§678-688). [Cal. Corp. Code §800(d)]

(a) **Limitation:** Some states limit the total amount of security that may be required. [*See, e.g.,* Cal. Corp. Code §800(d)—$50,000]

(4) **When liability or security matures:** [§656] Under some statutes, it is enough that the plaintiff-shareholder loses the derivative suit, *i.e.*, the defendant corporation is *automatically* entitled to recourse against the bond or other security, although the amounts are to be determined by the court. [Wash. Bus. Corp. Act §23A.08.460]

(a) **Compare:** Other statutes are more restrictive, allowing recourse against the plaintiff only if the court finds that the derivative suit was brought "without reasonable cause." [Tex. Bus. Corp. Act §5.14]

(5) **Applicability of state statutes to derivative suits in federal court**

(a) **In diversity cases:** [§657]   State security-for-expenses statutes are deemed "substantive" for purposes of the *Erie* doctrine. Thus, in federal derivative suits based on diversity of citizenship jurisdiction, the federal court must apply whatever security statute is applied in the local state courts. [Cohen v. Beneficial Industrial Loan Corp., 337 U.S. 541 (1949)]

(b) **In cases under federal securities act:** [§658]   However, state security-for-expenses statutes do not apply where the derivative suit is based on violation of the Securities Act of 1934. Here, the federal court is exercising federal question jurisdiction, and the Act has been held to reflect a congressional intent that shareholders be afforded access to federal tribunals without constraint on such state statutes. [McClure v. Borne Chemical Co., 292 F.2d 824 (3d Cir. 1961)]

(6) **Compare—liability for court costs:** [§659]   Quite apart from security-for-expenses statutes, a plaintiff-shareholder who loses is liable for the court costs incurred by the prevailing parties—the same as any other litigant. (*See* Civil Procedure Summary.)

(a) **No attorneys' fees:** [§660]   In most states, however, recoverable court costs do not include attorneys' fees. (Some states are contra. Under section 7.40(d) of the Model Act, the court may order payment of reasonable attorneys' fees incurred by defendants if it finds that a derivative action was brought "without reasonable cause." (*See also* Fed. R. Civ. Proc. 11, discussed in Civil Procedure Summary.)

f. **Defenses:** [§661]   In general, any defense that could have been asserted had the corporation brought the action can also be asserted in the plaintiff-shareholder's derivative suit—plus certain equitable defenses assertable only against the plaintiff personally.

(1) **Statute of limitations:** [§662]   In most states, the period applicable to the corporation's cause of action is applied. (A few states have special limitations periods for derivative suits. [*See e.g.,* N.Y. Civ. Prac. Law §213(7)—six years])

(a) **Period of statute:** [§663]   The statute of limitations runs from the time of the alleged wrongful act—unless the underlying cause of action is equitable or for fraud or defendants have concealed their wrongdoing, in which cases it may be held to run from the time the alleged wrong reasonably should have been discovered.

(2) **Personal defenses:** [§664]   A derivative suit is a proceeding in equity, and laches, unclean hands, pari delicto, and other so-called equitable defenses may therefore be asserted to bar the plaintiff's action.

(a) **Example:** Thus, a shareholder who *participated* or *acquiesced* in the wrong complained of cannot maintain a derivative suit on behalf of the corporation. Her conduct would be viewed as "unclean hands," precluding equitable relief. [*But see* Kullgren v. Navy Gas & Supply Co., 149 P.2d 653 (Colo. 1934)—contra]

(b) **Example:** Unreasonable delay by the plaintiff-shareholder in filing the action may constitute laches, barring the action, at least where the delay has been *prejudicial* to the defendants. (But unreasonable delay by one plaintiff-shareholder will not bar suit by some other qualified shareholders for the same wrong.)

(c) **Note:** Ordinarily, the *motives* of the plaintiff-shareholder are *immaterial* to the right to maintain the action. But if it could be shown that the plaintiff is acting at the instance of some rival corporation, rather than in the bona fide interest of her own corporation, "unclean hands" might bar the action. Under the Federal Rules, an improper motive may disqualify plaintiff from maintaining the suit. [Fed. R. Civ. P. 23.1; *see supra,* §631]

g. **Res judicata:** [§665] Judgment on the merits or a court-approved settlement in a derivative suit is res judicata to the claims asserted therein. Since the suit was maintained on behalf of the corporation, judgment on the merits *for or against* the defendants bars any further suits for the same wrong—either by the corporation itself, or by any other shareholders in derivative suits.

h. **Settlement and recovery:** [§666] Since the cause of action belongs to the corporation, so does any settlement or judgment (except in the "unusual circumstances" noted below). The plaintiff-shareholder benefits only indirectly, through any increase in the value of stock.

(1) **Private settlements barred:** [§667] If a plaintiff-shareholder personally receives any consideration to discontinue the action, it is held in trust for the corporation and must be paid over. [Clarke v. Greenberg, 296 N.Y. 146 (1947)]

(2) **Procedural requirements:** [§668] Most states require that settlement or dismissal of derivative suits be subject to *court approval* after some form of notice to all shareholders. [Fed. R. Civ. P. 23.1]

(a) **Without notice and court approval:** [§669] Absent such notice and approval, the settlement or dismissal will not be given res judicata effect; *i.e.,* other shareholders or the corporation may be permitted to sue again. [Papilsky v. Berndt, 466 F.2d 251 (2d Cir. 1972)]

(b) **Collateral attack:** [§670] Even though a settlement receives court approval after notice to the shareholders, it may still be collaterally attacked by a shareholder on the ground that it was fraudulent. [Clayton v. Mimms & Co., 386 N.E.2d 452 (Ill. 1979)]

(3) **Under "unusual circumstances," recovery may go to shareholders rather than corporation:** [§671] Under special circumstances, recovery in a derivative suit may be ordered paid directly to certain shareholders rather than to the corporate treasury.

    (a) **Corporation dissolved:** [§672] If the corporation has been dissolved and *all creditors paid,* no purpose would be served by ordering it paid to the corporation, and therefore the court may properly order any recovery paid to the shareholders.

    (b) **Corporate recovery would benefit those not entitled:** [§673] Where a corporate recovery would benefit certain shareholders not entitled to it, the court may order the money paid to other shareholders. *See,* for example, *Perlman v. Feldmann (supra,* §588), where a shareholder sold "control" of the corporation to a buyer who made it a captive supplier and thereby deprived the corporation of profits it otherwise would have made. The former controlling shareholder was ordered to account for the improper profits he made on the sale. However, these profits were ordered paid to the remaining shareholders rather than to the corporation to prevent the buyer (new controlling shareholder) from participating therein.

    (c) **Comment:** This kind of "bypass" of the corporate treasury is tantamount to the court's declaring a dividend from the corporation to the innocent shareholders. It will ordinarily be done only when the rights of creditors are not prejudiced.

i. **Reimbursement to plaintiff for litigation expenses:** [§674] If victorious, the plaintiff-shareholder may be entitled to reimbursement from the corporation for litigation expenses, including reasonable attorneys' fees.

(1) **Common fund doctrine:** [§675] At least where the derivative suit results in a monetary recovery to the corporation, such reimbursement is based on the equitable doctrine that one who has obtained a "common fund" for the benefit of others (here, the other shareholders) is entitled to reimbursement. [Fletcher v. A.J. Industries Inc., 266 Cal. App. 2d 313 (1968)]

(2) **"Substantial benefit" to corporation:** [§676] Even in the absence of a monetary recovery, many courts order reimbursement to a successful plaintiff if the derivative suit has resulted in a *substantial benefit* to the corporation. [Bosch v. Meeker Cooperative Light & Power Association, 101 N.W.2d 423 (Minn. 1960)—election of directors held illegal; Mills v. Electric Auto-Lite Co., *supra,* §476—management's proxy statement held violative of proxy rules]

(3) **Amount of fee:** [§677] Courts have used two basic approaches in determining the amount of the fee to be awarded. Some courts emphasize the amount recovered for the corporation. [Angoff v. Goldfine, 270 F.2d 185 (1st Cir. 1959)] However, the majority approach today focuses on the time counsel spent on the case, adjusted to reflect the quality of the work done and the risk assumed by the

lawyer. [Lindy Bros. Builders v. American Radiator & Standard Sanitary Corp., 487 F.2d 161 (3d Cir. 1973)]

j. **Indemnification of officers and directors:** [§678] Statutes in all states govern the extent to which the corporation may properly indemnify its directors or officers (or other employees or agents) for expenses incurred in defending suits against them for conduct undertaken in their official capacity. These statutes apply not only to derivative suits, but also to direct actions by the corporation, its shareholders, or third parties (*e.g.,* the state for a criminal violation; or an injured party for a tort).

(1) **Statute as exclusive basis for indemnification:** [§679] In some states, such statutes constitute the exclusive basis upon which indemnification is permitted. Any broader provision in the corporation's articles or bylaws is void as contrary to public policy. [Cal. Corp. Code §317(g)]

 (a) **Compare:** Other states permit the subject to be governed by the articles or bylaws, shareholder agreements, or votes of the shareholders or directors. [Del. Gen. Corp. Law §145; N.Y. Bus. Corp. Law §721]

(2) **Where defendant wins:** [§680] As long as the director or officer accused of wrongdoing *wins on the merits,* there is generally no problem. Every state permits the corporation to reimburse or indemnify him for his litigation expenses, inlcuding attorneys' fees, in defending the action.

 (a) **Rationale:** Public policy favors indemnification where the director or officer is vindicated. Indemnification encourages capable directors and officers to seek and retain corporate office and to resist unfounded charges against them. Moreover, it discourages minority shareholders from filing frivolous derivative suits, knowing that the defendants will contest such suits vigorously because their expenses will be paid by the corporation if they win. [Solimine v. Hollander, 19 A.2d 344 (N.J. 1941)]

 (b) **Indemnification as discretionary or mandatory:** [§681] In some states, reimbursement is discretionary with the board. But under many statutes, the corporation is required to indemnify a director or officer where successful on the merits (some add "or otherwise") in defense of a derivative suit or direct action against her in her capacity as director or officer. [Cal. Corp. Code §317(d); N.Y. Bus. Corp. Law §724; Del. Gen. Corp. Law §145]

(3) **Where defendant settles or loses:** [§682] The statutes vary significantly on the extent to which the indemnification is permissible where the officer or director loses the lawsuit or the suit is settled. Many statutes distinguish between third-party suits and derivative suits:

 (a) **Third-party suits:** [§683] Where the suit against the director or officer is by an outsider (*e.g.,* state in criminal action; injured party in tort action), statutes generally permit indemnification for both litigation expenses and whatever civil or criminal liabilities are incurred (money paid out in settlement, judgment or fines) provided that the disinterested directors or shareholders (or independent legal counsel) determine that the defendant director or officer acted in *good faith* for a purpose reasonably believed to be in the best interests of the corporation and (where a criminal action was involved) there was no reason to believe that the action involved was unlawful. [N.Y. Bus. Corp. Law §722; Del. Gen. Corp. Law §145(a); *and see* Cal. Corp. Code §317(b)]

1) **Bylaw requires reimbursement:** [§684] If the *statute is not the exclusive basis for indemnification,* and if a bylaw unqualifiedly requires the corporation to reimburse all expenses and amounts paid in settlement, it has been held that the corporation must indemnify a director for the sum he paid to settle an alleged rule 10b-5 violation. [B&B Investment Club v. Kleinert's, Inc., 472 F. Supp. 787 (E.D. Pa. 1979)]

(b) **Derivative suits:** [§685] However, where the suit against the director or officer is a derivative action charging him with wrongdoing toward the corporation, the statutes in most states are much stricter.

1) **Suit settled:** [§686] If the derivative suit is settled prior to judgment, most statutes permit indemnification of the officer or director for his *litigation expenses,* including attorneys' fees, provided (i) the settlement was made with court approval, and (ii) the defendant is determined to have acted in good faith, with reasonable care, and with the belief that he was acting in the best interest of the corporation, such determination being made by a majority of the disinterested directors or shareholders, or by the court. [Cal. Corp. Code §§317(c), (e)]

a) **Amount paid in settlement:** [§687] If the above (or similar) conditions are met, some states also permit the corporation to indemnify the director or officer for amounts paid in settlement. [N.Y. Bus. Corp. Law §722(c)]

2) **Judgment against defendant:** [§688] Where a director or officer in a derivative suit is adjudged to have acted dishonestly, or in bad faith, or to have obtained an improper personal gain, some statutes *prohibit* indemnification by the corporation, and this applies to both his litigation expenses and any liability imposed upon him. [N.Y. Bus. Corp. Law §721]

a) **Rationale:** It would destroy the purpose of the derivative suit if the corporation could make the errant director or officer "whole" for the consequences of this breach of duty to the corporation.

b) **Compare:** Other statutes allow the corporation to indemnify the errant director or officer for his litigation expenses including attorneys' fees (but not the damages assessed against him) in the derivative suit—if the court finds "such person is fairly and reasonably entitled to such indemnity." [Del. Gen. Corp. Law §145; Cal. Corp. Code §317(c)(1); N.Y. Bus. Corp. Law §722]

k. **Insurance against derivative suit liability:** [§689]   A number of states now have statutes that authorize a corporation to purchase and maintain insurance to protect the corporation against liability to its directors and officers for indemnification as authorized by law, and to protect the directors and officers against *any liability* arising out of their service to the corporation and against the expense of defending suits asserting such liability. (Sometimes, but not always, the directors and officers pay a portion of the insurance premium to reflect the cost of their coverage.)

(1) **Statutes:** [§690]   Some statutes are quite permissive and permit the corporation to maintain such insurance against any liability or expense incurred by a director or officer acting in an official capacity. [Del. Gen. Corp. Law §145(g); Cal. Corp. Code §317(i)]

(a) **Compare:** Other statutes prohibit a corporation's insuring its officers or directors against liability for acts involving deliberate dishonesty or where the wrongdoer "personally gained a financial profit or other advantage to which he was not legally entitled." [N.Y. Bus. Corp. Law §726(b)]

(b) **Comment:** To the extent that such insurance is permitted, it may enable a corporation to do indirectly (by paying insurance premiums) that which it could not do directly (indemnifying officers and directors against liability for breach of duty to corporation).

(c) **Public policy:** [§691]   Merely insuring against liability for acts of negligence is no doubt permissible. But if the insurance purports to insure against liability for intentional dishonesty or self-dealing by directors, it may be unenforceable as contrary to public policy.

4. **Compare—Suits by Directors or Officers:** [§692]   Some state statutes permit directors or officers to bring suits on behalf of the corporation. These are generally subject to fewer restrictions than shareholders' derivative suits (*e.g.,* no prior demand on the board of directors or shareholders is required). [N.Y. Bus. Corp. Law §720(b)]

5. **Compare—Creditor's Bill in Equity:** [§693]   A few cases permit a creditor, having obtained a judgment against the corporation and execution upon the judgment being returned unsatisfied, to assert a corporate cause of action in proceedings similar to a derivative suit.

a. **Other remedies:** [§694]   Futhermore, some statutes authorizing a creditor to attach or execute upon a debtor's property may permit a judgment creditor to enforce a corporate cause of action—by garnishing such sums as are due the corporation from the defendant, and then litigating the enforceability of the claim.

VIII. CAPITALIZATION OF THE CORPORATION

chapter approach

This chapter concerns the capitalization of the corporation through the issuance of shares, and the regulations incident thereto. Some important areas for exam purposes are as follows:

1. **Stock Subscriptions:** Subscriptions are agreements to purchase shares from the corporation. If such an agreement appears on your exam, first determine whether the agreement was entered into before or after formation of the corporation. ***Post-incorporation*** agreements are binding contracts; ***pre-incorporation*** agreements, however, vary in enforceability. If the pre-incorporation subscription is part of the articles, it is enforceable by the corporation once the articles are filed. If, however, the subscription is a separate agreement, it may be found to be merely a continuing offer and, thus, unenforceable.

2. **Consideration Required To Be Paid for Shares:** Statutes generally regulate the form and the amount of consideration the corporation must receive for its shares.

   a. **Form:** Remember that "money paid, labor done, or property actually acquired" is valid consideration, while an executory promise is not.

   b. **Amount:** A corporation must receive full payment for its shares. To determine whether shares have been paid for in full, start by checking to see whether the shares are par or no-par value shares. Remember that, ordinarily, par value shares must be sold for at least par value, or they are considered "watered." Watch out for stock that has either been sold for ***less than par value*** (discount shares) or issued in exchange for ***overvalued property or services.*** Recall that most courts allow subsequent creditors to recover from the issuee of the watered stock and any of her transferees who participated in or had knowledge of the watering. ***No-par*** value stock eliminates the watered stock problem because it may be sold at whatever price is deemed ***reasonable*** by the board.

3. **Fiduciary Duties of Promoters:** If an exam question concerns a promoter selling property to the corporation, note that the promoter has a fiduciary duty of ***full disclosure.*** If the promoter fails to make a full disclosure with respect to his dealings with the corporation, the corporation may sue for either rescission or damages.

4. **Preemptive Rights:** Ordinarily, a shareholder has a right to subscribe to the number of shares in a ***new*** issuance that will preserve his proportionate interest in the corporation. Remember that, when recognized, preemptive rights can be enforced by specific performance to compel issuance to plaintiff, damages, or an injunction against the issuance of shares in violation of preemptive rights.

5. **Statutes Regulating Issuance of Shares:** State statutes regulating the issuance of shares are known as "blue sky" laws. Some impose civil or criminal penalties for fraud in connection with the issuance of shares. All require that persons who sell securities be licensed. The most comprehensive blue sky laws require that the stock be registered with the appropriate state official.

Probably more important for exam purposes are the *federal securities laws.* The Securities Act of 1933 establishes the framework for federal regulation. The most important thing to remember is that no interstate facilities or mails may be used to offer to sell a security unless a *registration statement* has been filed with the SEC. You should also know that *written* offers to sell must always satisfy the requirements for a statutory prospectus (*i.e.,* set forth the key information from the registration statement), and actual sales or deliveries of securities may be made only after the effective date of the registration statement and a prospectus must accompany or precede the delivery of any security.

Be aware, however, that certain securities and transactions are *exempt from the registration requirements.* In particular, watch for the following *exempt transactions:* (i) ordinary trading transactions between individual investors in securities that have already been issued, (ii) transactions by a securities broker, provided she is not acting as an underwriter and the time for initial distribution of the securities has passed, (iii) transactions by an issuer not involving a public offering (*i.e.,* private placements), and (iv) offerings made entirely to residents of the issuer's state.

Finally, note that a question may ask you to consider the remedies for a violation of the securities laws. If so, first ask yourself whether the securities are required to be registered. If so and if the registration statement contains a misstatement or omits a material fact, recall that *any person* acquiring the securities without knowledge thereof has an action for damages against those connected with the issuance of shares or the registration statement (*e.g.,* the corporation, directors, underwriters, experts, etc). Note that the corporation is absolutely liable, but the others may defend on the ground that they exercised due diligence. If the securities are exempt, only the original purchaser is entitled to recover and only the issuer or other sellers may be held liable. Also, the purchaser has a cause of action against a seller for failure to comply with the federal requirements (*e.g.,* registration, delivery of prospectus, etc.).

A. SHARES—IN GENERAL [§695]

A "share" represents the stockholder's proprietary interest in the corporation. It arises from acceptance by the corporation of the consideration offered by the subscriber.

1. **What a Share Represents:** [§696] Specifically, a share represents the right to receive dividends as declared by the board, the right to receive a portion of the corporate assets on liquidation and, if voting shares are involved, the right to vote.

2. **What a Share Does Not Represent:** [§697] Ownership of a share does *not* entitle the holder to any specific asset of the corporation or any interest in its assets as a whole. Title to corporate assets is in the corporation and cannot be conveyed by the shareholders.

B. CLASSES OF SHARES—PREFERENCES

1. **Introduction:** [§698] Shares of one or more classes may be authorized in the articles. All shares have equal rights except as otherwise provided in the articles.

2. **Common:** [§699]   Common stock represents the residual ownership of the corporation. The common stockholders are entitled to pro rata dividends, without priority or preference over any other stock. Normally, the common stockholders have voting rights and are entitled to share in the distribution of assets on liquidation.

    a. **Classes:** [§700]   A corporation may have more than one class of common stock (*e.g.,* "Common A" and "Common B"), with one class having certain rights that the other does not, or with one class entitled to certain priorities over the other. In such cases, the stock with the rights or priorities is, in effect, "preferred stock" (below).

3. **Preferred:** [§701]   Preferred stock is a class of stock having some sort of preference over other classes of stock—generally as to dividends or liquidation rights.

    a. **Classes or series:** [§702]   There may be several classes or series of preferred (*e.g.,* "Preferred A" and "Preferred B")—one with distinct priorities over the other, and both with priority over the common stock.

    b. **Redemption rights:** [§703]   Preferred stockholders may be given the right to compel the corporation to repurchase the shares if it has legally available funds to do so. (*See infra,* §§938-946.) This is known as a right of redemption. Frequently, the articles will require the corporation to maintain a ***sinking fund*** for this purpose (*i.e.,* accumulations of earnings not available for dividend distribution).

    c. **Particular preferences:** [§704]   The following are the special rights or priorities (preferences) most often given to preferred stock. As indicated above, these rights exist only where expressly conferred by the articles.

        (1) **Preference in receipt of dividends:** [§705]   The most frequent preference (and the most important) is to give preferred stock the right to receipt of dividends— *i.e.,* dividends must be paid to it at a specified rate (*e.g.,* 5% of par value or $5 per share) before dividends are paid to the holders of common stock. Whether the right to dividends is cumulative or noncumulative depends on what is provided in the articles.

            (a) **Cumulative:** [§706]   Holders of cumulative preferred shares have the right to receive payment of the designated dividend each year, whether or not there are sufficient earnings to pay it. Nonpayment in a given year does not destroy the right; the dividends "cumulate" until paid. Although there is ordinarily no method of forcing the corporation to pay (absent abuse of discretion by the directors, below), no amounts may be paid as dividends on inferior classes of stock until the current dividend and all arrears are paid on the cumulative preferred shares.

            (b) **Noncumulative:** [§707]   The general view is that where dividends are determined to be "noncumulative," the shareholder is entitled to dividends only if and when declared by the board. The right does not accumulate and is completely lost as to any year in which a dividend is not declared.

This is true even though there are earnings available from which to pay such dividends. Absent an abuse of discretion, the shareholder cannot force the directors to declare dividends. [Guttman v. Illinois Central Railroad, 189 F.2d 927 (2d Cir. 1951)]

1) **Limitation:** [§708] Note, however, that if the board fails to vote payment of a noncumulative preferred stock dividend, it cannot vote payment of a common stock dividend during the same year.

2) **Minority view—"dividend credit rule":** [§709] New Jersey courts have held that even though noncumulative preferred shareholders have no legal right to dividends until declared by the board, they still have an *equitable* right to such dividends in any year in which the corporation had earnings adequate to pay dividends and funds legally available for their payment. Until such dividends are paid, no dividends may be paid on the common stock. [Sanders v. Cuba Railroad, 120 A.2d 849 (N.J. 1956)]

(2) **Participation rights:** [§710] In addition to preference in receipt of dividends, holders of preferred shares are sometimes given the right to participate with the common shares in any remaining funds available for distribution after the preferred dividend has been paid. Again, the terms and extent of such participation (whether pro rata, or different amounts for each class) are as fixed in the articles.

C. AUTHORIZATION AND ISSUANCE OF SHARES [§711]

This portion of the summary deals primarily with so-called "primary" stock sales; *i.e.,* the *original issuance* of shares by a corporation, as distinguished from later resale of the shares by the issuee.

1. **Authorization:** [§712] Whatever shares are issued must be *authorized* by the articles or charter of the corporation (*e.g.,* "This corporation shall be authorized to issue 1,000 shares of capital stock, each share shall have a par value of $100, and the par value of all shares authorized shall be $100,000").

   a. **When all authorized shares issued:** [§713] If all of the shares authorized under the articles have already been issued, no further shares can be issued until there is an *amendment* to the articles (*infra,* §1035) authorizing a larger number of shares.

2. **Issuance:** [§714] Issuance is the process by which all or part of the corporation's authorized shares are sold. Issuance requires action by the board of directors accepting an offer to subscribe for shares of the corporation, and directing the secretary to issue appropriate share certificates upon receipt of the specified consideration.

   a. **Legislative control:** [§715] The sale and issuance of shares by a corporation is subject to detailed regulation under federal and state statutes. (*See* discussion below.)

b. **Shares outstanding:** [§716]   Once shares have been issued, they are referred to as "outstanding."

c. **Repurchase of shares outstanding:** [§717]   Under certain circumstances, the corporation may be authorized to repurchase its shares. (*See infra,* §§947-967.) If it does so, it may either:

(1) *Cancel the shares* (in which case the shares would no longer be issued, thereby increasing the number of shares the corporation could thereafter issue within its authorized capital); or

(2) *Simply hold repurchased shares as treasury stock.* Such stock is no longer outstanding, but the shares are still considered to be issued. Treasury stock may, however, be resold by the corporation subject to rules different from those for the sale of unissued shares.

D. STOCK SUBSCRIPTIONS

1. **Definition:** [§718]   Stock subscriptions are agreements by subscribers to purchase stock or other securities to be issued by the corporation. Such agreements may be made prior to incorporation (it is often one of the functions of a promoter to obtain such subscriptions); or they may be made after formation as the corporation seeks to obtain or increase its capital.

2. **Offer and Acceptance Problems**

a. **Post-incorporation subscriptions:** [§719]   Where a subscription agreement is made between a subscriber and a corporation already in existence, it plainly constitutes a binding contract obligating the subscriber to purchase (and the corporation to issue and sell) the securities in question. Ordinary contract principles of offer and acceptance apply.

b. **Pre-incorporation subscriptions:** [§720]   Whether a subscription for shares in a corporation yet to be formed constitutes an enforceable contract is less clear.

(1) **Subscription contained in articles of incorporation:** [§721]   If the subscription for shares is part of the articles of incorporation (as where the incorporators agree to purchase shares from the corporation to be formed), the subscription is usually irrevocable once the articles are filed, and it can be enforced by the corporation. [Samia v. Central Oil Co., 158 N.E.2d 469 (Mass. 1959)]

(2) **Separate subscription agreement:** [§722]   Where the pre-incorporation subscription is contained in a separate agreement between the subscriber and the corporation to be formed, courts are split on whether the subscription is binding.

(a) **Majority view—subscription as "continuing offer":** [§723] Most courts at common law hold that a pre-incorporation subscription is **not** an enforceable agreement on the theory that since the corporation is not yet in existence (and the promoters have no power to bind the corporation, *see supra*, §§74-80) there is no contract. Thus, a pre-incorporation subscription is considered a mere "continuing offer" by the subscriber to purchase shares of the corporation—when, as, and if it comes into existence.

1) **Effect:** Until the corporation is formed and **accepts** the offer, it is **revocable** by the subscriber. And under normal contract principles, the subscriber's death or insanity would revoke it by operation of law. [Collins v. Morgan Grain Co., 16 F.2d 253 (9th Cir. 1927)]

2) **Criticism:** Allowing revocability may work hardships on other subscribers. It may cause the corporation to be undercapitalized, thereby jeopardizing the investment of those who do not revoke.

(b) **Minority view—subscription irrevocable as contract among subscribers:** [§724] To avoid the latter result, some courts hold that a pre-incorporation subscription has a dual character. In addition to being an offer to the corporation (above), it is deemed to be a **contract among the subscribers** to become shareholders upon formation of the corporation and acceptance of their offers. As such, it is binding and irrevocable at the outset.

1) **Effect:** Under this theory, a subscriber who fails to take the subscribed shares is **liable to the other shareholders** for any increased liability or loss that they bear as a result of the refusal (*e.g.*, statutory liability for debts of corporation).

2) **Compare:** And some courts hold that pre-incorporation subscriptions among several subscribers can be enforced **by the corporation** after it comes into existence, as a **third-party beneficiary** (the subscription contract having been entered into primarily for the benefit of the corporation). [Coleman Hotel Co. v. Crawford, 3 S.W.2d 1109 (Tex. 1928)]

(3) **Statutes:** [§725] Statutes in most states today eliminate the problem by making pre-incorporation subscriptions irrevocable for a designated period of time in the absence of contrary agreement. [*See, e.g.,* Del. Gen. Corp. Law §165—six months]

3. **Status of Subscribers as "Shareholders":** [§726] Pre-incorporation subscribers are not entitled to shareholder status (with attendant shareholder rights) until after the corporation has been formed and has accepted the subscription. On the other hand, post-incorporation subscribers are generally considered owners of the shares as soon as the subscription

agreement is entered into—even where their payment of the subscription price is deferred. [Reagan v. Midland Packing Co., 298 F. 500 (N.D. Iowa 1924)]

a. **Limitations:** [§727]   However, even for post-incorporation subscribers, certain rights and privileges of full shareholder status (*e.g.,* possession of the stock certificate, receipt of dividends, voting) are often limited by statute or terms of the subscription contract until the full subscription price is paid.

b. **Compare—purchasers:** [§728]   Stock subscriptions must also be distinguished from executory contracts to purchase and sell stock. Unlike a subscriber, the executory purchaser attains shareholder status only when he obtains *title* to the stock certificate, upon making full payment. [Stern v. Mayer, 207 N.W. 737 (Minn. 1926)]

   (1) **Note:** Whether a particular transaction will be treated as a subscription or an executory contract to purchase turns on the ***intention of the parties;*** *i.e.,* whether it was intended that the purchaser have shareholder status immediately (subscription) or only after the shares were paid for (executory contract). [Stern v. Mayer, *supra*]

4. **Remedies for Breach of Subscription Contract**

a. **Suit by corporation:** [§729]   If a subscriber breaches the subscription contract, the corporation can recover the ***full subscription price.*** No showing of actual or prospective damages is necessary. [RMBCA §6.20(d)]

b. **Suit by (or on behalf of) corporate creditors:** [§730]   If the corporation has become insolvent, judgment creditors of the corporation—or a receiver or trustee in bankruptcy representing all creditors—may enforce unpaid stock subscriptions, compelling the subscribers to pay whatever is owing. The subscription agreements are treated as assets of the corporation (money due the corporation), and may be enforced whether the shares have actually been issued or are being held pending full payment.

   (1) **Insolvency no defense:** [§731]   The corporation's insolvency is no defense to the creditors' suit to enforce the subscription. *Rationale:* Since a subscriber is treated as owner of the shares from the time of subscription (above), he is also subject to the liabilities attendant to such status.

      (a) **Compare—purchaser:** [§732]   On the other hand, some courts have held that one who has entered into an executory contract to purchase shares (as distinguished from a subscriber—*supra*, §728) may be excused from his contract in the event of the corporation's insolvency. Since the corporation cannot deliver a certificate having any value, there is a failure of consideration. [Stern v. Mayer, *supra*, §728]

         1) **Note:** Other courts have rejected this distinction. They hold that a contract to purchase unissued shares from a corporation constitutes a commitment to contribute the entire purchase price. Such agreement

is to be treated as a subscription and not as an executory contract. Consequently, the defendant is liable for the full amount due. [Martin v. Schuler, 573 P.2d 260 (Okla. 1977)]

E. CONSIDERATION REQUIRED TO BE PAID FOR SHARES

Statutes in most states regulate both the *form* and *amount* of consideration that the corporation must receive on issuance of its shares.

1. **Form of Consideration:** [§733]   Most states have constitutional or statutory restrictions on the kinds of consideration for which shares may be issued. Typically, shares may be issued only for *"money paid, labor done, or property actually acquired."*

    a. **Executory consideration:** [§734]   Executory promises generally are *not* legal consideration for the issuance of shares. Thus, *unsecured promissory notes* (executory promises to pay in the future) and executory promises to transfer assets or render services in the future are not lawful consideration.

        (1) **Rationale:** The reason executory promises are not legal consideration is to assure that a corporation's capital consists of substantial assets and to prevent the issuance of stock as "fully paid" when the corporation has not actually acquired that which was promised. [Sohland v. Baker, 141 A. 277 (Del. 1927)]

        (2) **Compare—secured obligations:** [§735]   An adequately secured promissory note is generally regarded as legal consideration for share issuance, the *collateral* being regarded as "property actually acquired." [General Bonding & Casualty Insurance Co. v. Moseley, 222 S.W. 961 (Tex. 1920)]

        (3) **Exceptions:** [§736]   Some statutes permit issuing shares in exchange for a promise of future payment or services. [RMBCA §6.21(b); Mich. Bus. Corp. Act §315; Va. Stock Corp. Act §17]

    b. **Consequences of issuing shares for improper consideration:** [§737]   Shares issued in violation of the above restrictions are said to be "void" as between the corporation and the issuee, and are subject to cancellation by the corporation. [Sohland v. Baker, *supra*] However, a few courts have held that such shares are only "voidable," and have permitted the corporation to recover the amount due thereon. [Maclary v. Pleasant Hills, Inc., 109 A.2d 830 (Del. 1954)]

        (1) **Effect of corporate bankruptcy:** [§738]   Furthermore, most courts hold that if the corporation becomes bankrupt, the issuee must pay the corporation's *creditors* the amount due for the shares—*i.e.*, their par or stated value. [McCarty v. Langdeau, 337 S.W.2d 407 (Tex. 1960); *but see* Stone v. Hudgens, 129 F. Supp. 273 (W.D. Okla. 1955)—contra]

2. **Amount of Consideration:** [§739]   The price that the corporation must receive for shares issued as "fully paid" depends on whether the shares have a par value.

a. **Par value shares:** [§740] Most statutes require that par value shares be sold *at least at par.* [Del. Gen. Corp. Law §153(a)]

(1) **Exception—to remedy impairment of capital:** [§741] Some courts hold that a going concern (as distinguished from one just beginning business) whose *capital is impaired* may sell its shares at "the best price obtainable"—even for less than par—for the purpose of recuperating itself. [Handley v. Stutz, 139 U.S. 417 (1891)]

(2) **"Watered stock" liability:** [§742] Except in the circumstance just noted, par value shares sold for less than par are *not* "fully paid" (regardless of what the share certificate itself may state). Such stock is said to be "watered."

(a) **Types of "watering":** [§743] Par value shares may be "watered" in either of two ways:

1) **Discount or bonus shares:** [§744] Shares may be issued for *consideration that is not even nominally equivalent* to their par value (*e.g.,* shares having par value of $1,000 issued for $500). These shares are often called "discount shares," and if no consideration at all is paid the shares may be referred to as "bonus shares."

2) **Property or services overvalued:** [§745] Shares may be issued in exchange for property or services that are nominally equivalent to par value but only because the property or services are overvalued (*e.g.,* shares having par value of $1,000 issued for property or services actually worth $500). This is the classic situation of "watered stock."

(b) **Corporation cannot complain:** [§746] Ordinarily, neither the corporation nor minority shareholders in a derivative suit (*supra,* §592) can complain of stock "watering." If the corporation issued shares as "fully paid," it is thereafter *estopped* to claim otherwise and cannot require the issuee to pay the difference.

1) **Compare:** Of course, this does not apply where the transferor-shareholder defrauded the corporation (intentional misrepresentation) or breached a fiduciary duty to it. (*See supra,* §§207 *et seq.*) In such cases, the corporation may institute an appropriate action for damages or to rescind the issuance of its shares.

2) **But note:** A few courts are simply contra on the general rule above: They *allow* the corporation (or a shareholder in a derivative suit) to sue the issuee for the amount of "water" in every case. [Scully v. Automobile Finance Co., 109 A. 49 (Del. 1920)]

(c) **Remedies for creditors:** [§747] If the corporation becomes insolvent, its creditors may be able to recover from the shareholders the amount by which their shares were "watered."

1) **Which creditors may sue:** [§748] The courts are split on whether all corporate creditors may impose such liability, or only those who extended credit *after* the shares were issued; *i.e.,* the issue is whether prior creditors can be said to have been prejudiced by the issuance of watered stock. The answer depends on which theory of liability the court adopts:

a) **Misrepresentation theory—subsequent creditors:** [§749] Most courts regard the issuance of stock as an implied representation to its creditors that the corporation has received assets equivalent in value to the par value of the shares issued, and treat shareholders receiving such shares as *parties to this implied misrepresentation.* Under this approach, only those creditors who extended credit after the shares were issued are entitled to complain of watered stock. Those who had already extended credit (prior creditors) cannot be said to have been misled by the issuance. [Handley v. Stutz, *supra,* §741]

1/ **Reliance:** [§750] Moreover, some courts hold that reliance by the creditor is an essential element of the action. Thus, to recover, the creditor must prove not only that he extended credit after the "watering," but also that in extending credit he *relied* on the corporation having received par value for its shares. [Bing Crosby Minute Maid Corp. v. Eaton, 46 Cal. 2d 484 (1956)]

2/ **Some courts presume reliance:** [§751] Other courts are more liberal and presume that subsequent creditors extended credit on such reliance, even in the absence of proof to that effect. However, the defendant-shareholder may prove that the subsequent creditor did not rely. [Hospes v. Northwestern Manufacturing & Car Co., 50 N.W. 1117 (Minn. 1892)]

b) **Trust fund theory—all creditors:** [§752] A minority view imposes liability for stock watering on the theory that the capital stock of the corporation constitutes a trust fund for all of its creditors. Under this theory, a shareholder who has received shares having a par value in excess of the assets transferred to the corporation is liable to *any creditor*—prior or subsequent—with or without notice, and irrespective of reliance.

c) **Statutory obligation:** [§753] A few statutes have been interpreted as codifying the trust fund theory. [Del. Gen. Corp. Law §162; DuPont v. Ball, 106 A. 39 (Del. 1918); *and see* Easton National Bank v. American Brick & Tile Co., 64 A. 917 (N.J. 1906)]

2) **Who may be held liable**

a) **Liability of issuee:** [§754] The original shareholder is liable for stock watering *even though he may have transferred* his shares to another. *Rationale:* The original shareholder was a party to the deception of the corporate creditors (misrepresentation theory, *supra*) and is not permitted to escape liability by disposing of the shares he obtained through the deception. [Del. Gen. Corp. Law §162(c)]

b) **Liability of transferee:** [§755] A transferee of watered stock is *not* liable under any theory unless she *participated in or had knowledge of* the watering, *i.e.,* knowledge that the shares were issued for assets worth less than their par value. Again, the rationale is that the basis for watered stock liability in most states is the deception of creditors (misrepresentation theory, *supra*); but an innocent transferee of the shares is not a party to the deception and hence not liable to the corporation's creditors. [Rhode v. Dock Hop Co., 184 Cal. 367 (1920); Del. Gen. Corp. Law §162(c)]

3) **Extent of liability—determining value of consideration:** [§756] Where the watering results from the corporation having issued par value shares for property or services, two different approaches have been taken by the courts in determining the *value* of consideration furnished:

a) **True value rule (minority):** [§757] At common law, a few cases held that *any substantial variance* between the market value of the properties or services transferred to the corporation and the par value of the shares issued was water—*regardless of the good faith* of the corporation or the subscriber in fixing the value of the assets transferred.

b) **Good faith rule (majority):** [§758] Most courts, however, held that if the parties in good faith believed that the value of the property or services given to the corporation was equal to the par value of the shares issued, the stock was not watered. The effect is that watered stock liability exists only where there is *intentional overvaluation* of the assets being received by the corporation. [Clinton Mining & Mineral Co. v. Jamison, 256 F. 577 (3d Cir. 1919)]

1/ **Note:** Most states today have statutes embodying this rule. For example, the Delaware statute provides, "In the absence of actual fraud in the transaction, the judgment of the directors as to the value of such consideration shall be *conclusive.*" [Del. Gen. Corp. Law §152]

4) **Statute of limitations:** [§759] Since watered stock liability exists for the protection of creditors, the statute of limitations on any action against shareholders generally runs *from the date the creditor extended credit* to the corporation—which might be many years after the "watering." [Townley Metal & Hardware Co. v. Cramer, 37 P.2d 915 (Okla. 1934)] Some states, however, place an outside limit, *e.g.,* no more than six years after the shares were issued or subscribed. [*See* Del. Gen. Corp. Law §162(e)]

b. **No-par value shares:** [§760] All states today authorize the issuance of no-par value stock. One purpose of no-par stock is to permit a corporation to issue stock in return for assets that have a small or doubtful value at present, but a high speculative return. In other words, no-par was developed to *eliminate* the problem of watered stock liability. No-par shares may be sold at *whatever price* is determined to be *reasonable* by the board of directors. "Reasonableness" must reflect the value of the corporation's assets at the time of issuance, its earnings record, etc.

(1) **Discretion of board:** [§761] In the absence of fraud or self-dealing on the part of the directors, their determination as to the reasonableness of consideration for an issuance of no-par stock is almost always upheld. [Bodell v. General Gas & Electric Corp., 140 A. 264 (Del. 1927)]

(2) **Effect of statutes requiring stated value:** [§762] Most statutes require that the directors (or shareholders) determine (or state) the value of the consideration to be received by the corporation for no-par shares. [Del. Gen. Corp. Law §153] In such event, no-par shares cannot be issued unless the assets are in fact worth their stated value; otherwise, the shares are "watered" and all the rules and consequences discussed above apply. [G. Loewus & Co. v. Highland Queen Packing Co., 6 A.2d 545 (N.J. 1939)]

c. **Actual situation today:** [§763] Watered stock liability suits are much less frequent today than in the past. One reason is that many states have some sort of regulatory statute ("blue sky" laws, *infra,* §§811-817) controlling the form and amount of consideration for which shares may be issued. The result is that shares are rarely issued for less than a fair and adequate consideration to the corporation.

d. **Model Act and California rule:** [§764] The Model Act and California have *eliminated* the designations of par and no-par. Shares may be sold at *whatever* *price* the board of directors determines in good faith to be their value. [RMBCA §6.21; Cal. Corp. Code §409(a)]

F. FIDUCIARY DUTIES OF PROMOTERS

1. **Duty to Corporation:** [§765]   Promoters also owe a fiduciary duty to the corporation they form. Problems typically arise when, after formation, a promoter sells property that he owns to the corporation (for cash or for shares).

   a. **Duty of disclosure:** [§766]   A promoter owes the corporation a fiduciary duty of ***full disclosure*** as to any dealings with it in which he has a personal interest. This requires a full revelation of the promoter's interest in the property being sold to the corporation, and ***all material facts*** that might affect the corporation's decision to purchase—perhaps including the extent of the promoter's profit on the transaction.

      (1) **To whom disclosure must be made:** [§767]   Disclosure must be made to either (i) ***an independent board of directors*** (not mere dummies, controlled by the promoter); ***or*** (ii) ***all existing shareholders*** and any persons then known to be planning to become shareholders.

      (2) **Remedy for breach of duty:** [§768]   If full disclosure is not made, the corporation has a cause of action against the promoter. [Pipelife Corp. v. Bedford, 145 A.2d 206 (Del. 1958)] If the corporation fails to sue (*e.g.,* as where the promoter controls the board), a shareholder's derivative suit may be available. (*See supra,* §592.)

   b. **Effect of promoters taking all stock with no plan to issue additional shares:** [§769]   Where the promoters become the ***sole*** shareholders of the corporation, and there is no plan to issue shares to others as part of the original capitalization, a failure to disclose their adverse financial interest is not deemed a violation of their fiduciary duty to the corporation—on the theory that they cannot conceal something from themselves.

      (1) **Common law:** [§770]   Thus, even where the promoters sold assets to the corporation at a highly inflated value, if they were the sole shareholders of the corporation, the ***corporation*** had no cause of action against them at common law. This was true even where the promoters then sold others the shares that they had received from the corporation at a price reflecting the inflated value of such assets. The ***purchasers of the shares*** might have a cause of action against the promoters for nondisclosure (*supra,* §§279 *et seq.*), but the corporation itself does not, since it was not a party to the transaction that involved the nondisclosure (the resale of the shares). [Hays v. The Georgian, Inc., 181 N.E. 765 (Mass. 1932)]

      (2) **Compare—rule 10b-5:** [§771]   However, the ***corporation itself*** has been held to have a cause of action against its promoters under rule 10b-5 for nondisclosure. Taking the entire original share issuance does ***not*** insulate them from liability under this rule.

c. **Effect of plan to issue additional shares:** [§772]   The result may be different where, although the promoters were the only stockholders at the outset, a ***further issue*** to innocent subscribers was contemplated as ***part of the original capitalization***. Initially, there was a split of authority on whether the ***corporation*** (under a new board of directors or through a derivative suit) can maintain an action against the original shareholders (promoters) for nondisclosure.

   (1) **Massachusetts rule:** [§773]   Most courts follow the "Massachusetts rule," which permits the corporation to maintain such an action. [Old Dominion Copper Mining & Smelting Co. v. Bigelow, 89 N.E. 193 (Mass. 1909)]

      (a) **Rationale:** The original capitalization of the corporation is viewed as a single transaction even though the shares are issued in stages, and sale to innocent subscribers is viewed to have been intended as part thereof, so that the promoters' sale of their assets will not be deemed to have been approved by ***all*** the shareholders absent full disclosure to them.

   (2) **Federal rule:** [§774]   The federal courts formerly held that no action could be maintained by the corporation. [Old Dominion Copper Mining & Smelting Co. v. Lewisohn, 210 U.S. 206 (1908)]

      (a) **Rationale:** The corporation was considered a legal entity whose status could not be affected by a subsequent enlargement of its membership. Since the corporation could not sue before the innocent shareholders came in, it could not sue afterwards.

      (b) **But note:** Later decisions cast doubt on the validity of this position. [*See* McCandless v. Furlaud, 296 U.S. 140 (1935)] In any event, since *Erie Railroad v. Tompkins,* 304 U.S. 64 (1938), the federal courts in diversity cases must follow the local state rule, and as indicated, most states adopt the Massachusetts rule, above. [San Juan Uranium Corp. v. Wolfe, 241 F.2d 121 (10th Cir. 1957)]

d. **Nature of recovery by corporation:** [§775]   If the promoters breach their fiduciary duty to the corporation by failing to make full disclosure in respect to their dealings with it (so that such dealings have not been approved by an independent board or by all disinterested shareholders), the corporation may sue for either rescission or damages.

   (1) **Rescission:** [§776]   Here, the corporation restores the property to the promoter and cancels the shares issued to him. (This is the preferred remedy for the corporation where the shares have ***increased*** in value.)

   (2) **Damages:** [§777]   Suppose the corporation issued $10,000 par value stock for property the promoter had purchased for $1,000, and which in fact had a fair market value of $5,000 at the time of his sale to the corporation. What is the measure of damages?

(a) **Fair market value:** [§778] Most courts limit the corporation's recovery to the *difference* between the value of the property transferred by the promoters to the corporation and the amount paid them (or par value of shares issued to them) for it—which would limit recovery in the above example to $5,000. [Old Dominion Copper Mining & Smelting Co. v. Bigelow, *supra,* §774]

(b) **Penalty measure:** [§779] However, some decisions allow the corporation to recover the difference between the amount *originally paid* by the promoter for the property and the amount paid him (or par value of shares issued to him) by the corporation for the property—in the example above, $9,000. The promoter is *penalized* because he is denied any increase in value on his investment; he loses the amount of profit he could have made if he had sold to a third party. [Victor Oil Co. v. Drum, 184 Cal. 226 (1920)]

1) **When imposed:** [§780] "Penalty-type" damages are most often imposed when it appears that the promoter acquired the property *in order to resell* it to the corporation as opposed to the situation where the promoter owned the property before plans to form the corporation. In the former instance, there was a fiduciary relationship between promoter and corporation at the time the promoter acquired the property and thus reason to deprive him of all profit on the transaction.

(3) **Effect of no-par value stock:** [§781] Where the shares issued to a promoter for his property have no par value, the corporation has been held not entitled to recover any damages since such stock *has no set value; i.e.,* there is no way of proving that the corporation suffered damages because the value of shares issued is equal to the value of the property *exchanged for them.* (*See supra,* §760.) [Piggly-Wiggly Delaware, Inc. v. Bartlett, 129 A. 413 (N.J. 1925)]

2. **Effect of Securities Laws:** [§782] The whole problem of promoters' fiduciary duties to a corporation organized by them is now also governed by state and federal laws regulating the issuance of corporate securities. (*See* full discussion *infra,* §§810 *et seq.*) In general, these laws make *mandatory* full disclosure of all material facts affecting the value of property received by the corporation in consideration for issuance of its shares. In particular, the Securities Act of 1933 requires disclosure of any shares issued or amounts paid to promoters within the previous two years and the consideration given by the promoter therefor. Furthermore, some state laws stipulate that the corporation *must* receive a *fair and adequate consideration* for each issuance.

a. **Result of violation:** [§783] Violation of such laws may result in penal sanctions against the promoters. Civil remedies are also available to the corporation and/ or the innocent shareholders allowing them to recover the amount by which they have been damaged.

G. PREEMPTIVE RIGHTS

1. **Definition:** [§784] A shareholder's preemptive right is the right to subscribe to that amount of shares in a new issuance that will preserve his existing proportionate interest in the corporation. In this way, preemptive rights protect the shareholder's voting percentage and proportionate interest in the net worth of the corporation.

    a. **Common law:** [§785] At common law, preemptive rights were *inherent*—they existed even if not provided for in the articles or bylaws. [Stokes v. Continental Trust Co., 186 N.Y. 285 (1906)]

    b. **Statutes:** [§786] Today, statutes in practically every state regulate preemptive rights.

        (1) **Implied:** [§787] Some statutes reflect policies favoring preemptive rights, and thus provide that such rights exist unless expressly denied in the articles. [N.Y. Bus. Corp. Law §622]

        (2) **Expressly granted:** [§788] Other statutes are aimed at restricting preemptive rights because they hinder financing, and accordingly provide that no shares shall have preemptive rights unless expressly granted in the articles. [Del. Gen. Corp. Law §102(b)]

        (3) **Close corporations:** [§789] Preemptive rights are more important in the case of small, closely held corporations. Where close corporations are treated separately by statute, preemptive rights are almost always provided.

2. **When More Than One Class of Shares Exists:** [§790] If a corporation has more than one class of shares (*e.g.*, common and preferred) and each class has different rights as to voting, dividends, and liquidation, it may be impossible to preserve the proportionate interest of each class exactly when a new class of shares possessing such rights is issued.

    a. **Common law:** [§791] Absent a clear provision in the articles resolving the problem, some decisions hold that all classes are equal and thus have preemptive rights in any new issue. [Thomas Branch & Co. v. Riverside & Dan River Cotton Mills, Inc., 123 S.E. 542 (Va. 1924)] Other courts hold that preemptive rights extend only to the class whose shares are the same as those of the new issue. [Niles v. Ludlow Valve Manufacturing Co., 202 F. 141 (2d Cir. 1913)]

    b. **Statutes:** [§792] Some statutes simply allow this problem to be resolved in the articles. [Del. Gen. Corp. Law §102(b)] Others authorize the board to apportion the new issues so as to "preserve as nearly as practicable" the relative rights of the different classes—and make the board's apportionment final absent fraud or bad faith. [N.Y. Bus. Corp. Law §622(d)]

3. **Authorized But Unissued Shares:** [§793] The general rule at common law was that preemptive rights applied only to new issues resulting from an *increase in the authorized capital* of the corporation.

a. **Preemptive rights denied:** [§794] Thus, where the shares involved had been previously authorized but were not issued at the time of the original stock issuance, preemptive rights were denied—on the theory that the proportionate interest of each shareholder should be calculated in terms of the number of shares originally authorized.

(1) **Note—some cases contra:** Other courts rejected this arbitrary approach. Some recognized preemptive rights when the new issue of previously authorized shares came long after the original issue, *i.e.,* at a time after the original issue had terminated. [Yasik v. Wachtel, 17 A.2d 309 (Del. 1941)] Some held that preemptive rights attached in a new issue of previously authorized shares if the purpose of the subsequent issues was to expand the business rather than simply to provide additional working capital. [Dunlay v. Avenue M Garage & Repair Co., 253 N.Y. 274 (1930)]

b. **Statutes:** [§795] Some statutes resolve the problem by providing that, unless otherwise stated in the articles, there are no preemptive rights in shares sold within two years of their original authorization. Thereafter, preemptive rights apply. [N.Y. Bus. Corp. Law §622(e)]

4. **Treasury Shares:** [§796] Most courts have also refused to recognize preemptive rights in a corporation's sale of treasury stock (stock previously issued, but later reacquired by the corporation). [Borg v. International Silver Co., 11 F.2d 147 (2d Cir. 1925)]

5. **Shares Sold for Consideration Other Than Cash:** [§797] Most courts hold that preemptive rights apply only to shares issued for cash, and not to shares issued in exchange for property or personal services rendered to the corporation or shares issued to accomplish a merger. *Rationale:* It is more important to allow the corporation to obtain unique property or services by issuing its shares than to protect minority shareholders against dilution. [Thom v. Baltimore Trust Co., 148 A. 234 (Md. 1930)]

a. **Statutes:** [§798] Of those statutes that deal with the problem at all, most deny preemptive rights in shares issued for noncash consideration or in connection with a merger or consolidation unless otherwise provided in the articles. [N.Y. Bus. Corp. Law §622(e)]

6. **Remedies:** [§799] When recognized, preemptive rights can be enforced either by (i) suit for *specific performance* to compel issuance to the plaintiff of authorized shares in an amount necessary to retain his proportionate interest; (ii) *damages* computed on the basis of the difference between the subscription price of that amount of newly issued shares and their market value (on the theory that plaintiff can then acquire the shares on the market); or (iii) a court of equity *enjoining* the corporation from issuing shares in violation of the preemptive rights. [Stokes v. Continental Trust Co., *supra,* §785]

a. **Compare—cancellation:** When the shares already have been issued and are unavailable on the market (*e.g.,* in a close corporation), the shareholder may be entitled to cancellation of shares issued in violation of his preemptive rights—at least when such shares are held by those who participated in the wrongdoing.

7. **Equitable Limitations on Issuance of New Shares:** [§800] Regardless of whether preemptive rights are recognized, courts generally do not permit majority shareholders or directors to cause an **unfair dilution** of the minority's interest by issuing shares to themselves at less than fair value. [Ross Transport, Inc. v. Crothers, 45 A.2d 267 (Md. 1946)]

    a. **Example:** X Corp. has 600 shares outstanding, owned equally by A, B, and C. The value of the shares is $10 each. A and B (also directors) cause X Corp. to issue to them 600 new shares for $5 each. C's interest is diminished in value from $2,000 to approximately $1,500.

    b. **"Quasi-preemptive rights":** [§801] Where preemptive rights are not otherwise provided or recognized, some courts have accomplished essentially the same result by recognizing "quasi-preemptive rights" to protect against such unfair dilution. [Shaw v. Empire Savings & Loan Association, 186 Cal. App. 2d 401 (1960)]

        (1) **Dilution of control:** [§802] Quasi-preemptive rights have also been recognized as preventing the directors from issuing stock to themselves or their associates (to the exclusion of other shareholders) for the purpose of obtaining or perpetuating control. [Sheppard v. Wilcox, 210 Cal. App. 2d 53 (1962)]

    c. **Fiduciary obligation:** [§803] Other courts have simply held that the majority (as directors and as shareholders) owe a fiduciary duty to the minority, and that their issuing shares to themselves for less than fair value, or to obtain or perpetuate control is a "fraud" upon the minority shareholder. Under this approach, a court of equity may **set aside the unfair issuance** even if there were preemptive rights, which the minority failed to exercise. [Katzowitz v. Sidler, 24 N.Y.2d 512 (1969)—new shares issued at $100 per share, when book value was $1,800; but minority shareholder lacked funds to exercise his preemptive rights]

        (1) **Breach of duty:** [§804] Thus, it is a breach of fiduciary duty, irrespective of the existence of preemptive rights, for directors to obtain control by issuing shares to themselves or their associates, even at a fair price, unless the directors can show a bona fide corporate purpose for such issuance, which purpose could not have been accomplished substantially as effectively by alternative means. [Schwartz v. Marien, 34 N.Y.2d 487 (1975)] (For further discussion of fiduciary duties owed by majority shareholders to minority, *see supra,* §§559 *et seq.*)

    d. **Significance of rule 10b-5:** [§805] Apart from common law "equitable limitations," it is a violation of rule 10b-5 for directors to cause the corporation to issue stock to themselves or their associates at an unfairly low price or for the purpose of obtaining or perpetuating control. Such an issuance is a "fraud" on the corporation within the meaning of rule 10b-5, and if the corporation fails to sue, a derivative action may be filed by a minority shareholder against the directors involved. (*See supra,* §598.)

H. UNDERWRITING

1. **Defined:** [§806]   Underwriting is the process whereby a securities dealer takes stock from a corporate issuer and arranges for its sale to the public.

2. **"Firm Commitment" Underwriting:** [§807]   In a "firm commitment" underwriting, the underwriters insure the sale of the entire issue by purchasing it outright from the corporation. The underwriters then seek to market the stock to the public.

3. **"Best Efforts" Underwriting:** [§808]   In a "best efforts" underwriting, the underwriters are bound only to use their special skills and efforts to attempt sale of the issue, and are not responsible for any unsold stock.

4. **Statutory Regulation:** [§809]   Underwriters are subject to strict regulation under both federal and state laws, which (among other things) generally require full disclosure of the compensation arrangements with the issuer and subject the underwriter to the same anti-fraud prohibitions applicable to the issuer (below).

I. STATUTES REGULATING ISSUANCE OF SHARES

1. **In General:** [§810]   Both state and federal laws have been enacted regulating the issuance of securities. Since federal laws expressly do *not* preempt the field [Securities Act of 1933 §18], a corporate issuer must often comply with *both* state and federal regulations.

2. **State Regulation—"Blue Sky" Laws:** [§811]   State statutes regulating the issuance of securities are known as "blue sky" laws (their constitutionality resting on the legitimate state interest in preventing "schemes which have no more basis than so many feet of blue sky"). [Hall v. Geiger-Jones Co., 242 U.S. 539 (1917)] Every state has some type of blue sky law; many have special regulatory bodies charged with administration and enforcement of these laws. There are three basic types of blue sky laws (states combining the features of more than one type):

   a. **Fraud type:** [§812]   Some laws simply impose civil or criminal sanctions for fraud in connection with the issuance of securities. No permit or registration is required to issue securities, and there is generally no special administrative agency charged with enforcement of the statute. No state uses this method alone.

   b. **License type:** [§813]   All states have laws requiring that various persons who sell securities—brokers, dealers and agents of corporate issuers—register with the state and submit certain information.

   c. **Securities registration type:** [§814]   The most comprehensive type of blue sky law requires that stock be registered (or "qualified") with an appropriate state officer or agent prior to issuance.

      (1) **Registration by notification:** [§815]   Some of these laws require a complete description of the issuer and shares to be issued, and the shares must be sold as described. The purpose of such laws is simply disclosure; *i.e.,* there is generally no discretion in the state to deny permission to issue the stock.

(2) **Registration by qualification:** [§816]   However, other laws of this type provide for *substantive review* of the proposed issuance by a state official who can prevent issuance if it fails to meet statutory requirements, *e.g.,* that it is "fair, just, and equitable."

(3) **Registration by coordination:** [§817]   Some states provide that securities registered under the federal scheme may be issued by submitting to the state official essentially the same information as is required under the Securities Act of 1933.

3. **Federal Regulation:** [§818]   The *Securities Act of 1933* [15 U.S.C. §77] establishes the basic framework for federal regulation of the public distribution of securities through use of interstate commerce or the mails. It provides for a *registration-type* system of regulation, the purpose of which is to assure *full disclosure* of all pertinent facts to any prospective investor. The agency charged with enforcement is the Securities and Exchange Commission (SEC). Note that the SEC has no power to disapprove a proposed issuance; its only power is to compel *disclosure* of all pertinent details.

a. **Registration statement:** [§819]   Basically, the 1933 Act forbids the use of interstate facilities or the mails to offer to sell a security, unless a registration statement has been filed with the SEC. [Securities Act §5(c)]

(1) **Waiting period:** [§820]   During the time between filing the registration statement and the date that it becomes "effective" (a time known as the "waiting period"), no *written* offer to sell a security may be made through interstate facilities or the mails unless it satisfies the requirements for a "statutory prospectus." (This rule on written offers also applies after the effective date.) [Securities Act §5(b)(1)]

(2) **After effective date:** [§821]   Actual sales of securities, or deliveries after sale, through interstate facilities or the mails may only be made after the "effective date" [Securities Act §5(a)]—and a prospectus must either accompany or precede the delivery of any security [Securities Act §5(b)(2)].

b. **Integrated disclosure:** [§822]   Corporations subject to the reporting requirements of the Securities Exchange Act of 1934 whose shares are actively traded (as defined) may incorporate by reference their 1934 Act filings in their 1933 Act registration statements. [Securities Act Release No. 6235 (1980)]

(1) **"Shelf" registration:** [§823]   Corporations may also offer securities over a two-year period after the effective date of a registration statement that automatically incorporates by reference subsequently filed 1934 Act reports. [Rule 415] This permits these corporations to sell securities "off the shelf" when they feel market conditions are favorable.

c. **Relevant terms**

(1) **"Offer to sell":** [§824]   This term includes "every attempt or offer to dispose of, or solicitation of an offer to buy, a security or interest in a security, for value." [Securities Act §2(3)] It has been broadly interpreted to include all activities which, under the circumstances, are designed to stir public interest in a security. [*In re* Carl M. Loeb, Rhoades & Co., 38 S.E.C. 843 (1959)—publicity in advance of a proposed issuance]

(2) **"Security":** [§825]   This includes not only stock, bonds, and most promissory notes, but also any offering that constitutes an investment contract or certificate of interest or participation in any profit-sharing agreement, regardless of form. [Securities Act §2(1)]

   (a) **Test:** [§826]   The test is "whether the scheme involves an investment of money in a common enterprise with profits to come *solely* from the efforts of others." [SEC v. W.J. Howey Co., 328 U.S. 29 (1946)] Some courts have expanded this to include profit schemes wherein "the efforts made by those other than the investor are the undeniably significant ones." [SEC v. Glenn W. Turner Enterprises, Inc., 474 F.2d 476 (9th Cir. 1973)]

   (b) **Application:** [§827]   The term "security" has thus been applied to a wide variety of interests—*e.g.,* fractional interests in oil royalties or mineral leases, percentages of patent rights or fruit orchards, and interests in limited partnerships, mortgages or deeds of trust. But it has been held not to apply to an employer-financed pension plan because the employee made no monetary investment and the fund's income came mainly from employer contributions rather than the efforts of the fund's managers. [International Brotherhood of Teamsters v. Daniel, 439 U.S. 551 (1979)]

      1) **Sale of business:** [§828]   Sale of all the stock of a company *is* the sale of "securities." Even though the sale is simply a method to transfer ownership of a business, the stock has all the traditional characteristics of a security. [Landreth Timber Co. v. Landreth, 471 U.S. 681 (1985)]

(3) **"Registration statement":** [§829]   A registration statement is a detailed statement of all matters pertaining to the proposed issuance. The form is designed to force *disclosure* of all factors that may affect the fairness of the issue and the financial status of the corporation. Full details must be provided as to the issuer's property and business; the identity and background of all corporate officers and directors; the compensation they receive; the nature of the security being offered; sales costs, underwriting commission and discounts; and the like. [Securities Act §7]

(4) **"Statutory prospectus":** [§830]   A statutory prospectus is a document, filed with the registration statement, that sets forth the key information contained in the statement. [Securities Act §10] As noted above, a copy of the prospectus

(but not the registration statement) must be given to every buyer of securities covered by the registration statement.

(5) **"Effective date":** [§831] The registration statement becomes effective 20 days after filing unless the SEC agrees to an earlier date. If the SEC requires further information, it notifies the corporation that amendments to the registration statement are necessary. Such amendments start the 20-day period again, unless the SEC consents to an acceleration of the effective date. [Securities Act §8]

d. **Exempt securities:** [§832] The Act lists a number of types of securities that are exempt from the Act's registration requirements, *e.g.,* certain short-term commercial paper, securities issued by governmental bodies or charitable institutions, and securities subject to other government regulation (such as bank securities or insurance policies). [Securities Act §3(a)]

(1) **But note:** Even exempt securities are subject to the Act's *anti-fraud* rules. (*See infra,* §880.)

e. **Exempt transactions:** [§833] The following types of transactions are exempted from the registration requirements of the 1933 Act. (*Note:* The *anti-fraud rules* of the Act may still apply; *see infra,* §880.)

(1) **Ordinary trading transactions ("casual sales" exemption):** [§834] The Act exempts "*transactions* by any person *other than* an issuer, underwriter, or dealer." [Securities Act §4(1)] This covers ordinary trading transactions between individual investors in securities that have already been issued—in contrast to sales by issuers and others participating in transactions connected with the initial distribution of securities. [SEC v. Chinese Consolidated Benevolent Association, 120 F.2d 738 (2d Cir. 1941)]

(a) **Not applicable to secondary distributions:** [§835] The exemption does *not* cover public offerings by a person who acquired the shares from an issuer in a "private placement" (below) if that person took the shares with a *view to public distribution.* Such persons are considered underwriters regardless of whether they are otherwise engaged in the securities business. [Securities Act §2(11); Gilligan, Will & Co. v. SEC, 267 F.2d 461 (2d Cir. 1959)]

(b) **Not applicable to sales by control persons:** [§836] The exemption also does not cover public offerings by persons who have a *control relationship* with the issuer. As to such offerings, the control persons are themselves considered issuers under the Act; and those who distribute the securities for them are underwriters. [*In re* Ira Haupt & Co., 23 S.E.C. 589 (1946)]

1) **"Casual sales" by control persons:** [§837] However, SEC *rule 144* exempts sales to the public by control persons of small amounts of securities within designated time periods. (For details on rule 144, *see infra,* §§844-849.)

(2) **Dealer sales:** [§838] Transactions by a dealer (securities broker) are exempt, except where (i) she is acting as an underwriter of the securities, or (ii) during the initial distribution of the securities (first forty days following registration). [Securities Act §4(3)]

(3) **Private placements:** [§839] Transactions by an issuer "not involving any public offering" are exempt. [Securities Act §4(2)] This applies to an offering to a relatively small number of private subscribers who are *sufficiently experienced or informed* that the disclosure requirements are not necessary for their protection (*i.e.,* they are "able to fend for themselves") and who are acquiring the shares *as an investment* rather than for resale to the public. [SEC v. Ralston-Purina Co., 346 U.S. 119 (1953)]

   (a) **Requirement of available information:** [§840] A high degree of business or legal sophistication by the offerees is not enough to gain the private placement exemption. The offerees *must* have either (i) *full disclosure* of the information that a registration statement would have provided, or (ii) *access* to such information (through an employment or family relationship or by economic bargaining power). [Doran v. Petroleum Management Corp., 545 F.2d 893 (5th Cir. 1977)]

      1) **Note—number of offerees not decisive:** The number of offerees is *not* decisive. Depending on the availability of information, an offering to a few persons may be public and an offering to many persons may be private. In addition, the *size of the offering* is a significant factor. [Doran v. Petroleum Management Corp., *supra*]

      2) **And note:** Under rule 506, an issuer may sell an *unlimited* amount of securities to "accredited investors" (defined *infra,* §841) and up to 35 other purchasers, but the issuer must reasonably believe that these other purchasers (or their purchaser representatives) have such knowledge and experience that they are capable of evaluating the offering *and* they must be furnished detailed information (as defined).

   (b) **Small offerings under regulation D:** [§841] During any 12-month period, an issuer may, without providing *any* information, sell securities:

      1) Up to $500,000 to *any number* of purchasers [Rule 504]; or

      2) Up to $5 million to *accredited investors.* [Securities Act §4(6)] "Accredited investors" include financial institutions, business development companies, large charitable or educational institutions, the issuer's directors and executive officers, and wealthy individuals (as defined). [Rules 501, 505] In addition to accredited investors, the issuer may add up to *35 ordinary purchasers* if it provides detailed information (as defined) to all purchasers. [Rule 505]

(c) **Investment intent:** [§842]   Each purchaser in a private offering or one under rule 506 or regulation D must acquire the securities as an investment, and not for resale or distribution to the public. Ordinarily, each purchaser is required to sign a letter of intent to this effect so that shares issued pursuant to this exemption are commonly known as "letter stock" or "restricted securities."

1) **Legal imprint:** [§843]   To assure that the purchasers take the shares for investment, many corporations print a notice on the face of the share certificates to the effect that "these shares have been issued pursuant to an exemption from registration, and may not be freely traded until registered, or further exemption established," and instruct their transfer agents not to transfer shares bearing such imprint.

2) **Resale of restricted securities—rule 144:** [§844]   Such legend imprint renders shares issued under a private offering exemption nonmarketable until registered, or until some further exemption from registration is established. Rule 144 creates an exemption for resale of such shares (and shares owned by control persons; *supra,* §837) if the following requirements are met:

   a) **Public information:** [§845]   There must be specified current public information concerning the issuer.

   b) **Holding period:** [§846]   No resales at all of restricted securities are generally permitted within the first two years following issuance of the shares.

   c) **Limitation on amount sold:** [§847]   Thereafter, purchasers who are control persons can sell during each *three-month* period shares equal to as much as 1% of the total shares outstanding in the same class (or 1% of the average weekly volume of shares traded on national securities exchanges or automated quotation systems during the preceding four weeks, whichever is greater).

   d) **Notice requirement:** [§848]   If more than 500 shares are to be sold, or if the sales price exceeds $10,000, the shareholder must file with the SEC a signed notice of intent to sell the securities concurrently with placing the sale order with the broker. The purpose is to allow the SEC to monitor the marketing of such securities.

   e) **Sales by noncontrol persons:** [§849]   Purchasers who are not control persons may sell *any* amount if (i) they have owned the securities for three years and they are listed on a national exchange or quoted through an approved automated system, or (ii) they have owned the securities for four years and the issuer has provided specified current public information.

(4) **Intrastate offerings:** [§850]   Where the offering and sale is made *entirely* to residents of the same state in which the issuer resides and is doing business, the issue is exempt from registration. (A corporation is said to "reside" in the state of incorporation.) [Securities Act §3(a)(11)]

    (a) **Note:** The exemption is strictly construed. Thus, it is lost where securities are inadvertently offered to an out-of-state resident, even if no sale is ever made to that person. Good faith reliance on the offeree's representation of residence is apparently no defense if it proves to be false. [Rule 147]

(5) **Other exemptions:** [§851]   The 1933 Act also authorizes the SEC to exempt other issuances where the SEC finds that registration is not necessary by reason of the small amount involved or the *limited character of the offering.* [Securities Act §3(b)]

    (a) **Regulation A:** [§852]   Where the total amount of the issue is *less than $1,500,000,* the SEC permits an *abbreviated offering circular* containing basic information about the stock and its issuer, in lieu of the more detailed registration statement otherwise required. After review by the SEC the offering circular must be distributed to prospective purchasers of the stock.

    (b) **Rule 145:** [§853]   Another provision provides *limited registration* requirements for securities issued pursuant to certain transactions *formally approved by the shareholders* of the issuer, pursuant to statute or the articles—*e.g.,* certain mergers, acquisitions, transfers of assets and reclassification of shares (*see infra,* §§992, 1026, 1035).

f. **Remedies—anti-fraud provisions:** [§854]   The 1933 Act provides both civil and criminal sanctions for violation of its registration requirements or any fraud in connection with the issuance of the securities or the filing of the registration statement.

(1) **False registration statement—section 11:** [§855]   If the registration statement, when it becomes effective, contains a *misstatement or omission of material fact,* any person acquiring the securities without knowledge thereof has an action for damages (the amount she lost on the investment) against various persons connected with the issuance.

    (a) **Who may sue:** [§856]   This remedy is granted to *any person who has acquired* the securities—not just the original issuee. But a person cannot sue if she *knew* of the misstatement or omission when she acquired the securities. [Securities Act §11(a)]

        1) **Privity not required:** [§857]   No privity is required between the plaintiff and the parties sought to be held liable.

        2) **Must prove shares were part of that offering:** [§858]   If plaintiff acquired her shares in the market *subsequent to distribution* of the registered offering, she must prove that the shares she acquired were *part of that offering,* rather than shares issued at some other time.

(b) **Elements of plaintiff's action:** [§859] Plaintiff need not prove fraud in the tort sense, or even any intentional wrongdoing. Subject to certain defenses (*see* below), plaintiff need only show that *some material fact was omitted or misrepresented* in the registration statement.

    1) **Materiality:** [§860] "Material" covers all matters that an average prudent investor needs to know before being able to make an intelligent, informed decision on whether to buy the security.

    2) **Reliance and causation need not be shown:** [§861] It is *not* necessary for plaintiff to prove that she *relied* on the misrepresentation or omission, or that it *caused* the loss in value of the security. The fact that it was "material" (above) is enough for liability.

        a) **Exception:** [§862] If plaintiff acquires her shares *after* the corporation publishes an earnings statement for the 12-month period following the effective date of registration, the plaintiff must prove reliance, *i.e.,* that the falsity in the registration statement *caused* her to purchase. [Securities Act §11(a)] (Even here, however, plaintiff need not prove she personally *read* the statement—she could have been relying on investment advice given her by others who had.)

(c) **Who may be held liable:** [§863] Liability may extend to the *corporation,* its *directors* and persons who are named as being or about to become its directors, all persons who *sign* the registration statement, the *underwriter,* and *experts*—such as accountants, engineers, and other professionals (including *lawyers*)—who are identified as having prepared or certified the registration statement or any report or valuation in connection therewith. [Securities Act §11(a)]

    1) **Liability of experts:** [§864] The responsibility of lawyers, accountants, and other experts is normally limited to those parts of the registration statements *made on their authority.* [Securities Act §11(a)]

(d) **Defenses**

    1) **Corporation:** [§865] The issuer is *absolutely liable* for any material misstatement or omission in the registration statement. [Securities Act §11(b)] The only possible issuer defense is that plaintiff *knew* of the untruth or omission at the time she acquired the shares (*see* above).

    2) **Others—"due diligence" defense:** [§866] All other persons to whom liability extends under section 11 (above) may avoid liability by *proving* that they exercised *due diligence* with respect to the information in that part of the registration statement for which they are sought to be held liable.

a) **Signers, directors, underwriters, etc.:** [§867] Generally, these persons must prove that, after reasonable investigation, they had reasonable ground to believe that the statements were true and complete as required. [Securities Act §11(b)(3)(A)] Again, the standard of "reasonableness" is that required of a prudent person in the management of her own property. [Securities Act §11(c)]

1/ **Personal investigation required:** [§868] It is *no* defense that these persons had no knowledge of the misstatements or omissions or that they had been associated with the issuer for only a limited time. They must show not merely that they made inquiry of responsible corporate officers or employees, but also that they *reasonably investigated* the corporation's affairs *personally.* The defendant cannot escape liability by taking management's representations at face value. [Escott v. Barchris Construction Corp., 283 F. Supp. 643 (S.D.N.Y. 1968)]

2/ **Compare—portions made on authority of expert:** [§869] However, as to those portions of a registration statement made on the authority of an *expert* (*e.g.,* financial statements certified by accountant or valuations certified by appraiser), "due diligence" is established as long as the party-defendant had no reasonable ground to disbelieve the expert's statement. [Securities Act §11(b)(3)(C)]

b) **Experts:** [§870] As to those parts of the registration statement made on their authority, experts must prove that, after reasonable investigation, they had reasonable ground to believe such parts were true and complete. [Securities Act §11(b)(3)(B)]

(e) **Measure of recovery:** [§871] The plaintiff is entitled to *actual damages.* This is considered to be purchase price minus resale price, but if she has not sold by the time she sues, damages may not exceed the difference between purchase price and the market value of the security at the time suit is brought. [Securities Act §11(e)]

1) **Reduction of damages:** [§872] A defendant may reduce liability by proving that plaintiff's damages were not attributable to the part of the registration statement as to which the liability is asserted. [Securities Act §11(e)]

(2) **General civil liability—section 12:** [§873] The 1933 Act expressly imposes civil liability on any person who *offers or sells* a security (i) in violation of section 5 (requiring registration, delivery of a prospectus, etc.) [Securities Act §12(1)], or (ii) through means of interstate commerce or the mails by use of

material misstatements or omissions (*i.e.*, not limited to the registration statement) [Securities Act §12(2)].

   (a) **Who may sue:** [§874] This right of action is afforded only to the original purchaser. There must be a showing of *privity* with the seller.

       1) **Compare:** Under section 11, above (misrepresentation or omissions in the registration statement), *any* holder is entitled to sue; no privity is required.

   (b) **Who may be held liable:** [§875] By its terms, section 12 applies only to "persons who offer or sell" a security so that only the *issuer and other sellers* apparently can be held liable thereunder.

       1) **Compare:** Under section 11, liability can be imposed on *any* person connected with the registration statement; thus, liability extends to officers, directors, lawyers, accountants, etc.

   (c) **Defenses:** [§876] Liability under section 12(2) for misstatements or omissions is conditioned on the plaintiff's proving that she did not know of them. Also there is no liability if the defendant proves that he did not and, in the exercise of reasonable care, could not know of them.

   (d) **Measure of recovery:** [§877] Plaintiff may sue to rescind or, if she no longer owns the security, to recover damages (the amount she lost on the investment).

(3) **Implied civil liability; criminal liability—section 17:** [§878] The 1933 Act also makes it unlawful for *any* person to offer or sell securities through the mails or in interstate commerce by means of "any device or scheme to defraud" or "by means of any misstatement or omission" of material fact. [Securities Act §17]

   (a) **Right of action implied:** [§879] Unlike sections 11 and 12, which expressly create a civil cause of action for violation, section 17 simply provides that the acts are "unlawful" (*i.e.*, criminal liability). However, some courts have *implied* a civil remedy against persons who violate section 17, although the scope of this remedy remains unclear.

(4) **Remedies applicable to exempt securities:** [§880] Note that the anti-fraud provisions of sections 12 and 17 apply to the "offer or sale" of securities *whether or not* the securities are required to be registered. Thus, they cover transactions and securities that are *exempt from the registration* requirements of the 1933 Act (*supra*, §§833-853) and therefore beyond the reach of section 11 (which applies only to omission and falsity in the registration statement; *see* above).

(5) **Indemnification agreements—enforceability:** [§881] Frequently, persons outside the issuing company who play some role in connection with a stock issuance (particularly underwriters) may bargain for an indemnification agreement—whereby the company and/or its controlling shareholders agree to hold the underwriters harmless from any liability they incur for Securities Act violations.

    (a) **Willful violations:** [§882] If the underwriter (or other indemnified party) has **knowledge** of the violations, the indemnification agreement is **unenforceable** as a matter of law. *Rationale:* One cannot insure himself against his own willful wrongdoing, and to allow indemnity in such cases would encourage flaunting of the Act. [Globus v. Law Research Service, Inc., 418 F.2d 1276 (2d Cir. 1969)]

(6) **Compare to rule 10b-5:** [§883] As discussed *supra* (§§285 *et seq.*), none of the anti-fraud provisions of the 1933 Act are as broad as section 10(b) of the 1934 Act and rule 10b-5 thereunder.

    (a) **Scope:** [§884] Rule 10b-5 protects **sellers** as well as buyers.

    (b) **Procedure:** [§885] Even as to buyers, an action under rule 10b-5 has certain **procedural advantages** over sections 11 and 12; *e.g.*, it **may** avoid the strictures on damages under the latter (*supra,* §§871, 877) as well as their short statute of limitations, *infra.*

    (c) **Costs:** [§886] Moreover, under sections 11 and 12, a court may assess **unsuccessful** plaintiffs with the **costs of suit** (including attorneys' fees) and may require plaintiffs to post advance **security** for such costs.

    (d) **Scienter:** [§887] Thus, despite the fact that sections 11 and 12 eliminate plaintiffs' need to prove scienter, most purchaser-plaintiffs prefer to maintain a civil action under rule 10b-5, rather than under the anti-fraud provisions of the 1933 Act.

IX. DISTRIBUTIONS TO SHAREHOLDERS

chapter approach

The subjects of this chapter, dividends and the redemption or repurchase of shares, are more likely to arise as subissues rather than as major exam topics. Nevertheless, it is important for you to know at least the following rules:

1. **Dividends:** In discussing issues concerning dividends, keep in mind that shareholders do not have a right to dividends; payment of dividends is within the business judgment of the directors. When a cash or property dividend has been declared, investigate the *source* of the dividend. In most states, these dividends may be paid only out of a surplus of net assets over stated capital. Check the surplus account from which the dividend is to be paid. Some states restrict the use of certain accounts, and most states prohibit the use of reappraisal surplus for dividends. Be aware that *all* states prohibit dividends when the corporation is insolvent or the payment of the dividend would render it insolvent.

   If the directors have declared an illegal dividend, recall that they are personally liable to the corporation to the extent of the injury to creditors and preferred shareholders. As for shareholder liability, if the corporation is solvent, shareholders who receive an illegal dividend without knowledge of its illegality are entitled to keep it, but if the corporation is insolvent, the shareholders who receive an illegal dividend are *absolutely* liable to return it.

2. **Redemption and Repurchase of Shares**

   a. **Redemption:** If a corporation wishes to retire certain shares (usually a preferred class) for the benefit of the common shares, consider redemption, by which the corporation pays the stipulated redemption price and the shareholders must relinquish their shares. Redeemed shares are canceled and stated capital reduced accordingly. Note that a corporation can redeem out of *any available funds* (surplus or stated capital). Most importantly, check to see that the corporation has the power to redeem—*i.e.,* is that power *expressly provided in the articles or bylaws?*

   b. **Repurchase:** All states have statutes authorizing corporations to *repurchase* their own shares. A provision in the articles or bylaws is *not* required. Repurchased shares are not automatically canceled; they remain issued as "treasury stock," with full rights to dividends, voting, etc., when resold. Unlike redemption, a repurchase may be made only under the same conditions that a cash or property dividend may be paid; *i.e.,* only when there is a surplus and only out of certain surplus accounts.

   c. **Limitations:** When faced with a redemption or repurchase problem, ask whether the corporation is *insolvent* or whether the redemption or repurchase will render it insolvent. If so, redemption and repurchase are not permitted. Then ask whether the redemption or repurchase will leave the corporation with *sufficient assets to cover liquidation preferences* of outstanding shares. If not, the redemption or repurchase generally will not be permitted. Finally, ask whether a discretionary redemption or repurchase serves a *bona fide corporate purpose,* rather than the personal interests of directors or insiders. Note that the remedies for unlawful redemption or repurchase are generally the same as those available for illegal dividends.

A. DIVIDENDS

1. **Definition:** [§888] A "dividend" is any distribution of **cash** or **property** paid to shareholders on account of their share ownership.

2. **Right to Dividends:** [§889] The general rule is that payment of dividends is a matter within the business judgment of the board of directors. The shareholders ordinarily have no right to dividends even if funds are available. The directors alone determine if and when dividends are to be declared, and the amounts thereof. [Gottfried v. Gottfried, 73 N.Y.S.2d 692 (1947)]

   a. **Equitable limitation:** [§890] If a complaining shareholder can show that the board's refusal to declare dividends is in *bad faith* or so unreasonable as to amount to an *abuse of discretion,* a court of equity may intervene. Thus, if the directors (on behalf of the majority shareholders) are attempting to abuse the minority by refusing to declare dividends notwithstanding huge earned surpluses (and/or generous salaries to the majority), equity may intervene to protect the minority by compelling distribution of some reasonable portion of the available surplus. [Dodge v. Ford Motor Co., *supra,* §92]

      (1) **Caution:** It should be emphasized that equity will not intervene unless there is palpable abuse or bad faith by the directors. The *Dodge* case is one of the few reported decisions where this has been found. [*See also* Miller v. Magline, Inc., 256 N.W.2d 761 (Mich. 1977)]

      (2) **Fiduciary duty in close corporations:** [§891] The duty that shareholders of a close corporation owe each other (*supra,* §565) may affect the power to declare dividends held by the majority shareholders (or a minority that has a veto power). [Smith v. Atlantic Properties, Inc., 422 N.E.2d 798 (Mass. 1981)—court may order declaration of dividends to avoid federal tax penalty for undue accumulation of earnings]

      (3) **Statutes:** [§892] A few states have statutes regulating dividend declaration in close corporations. For example, the North Carolina statute requires directors of a close corporation to *justify* their refusal to pay less than one-third of annual net profits in dividends, where holders of 20% or more of the shares complain. [N.C. Bus. Corp. Act §55-50]

   b. **Preferred dividends may be mandatory:** [§893] Although preferred shareholders have no inherent right to dividends, the articles *may* give them such a right if the earnings of the corporation are sufficient for payment ("payment mandatory if earned"). [New England Trust Co. v. Penobscot Chemical Fiber Co., 50 A.2d 188 (Me. 1946)]

3. **Source of Lawful Dividends:** [§894]   The problem most frequently encountered with regard to payment of cash or property dividends is whether ***funds of the proper type*** are available for distribution. Statutes in virtually all states restrict the ***sources*** from which cash or property dividends may be paid. These restrictions seek to protect corporate creditors and, often, preferred shareholders. Violation of the restrictions may result in personal liability for the directors who authorize the dividends and the shareholders who receive them.

a.   **Restriction on dividends when capital account impaired**

(1)   **Majority view:** [§895]   In most states, cash or property dividends are payable only when the corporation has a surplus—an excess of net assets (total assets minus total liabilities) over stated capital. In these states, dividends cannot be paid out of the corporation's stated capital.

(a)   **Rationale:** Traditionally, a corporation's stated capital represented amounts contributed by the shareholders to allow the corporation to operate. Creditors were entitled to rely on such amounts for payment of debts incurred by the corporation. Therefore, except under designated special circumstances (*infra*, §§916-919), stated capital could not be returned to the shareholders as dividends—at least while creditors of the corporation remained unpaid.

(b)   **"Stated capital" defined:** [§896]   Stated capital is the ***aggregate par value*** of all shares issued having a par value and the ***aggregate stated value*** of all no-par shares. If the directors fail to set a stated value for no-par stock, it is deemed to be the value of the consideration received for such stock.

1)   **Example:** XYZ Corp. sells 1,000 shares of its $10 par value stock for $10,000. It also sells 1,000 shares of its no-par stock for property worth $5,000; and the directors fail to designate a stated value for the no-par shares. The corporation's capital account (stated capital) is $15,000.

2)   **Application:** In the previous example, XYZ Corp. generally cannot pay a cash or property dividend unless its net assets (total assets minus total liabilities) exceed $15,000.

(c)   **"Nimble dividends" prohibited:** [§897]   In most jurisdictions, the restriction on paying dividends out of stated capital prevents so-called "nimble dividends" (*infra*, §904). If the corporation's capital account has become impaired (by virtue of operating losses, depreciation write-offs, or otherwise), it cannot declare dividends even though it has ***current net*** *profits.* The current profits must be used to "repair" the deficit in the stated capital.

    1) **"Net profits" defined:** [§898] A corporation's "net profits" means its earnings during the accounting period, with adjustments as required by good accounting practice (*e.g.,* appropriate reserves for depreciation, bad debts, etc.).

  (d) **"Wasting asset" corporations:** [§899] Many states have special dividend rules for corporations engaged in the exploitation of a "wasting asset," *i.e.,* an asset such as an oil well or patent that is to be consumed over a period of time and not replaced. [Del. Gen. Corp. Law §170(b)]

    1) **Permit return of capital:** [§900] These statutes permit the corporation's net profits to be computed without a deduction for the depletion (*i.e.,* depreciation) of the value of the wasting asset. In effect, they permit a return of capital to the shareholders in the form of dividends.

    2) **Limitation:** [§901] Some statutes require that the corporation's net assets remaining after a dividend is paid be sufficient to cover any liquidation preferences that preferred stock has. [N.Y. Bus. Corp. Law §510(b)]

    3) **Notice:** [§902] Some statutes require notice to shareholders that the dividend is being paid under these conditions.

(2) **Minority rules:** [§903] Some states have adopted a more liberal policy with respect to payment of dividends, permitting distributions under certain circumstances even though the corporation's stated capital is impaired.

  (a) **"Nimble dividends" permitted in some states:** [§904] Some states permit payment of dividends out of current net profits regardless of impairment of the capital account. Typically, these states broaden the accounting period over which the corporation's net profits are computed for dividend purposes. For example, Delaware permits dividends out of earnings during the current and preceding years (rather than during just the current accounting period). [Del. Gen. Corp. Law §170]

  (b) **California rule:** [§905] California has an even more liberal dividend policy. Broadly, a corporation is permitted to pay cash or property dividends as long as its total assets after such payment are at least equal to 1¼ times its liabilities *and* its current assets are at least equal to its current liabilities. [Cal. Corp. Code §500(b)]

    1) **Effect:** Under this rule, as long as the asset value requirements are met, dividends may be paid even though the corporation has no current

profits, and even though the amount contributed as its capital is impaired.

2) **Enterprise as a whole:** [§906] Moreover, assets and liabilities are determined with reference to the business as a whole including not only the corporation itself, but also all subsidiaries that could properly be included in its financial statements under generally accepted accounting principles. [Cal. Corp. Code §114]

3) **Valuation of assets:** [§907] The value of corporate assets must be determined without goodwill and without capitalized research and development expenses. [Cal. Corp. Code §500(b)]

4) **Current assets:** [§908] "Current assets" are assets that are cash equivalents or may reasonably be expected to be converted into cash (*e.g.,* inventories and accounts receivable) within *one year.*

(c) **Model Act:** [§909] The Model Act authorizes cash or property dividends as long as the corporation's total assets are at least equal to its total liabilities. [RMBCA §6.40(c)]

1) **Valuation of assets:** [§910] The value of corporate assets may be based upon any "fair method that is reasonable in the circumstances." [RMBCA §6.40(d)]

(d) **Limitations:** [§911] Even under these liberal statutes, however, cash or property dividends are never proper where payment thereof would result in the corporation becoming *insolvent,* or, in many states, where the payment would endanger *liquidation priorities* of preferred stock. [Cal. Corp. Code §§501-502; Del. Gen. Corp. Law §170; RMBCA §6.40(c); *and see infra,* §§925-927]

1) **And note:** The California statute provides that dividends cannot be paid to any class of shares while cumulative dividends are in arrears on any preferred class. [Cal. Corp. Code §503]

(e) **Notice to recipient shareholder:** [§912] Where dividends are paid out of any source other than earned surplus (below), many states also provide that the corporation must notify the receiving shareholders as to the source of the funds distributed. [Cal. Corp. Code §507; N.Y. Bus. Corp. Law §510(c)]

b. **Restrictions as to type of surplus account from which dividends may be paid:** [§913] Besides the prohibition in most states on any dividend payment while capital is impaired, there are statutory restrictions on payment of cash or property dividends from certain kinds of surplus accounts.

(1) **Earned surplus:** [§914] "Earned surplus" is the total net profits retained by the corporation during all of its previous years of operation, *i.e.,* its profits offset by its losses, and further reduced by dividends paid out in previous years.

    (a) **Example:** XYZ Corp. has been in business three years. During the first year, it had an operating loss of $5,000. The second year it had profits of $20,000. The third year it broke even and, for the first time, paid a dividend of $10,000. XYZ now has an earned surplus of $5,000 (-$5,000 + $20,000-$10,000).

    (b) **As source of dividends:** [§915] Earned surplus is a proper source of cash and property dividends in all states. Indeed, earned surplus may ordinarily be the only proper source of such dividends in a few states.

(2) **Paid-in surplus:** [§916] "Paid-in surplus" occurs where par value shares are sold for more than par; where no-par value shares are sold for more than their stated value (so that not all of the consideration received for no-par shares is allocated to stated capital); or from gifts to the corporation.

    (a) **Example:** XYZ Corp. sells 1,000 shares of its $10 par value shares for $12,500. The $2,500 excess over par value is paid-in surplus. Similarly, if XYZ Corp. sells 1,000 shares of its no-par shares for $5,000, the directors designating $1,000 as the stated value of such shares, the $4,000 excess over stated value is paid-in surplus.

    (b) **As source of dividends:** [§917] *Most states permit a distribution of dividends out of paid-in surplus.* [N.Y. Bus. Corp. Law §510(b)] Again, it is often required that the corporation notify the shareholders receiving such dividends of their source. [N.Y. Bus. Corp. Law §510(c); Cal. Corp. Code §507] Other states are more restrictive. In some, dividends may not be paid out of paid-in surplus if there are arrearages in dividends on cumulative preferred shares or if the remaining net assets of the corporation would be reduced below the preferred's liquidation preference. [Pa. Bus. Corp. Act §1703] In others, dividends from paid-in surplus usually can be paid only to preferred shareholders if the corporation has more than one class of shares. [N.C. Bus. Corp. Act §55-50(a)(3)]

(3) **Capital reduction surplus:** [§918] Capital reduction surplus arises where the par value or stated value of no-par shares has been reduced by the corporation. There are a variety of methods for reducing capital. In most states, capital may be reduced by amending the articles of incorporation. (*See infra,* §§1033-1049.) In some states, capital reduction can be accomplished only pursuant to special statutory procedures. [Del. Gen. Corp. Law §§242, 244]

    (a) **Purpose:** A frequent reason for reducing stated capital is to remedy a capital impairment (*e.g.,* deficits incurred by operating losses in past years). When capital is reduced, the surplus created by the reduction is "capital reduction surplus." Such surplus can be used to offset the prior deficit so that future earnings can be available for dividends, instead of having to be used to "repair" the deficit in the capital account.

(b) **As source of dividend:** [§919]   In most states, any capital reduction surplus in excess of that needed to "repair" the capital account may properly be used as a source of cash and property dividends to the shareholders—subject, however, to restrictions similar to those for dividends from paid-in surplus (*supra*, §916).

(c) **Shareholder approval:** [§920]   If the capital reduction is accomplished by amending the articles of incorporation, shareholder approval is required. Some states require such approval for *all* methods of capital reduction. [Pa. Bus. Corp. Law §706] Other states allow the board of directors to reduce capital without shareholder approval, *e.g.*, by canceling stock that has been reacquired. [N.Y. Bus. Corp. Law §515]

(d) **Appraisal rights:** [§921]   Some statutes give preferred shareholders appraisal rights if a capital reduction adversely affects their interests (*e.g.*, preference on liquidation). [N.Y. Bus. Corp. Law §806(b)(6); Matter of Kinney, 279 N.Y. 423 (1939)]

(4) **Reappraisal (revaluation) surplus:** [§922]   Surplus may also be created by a corporation revaluing assets that have appreciated in value over acquisition cost.

(a) **Example:** XYZ Corp.'s home office is located on land that cost the corporation $100,000 but now has a fair market value of $500,000. By changing the balance sheet value of the land, a "revaluation" surplus of $400,000 is created.

(b) **As source of dividend:** [§923]   Surplus created by unrealized appreciation in asset value is not a proper source of dividends in many states. [Kingston v. Home Life Insurance Co., 101 A. 898 (Del. 1917)]

1) **Minority view:** [§924]   Some states allow surplus from reappraisal of assets to be used like paid-in surplus or capital reduction surplus. [Randall v. Bailey, 23 N.Y.S.2d 173 (1940)]

c. **Insolvency as restriction on dividends:** [§925]   Virtually all states forbid dividends of any type where the corporation is in fact insolvent, or where payment of the dividend would render the corporation insolvent. [N.Y. Bus. Corp. Law §510(a)]

(1) **"Insolvency" defined:** [§926]   "Insolvency" is defined in two ways. In the bankruptcy sense, a corporation is insolvent when its *liabilities exceed its assets.* In the equity sense, a corporation is insolvent if it is unable to meet its debts as they mature, *i.e., insufficient cash* to pay its bills, regardless of the value of its assets. [N.Y. Bus. Corp. Law §102(a)(8)] If a corporation is insolvent—or a dividend payment would render it insolvent—in either sense, it may not legally pay a dividend.

d. **Protection of preferred stock as restriction on dividends:** [§927]   In some states, a corporation cannot pay a cash or property dividend from any source where the payment would endanger the liquidation preference of shares having such a preference (*i.e.*, where net assets after the payment would be less than the liquidation preference) unless the dividend is paid to that class of shares alone. [Cal. Corp. Code §502; Pa. Bus. Corp. Law §1701(B)(5)]

(1) **Effect:** Wherever there is preferred stock having some priority in the event of liquidation, and the corporation's stated capital has become impaired (due to operating losses, depreciation write-off, or any other cause), to the extent that it does not at least cover the preferred's liquidation preference, dividends can be distributed only to the preferred shares—until sufficient earnings are accumulated to cover the full amount due the preferred shareholders on liquidation.

e. **Contractual restrictions on dividends:** [§928]   Especially because of the ease in creating capital reduction surplus to "repair" deficits from previous operating losses (*see supra*, §§918-919), dividend statutes provide relatively little protection to creditors as long as the corporation is not insolvent (*see supra*, §§925-926). As a consequence, institutions that make large, long-term loans may place protective covenants in the loan agreement limiting dividends that might jeopardize repayment of the loan. Similar provisions may be required by underwriters in connection with the public issuance of bonds or preferred stock.

4. **Remedies for Illegal Dividends**

a. **Personal liability of directors:** [§929]   Directors who declare a dividend from an unlawful source (or under other conditions rendering payment illegal) are jointly and severally liable to the corporation for the benefit of creditors or preferred shareholders affected thereby.

(1) **Defenses:** [§930]   Early cases held that the directors' liability was absolute. But modern statutes and cases recognize a number of defenses. Usually directors are not liable if they voted against the distribution, were absent from the meeting, or relied in good faith (*i.e.*, after making inquiries reasonable under the circumstances) on financial statements showing the availability of a proper source of funds for the payment. [Del. Gen. Corp. Law §§172, 174; N.Y. Bus. Corp. Law §§717, 719]

(2) **Amount of liability:** [§931]   Some statutes allow the corporation to recover the full amount of the unlawful dividend. [RMBCA §8.33] Most, however, limit the recovery to the amount of injury suffered by the creditors and preferred shareholders, *e.g.*, the amount of liabilities owed to the creditors, and the amount by which the dividend impaired liquidation preferences of the preferred shares. [N.Y. Bus. Corp. Law §719]

(3) **Contribution among directors:** [§932]   Any director held liable for unlawful dividends is normally entitled to compel contribution from other directors who

could also be held liable (*i.e.,* those with no defense). [RMBCA §8.33; Del. Gen. Corp. Law §174(b)]

    (a) **Contribution from shareholders:** [§933] Most statutes also permit directors held liable to compel contribution from shareholders who received the unlawful dividend **with knowledge** of the illegality. [RMBCA §8.33(b); N.Y. Bus. Corp. Law §719(d)]

b. **Personal liability of shareholders**

    (1) **Where corporation insolvent:** [§934] If the corporation is insolvent (or is rendered insolvent by the dividend distribution), the shareholders who receive the illegal dividend are often held absolutely liable to return it to the corporation for the benefit of the creditors or preferred shareholders affected thereby. [Pa. Bus. Corp. Law §1707(B)]

        (a) **Absolute liability:** [§935] Liability here is absolute, and it is therefore no defense that the shareholders received the payment in good faith and without knowledge of the corporation's insolvency. *Rationale:* The distribution by an insolvent corporation constitutes a **fraudulent conveyance** (no consideration given by the shareholder), and such a conveyance is void against creditors or those entitled to priority. [Woody v. National City Bank, 24 F.2d 661 (2d Cir. 1928)]

        (b) **Direct action possible:** [§936] Creditors (or preferred shareholders) affected thereby can bring a direct action against the shareholders receiving the illegal dividend. [Unif. Fraud. Transfer Act §7]

    (2) **Where corporation solvent:** [§937] Where the corporation's solvency is not affected by the distribution, shareholders who receive the payments innocently—not knowing the dividend is from an improper source or under illegal conditions—are generally held entitled to retain them. [McDonald v. Williams, 174 U.S. 397 (1899)]

        (a) **But note:** The result is contra where the shareholders know or should have known of the illegality or are charged with such knowledge (as where they hold controlling shares). [Pa. Bus. Corp. Law §1707(B)]

B. REDEMPTION AND REPURCHASE OF SHARES

1. **Redemption:** [§938] A "redemption" involves the corporation's acquisition of some or all of a class of its outstanding shares by paying a stipulated redemption price (usually something in excess of par or stated value) to the shareholders, who must then surrender their certificates. Redeemed shares are usually canceled, and stated capital (shares outstanding) reduced accordingly. The chief purpose of redemption is usually to retire shares with dividend preferences, for the benefit of the common shares.

a. **Power to redeem:** [§939]   A corporation has the power to redeem shares only where it is *expressly provided* in the articles or bylaws; *i.e.,* there is no implied or inherent power to redeem.

   (1) **One class of stock:** [§940]   If there is only one class of shares outstanding (common), it is generally *not redeemable.* To allow redemption in such a case would give the directors the power to eliminate the shareholders to whom they are ultimately responsible. [American Hair & Felt Co. v. Starring, 2 A.2d 249 (Del. 1937); *and see* N.Y. Bus. Corp. Law §512(c)]

     (a) **Compare:** Redemption of some common shares, pursuant to resolution of the board acting in good faith, has been permitted when previously agreed to by the shareholders on occurrence of a designated event. [Lewis v. H.P. Hood & Sons, 121 N.E.2d 850 (Mass. 1954)]

   (2) **Redeem part of a class:** [§941]   Where the corporation is authorized to redeem less than all of a class of shares outstanding (*e.g.,* "10,000 of the 30,000 Class A preferred shares issued"), it generally must be done either *by lot or ratably* among all shares in the class subject to redemption. It usually cannot be used discriminatorily to "get rid" of a particular shareholder or shareholders. [State *ex rel.* Waldman v. Miller-Wohl Co., 28 A.2d 148 (Del. 1942)]

b. **Mandatory vs. optional redemption:** [§942]   Usually, the right to redeem is *optional* with the corporation, and exercise of the right is therefore entirely discretionary with the directors.

   (1) **Mandatory redemption:** [§943]   Nevertheless, provisions in the articles for compulsory or mandatory redemption (*e.g.,* on a specified date or event) are valid in most states. They are treated as a binding contractual commitment between the corporation and its shareholders. Where mandatory redemption is required, the articles often contain provisions requiring the corporation to deposit a portion of its net earnings in a *sinking fund* which can be used solely for redemption purposes.

c. **Source of funds to redeem:** [§944]   In most states, a corporation is permitted to redeem out of *any available funds, i.e.,* any kind of surplus or even stated capital. [N.Y. Bus. Corp. Law §513(c)]

   (1) **Rationale:** Having conferred upon the corporation the power to redeem, the shareholders are deemed to consent even to the impairment of capital if required for this purpose. Similarly, since redemption must be expressly authorized in the articles or bylaws (*supra,* §939), creditors are deemed to have notice of the possibility that capital will be reduced thereby.

   (2) **Limitations:** [§945]   However, a redemption may not be allowed where it would otherwise prejudice the rights of creditors. (*See infra,* §§955-966.)

d. **Effect of redemption:** [§946]   Statutes often provide that once redeemed, the shares are automatically canceled and stated capital (shares outstanding) reduced accordingly. However, this does not affect the corporation's "authorized capital" (*supra*, §§712-717), so that the corporation normally would have the power to issue new shares in replacement of those canceled up to the amount of its authorized capital.

2. **Repurchase of Shares:** [§947]   A "repurchase" of shares by the corporation is distinguished from a "redemption" in that a repurchase is not effected pursuant to a provision in the articles, and most statutes do not provide that the shares are automatically canceled. They remain issued (hence no effect on stated capital), although held by the corporation as "treasury stock" (*supra*, §717) with the full right to dividends, voting, etc., when resold. [*Compare* Cal. Corp. Code §510(a); RMBCA §6.31(a)—shares that have been repurchased are canceled and revert to the status of authorized but unissued stock]

a. **Power to repurchase:** [§948]   Whereas the power to redeem shares must be expressly reserved in the articles (*supra*, §939), at common law, a corporation generally was deemed to have the inherent right to repurchase its own shares, providing it acted in good faith. (*See infra*, §963.) All states now have statutes authorizing the corporation to repurchase its own shares.

b. **Validity of repurchase agreements:** [§949]   The corporation usually may validly obligate itself at the time of subscription, or later, to repurchase particular shares (either absolutely, or upon demand or at the option of the shareholder), provided that there is a legal source of funds with which to repurchase. Courts have upheld the corporation's obligation to repurchase even when the other shareholders had no knowledge of the corporation's agreement to repurchase and the repurchase results in some shareholders getting a preferential price. [Grace Securities Corp. v. Roberts, 164 S.E. 700 (Va. 1932); *but see* Hoops v. Leddy, 182 A. 271 (N.J. 1936)—contra]

c. **Source of funds for repurchase:** [§950]   Most statutes permit a corporation to repurchase its shares under the same conditions that they permit payment of a cash or property dividend, *i.e.*, only if the corporation has a surplus. [N.Y. Bus. Corp. Law §513(a); Pa. Bus. Corp. Law §1701(B)]

(1) **Type of surplus account:** [§951]   Just as most states today permit cash or property dividends to be paid out of either earned, paid-in, or capital reduction surplus accounts (*supra*, §§915, 916, 919), any of these accounts generally may be used for the repurchase of outstanding shares.

(a) **California and Model Act rules:** [§952]   Under the California and Model Act rules, repurchase or redemption of shares is conditioned on the valuation of remaining assets, just as with payment of cash or property dividends (*supra*, §§905-908).

(2) **Restriction of surplus account:** [§953]   Since the shares purchased become treasury stock of the corporation available for resale, there is no automatic diminution in the surplus account. However, most statutes provide that when a corporation repurchases its own stock, the surplus account is "restricted" by the amount of the repurchase price, meaning that it cannot be used for the payment of dividends or other repurchases. [Pa. Bus. Corp. Law §1701(E)]

    (a) **Note:** Such surplus may again become unrestricted when the corporation either resells these shares (in exchange for cash or property) or cancels them (thus reducing stated capital). Once unrestricted, the surplus account may again be used as a source of funds to pay dividends or repurchase other shares.

(3) **Exceptions—repurchases out of stated capital:** [§954]   Generally, repurchases cannot be made where there is no surplus. However, many statutes authorize a corporation to repurchase its own shares out of stated capital for the following limited purposes:

    (i) To collect or compromise a *debt, claim, or controversy with a shareholder;*

    (ii) To pay dissenting shareholders for *appraisal rights* in merger proceedings (*infra,* §§969-985); or

    (iii) To *eliminate fractional shares.*

[N.Y. Bus. Corp. Law §513(b)]

3. **Further Limitations on Repurchase and Redemption:** [§955]   A repurchase or redemption of shares has the same effect as a dividend—*i.e.,* distributing assets of the corporation to shareholders, thereby putting them beyond the reach of creditors and, often, of senior shareholders. Thus, limitations similar to those imposed on dividend distributions (*supra,* §§894-927) are imposed on redemptions and repurchases of shares.

    a. **Insolvency limitation:** [§956]   No redemption or repurchase is permitted where the corporation is insolvent, or where the effect of the redemption or repurchase would be to render the corporation insolvent in either the bankruptcy or equity sense. [N.Y. Bus. Corp. Law §513(a)]

        (1) **Time of valuation:** [§957]   The corporation's solvency has usually been determined at the time that payment on the redemption or repurchase is made, rather than at the time the corporation bound itself to redeem or repurchase. Thus, even if the corporation was solvent when it entered into an agreement to repurchase certain shares in the future, the agreement is unenforceable if at the time payment is due, the corporation has become insolvent. [Neimark v. Mel Kramer Sales, Inc., 306 N.W.2d 278 (Wis. 1981)]

            (a) **Promissory note:** [§958]   Pursuant to this rule, most courts have held that if a solvent corporation gives a promissory note in repurchasing its shares, the note can be enforced only as long as the corporation remains solvent. If the corporation becomes insolvent, further payments are unenforceable. [McConnell v. Estate of Butler, 402 F.2d 362 (9th Cir. 1968)—on bankruptcy of corporation, holder of note issued to repurchase shares was subordinated to claims of other corporate creditors; *but see* Williams v. Nevelow, 513 S.W.2d 535 (Tex. 1974)—contra]

1) **Statutes:** [§959]   Some statutes have adopted the contrary view. If the promissory note was given when the corporation could properly repurchase its shares, the note may subsequently be enforced as an ordinary debt of the corporation. [Del. Gen. Corp. Law §160; N.J. Bus. Corp. Act §14A7-16(6); RMBCA §6.40(e)]

(b) **Compare—secured instrument:** [§960]   Some courts have held that if the note was *secured* and issued in *good faith,* and the corporation was solvent when the security was given, the noteholder can retain the collateral even though the corporation later becomes insolvent. [Tracy v. Perkins-Tracy Printing Co., 153 N.W.2d 241 (Minn. 1967); *In re* National Tile & Terrazzo Co., 537 F.2d 329 (9th Cir. 1976)]

(c) **Surplus requirement:** [§961]   In addition to the rule that a repurchase agreement cannot be enforced at a time when the corporation is insolvent, some courts have also held that the corporation must meet the *surplus test* when each payment is made. [Mountain State Steel Foundries, Inc. v. Commissioner, 284 F.2d 737 (4th Cir. 1960); *but see* Neimark v. Mel Kramer Sales, Inc., *supra*—contra]

b. **Protection of liquidation preferences:** [§962]   Redemption or repurchase is generally not allowed where the effect would be to leave the corporation with insufficient net assets to cover the liquidation preferences of outstanding shares entitled to such preferences. [Pa. Bus. Corp. Law §1701(B)(5)]

c. **Bona fide corporate purposes—equitable limitations:** [§963]   In addition to the foregoing restrictions, courts have held that any discretionary redemption or repurchase must serve some bona fide *corporate purpose* (such as to eliminate dissident shareholders)—rather than merely to serve the *personal interests* of the directors or "insiders."

(1) **Repurchase or redemption favoring "inside" shareholders prohibited:** [§964]   A repurchase or redemption cannot be used to favor "inside" shareholders at the expense of others (*e.g.,* buying out the shares of "insiders" when the outlook for the corporation is bleak, or conversely, buying out "outsiders" when prospects for the corporation are bright). [Zahn v. Transamerica Corp., *supra*, §569]

(2) **Protection from corporate "raider":** [§965]   A corporate purpose must be shown when a corporation purchases the shares of a "corporate raider" to prevent his obtaining control, *e.g.,* when directors cause the corporation to

purchase shares from a shareholder who otherwise threatens to seize control; or the directors cause the corporation to purchase shares of other shareholders to prevent the "raider" from obtaining them. If the purchases are made solely for the purpose of perpetuating the officers and directors in their jobs, this is not a bona fide corporate purpose. But if there is reason to believe that the corporate takeover by the "raider" would jeopardize the interests of the corporation generally, the repurchase may be justified. [Cheff v. Mathes, 199 A.2d 548 (Del. 1964)]

(a) **Compare—rule 10b-5:** [§966] Where directors cause the corporation to repurchase or redeem shares for the personal benefit of the directors rather than for bona fide corporate purpose, the corporation as purchaser of the shares is deemed "defrauded," and is entitled to maintain an action against the directors under rule 10b-5.

4. **Remedies for Unlawful Redemption or Repurchase:** [§967] Generally, the same remedies available for illegal dividends are available against directors and shareholders for unlawful redemptions or repurchases of shares. (*See* detailed discussion *supra*, §§929-937.)

X. FUNDAMENTAL CHANGES IN CORPORATE STRUCTURE

chapter approach

This chapter details fundamental corporate changes (*e.g.*, mergers, sale of substantially all assets, articles amendments, and dissolution), as well as the shareholder rights they trigger. The most important areas for exam purposes are as follows:

1. **Appraisal Rights of Shareholders:** Whenever you encounter a fundamental corporate change on an exam, consider whether the dissenting shareholders (or which dissenting shareholders) have appraisal rights requiring the corporation to buy their shares at "fair value" (or sometimes "fair market value"). Keep in mind that appraisal rights involve a rather elaborate procedure, which usually includes notice by the shareholder of intent to demand payment, notice by the corporation that the proposed action was authorized, demand for payment by the dissenters, and payment by the corporation of the amount it determines to be the fair value of the shares. If the dissenting shareholders reject the corporation's estimate of fair value, the corporation must turn to the court for a determination of value.

2. **Statutory Merger:** A statutory merger occurs when one corporation is absorbed into another. This is normally accomplished by the "surviving" corporation issuing its shares to the shareholders of the "disappearing" corporation. In a merger situation, ask whether the shareholders of each corporation have the ***right to approve*** the merger and whether they have ***appraisal rights*** if they do not approve. Generally, after the merger plan is approved by the board, it is submitted to the shareholders of each corporation, who must usually approve it by a ***majority of the outstanding shares*** (sometimes two-thirds of the outstanding shares is required).

   Dissenters are usually entitled to appraisal rights. Note, however, that in ***short-form*** mergers neither corporation's shareholders are entitled to vote on the plan and only the subsidiary's shareholders have appraisal rights. Under many statutes, only the shareholders of the disappearing corporation in a ***small-scale*** merger have approval and appraisal rights. And note that some statutes ***deny*** appraisal rights if the corporation's stock is listed on a national securities exchange or is held by over 2,000 shareholders.

3. **De Facto Mergers:** Watch for a question where a corporation attempts to circumvent the approval and appraisal rights of shareholders by (i) acquiring substantially all of a corporation's assets in exchange for stock or (ii) acquiring a majority of a corporation's stock in exchange for stock. Remember that many courts have held that a transaction that has the ***effect*** of a merger is deemed to be a merger for purposes of voting and appraisal rights.

4. **Triangular Mergers:** When a merger is desired but the acquiring corporation wishes to insulate itself from the disappearing corporation's liabilities, consider a triangular merger, whereby the merger is accomplished through a subsidiary of the acquiring corporation. Note that these mergers also affect voting and appraisal rights of shareholders of the acquiring corporation.

5. **Sale of Substantially All Assets:** A sale, not in the ordinary course of business, of substantially all of the corporation's assets requires the approval of the majority (sometimes two-thirds)

of outstanding shares. Note that most statutes grant appraisal rights for shareholders dissenting to a sale of substantially all of the corporate assets.

6. **Amendment of Articles:** Generally, amendments to the articles of incorporation must be approved by the board **and** a majority (or two-thirds) of the outstanding shares. If the change will particularly affect a certain class, the approval of that class may also be required. Many states and the Model Act give appraisal rights to dissenters where, for example, the amendment adversely alters or abolishes a preferential right; excludes or limits a right to vote; alters or abolishes a preemptive right; or creates, alters, or abolishes a redemption right. Remember, however, that some states do not provide appraisal rights for any article amendments.

7. **Dissolution and Liquidation:** Dissolution terminates the corporation's status as a legal entity; liquidation terminates the corporation's business. For **voluntary** dissolution, approval by the board and a majority of the outstanding shares is normally required. Shareholders usually may bring an action for **involuntary** dissolution when, for example, the directors are deadlocked and irreparable injury is threatened; the directors are acting in an illegal, oppressive, or fraudulent manner; the shareholders are deadlocked; or the corporate assets are being misapplied or wasted. Most statutes also allow the state to institute dissolution proceedings on specified grounds (*e.g.,* fraud in obtaining the certificate of incorporation).

After dissolution, the corporation must "liquidate" or "wind up" its affairs by paying its debts and distributing the remaining assets. On liquidation, every shareholder is generally entitled to a pro rata portion of the net assets remaining after creditors have been paid. However, preferred shares usually have a liquidation preference which entitles their holders to payment before any distribution to holders of common stock. Remember that creditors are paid first. Known creditors must be given notice of dissolution. Creditors with notice must present their claim within a given time period or their claim will be barred.

8. **Limitations on Power of Controlling Shareholders:** Fundamental changes that increase the ownership or change the rights of controlling shareholders, directors, or officers are subject to judicial review for fairness. Such changes may, for example, provide a way for controlling shareholders to "freeze out" minority shareholders, *e.g.,* through sale of substantially all assets, cash-out mergers, and reverse stock splits. To be permissible, most courts require that the freezeout serve a **legitimate business purpose;** other courts require that the transaction meet the standard of **entire fairness.** Note that "going private" transactions, either through freezeouts or self-tenders (tender offers by corporation for minority shares), are subject to extensive federal regulation, which includes disclosure provisions and an anti-fraud provision similar to rule 10b-5.

9. **Tender Offers:** A tender offer asks the shareholders of a target corporation to tender their shares for cash or securities. Since a tender offer addresses the shareholders in their individual capacities, it is not a corporate transaction from the target's perspective and gives rise to neither shareholder voting nor appraisal rights in the target's shareholders. Similarly, a tender offer generally does not give rise to approval or appraisal rights in the bidder's shareholders unless it amounts to a de facto merger.

Keep in mind that tender offers are regulated in many ways by federal securities laws. For example, a person (or group) who acquires more than 5% of a corporation's securities that are registered under the 1934 Act must file a schedule 13D disclosure form. Similarly, anyone making a tender offer for registered securities must file a schedule 14D disclosure form. Furthermore, the Securities Exchange Act regulates the terms of such tender offers—*e.g.,* to whom they must be offered or the period they must remain open—and requires the target corporation's management to (i) recommend acceptance or rejection of the offer to the shareholders, (ii) remain neutral, or (iii) state that it is unable to take a position.

Remember too that section 14(e) prohibits material misstatements or omissions and fraudulent or manipulative acts in connection with a tender offer or a solicitation favoring or opposing a tender offer. Since this was designed to protect the *shareholders* of the target, neither the bidder nor the target corporations may sue for damages under section 14(e), although they may seek injunctive relief. The target's shareholders who tender their shares based on misleading information may sue for both damages and injunctive relief; nontendering shareholders may also be able to sue, provided they can show damages.

Besides federal regulations, your question may involve a state statute regulating tender offers. If so, determine whether it violates either the Supremacy Clause (by conflicting with the federal regulations) or the Commerce Clause (by regulating interstate commerce or imposing an excessive burden on interstate commerce) of the U.S. Constitution.

A. INTRODUCTION [§968]

Fundamental changes in a corporation's structure are subject to special statutory requirements. The major fundamental changes are mergers, sales of substantially all assets, amendment of the articles (certificate) of incorporation, and dissolution. Tender offers are also subject to special rules.

B. APPRAISAL RIGHTS OF SHAREHOLDERS

1. **In General:** [§969]   Statutes in most states provide that shareholders who *dissent* from mergers or certain other kinds of fundamental corporate changes may require the corporation to purchase their shares at the "fair value" or "fair market value" of the shares—usually excluding any element of appreciation or depreciation resulting from anticipation or execution of the merger or other change. [Del. Gen. Corp. Law §262; RMBCA §§13.01-13.03, 13.20-13.28, 13.30-13.31; Cal. Corp. Code §§1300 *et seq.*]

2. **Valuation:** [§970]   Most statutes provide that a dissenting shareholder has the right to be paid the "fair value" of his stock. Some statutes provide that a shareholder has the right to be paid the "fair market value" of his stock.

   a. **"Fair value" statutes:** [§971]   Under statutes that provide that a dissenter shall be paid the fair value of his shares, the two leading methods of valuation are the "Delaware block method" and the methods of modern finance.

(1) **Delaware block method:** [§972]   Traditionally, fair value has been determined by applying the so-called "Delaware block method" of valuation. Under this method, the court determines the elements of value of a corporation's stock and assigns a weight to each element. The value of the stock is then calculated as the weighted average of these elements. For example, in *Piemonte v. New Boston Garden Corp.*, 387 N.E.2d 1145 (Mass. 1987), the Massachusetts Supreme Court approved the following weighting by the lower court of the usual elements of value:

> Market Value   — 10%
>
> Earnings Value — 40%
>
> Net Asset Value — 50%

  (a) **Market value:** [§973]   The market value is the price at which the corporation's shares were being traded on the market just prior to announcement of the transaction. The weight given to market value will depend in part on how deep the market was, *i.e.*, whether there was extensive or only limited trading in the corporation's stock.

  (b) **"Investment" or "earnings" value:** [§974]   "Investment" or "earnings" value is measured by determining the corporation's average annual earnings during some number of years (usually five) before the event that triggers appraisal rights, and then capitalizing (*i.e.*, multiplying) that average by a selected multiplier. [Tri-Continental Corp. v. Battye, 74 A.2d 71 (Del. 1950); Francis I. duPont & Co. v. Universal City Studios, Inc., 312 A.2d 344 (1973), *aff'd,* 334 A.2d 216 (Del. 1975)]

  (c) **Asset value:** [§975]   Asset value is normally based on the liquidation value of the corporation's assets. [Poole v. N.V. Deli Maatschappij, 243 A.2d 67 (Del. 1968)]

  (d) **Dividend value:** [§976]   Dividend value is sometimes taken into account, but often no separate weight is given to this element, on the ground that it largely reflects the same value as earnings. [Francis I. duPont & Co., *supra*, §974]

(2) **Modern finance methods:** [§977]   A more modern approach to the valuation of stock for appraisal purposes is to allow proof of value to be made by any technique or method that is generally considered acceptable in the financial community and otherwise admissible in court. This approach was adopted by Delaware in *Weinberger v. UOP,* 457 A.2d 701 (Del. 1983), and is also adopted in New York by statute [N.Y. Bus. Corp. Law §623(h)(4)]. However, non-Delaware courts that have used the Delaware method in the past may continue to do so. [*See* Leader v. Hycor, Inc., 479 N.E.2d 173 (Mass. 1985)]

b. **"Fair market value" statutes:** [§978]   Some statutes provide that a dissenter should be paid fair market value. Under such statutes, market price may be determinative, unless the market is very thin or reflects aberrational factors.

3. **Procedure:** [§979]   Not every shareholder who votes against a merger or other fundamental change is a "dissenting shareholder" for purposes of the appraisal statutes. To qualify as a dissenter, the shareholder must follow an elaborate statutory procedure. The corporation must also follow an elaborate procedure in response. Details vary from state to state, but the procedure stated in the Revised Model Business Corporation Act is typical.

a. **Notice to the corporation:** [§980]   First, the shareholder must deliver to the corporation, before the vote is taken, written notice of her intent to demand payment for her shares if the proposed action is effectuated, and must not vote her shares in favor of the proposed action. [RMBCA §13.21(a)]

b. **Notice by the corporation:** [§981]   If the proposed corporate action is authorized at a shareholders' meeting, the corporation must deliver a written dissenters' notice to all shareholders who delivered the notice of intent to demand payment and did not vote in favor of the transaction. The notice to dissenters must be sent no later than 10 days after the corporate action was taken, and must:

   (i)   State the *address* to which a demand for payment must be sent, and where and when stock certificates must be deposited;

   (ii)   Inform shareholders to what *extent transfer of their shares will be restricted* after their demand for payment is received;

   (iii)   Supply a *form* for demanding payment;

   (iv)   *Set a date* by which the demand for payment must be made, which may not be less than 30 nor more than 60 days after the date the notice to the shareholder is delivered; and

   (v)   Be accompanied by a copy of the *relevant statutory provisions.*

   [RMBCA §13.22]

c. **Duty to demand payment:** [§982]   The shareholder must then demand payment and deposit her stock certificates. [RMBCA §13.23]

d. **Corporate response:** [§983]   As soon as the proposed corporate action is taken, or upon receipt of a demand for payment, the corporation must pay each dissenter who has complied with the procedural requirements the amount the corporation estimates to be the fair value of the shares, plus accrued interest. The payment must be accompanied by:

   (i)   Designated *financial statements and income statements;*

    (ii)   A statement of the ***corporation's estimate of the fair value*** of the shares;

    (iii) An ***explanation of how the interest was calculated;***

    (iv) A statement of the ***dissenter's rights;*** and

    (v)   A copy of the ***relevant statutory provisions.***

[RMBCA §13.25]

e.   **Appraisal proceedings:** [§984] If a dissenting shareholder is unwilling to accept the corporation's estimate of fair value, the corporation must petition the court to determine fair value. All dissenters whose demands remain unsettled must be made parties to the proceeding. The court may appoint one or more appraisers to receive evidence and recommend a decision on the question of fair value. The dissenters are entitled to the same discovery rights as parties in other civil proceedings. [RMBCA §13.30]

f.   **Costs:** [§985] The costs of an appraisal proceeding, other than counsel and expert fees, are assessed against the corporation, except that the court may assess these costs against all or some of the dissenters, in amounts the court finds equitable, to the extent the court finds the dissenters acted arbitrarily, vexatiously, or not in good faith. The court may also assess counsel and expert fees, in amounts the court finds equitable, against the corporation if the court finds the corporation did not substantially comply with the statutory requirements, or against either the corporation or a dissenter if the court finds that the party acted arbitrarily, vexatiously, or not in good faith. [RMBCA §13.31]

C. STATUTORY MERGERS

1.   **In General:** [§986] A statutory merger is a corporate combination in which one corporation is legally absorbed into another. To accomplish a statutory merger, the corporation that will survive the merger (the "survivor") issues shares of its stock or other securities to shareholders of the other constituent corporation (the "disappearing corporation"). Under the statute, the disappearing corporation is thereby absorbed into the survivor, and the disappearing corporation's shareholders become shareholders in the survivor. [Del. Gen. Corp. Law §251(a)(e); RMBCA §§11.01, 11.03, 11.05, 11.06]

    a.   **Consolidation:** [§987] A consolidation is similar to a merger, except that in a consolidation two or more existing corporations combine to form a wholly new corporation. Since the requirements for merger and consolidation are virtually identical, and the consolidation technique is rarely employed, the balance of this section will focus on mergers.

2.   **Effect of Merger:** [§988] When a merger becomes effective, the disappearing corporation ceases to exist. The survivor succeeds, by operation of law, to all of the disappearing corporation's rights, assets, and liabilities. [Del. Gen. Corp. Law §259; RMBCA §11.06; Cal. Corp. Code §1107(a)]

a. **Effect on corporate contracts:** [§989] Because the survivor succeeds to the disappearing corporation's rights, assets, and liabilities by operation of law, the disappearing corporation's contracts—even contracts that are not ordinarily assignable, and indeed, even contracts that are not assignable by their terms—are generally taken over by the survivor.

    (1) **Exception:** [§990] A contract may specifically provide that it is not assignable in a merger. Furthermore, a court may imply such a term in an appropriate case.

3. **Board Approval:** [§991] A merger is begun when the board of directors of each constituent corporation adopts a plan or agreement of merger. Normally, this plan or agreement must set forth:

    (i) The *terms and conditions* of the merger, including the manner of converting shares of the constituents into shares of the survivor;

    (ii) The *mode* of putting these terms into effect;

    (iii) A statement of any *amendments to the survivor's articles (certificate) of incorporation* to be effected by the merger; and

    (iv) Any *other terms* agreed upon.

[Del. Gen. Corp. Law §251(b); RMBCA §11.01; Cal. Corp. Code §1101]

4. **Shareholder Approval:** [§992] After the merger plan or agreement is adopted by the board, it normally must be submitted to the shareholders of each constituent corporation for their approval.

a. **Percentage of approval required:** [§993] Because of the importance of mergers, most statutes require approval by a majority of the *outstanding stock*—not simply a majority of the shares present at a meeting. [Del. Gen. Corp. Law §251(c); RMBCA §11.03] Many statutes require that a merger be approved by two-thirds of the outstanding stock of each corporation.

b. **Class voting:** [§994] A number of statutes require that under certain conditions a merger be approved not only by a majority or two-thirds of the outstanding stock, but also by a designated percentage of each class of shareholders, whether or not otherwise entitled to vote. [RMBCA §11.03; Cal. Corp. Code §1201—approval by majority of each class required, except that no approval by nonvoting preferred shareholders is necessary if no change in the rights, privileges, or preferences of the class]

c. **Appraisal rights:** [§995] Shareholders who dissent from a merger, and follow certain procedures, normally have a right to be paid the fair value of their shares. (*See supra*, §§969-985.)

d. **Mergers that do not require shareholder approval:** [§996]   There are two kinds of cases in which shareholder approval may not be required for a merger.

(1) **Short-form mergers:** [§997]   Many statutes provide special rules for the approval of a merger between a parent and a subsidiary in which the parent owns a designated percentage of the stock—normally 90%. [Del. Gen. Corp. Law §253; RMBCA §11.04; Cal. Corp. Code §1110(b)] Such mergers are known as "short-form" mergers.

(a) **Merger effected by boards of directors:** [§998]   Under these statutes, a short-form merger does not require the approval of either the parent's or the subsidiary's shareholders. Instead, the merger can be effected simply by the boards of the parent and the subsidiary, or, under some statutes, by the board of the parent alone.

1) **Rationale:** Since the parent owns almost all the subsidiary's stock, approval of the subsidiary's shareholders would be a foregone conclusion.

(b) **Appraisal rights:** [§999]   Although the subsidiary's shareholders do not have the right to vote on a short-form merger, they do have appraisal rights. However, the parent's shareholders have neither voting nor appraisal rights.

(2) **Small-scale mergers:** [§1000]   Some statutes provide that approval by the shareholders of the *survivor* corporation is not required if:

(i) The *voting stock of the survivor issued* to effect the merger *does not constitute more than a certain percentage*—usually one-sixth—of the outstanding shares of the voting stock immediately after the merger, *and*

(ii) The merger *does not make any change in the survivor's articles (certificate) of incorporation.*

[Del. Gen. Corp. Law §251(f); RMBCA §11.03(g); Cal. Corp. Code §1201(b)]

(a) **Rationale:** Such mergers are not economically significant to the survivor and its shareholders.

(b) **Appraisal rights:** [§1001]   Following this same rationale, the survivor's shareholders have no appraisal rights.

(c) **Shareholders of disappearing corporation:** [§1002]   The small-scale merger statutes affect only the survivor corporation. Approval by shareholders of the disappearing corporation is still required, because the merger is economically significant to that corporation. These shareholders also have appraisal rights.

e. **Mergers that do not trigger appraisal rights:** [§1003] Some statutes deny appraisal rights for certain types of mergers or certain types of corporations.

(1) **Exceptions based on nature of merger:** [§1004] As noted above, in a *short-form merger,* the minority shareholders of the *subsidiary* have appraisal rights, but the parent's shareholders do not. (*See supra,* §999.) Likewise, in a *small-scale merger,* the shareholders of the *disappearing corporation* have appraisal rights, but the shareholders of the survivor do not. (*See supra,* §1001.)

(2) **Exceptions based on nature of stock**

  (a) **Stock listed on national exchange:** [§1005] Some statutes provide that a merger does not give rise to appraisal rights in the case of a corporation whose stock is listed on a national securities exchange.

    1) **Rationale:** The theory of this exception is that in such cases the shareholder has an assured market for the stock, and therefore does not need an appraisal right to be able to get out of the corporation when it undergoes a fundamental change. Moreover, it is thought, where stock is traded on an organized market it is unlikely that the appraisal price would differ significantly from the market price.

  (b) **Stock held by over 2,000 shareholders:** [§1006] Some statutes also eliminate appraisal rights in the case of any corporation with 2,000 or more shareholders, whether or not the stock is listed on a securities exchange. [Del. Gen. Corp. Law §262(k)]

    1) **Rationale:** With that many stockholders, the market is likely to be about as deep as it is on some stock exchanges.

  (c) **Carve-out from exception:** [§1007] The California statute eliminates appraisal rights as to shares traded on the New York or American Stock Exchanges, and as to certain over-the-counter stocks, *except* where the appraisal is demanded by shareholders holding 5% or more of the outstanding shares. [Cal. Corp. Code §1300(b)]

    1) **Rationale:** If a block of shares this large entered the market, it would sell at a distress price, even in a well-organized market. Furthermore, the fact that so many shareholders prefer appraisal rights to selling their stock on the market provides a good indication that appraisal is not being sought merely as a nuisance tactic.

f. **Exclusivity of appraisal rights:** [§1008] Under some statutes, dissenting shareholders who have an appraisal right may not be permitted to invoke another remedy to challenge or upset the merger. (*See infra,* §1091.)

D. DE FACTO MERGERS

1. **Introduction:** [§1009]   The explicit statutory rules that govern voting and appraisal rights in mergers differ considerably from the explicit statutory rules that govern voting and appraisal rights for other kinds of corporate combinations, such as acquisitions by one corporation of the stock or assets of another. For example, a merger normally requires shareholder approval. In contrast, under the literal terms of most statutes, an acquisition of assets or stock normally does not. A merger normally triggers appraisal rights. In contrast, under the literal terms of most statutes, an acquisition of stock or assets normally does not. Under a few statutes, including Delaware, even a *sale* of substantially all assets does not trigger appraisal rights. Accordingly, there are certain gaps in the statutes, in that if only the explicit rules are considered, corporate combinations that are virtually identical in substance give rise to radically different shareholder rights, depending solely on the form in which management chooses to cast the combination. This difference in treatment sometimes seems anomalous, because a transaction that is cast in the form of an acquisition by one corporation of another corporation's assets or stock may have the practical effect of a merger. To help fill these gaps, the courts have created the de facto merger doctrine.

2. **Acquisition of Substantially All Assets in Exchange for Stock:** [§1010]   Suppose one corporation acquires substantially all the assets of another in exchange, not for cash, but for its own stock. In that case, the two corporations are combined, as in a merger: the transferor corporation disappears, as in a merger; and the shareholder groups of the two corporations are combined, as in a merger. [Farris v. Glen Alden Corp., 143 A.2d 25 (Pa. 1958); Rath v. Rath Packing Co., 136 N.W.2d 410 (Iowa 1965)]

    a. **Comment:** It is true that in an acquisition of assets, stock in the acquiring corporation is issued to the transferor corporation; while in a merger, stock in the survivor corporation is issued directly to the transferor corporation's shareholders. However, if, as is often the case, the agreement requires the transferor corporation to immediately liquidate and distribute the stock to its shareholders, this difference is only one of form.

3. **Acquisition of Majority Stock in Exchange for Stock:** [§1011]   Alternatively, suppose an acquiring corporation acquires a majority of the stock of another corporation in exchange for its own stock. From the perspective of the acquiring corporation's shareholders, the transaction is functionally equivalent to a merger, at least where the acquired corporation is then dissolved. The two corporations are combined, as in a merger; one corporation disappears, as in a merger; and the two shareholder groups are combined, as in a merger. [Applestein v. United Board & Carton Corp., 159 A.2d 146 (1960), *aff'd*, 161 A.2d 474 (N.J. 1960)]

4. **De Facto Merger Doctrine:** [§1012]   To protect the rights of shareholders in stock-for-assets and stock-for-stock combinations, many courts hold that a transaction that has the *effect* of a merger is *deemed to be a merger* for purposes of voting and appraisal rights. Under this de facto merger doctrine, if one corporation acquires substantially all of another corporation's assets in exchange for stock that is distributed to the transferor corporation's shareholders, the transaction will require the approval of the acquiring

corporation's shareholders and will trigger appraisal rights for those shareholders. The same rule would apply to an acquisition of another corporation's majority stock in exchange for a majority of the acquiring corporation's stock. The test is whether the transaction has "all the characteristics and consequences," or the "indicia," of a merger. [Farris v. Glen Alden Corp., *supra*, §1010; Applestein v. United Board & Carton Corp., *supra*; Rath v. Rath Packing Co., *supra*, §1010]

5. **"Equal Dignity" Rule:** [§1013] Some courts have rejected the de facto merger doctrine. In particular, the Delaware courts say that the various forms for combinations all have "equal dignity," and the requirements of one form are irrelevant to others. Under this view, the form and label that management attaches to a corporate combination determines whether the transaction requires shareholder approval and triggers appraisal rights. [Hariton v. Arco Electronics, Inc., 188 A.2d 123 (Del. 1963); Heilbrunn v. Sun Chemical Corp., 150 A.2d 755 (Del. 1959)]

6. **Statutes:** [§1014] Several states have statutes that effectively eliminate the de facto merger problem by treating corporate combinations on the basis of substance rather than form.

   a. **California:** [§1015] The California statute illustrates this approach.

      (1) **Reorganizations:** [§1016] The statute creates a new category of corporate combinations, called "reorganizations." [Cal. Corp. Code §§181, 1200] The following are all considered "reorganizations" under the California statute:

         (i) *Merger reorganizations*—A merger, other than a short-form merger.

         (ii) *Exchange reorganizations*—An acquisition by one corporation of more than 50% of the stock in another, wholly or partly in exchange for shares of the acquiring corporation.

         (iii) *Sale-of-assets reorganization*—An acquisition by one corporation of substantially all of the assets of another, wholly or partly in exchange either for the acquiring corporation's shares or for debt securities that are not adequately secured and have a maturity greater than five years.

      (2) **Shareholder rights:** [§1017] If a combination is a reorganization, as defined above, shareholders have the following voting and appraisal rights under the California statute:

        (a) **Shareholder approval required:** [§1018] A merger or sale-of-assets reorganization must be approved by a majority of the shareholders of both constituent corporations. [Cal. Corp. Code §§117, 152] An exchange reorganization must be approved by shareholders of the acquiring corporation. [Cal. Corp. Code §§1200, 1201(a)]

           1) **Exception—small-scale acquisitions:** [§1019] Approval by the shareholders of the acquiring corporation is not required if the corporation (or the persons who were its shareholders immediately

before the reorganization) ends up owning at least five-sixths of the stock of the surviving corporation, provided the reorganization does not require amendment of the corporation's articles.

(b) **Appraisal rights:** [§1020] If a reorganization requires approval by a corporation's shareholders under the California statute, the shareholders of that corporation are also given appraisal rights if they dissent from the proposed reorganization (subject to the California exceptions for securities traded on national exchanges (*supra*, §1007)). [Cal. Corp. Code §1300(a), (b)]

7. **New York Stock Exchange Rules:** [§1021] The rules of the New York Stock Exchange, like the California statute, require shareholder approval of corporate combinations regardless of form. Under these rules, securities to be issued by a company listed on the Exchange in connection with the direct or indirect acquisition of a business, a company, tangible or intangible assets, or property or securities representing any such interests cannot be listed unless the acquisition is approved by the shareholders, if the issuance of common stock used to effect the acquisition could result in an increase in outstanding common shares of 18-1/2% or more, or has a fair value of 18-1/2% or more of the market value of the outstanding common shares of the issuing corporation. The American Stock Exchange has a comparable rule.

E. TRIANGULAR MERGERS [§1022]

The triangular merger is a recent development in the merger area. There are two types of triangular mergers—conventional and reverse.

1. **Conventional Triangular Merger:** [§1023] A conventional (or "forward") triangular merger works like this: Assume that Corporations A and X want to engage in a merger in which A will be the survivor. X's shareholders will end up with 100,000 shares of A. In a normal merger, this would be accomplished by having A issue 100,000 shares to X's shareholders. In a conventional triangular merger, A instead begins by creating a new subsidiary, B. A then transfers 100,000 shares of its own stock to B, in exchange for all of B's stock. X is then merged not into A, but into B. However, instead of issuing its *own* stock to X's shareholders, B issues its 100,000 shares of A stock. The net result is that X's business is owned by A indirectly—through B, its wholly owned subsidiary—rather than directly by A itself, as in a normal merger. X's shareholders end up with 100,000 shares of A stock, just as they would in a normal merger with A itself.

a. **Purpose:** A major purpose for using this technique is that A may want to avoid assuming X's liabilities. In a conventional merger between A and X, A would succeed to X's liabilities by operation of law. By using a triangular merger, A may be able to insulate itself from direct responsibility for X's liabilities, since X is merged into B, not into A.

2. **Reverse Triangular Merger:** [§1024] A reverse triangular merger begins like a conventional triangular merger. A creates a subsidiary, B, and transfers 100,000 shares of A stock to B in exchange for all of B's stock. In a conventional triangular merger,

X would then be merged into B. In a reverse triangular merger, however, B is merged into X. The merger agreement provides that all previously outstanding X shares are automatically converted into the 100,000 shares of A held by B. All shares in B are automatically converted into shares in X. As a result, B disappears, because it is merged into X. X becomes a wholly owned subsidiary of A, because A owned all the shares of B, and all the shares in B are converted into shares in X. X's shareholders own 100,000 shares of A stock, because all shares in X are converted into shares in A.

    a.   **Purpose:** Like a conventional triangular merger, a reverse triangular merger may insulate A from X's liabilities, since X ends up as a subsidiary of A, rather than merging into A. In addition, however, X's legal status as a corporation is preserved. This could be important where X has valuable rights under contracts, leases, licenses, or franchises that might be lost in a merger in which it was not the survivor.

3.   **Voting and Appraisal Rights in Triangular Mergers:** [§1025]   Triangular mergers may be used to erode voting and appraisal rights. For example, in a merger of B into X, the subsidiary (B), rather than the parent (A), is a party to the merger. Literally, therefore, only B's shareholders have voting and appraisal rights. Since B's only shareholder is A, and since A obviously will vote its stock in B in favor of the merger, A's shareholders would not have voting or appraisal rights. It has been argued that such a merger is a de facto merger as to A, but the court rejected this argument, at least under the (Pennsylvania) statute that governed the transaction, which had earlier been amended with the apparent purpose of rejecting the de facto merger theory. [Terry v. Penn Central Corp., 668 F.2d 188 (3d Cir. 1981)]

F.   SALE OF SUBSTANTIALLY ALL ASSETS

1.   **Shareholder Approval**

    a.   **Approval normally required:** [§1026]   At common law, a sale of substantially all assets normally required unanimous shareholder approval, on the theory that it violated an implied contract among the shareholders to maintain the corporation in business. Today, virtually every state has a statute authorizing such a sale upon approval by the board and a requisite percentage (but less than all) of the shareholders. In most states, a majority of the outstanding shares is required. [Del. Gen. Corp. Law §271; RMBCA §§12.01, 12.02, 13.02; Cal. Corp. Code §1001(a)] In some states, approval by two-thirds of the outstanding shares is required.

    b.   **Exception for sales made in ordinary course of business:** [§1027]   Some statutes explicitly exclude sales in the ordinary course of business from the requirement of shareholder approval. [RMBCA §12.01; Cal. Corp. Code §1001(a)(2)] Under such a statute, if a corporation was organized to build and sell a single office building, a sale of the building would not require shareholder approval. Even where the statutes do not explicitly so provide, courts have treated sales in the ordinary course of business as outside the statutory requirement of shareholder approval, on the theory that even at common law, where unanimous shareholder approval was required, sales made in the ordinary course of business were excepted, since they were deemed to be in furtherance (rather than in breach) of the implied contract among the shareholders. [Jeppi v. Brockman Holding Co., 34 Cal. 2d 11 (1949)]

c. **Exception for corporations in failing circumstances:** [§1028]   There is a split of authority on whether the requirement of shareholder approval applies where a corporation is insolvent or in failing circumstances or financial distress. [*See* Teller v. W.A. Griswold Co., 87 F.2d 603 (6th Cir. 1937)—statute inapplicable; Michigan Wolverine Student Cooperative v. William Goodyear & Co., 22 N.W.2d 884 (Mich. 1946)—contra]

d. **Exception for mortgages, pledges, etc.:** [§1029]   Most statutes do not require shareholder approval for the corporation's execution of a mortgage or other lien on corporate assets for the purpose of securing a corporate obligation. [RMBCA §12.01; Cal. Corp. Code §1000]

2. **Appraisal Rights:** [§1030]   Where a sale of substantially all assets requires shareholder approval, most statutes also provide dissenting shareholders with appraisal rights.

a. **Exceptions:** [§1031]   A few statutes do not confer appraisal rights in connection with the sale of assets. [*See* Del. Gen. Corp. Law §262] Furthermore, some statutes that confer appraisal rights generally make exceptions for certain kinds of sales. [Cal. Corp. Code §§181, 1300—no appraisal rights where corporate assets are sold *entirely* for cash or adequately secured, short-term debt securities]

3. **What Constitutes "Substantially All Assets":** [§1032]   In determining whether a sale of assets includes "substantially all assets" for purposes of the statute, the question is not simply the percentage of assets sold, but whether the assets sold constitute substantially all of the corporation's operating assets, account for most of the corporation's revenues, or are vital to the operation of the corporation's business. [Katz v. Bregman, 431 A.2d 1274, *appeal denied,* 435 A.2d 1044 (Del. 1981)]

G. AMENDMENT OF ARTICLES

1. **In General:** [§1033]   Fundamental changes in the corporate structure may be effected through amendment of the corporate articles. Some amendments may of course be pure formalities (*e.g.,* changing the name of the corporation). Others may substantially change or impair the rights of the shareholders (*e.g.,* making cumulative preferred shares noncumulative). Still others may substantially affect the corporation itself (*e.g.,* changing its business purposes).

2. **Vote Required:** [§1034]   An amendment of the corporation's articles normally must be approved by (i) the board and (ii) a majority or (under some statutes) two-thirds of the outstanding shares.

a. **Class voting:** [§1035]   Many statutes require that amendments that would have certain designated effects on the shares of a given class be approved not only by the shareholders as a whole, but also by the class voting separately—whether or not stock of the class is otherwise entitled to vote. For example, under the Model

Act, an amendment to the articles of incorporation requires the approval of each class of shareholders—even those classes not entitled to vote under the articles of incorporation—if it would increase or decrease the authorized shares of the class; limit or deny a preemptive right; change shares of the class into a different number of shares of the same class; change the rights, preferences, or limitations of the class; create a new class of shares having superior or substantially equal financial rights or preferences; or increase the rights, preferences, or number of shares of any class that have superior or substantially equal financial rights or preferences. [RMBCA §§10.04, 11.03(f)(1)]

b. **Special provisions:** [§1036]   Statutes may also contain special provisions placing limitations on certain kinds of articles amendments. For example, under the Delaware statute, an amendment restricting transferability of shares is not binding on shares already issued, unless approved by the holders of the shares in question. [Del. Gen. Corp. Law §202(b)] Under the California statute, an amendment reducing the number of directors cannot be adopted over the opposition of whatever number of shares would have been sufficient, prior to the amendment, to elect at least one director with cumulative voting. [Cal. Corp. Code §212(a)]

c. **Effect of provision in articles requiring higher percentage:** [§1037]   The articles may validly require a higher (but not a lower) percentage of shareholder approval for any proposed amendment than would otherwise be required by the statute. [Del. Gen. Corp. Law §§216, 242(b)(1); RMBCA §727; Cal. Corp. Code §204(a)(5)] Similarly, most courts will enforce shareholder agreements requiring a higher percentage of shareholder approval than would otherwise be required by statute. (*See supra,* §502.)

3. **Appraisal Rights:** [§1038]   Many states give appraisal rights in connection with certain kinds of article amendments. For example, under the Model Act, shareholders have a right to be paid the fair value of their shares if they dissent from an amendment that materially and adversely alters or abolishes a preferential right; excludes or limits the right to vote on any matter; alters or abolishes a preemptive right; or creates, alters, or abolishes a right of redemption. [RMBCA §13.02(a)(4)] Many statutes, however, do not provide appraisal rights in connection with article amendments.

4. **Constitutional Issues**

a. **Contract between state and corporation:** [§1039]   For purposes of constitutional law, a certificate of incorporation is a contract between the incorporating state and the corporation, and therefore is within the Contract Clause, which prohibits states from impairing the obligation of contracts. [Trustees of Dartmouth College v. Woodward, 17 U.S. 518 (1819); U.S. Const. art. I, §10]

b. **Contract among shareholders:** [§1040]   Subsequently, the United States Supreme Court held that the certificate of incorporation was also a contract *among the shareholders,* thus it could not be changed without their unanimous consent. [Geddes v. Anaconda Copper Mining Co., 254 U.S. 590 (1921)]

c. **Result—limited state power:** [§1041]   The result was to set limits on the power of a state to regulate corporations organized under its laws and also on the power of the shareholders—absent unanimity—to amend the articles of incorporation or make any fundamental change in the corporation that could be regarded as a change in their "contract."

d. **Reserved power clauses:** [§1042]   In response, the states amended their general corporation laws to include "reserved power clauses," *i.e.,* provisions reserving to the state the power to alter, amend, or repeal its corporation laws as regards corporations incorporated after the adoption of such provisions. These reserved power clauses are deemed to be part of the "contract" between the state and the corporation, and are therefore given effect by the courts.

e. **Shareholder amendment:** [§1043]   State corporations laws were also amended to permit the shareholders of corporations organized thereunder to amend the articles of incorporation or adopt other fundamental changes with less-than-unanimous consent. These provisions were also given effect.

f. **Today:** [§1044]   Most existing corporations have been either organized or reorganized under statutes that contain reserved power and shareholder amendment provisions. Since the granting of any corporate charter is subject to these provisions, the incorporators are deemed to have consented to them. Hence, the problem of whether an amendment to the articles of incorporation constitutes an impairment of contract is relatively minor today.

g. **Remaining problems:** [§1045]   The remaining problems are (i) whether there are any constitutional or implied contractual limitations on the power of the state to amend its laws in a way that affects corporations incorporated prior to the adoption of a reserved power clause, and (ii) whether there are any limits on the power of a state to regulate, or on the power of shareholders to amend the articles of, corporations incorporated after adoption of a reserved power clause.

   (1) **Limitations on powers of state**

      (a) **Changes affecting corporation's business:** [§1046]   In the case of *general* laws that apply only to the corporation's business activities, as opposed to the rights and duties of shareholders, etc., it is clear today that the state's power to change the law is not limited by *Dartmouth College (see supra,* §1039). For example, the state may enact general laws restricting or prohibiting certain businesses even though such businesses were proper at the time the corporation was originally organized, and even though the law affects a corporation incorporated prior to the adoption of a reserved power clause.

      (b) **Changes affecting persons:** [§1047]   On the other hand, there may still be some limitations on the state power to regulate the rights of shareholders, directors, officers, or corporate creditors, as such, even where reserved power clauses are in effect. Specifically, a state cannot eliminate "vested property rights" or "impair the obligations of contract of third persons." [Coombes v. Getz, 285 U.S. 434 (1932)] In *Coombes,* creditors of the corporation filed an action against its directors under a provision of state law that made directors liable for corporate funds embezzled or misappropriated by officers. While the action was pending, the relevant state law provision was repealed. The Supreme Court held that the repeal was ineffective as to the plaintiff-creditors; it would not be permitted to affect their "vested" rights against the directors.

1) **Rationale:** The rationale of *Coombes v. Getz* was that the exercise of a state's reserved powers is still subject to the limitations of the United States Constitution. Such state action may constitute a taking without compensation in violation of the Due Process Clause.

(2) **Limitations on shareholders' power**

(a) **"Vested property rights" theory:** [§1048] In the past, the vested property rights theory also constituted a significant limitation on shareholder power to amend the certificate. Many cases struck down article amendments that seriously altered shareholder rights—particularly the rights of preferred shareholders to receive accrued but unpaid dividends—where the type of amendment in question was not *explicitly* authorized by the statute in force at the time the corporation was organized. [Keller v. Wilson & Co., 190 A. 115 (Del. 1936)] However, other courts rejected this approach [McNulty v. W. & J. Sloane, 34 A.D.2d 284 (1945)], and even those courts that accepted it allowed equivalent results to be reached through other techniques, such as mergers. [Federal United Corp. v. Havender, 11 A.2d 331 (Del. 1940)] This problem is largely historical today, since most existing corporations have been organized or reorganized under statutes that explicitly authorize almost every conceivable type of shareholder amendment, and because modern courts are generally unsympathetic to the vested rights theory.

(b) **Fairness:** [§1049] A much more significant limitation is that of fairness. Where a controlling shareholder causes a corporation to amend its articles in a manner that arguably benefits that shareholder, a minority shareholder can complain that the amendment is fraudulent or unfair. [Bove v. The Community Hotel Corp., 249 A.2d 89 (R.I. 1969)] Fairness is frequently an issue in attempts to recapitalize a corporation in a manner that adversely affects the rights, preferences, or privileges of a certain class of shareholders—*e.g.,* reducing the dividend rate on preferred shares, making the dividends noncumulative instead of cumulative, or issuing a new class of preferred with priorities senior to the class already outstanding.

H. DISSOLUTION AND LIQUIDATION

1. **Introduction:** [§1050] Dissolution involves the termination of a corporation's status as a *legal entity.* Dissolution falls into two basic categories, *voluntary* and *involuntary.*

Voluntary dissolution occurs as a result of a decision of the corporation acting through appropriate corporate organs. Involuntary dissolution is forced upon the corporation by the courts. To be distinguished from dissolution is the related process of *liquidation,* which involves termination of the corporation's business.

2. **Voluntary Dissolution:** [§1051]   For voluntary dissolution, the statutes typically require a vote of the board recommending a plan of dissolution to the shareholders, and approval of the plan by a majority of the outstanding shares. [RMBCA §14.03] Some states have much different requirements. For example, in California, board approval is not required, and 50% shareholder approval is sufficient. [Cal. Corp. Code §1900]

3. **Involuntary Dissolution:** [§1052]   Involuntary dissolution may be precipitated by shareholders, the state, or, under some statutes, the directors.

   a. **Action by shareholders or directors**

      (1) **Nonstatutory involuntary dissolution:** [§1053]   The original rule at common law was that, absent statutory authority, courts had no jurisdiction to grant dissolution at the request of a minority shareholder. [Leventhal v. Atlantic Finance Corp., 55 N.E.2d 20 (Mass. 1944)] Eventually, however, most (although not all) courts took the position that they could grant dissolution for fraud, dissension, deadlock, abuse to minority shareholders, or gross mismanagement. [Miner v. Belle Isle Ice Co., 53 N.W. 218 (Mich. 1892); Lichens Co. v. Standard Commercial Tobacco Co., 40 A.2d 447 (Del. 1944)] However, nonstatutory dissolution is rarely granted.

      (2) **Involuntary dissolution under statute:** [§1054]   Today, statutes in most states set forth grounds under which shareholders can bring judicial proceedings to force dissolution.

         (a) **Grounds:** [§1055]   These statutes vary widely as to the grounds for involuntary dissolution. However, the Model Act includes many of the typical grounds. It provides that a court can dissolve a corporation in a proceeding by a shareholder if any of the following grounds are established:

            (i) The *directors are deadlocked in the management* of the corporate affairs, the shareholders are unable to break the deadlock, and irreparable injury to the corporation is threatened or being suffered, or the business and affairs of the corporation can no longer be conducted to the advantage of the shareholders generally, because of the deadlock.

            (ii) The directors or those in control of the corporation have acted, are acting, or will act in a manner that is *illegal, oppressive, or fraudulent.*

(iii) The **shareholders are deadlocked** in voting power and have failed, for a period that includes at least two consecutive annual meeting dates, to elect successors to directors whose terms have expired.

(iv) The corporate **assets are being misapplied or wasted.**

[RMBCA §14.30(2)]

(b) **Application to close corporations:** [§1056] As a practical matter, involuntary dissolution is highly unlikely to be ordered except in closely held corporations. In such corporations, however, dissolution is a very important remedy, especially for oppression by those in control. The statutes are gradually increasing the grounds for involuntary dissolution to include oppression and like grounds, and the courts are increasingly giving the statutes an expansive reading and are readier than in the past to order dissolution. Although some cases focus on the wrongfulness of the conduct of those who are in control [Baker v. Commercial Body Builders, Inc., 507 P.2d 387 (Or. 1973)], the trend is to focus on whether the conduct of those in control frustrates the **reasonable expectations** of those not in control [*In re* Kemp & Beatley, Inc., 64 N.Y.2d 63 (1984); Meiselman v. Meiselman, 307 S.E.2d 551 (N.C. 1983)].

(c) **Who can bring action:** [§1057] Under some statutes, there is a limitation on shareholder standing to sue for involuntary dissolution. Under the California statute, for example, a shareholder petition for dissolution can be filed only by one of the following:

(i) **One-third** of the shareholders, other than those alleged to have participated personally in **management wrongdoing,** where that is the ground on which dissolution is sought.

(ii) **Any** shareholder of a **statutory close corporation.**

(iii) **Any** shareholder of **any** corporation, where the ground for dissolution is **expiration** of the period for which the corporation was formed.

(iv) Any other **person authorized in the articles** to bring such an action.

[Cal. Corp. Code §1800(a)]

(d) **Purchase of plaintiff's shares as bar to dissolution:** [§1058] Under some statutes, noncomplaining shareholders may avoid involuntary dissolution by purchasing (or causing the corporation to purchase) the shares of the complaining shareholders at their fair cash value as determined by the court. [Cal. Corp. Code §2000]

1) **Compare—voluntary dissolution:** [§1059] A similar right exists under the California statute where voluntary dissolution is initiated by exactly 50% of the shareholders. The other 50% of the shareholders

have the option to prevent dissolution by purchasing the shares of those who want to dissolve. [Cal. Corp. Code §2000]

4. **Dissolution Under Shareholder Agreement:** [§1060]   Courts may also order dissolution to effect a preexisting agreement among the shareholders. For example, close corporation agreements sometimes provide that upon the happening of certain defined events (*e.g.,* completion of a certain project), each shareholder (or certain designated shareholders) shall have the option to require dissolution of the corporation. Such agreements are valid and will be given effect, even if not specifically authorized by statute. [Leventhal v. Atlantic Finance Corp., *supra,* §1053]

5. **Action by Directors:** [§1061]   Some statutes permit directors to petition for involuntary dissolution on specified grounds. [Cal. Corp. Code §1800(a)—one-half of the directors can petition on same grounds as shareholders]

6. **Action by State:** [§1062]   Most statutes also allow designated state officials to institute dissolution proceedings on specified grounds. For example, the Model Act authorizes dissolution in a proceeding by the attorney general, if it is established that the corporation obtained its articles of incorporation through fraud or the corporation has continued to exceed or abuse the authority conferred upon it by law. [RMBCA §14.30] The Model Act also authorizes the secretary of state to begin proceedings for administrative dissolution if a corporation does not pay any franchise tax within 60 days after it is due, or does not deliver its annual report to the secretary of state within 60 days after it is due. The corporation then has 60 days to correct the problem; if it fails to do so, the secretary can cause its administrative dissolution. [RMBCA §§14.20-14.21]

7. **Liquidation**

   a. **Nature of proceedings:** [§1063]   Dissolution does not in itself terminate the corporate business. After dissolution, the corporation must still "liquidate" or "wind up" its affairs, pay or make provision for payment of its debts, and distribute its remaining assets or sell the remaining assets and distribute the proceeds. Under the Model Act, for example, a dissolved corporation continues its corporate existence, and may carry on any business that is appropriate to wind up and liquidate its business affairs, including: (i) collecting its assets; (ii) disposing of properties that will not be distributed in kind to its shareholders; (iii) discharging or making provision for discharging its liabilities; (iv) distributing its remaining property among its shareholders according to their interests; and (v) doing every other act necessary to wind up and liquidate its business and affairs. However, the corporation may not carry on any business that is *not* necessary to wind up and liquidate its business affairs. [RMBCA §14.05]

   b. **Management:** [§1064]   During the liquidation or winding-up process, the corporation continues under the management of the board. However, if the directors continue to operate the business of the corporation after dissolution beyond the period reasonably required for the winding-up process, they may be held personally liable for the corporation's debts. [Borbein, Young & Co. v. Cirese, 401 S.W.2d 940 (Mo. 1966)]

c. Rights of shareholders on dissolution

(1) **Where corporation has only common stock:** [§1065] Where a corporation has only common stock, the general rule is that on liquidation every shareholder is entitled to a pro rata portion of the net assets remaining after the claims of creditors have been paid or provided for.

   (a) **Form of distribution:** [§1066] Under most statutes, liquidating distributions to the holders of common stock normally can be made either in cash or (if practicable) in property. [Cal. Corp. Code §2006] In the absence of unanimous consent, the corporation ordinarily cannot discriminate among shareholders by adopting a plan of distribution under which unique property is distributed to certain designated shareholders, while cash is distributed to others (*e.g.,* giving cash to minority shareholders, while giving irreplaceable corporate assets (patents, etc.) to majority shareholders). [*In re* San Joaquin Light & Power Co., 52 Cal. App. 2d 814 (1942)]

(2) **Where corporation has preferred stock:** [§1067] If there is a class of preferred stock outstanding, the certificate of incorporation will usually provide that shares of that class are entitled to a liquidation preference. This means that the net assets remaining after creditors have been paid must be applied to payment of the preferred stock's liquidation preference before any distribution is made to holders of common stock.

d. Rights of creditors

(1) **Notice:** [§1068] The corporation remains liable on its debts after dissolution. In winding up, the first priority is to pay these debts. To expedite liquidation, however, some statutes create a time limit within which a creditor who has been given proper notice of the dissolution must file a claim in the dissolution proceedings. Creditors who are on notice, and do not file a claim within this period, are thereafter barred from bringing suit on their claims.

   (a) **Disposition by written notice:** [§1069] The Model Act provides that a dissolved corporation may give known claimants written notice of dissolution. The notice must state a deadline, at least 120 days after the date of the notice, by which the dissolved corporation must receive a claim, and the notice must state that the claim will be barred if not received by the deadline. If a claimant who was given such notice does not present the claim to the dissolved corporation by the deadline, the claim is barred. The claim is also barred if a claimant whose claim was presented and rejected does not begin a proceeding to enforce the claim within 90 days from the effective date of the rejection notice. [RMBCA §14.06]

   (b) **Disposition by publication:** [§1070] The Model Act also provides that a dissolved corporation may publish notice of its dissolution in a newspaper of general circulation in the county and request that persons with claims against the corporation present them in accordance with the notice. The notice must describe the information that has to be included in a claim, provide a mailing address where the claim may be sent, and state that a claim will be barred unless a proceeding to enforce it is begun within five years after the publication of the notice. All claims against the dissolved corporation, including unknown claims, contingent claims, and known claims that were not the subject of individual written notice, are then barred unless a proceeding to enforce the claim is brought within five years after the newspaper notice. [RMBCA §14.07]

(2) **Right to trace corporate assets:** [§1071] If the corporation's assets are distributed prior to satisfaction of creditors' claims, an unpaid creditor who is not barred by the failure to present a timely claim may recover from the transferee shareholders.

I. LIMITATIONS ON POWER OF CONTROLLING SHAREHOLDERS TO EFFECT FUNDAMENTAL CHANGES IN CORPORATE STRUCTURE

1. **Fiduciary Duties Owed by Controlling Shareholders to Minority—Fairness:** [§1072] Recall that controlling shareholders owe a broad fiduciary duty to minority shareholders with respect to the exercise of corporate control (*supra*, §559). This duty is particularly relevant to fundamental changes in which the controlling shareholders are self-interested (*e.g.*, a merger between a corporation in which S owns a *majority* of stock and a corporation *wholly owned* by S). Such transactions are subject to the same requirement of fairness as ordinary business dealings between a corporation and its officers or directors, and can be set aside if unfair. [Sterling v. Mayflower Hotel Corp., 93 A.2d 107 (Del. 1952)]

   a. **Arm's-length combinations:** [§1073] A long line of Delaware cases hold that even an *arm's-length* corporate combination is subject to judicial review for fairness of consideration. However, in such cases, the burden of proof is on the plaintiff to show that there is such a gross disparity between the value of the assets sold and the consideration received "as will raise an inference of improper motives or reckless indifference to or intentional disregard of stockholders' interests." [Gimbel v. Signal Companies, 316 A.2d 599 (1974), *aff'd*, 316 A.2d 619 (Del. 1974)]

2. **Freezeouts:** [§1074] Often a controlling shareholder wishes to eliminate ("freeze out") minority shareholders from any further participation in the corporate enterprise. Among the techniques sometimes used to effect a freezeout of minority shareholders are the following.

   a. **Sale of substantially all assets:** [§1075] A sale of substantially all assets may be used to freeze out minority shareholders, by causing the corporation to sell its assets to the controlling shareholder or to a corporation it controls. The minority shareholders end up with stock in a corporation that holds only cash (and which is normally dissolved), while the controlling shareholder ends up with 100% ownership of the corporate business. [Theis v. Spokane Falls Gaslight Co., 74 P. 1004 (Wash. 1904); Matteson v. Ziebarth, 242 P.2d 1025 (Wash. 1952)]

b. **Mergers:** [§1076]   Most merger statutes now permit the surviving corporation in a merger to issue cash, rather than stock, in exchange for stock of the disappearing corporation. This creates another freezeout technique: Assume the controlling shareholder of Corporation C owns all the stock of Corporation D as well. The controlling shareholder then arranges a cash-out merger of C into D, in which D issues cash rather than stock to C's minority shareholders. Here again, the minority shareholders end up with stock in a corporation that holds only cash, and the controlling shareholder ends up with all of the corporate business. [Weinberger v. UOP, Inc., *supra*, §977] (Much the same result can be achieved if D issues debentures or redeemable preferred instead of cash.)

c. **Reverse stock splits:** [§1077]   Most statutes empower a corporation to involuntarily eliminate fractional shares (*i.e.,* shareholdings representing less than one full share) by paying any holder of fractional shares the value of the fractional shares in cash. This gives rise to another freezeout technique. Under this technique, the corporation effects a reverse stock split by amending its articles to drastically reduce the number of outstanding shares, and then pays off (and thereby ousts) shareholders who own fractional shares as a result of the reverse split.

   (1) **Example:** Corporation C amends its certificate to cause every 1,000 existing shares to become 1 share. Each person holding less than 1,000 shares thus ends up owning a fractional share and then is frozen out when C exercises its right to eliminate fractional shares.

d. **Two kinds of freezeout:** [§1078]   Freezeouts can be placed into two categories. In some cases, the freezeout is effected by a *combination of two preexisting enterprises* (not simply two preexisting corporations). In other cases (*e.g.,* reverse stock splits or cash-out mergers into shell corporations), there is *no change in the enterprise,* but only a change in the corporate entity and its ownership.

e. **Permissibility of freezeouts:** [§1079]   The courts have taken different lines on whether freezeouts are permissible.

   (1) **Legitimate business purpose:** [§1080]   Most courts hold that a freezeout is permissible if, but only if, it is effected for a legitimate business purpose. [Coggins v. New England Patriots Football Club, Inc., 492 N.E.2d 1112 (Mass. 1986)] Normally, the business purpose test requires a showing that eliminating the minority shareholders will increase corporate income or assets, *i.e.,* will make the pie bigger, rather than simply redistributing the value of the enterprise from the minority shareholders to the controlling shareholders.

      (a) **Operating efficiency:** [§1081]   The clearest business purpose for a freezeout is a combination between two preexisting enterprises (most typically, a controlling parent and a partially owned subsidiary) that arguably will result in operating efficiencies.

      (b) **Increase corporate income or assets:** [§1082]   Some cases accept a business purpose even in the absence of a combination of two different enterprises, where it can be shown that elimination of the noncontrolling shareholders will increase corporate income or assets. [Alpert v. 28 Williams St. Corp., 63 N.Y.2d 557 (1984)] At least one case permitted a reverse stock split technique to be used for elimination of a very small minority interest (0.01%) by analogizing to short-form mergers. [Teschner v. Chicago Title & Trust Co., 322 N.E.2d 54 (Ill. 1974)] In another case, however, it was held that such a transaction was subject to attack if no compelling business purpose was shown. [Clark v. Pattern Analysis & Recognition Corp., 87 Misc. 2d 385 (1976)]

(2) **Entire fairness:** [§1083]   Delaware does not require a business purpose. However, any self-interested combination must meet the standard of entire fairness. [Weinberger v. UOP, Inc., *supra,* §977; Rabkin v. Philip A. Hunt Chemical Corp., 498 A.2d 1099 (Del. 1985)]

3. **Effect of Securities Acts:** [§1084]   In addition to rights under state law—or even when the only right under state law is to ask for appraisal—a shareholder objecting to a merger (or other fundamental change) may be able to bring an action for violation of rule 10b-5 or the federal proxy rules if the controlling shareholder is guilty of deceptive conduct. (*See supra,* §§285-379, 462-486.) However, where there has been full disclosure of all material facts surrounding the merger or change in the corporate structure, a complaining shareholder's remedies, if any, must be found under state law.

4. **Self-Tender:** [§1085]   Another technique for effectively eliminating most or all minority shareholders is to cause the corporation to make a tender offer for the minority shares (a "self-tender"). This is technically not a freezeout, because it is not involuntary: A shareholder is not legally required to tender her shares in a self-tender. However, as a practical matter, she may have little economic alternative, because the self-tender may have an adverse effect on nontendering shareholders by drying up the market for their stock, causing delisting, etc.

5. **Going-Private Transactions—Rule 13e-3**

   a. **In General:** [§1086]   Transactions that eliminate public ownership, whether through a legally compulsory freezeout or through self-tender, are sometimes known as "going-private" transactions. Rule 13e-3 of the Securities Exchange Act governs going-private transactions involving corporations with equity securities registered under that Act.

   b. **Definition:** [§1087]   A "rule 13e-3 transaction" includes:

   (1) *A purchase* of any equity security by the issuer (*i.e.,* the corporation);

   (2) *A tender offer* for any equity security made *by the issuer*; and

   (3) *A solicitation of proxies* in connection with a merger or similar corporate transaction, a sale of substantially all assets, or a reverse stock split, *if* the effect of the transaction is (i) to cause any class of the corporation's equity securities registered under the 1934 Act to be held of record by *less than 300*

persons, or (ii) to cause any class of the corporation's equity securities that is listed on a national securities exchange to be *delisted.*

c. **Requirement of filing and disseminating information:** [§1088]   An issuer that proposes to engage in a rule 13e-3 transaction must file and disseminate a schedule 13e-3. This schedule 13e-3 must include information on *alternative means* to accomplish the relevant purpose, the *reasons* for the structure and timing of the transaction, and the *benefits and detriments* of the transaction to the issuer and minority shareholders (including the federal tax consequences). Schedule 13e-3 must also state "whether the issuer . . . reasonably believes that the rule 13e-3 transaction is fair or unfair to unaffiliated security holders" and must discuss "in reasonable detail the material factors upon which the belief . . . is based." According to an instruction to the schedule, such factors will normally include:

(1)   *Whether the consideration* offered minority shareholders constitutes *fair value,* in relation to current market prices, historical market prices, net book value, going concern value, and liquidation value.

(2)   *The purchase price paid by the issuer* for the securities during the preceding two fiscal years.

(3)   *Any report, opinion, or appraisal* obtained from outside parties.

(4)   *Firm offers* made by an outsider during the preceding 18 months in connection with a proposed combination.

d. **Anti-fraud rule:** [§1089]   If a going-private transaction falls under rule 13e-3, the transaction is made subject to an anti-fraud rule that is comparable to rule 10b-5 but does not contain the "in connection with the purchase and sale of securities" limitation of rule 10b-5.

6. **Effect of Appraisal Rights:** [§1090]   If a transaction triggers appraisal rights, those rights are sometimes deemed exclusive of other remedies. Just when, and to what extent, appraisal rights will be exclusive is a complex question that depends on the terms of the relevant statute, the ground on which the transaction is attacked, and the precise remedy sought.

a. **Statutes that explicitly make appraisal exclusive remedy:** [§1091]   Some statutes explicitly make appraisal rights an exclusive remedy. For example, the Pennsylvania statute provides that if a shareholder dissents from a transaction, he is limited to his appraisal rights, and if he does not dissent, he is conclusively presumed to have consented. [Pa. Bus. Corp. Act §1515(B)]

(1)   **But note:** Even under this kind of statute, the availability of appraisal rights normally does not preclude an attack based on the grounds that:

(a)   The transaction is *not authorized* by the statute;

(b) The ***procedural steps*** required to authorize the transaction were not properly taken; or

(c) Shareholder approval of the transaction was obtained through ***fraudulent misrepresentation*** or without disclosure of material facts.

b. **Statutes that do not explicitly make appraisal exclusive remedy**

(1) **Monetary damages:** [§1092]   Even statutes that do not explicitly make the appraisal remedy exclusive are often interpreted to ***preclude*** a shareholder from bringing a suit based on the transaction in which he asks for ***monetary damages measured by the value of his stock.*** [Adams v. United States Distributing Corp., 34 S.E.2d 244 (Va. 1945)]

(2) **Injunctive relief or rescission:** [§1093]   Some cases suggest that the availability of appraisal rights also precludes a suit for injunctive relief or rescission even in the absence of explicit statutory language. [Pupecki v. James Madison & Co., 382 N.E.2d 1030 (Mass. 1978); Blumenthal v. Roosevelt Hotel, Inc., 202 Misc. 988 (1952)] However, the general rule is that in the absence of explicit statutory language, the mere availability of appraisal rights does not preclude shareholders from seeking injunctive relief or rescission for fraud, using that term in the broad sense to include unfair self-dealing by fiduciaries.

(3) **Delaware view:** [§1094]   The Delaware courts recognize that although monetary remedies should be confined to an appraisal proceeding, the appraisal remedy may not be adequate in certain cases, particularly where fraud, misrepresentation, self-dealing, deliberate waste of corporate assets, or gross and palpable overreaching are involved. [Weinberger v. UOP, *supra*, §977; Rabkin v. Philip A. Hunt Chemical Co., *supra*, §1083]

   a) **Note:** It seems fairly clear, however, that in Delaware, as in most other states, appraisal is normally the exclusive remedy for monetary relief, and is almost without exception the exclusive monetary remedy of the subsidiary's shareholders in a short-form merger.

J.   TENDER OFFERS

1. **In General:** [§1095]   A tender offer is an offer to shareholders of a corporation (the "target corporation") asking them to tender their shares in exchange for either cash or securities. A tender offer is usually made by another corporation (the "bidder" or the "raider"). A tender offer almost invariably invites the tender of at least a majority of the target's shares, and frequently invites the tender of all of the target's shares.

a. **Conditions:** [§1096]   Typically, the terms of a tender offer provide that the bidder will acquire the shares that are tendered only if certain conditions are met. The most important of these conditions is that some specified minimum of shares must be tendered.

b. **Toehold stock acquisitions:** [§1097]   A tender offer is often preceded by a preliminary "toehold acquisition" of shares in the target on the open market.

c. **Second-step transactions:** [§1098] If a tender offer by a corporate bidder is successful, the target initially becomes a subsidiary of the bidder. However, a successful tender offer is frequently followed by a "second-step" or "second-stage" transaction, such as a merger, in which the target is merged into or otherwise combined with the bidder. Shares held by nontendering shareholders are often cashed out as part of the second step, through a freezeout transaction. (*See supra,* §§1074-1983.)

d. **Friendly vs. hostile tender offers:** [§1099] Tender offers are classified as friendly or hostile. A friendly tender offer is an offer that is supported by the target's board. A hostile tender offer is an offer that is opposed by the target's board.

e. **Approval required:** [§1100] Strictly speaking, neither type of tender offer is a *corporate* transaction from the target's perspective. Rather, the transaction is an offer to the target's shareholders in their individual capacities. Accordingly, in the absence of statute (*see infra,* §§1129-1135) a tender offer does not require a vote by the target's shareholders and does not give rise to appraisal rights in those shareholders. A tender offer also normally does not require the approval of, or give rise to appraisal rights in, the bidder's shareholders, unless it constitutes a de facto merger (*see supra,* §§1009-1021).

f. **Defensive tactics:** [§1101] Often, the board of a target company takes some defensive action to ward off a takeover. For example, the board may seek to combine with an alternative corporation (a "white knight"), or may agree to sell the business to management (a "management buyout"), or may give a third party or management an option ("lock-up") on a key division of the corporation ("the crown jewel"). Although the standards by which to review such defensive actions are still emerging, it seems relatively clear that they will be reviewed by an intermediate standard that is between the relatively strict duty of loyalty rule and the very liberal business judgment rule. A defensive action does not necessarily have to satisfy a standard of fairness, but it must at least be reasonable in terms of shareholder interests. The standard employed by the Delaware courts is that such an action must be "reasonable in relation to the threat posed." [Unocal Corp. v. Mesa Petroleum Co., 493 A.2d 946 (Del. 1985); Moran v. Household International, Inc., 500 A.2d 1346 (Del. 1985); Revlon, Inc. v. MacAndrews & Forbes Holdings, Inc., 506 A.2d 173 (Del. 1986)]

2. **Federal Securities Law—The Williams Act:** [§1102] Tender offers, and the toehold share acquisitions that often precede them, are regulated in a great number of respects by the Williams Act (and its amendments), which added sections 13(d), 14(d), and 14(e) to the Securities Exchange Act of 1934. A discussion of the obligations imposed by these sections follows.

a. **Notice of five percent ownership:** [§1103] Under section 13(d) of the Securities Exchange Act of 1934, a person who has acquired beneficial ownership of more than 5% of any class of equity securities registered under section 12 of the Act must file a Schedule 13D within 10 days of the acquisition.

(1) **Contents:** [§1104] The Schedule 13D must include the purchaser's identity and background; the amount and sources of the funds for the purchase; the

purpose of the purchase; any plans with respect to extraordinary corporate transactions involving the corporation whose stock has been acquired; and any contracts, arrangements, or understandings with other persons regarding the corporation's securities.

(2) **Formation of a group:** [§1105]   For this purpose, the term "person" includes a group. Merely combining existing shareholdings for the purpose of control, without more, is sufficient to constitute a "group," and trigger the filing requirements, if the members of the newly constituted group own more than 5% of the corporation's stock. [Rule 13-5(b); GAF Corp. v. Milstein, 453 F.2d 709 (2d Cir. 1971)]

(3) **Remedy:** [§1106]   A target corporation has an implied right of action for a violation of section 13(d). The appropriate remedy for such violation is an injunction to require a corrective amendment to the filing and to prohibit additional purchases until the filing is corrected. Normally, an injunction that prohibits the purchaser from voting the acquired shares, or requires that previously acquired shares be divested, is not an appropriate remedy, at least where the failure is cured by a subsequent filing. [Rondeau v. Mosinee Paper Corp., 422 U.S. 49 (1975); General Aircraft Corp. v. Lampert, 556 F.2d 90 (1st Cir. 1977)]

b.   **Tender offers under Williams Act:** [§1107]   The Williams Act also regulates tender offers. What constitutes a "tender offer" within the meaning of the Williams Act is not completely settled.

(1) **Eight-factor test:** [§1108]   Some courts have adopted the following eight-factor test to determine whether an offer to buy stock is a tender offer under the Act:

(i)   Did the purchaser engage in *active and widespread solicitation* of public shareholders?

(ii)   Is the solicitation made for a *substantial percentage* of the issuer's stock?

(iii)   Is the offer to purchase made at a *premium* over the prevailing market price?

(iv)   Are the terms of the offer *firm* rather than negotiable?

(v)   Is the offer *contingent* on the tender of a fixed number of shares?

(vi)   Is the offer open only for a *limited period of time?*

(vii)   Are the offerees under *pressure* to sell their stock?

(viii) Do public announcements of a purchasing program precede or accompany a rapid accumulation of large amounts of the target's securities?

[Wellman v. Dickinson, 475 F. Supp. 783 (S.D.N.Y. 1979), *aff'd on other grounds,* 682 F.2d 355 (2d Cir. 1982), *cert. denied,* 460 U.S. 1069 (1983); SEC v. Carter Hawley Hale Stores, Inc., 750 F.2d 945 (9th Cir. 1985)]

(2) **Alternative test—substantial risk of insufficient information:** [§1109] The Second Circuit has rejected the eight-factor test. It has held instead that the question of whether an offer to buy stock constitutes a tender offer under the Williams Act turns on whether there appears to be a likelihood that unless the Act's rules are followed, there will be a substantial risk that solicitees will lack information needed to make a carefully considered appraisal of the proposal put before them. [Hanson Trust PLC v. SCM Corp., 774 F.2d 47 (2d Cir. 1985)]

(a) **Example:** Applying the above standard, the Second Circuit held in *Hanson* that the transaction before it was not a tender offer because:

(i) The target had 22,800 shareholders and offers were made to only six. This *number was deemed miniscule* compared with the numbers involved in public solicitations of the type against which the Williams Act was directed.

(ii) At least five of the sellers were *highly sophisticated professionals,* knowledgeable in the market place and well aware of the essential facts needed to exercise their professional skills and to appraise the offer.

(iii) The sellers were *not pressured to sell* their shares by any conduct that the Williams Act was designed to alleviate, but only by the forces of the market place.

(iv) There was *no active or widespread advance publicity* or public solicitation.

(v) The price received by the six sellers was *not at a premium* over the then-market price.

(vi) The purchases were *not made contingent* upon acquiring a fixed minimum number or percentage of the target's outstanding shares.

(vii) There was *no time limit* within which the buyer would purchase the target's stock.

[Hanson Trust PLC v. SCM Corp., *supra*]

(3) **Open-market purchases:** [§1110] Purchases made anonymously on the open market almost certainly do not constitute a tender offer within the meaning of the Act. [Kennecott Copper Corp. v. Curtiss-Wright Corp., 584 F.2d 1195 (2d Cir. 1978); Calumet Industries, Inc. v. MacClure, Fed. Sec. Reg. Rep. (CCH)

¶96,434 (N.D. Ill. 1978)] However, the SEC has not entirely acquiesced in this position.

c. **Information statement by person who makes tender offer:** [§1111] Section 14(d) requires any person who makes a tender offer for a class of registered equity securities, which would result in that person owning more than 5% of the class, to file a schedule 14D containing specific information.

(1) **Contents:** [§1112] The schedule 14D must contain extensive disclosure of such matters as the offer; the identity of the bidder; past dealings between the bidder and the corporation; the bidder's source of funds; the bidder's purposes and plans concerning the corporation; the bidder's contracts and understandings or relationships with respect to securities of the corporation; financial statements of the bidder, if they are material and the bidder is not an individual; and arrangements between the bidder and those holding important positions with the corporation.

d. **Regulation of terms of tender offers:** [§1113] Section 14(d) of the Securities Exchange Act, and rules 14d and 14e, regulate the terms of tender offers. Under these provisions:

(1) *A tender offer must be held open for at least 20 days.*

(2) *A tender offer must be open to all security holders of the class* of securities subject to the tender offer (the "all holders rule").

(3) *Shareholders must be permitted to withdraw tendered shares* during the first 15 days of an offer, or after 60 days if the shares have not been purchased by then.

(4) *If the tender offer is oversubscribed,* the offeror must *purchase on a pro rata basis* from among the shares deposited during the first 10 days, or such longer period as the bidder may designate.

(5) *If the tender-offer price is increased, the higher price must be paid to all tendering shareholders*—even those who tendered in response to the lower price—and the offer must remain open at least 10 days after notice of the increase is first published.

e. **Obligations of target's management:** [§1114] Rule 14e-2 requires the target company, no later than 10 business days from the date the tender offer is first published, to give its shareholders a statement disclosing that the target either: (i) *recommends acceptance or rejection* of the tender offer; (ii) *expresses no opinion* and is remaining neutral toward the tender offer; or (iii) is *unable to take a position* with respect to the tender offer. The statement must also include the reason for the position or for the inability to take a position.

f. **Tender offers by issuers:** [§1115]   Under section 13(e) and rule 13e, corporations that tender for their own stock ("issuer" or "self" tenders) are subject to obligations similar to those imposed on outside bidders under rules 14d and 14e.

g. **Anti-fraud provision:** [§1116]   Section 14(e) prohibits material misstatements, misleading omissions, and fraudulent or manipulative acts, in connection with a tender offer or any solicitation in favor of or in opposition to a tender offer. Section 14(e) is closely comparable to rule 10b-5, except that it does not contain the limiting language, "in connection with the purchase or sale" of securities, found in rule 10b-5. It is not yet completely clear who may bring an action under section 14(e). A major Supreme Court decision, *Piper v. Chris-Craft Industries, Inc.,* 430 U.S. 1 (1977), lays down some important rules, but leaves a number of gaps.

(1)   **Suit by offeror**

(a)   **Damages:** [§1117]   Under *Piper v. Chris-Craft Industries, Inc.,* the bidder does not have standing to sue for damages under section 14(e), particularly a suit against the target corporation's management for false statements made in opposition to the tender offer.

1)   **Rationale:** The Williams Act was designed to protect shareholders of the target. It is not consistent with the underlying legislative purpose to imply a damages remedy for the bidder, particularly since the target's shareholders might end up bearing the burden of an award based on misrepresentations by the target's management.

(b)   **Injunctive relief:** [§1118]   In *Piper v. Chris-Craft Industries, Inc.,* the Court left open the question of suits by the bidder under section 14(e) for *injunctive* relief against the target or its management. Lower courts have held that such a suit will lie. [Weeks Dredging & Contracting, Inc. v. American Dredging Co., Fed. Sec. Reg. Rep. (CCH) ¶96,414 (E.D. Pa. 1978); Humana, Inc. v. American Medicorp, Inc., Fed. Sec. Reg. Rep. (CCH) ¶96,286 (S.D.N.Y. 1978)] The bidder can also bring a suit for injunctive relief against competing bidders. [Humana, Inc. v. American Medicorp, Inc., Fed. Sec. L. Rep. (CCH) ¶96,298 (S.D.N.Y. 1978)]

1)   **Rationale:** Unlike damages, an injunction does not impose any burden upon the target's shareholders. Furthermore, an injunction prior to the time when the target's shareholders must decide whether to accept the tender offer allows them to make their decision in an environment purged of false and misleading information. [Weeks Dredging & Contracting, Inc. v. American Dredging Co., *supra*]

(2)   **Suit by target corporation**

(a)   **Damages:** [§1119]   Since *Chris-Craft* was based on the conclusion that the Williams Act was designed to protect the target's ***shareholders,*** the target corporation itself would not have standing to sue the bidder for damages under rule 14e.

    (b) **Injunction:** [§1120] The target corporation **can** sue for an injunction against the bidder for violation of section 14(e), since such an injunction will protect the interests of the target's shareholders. [Gearhart Industries, Inc. v. Smith International, Inc., 741 F.2d 706 (5th Cir. 1984)]

  (3) **Suit by target's shareholders**

    (a) **Suit by tendering shareholders:** [§1121] Based on the Court's interpretation of the Williams Act in *Piper v. Chris-Craft Industries, Inc.*, shareholders of the target have standing to sue for both damages and injunctive relief if they tender their shares on the basis of false and misleading information.

    (b) **Suit by nontendering shareholders:** [§1122] The Court did not express a view on this issue in *Piper v. Chris-Craft Industries, Inc.*, but since the statute does not contain the purchaser-seller limitation associated with rule 10b-5, nontendering shareholders can probably sue under section 14(e), provided they can show damage resulting from a violation of that section.

3. **State Statutes Regulating Tender Offers:** [§1123] Many states now have statutes regulating takeover bids.

  a. **First-generation statutes:** [§1124] The so-called "first-generation" statutes imposed very stringent requirements on takeover bids. In *Edgar v. MITE Corp.*, 457 U.S. 624 (1982), the Supreme Court held one such statute, the Illinois Takeover Act, unconstitutional. The Court considered the following theories:

    (1) **Supremacy Clause:** [§1125] Three of the six judges who passed on the merits of the case held that the Illinois statute was unconstitutional under the Supremacy Clause, on the ground that a major objective of the Williams Act was maintaining a neutral balance between management and the bidder, and the Illinois Act violated this balance. (*See infra*, §§1131-1134.)

    (2) **Commerce Clause:** [§1126] All six judges who addressed the merits held that the Illinois Act violated the Commerce Clause, by:

      (a) Directly regulating commerce taking place across state lines, because it applied to prevent an offeror from making an offer even to non-Illinois shareholders; and

      (b) Imposing an excessive burden on interstate commerce, by permitting the secretary of state to block a nationwide tender offer.

b. **Second-generation statutes:** [§1127]   After the decision in *Edgar v. MITE Corp.*, a number of states adopted "second-generation" takeover statutes. These statutes fall into two major categories: "fair price" statutes and "control share acquisition" statutes.

   (1) **Fair price statutes:** [§1128]   Under the fair price statutes, an acquiror must pay all shareholders the "best price" paid to any one shareholder.

   (2) **Control share acquisition statutes:** [§1129]   Under control share acquisition statutes, if a designated stock-ownership threshold is crossed by an acquiring shareholder, he cannot vote the acquired shares without the approval of a majority of the disinterested shareholders.

      (a) *CTS* **case:** [§1130]   In *CTS Corp. v. Dynamics Corp. of America,* 481 U.S. 69 (1987), the Supreme Court upheld a control share acquisition statute adopted by Indiana. The Indiana statute is limited to targets incorporated in Indiana. The statute applies whenever a person acquires "control shares," *i.e.,* whenever a person acquires shares that (but for the operation of the statute) would bring the person's voting power in the corporation to or above any of three thresholds: 20%, 33-1/3%, or 50%. An acquiror that passes such a threshold cannot vote the acquired stock unless voting rights are approved by a majority of all disinterested shareholders voting at the next regularly scheduled meeting of the shareholders or at a specially scheduled meeting. The acquiror can require management of the corporation to hold such a special meeting within 50 days.

         1) **Supremacy Clause:** [§1131]   The Court held that the Indiana statute was not preempted by the Williams Act. The Illinois statute in *Edgar v. MITE Corp.* had three offending features, which the Indiana statute did not share.

            a) **Communicating with shareholders:** [§1132]   The Illinois statute provided for a 20-day precommencement period. During this time, management could disseminate its views on the upcoming tender offer to shareholders, but bidders could not publish their offers. This conflicted with the Williams Act, because Congress had deleted express precommencement notice provisions from the Williams Act. In contrast, the Indiana statute does not give either management or the bidder an advantage in communicating with shareholders about an impending tender offer.

            b) **Delay:** [§1133]   The Illinois statute provided for a hearing on a tender offer. Because no deadline was set for the hearing, management could indefinitely stymie a takeover. This conflicted with the Williams Act, because Congress anticipated that bidders would be free to go forward without unreasonable delay. In contrast, the Indiana statute does not impose an indefinite delay on tender offers. Nothing in the statute prohibits an offeror from consummating an offer on the 20th business day, the earliest day permitted under applicable federal regulations, and full voting rights will be vested or denied within 50 days after commencement of the tender offer.

c) **Fairness evaluation:** [§1134]   The Illinois statute provided for review of the fairness of tender offers by the Illinois Secretary of State. This conflicted with the Williams Act, because Congress intended investors to be free to make their own decisions. In contrast, the Indiana statute does not allow the state government to interpose its views of fairness between willing buyers and sellers of shares of the target company. Rather, the statute allows *shareholders* to collectively evaluate the fairness of the offer.

2) **Commerce Clause:** [§1135]   The Court in *CTS* also concluded that the Indiana statute does not violate the Commerce Clause, because it does not discriminate against interstate commerce and does not subject activities to inconsistent regulation. The statute applies only to Indiana corporations, and a state has authority to regulate domestic corporations, including the authority to define the voting rights of shareholders.

(3) **Other statutes:** [§1136]   Some new ("third generation") statutes do not fall into either the control-share acquisition or the fair-price patterns. For example, the New York statute provides for a five-year delay between the time a tender offer occurs and the time the target can be merged or otherwise combined with the bidder, unless the transaction was approved by the target's board of directors prior to the date control was acquired. [N.Y. Bus. Corp. Law §912] The Delaware statute imposes a prohibition on combinations between the bidder and the target, subject to certain exceptions, for three years. [Del. Gen. Corp. Law §103]

XI.   CONFLICT OF LAWS PRINCIPLES

chapter approach

Conflicts issues rarely arise on Corporations exams. However, you should remember that all questions concerning the internal affairs of the corporation are decided according to the law of the state of incorporation. Also keep in mind that a state may refuse to apply that law if it violates local public policy.

A.   GENERAL RULE

1. **Law of State of Incorporation Applies:** [§1137]   No matter where the litigation occurs, the general choice of law rule is that all questions concerning the organization or internal affairs of a corporation are decided according to the law of the state in which it was incorporated.

    a. **Example:** A corporation organized in state A has its principal office and place of business in state B. In litigation in state B (or elsewhere) involving the corporation's internal affairs, the court will generally refer to and apply the law of state A.

    b. **Effect:** This is the reason that many businesses choose to incorporate in Delaware, Nevada, or other states having laws deemed favorable to corporate management. As discussed earlier, Delaware law does away with mandatory cumulative voting (_supra,_ §443) and eases the limitations against a corporation indemnifying its officers and directors for liabilities incurred in office (_supra,_ §§682-688).

B.   LIMITATIONS

1. **Local Public Policy:** [§1138]   Nevertheless, local courts may refuse to apply the law of another state where this would validate some act strongly offensive to local public policy.

    a. **Example:** A California court has refused to permit a Delaware corporation to solicit shareholder approval for an amendment to its articles of incorporation that would have eliminated cumulative voting for directors. Even though such an amendment would have been permitted under Delaware law, the California court held that California had a legitimate interest in the matter since the corporation's principal business was in California and many of its shareholders resided there. Hence, the court insisted upon applying its own local laws prohibiting the amendment. [Western Air Lines v. Sobieski, 191 Cal. App. 2d 399 (1961)]

2. **Local Statutes:** [§1139]   A few states now have statutes that subject foreign corporations having substantial local "contacts" to various local regulations intended to protect shareholders and creditors. [Cal. Corp. Code §2115; N.Y. Bus. Corp. Law §§1306, 1317-1320]

a. **"Pseudo-foreign" corporations:** [§1140]   Under the California statute, if more than *half* of the corporation's business (average of its property, payroll, and sales) is done within the state and more than half of its shareholders have California addresses, it is treated as a "pseudo-foreign" corporation. Such corporations are subject to California law with respect to such matters as election and removal of directors, directors' standard of care and liability for unlawful distributions, shareholder rights to cumulative voting and inspection of records, shareholder approval and dissenters' rights in the case of reorganizations, and required corporate records and reports to shareholders. [Cal. Corp. Code §2115(b)]

b. **Constitutionality:** [§1141]   The validity of these statutes under the Full Faith and Credit and Commerce Clauses of the Constitution has been questioned, but not yet authoritatively resolved.

c. **Exemptions:** [§1142]   The "pseudo-foreign" corporation statute does not apply to out-of-state corporations whose shares are listed on national securities exchanges. These exchanges are deemed to have adequate "fairness" rules of their own, and their geographical shareholder-distribution requirements make it unlikely that more than half the shareholders would ever be residents of a single state. [Cal. Corp. Code §2115(e)]

REVIEW QUESTIONS

CHARACTERISTICS OF CORPORATIONS

1. If Smith owns 10% of the outstanding shares of XYZ Corporation, is Smith responsible for 10% of XYZ's debts? _____

2. Do shareholders in a corporation generally have management power and direct control of its affairs? _____

3. A, B, and C are the sole shareholders of ABC Corporation. A dies; B and C sell their shares to D and E, respectively. Does ABC Corporation still exist? _____

4. Are both corporations and partnerships "legal entities"? _____

5. In a limited partnership, does a limited partner have the same right to management and control as a partner in an ordinary partnership? _____

6. Able and Baker formed Acme Corp., a widget manufacturing business. Corporate formalities were observed when Acme Corp. was formed, but since then Able and Baker have neither held any meetings nor maintained any corporate records. Lately, Baker has been paying his household bills from Acme's account, and Able bought his wife a car with an Acme check. May C Corp., an Acme creditor who has not been paid for months, reach Able and Baker's personal assets to satisfy its claim? _____

7. Don, Ed, and Frank formed DEF Trucking Corporation, with investments of $250 each. They are the sole shareholders. They have observed all corporate formalities and have kept DEF's assets separate from their own. They have allowed DEF to run up debts of $100,000 in excess of its assets. Can the creditors "pierce the corporate veil" to reach the assets of Don, Ed, and/or Frank? _____

8. Does the "Deep Rock Doctrine" permit the creditors of an insolvent corporation to collect their debts directly from the shareholders? _____

9. Beulah is a major shareholder of the XYZ Corporation. XYZ owes Creditor $10,000. Can XYZ assert, as an offset against its debt, a claim that Beulah has against Creditor? Can XYZ sue in its own name on Beulah's claim? _____

ORGANIZING THE CORPORATION

10. Under typical statutes governing incorporation, must the articles of incorporation state:

    a. The specific business purpose for which the corporation is formed? _____

    b. The number of shares it proposes to issue? _____

11. Under typical statutes governing incorporation, is it required that the incorporators also be permanent directors? _____

12. Under typical statutes governing incorporation, must **both** the articles of incorporation and the bylaws be filed with an appropriate state official in order to create corporate status? _____

13. The incorporators of White Corporation inadvertently filed defective articles of incorporation but thereafter contracted and acted as a corporation. Assuming the statutory requirements had been met, which, if any, of the following parties can attack White's status as a corporation? _____

    (A) Its own shareholders.

    (B) Its creditors.

    (C) The state.

14. The "corporation by estoppel" doctrine operates only against a third party who has dealt with the corporation and only as to the particular dealing. True or false? _____

15. Where statutes provide that corporate status is conclusively presumed from a proper filing of articles of incorporation, may shareholders rely on the "de facto incorporation" doctrine if the articles are **not** properly filed? _____

16. During the promotion stage of Central Corporation, Promoter Perry enters into a contract on behalf of the corporation for the purchase of equipment from Manufacturer. After formation, Central rejects the contract and refuses to proceed with the purchase. Can Manufacturer enforce the contract against Central? _____

17. Same facts as above except that Central, after formation, ratified the promoter's contract. If it subsequently changes its mind, can it be held liable on the contract? _____

18. Can Central enforce the contract against Manufacturer? _____

19. If Central rejects the contract, is Perry liable individually? _____

POWERS AND LIABILITIES OF A CORPORATION

20. Can a corporation exercise powers other than those explicitly enumerated in its articles of incorporation? _____

21. Does a corporation have the **implied** power to enter into a partnership? _____

22. May a corporation validly make an educational or charitable gift that serves **no** direct corporate business purpose? _____

23. Can a **lawful** act ever be an "ultra vires" act? _____

24. If a corporate employee, in the course of employment, commits a tortious act that was within the scope of employment, but was unauthorized, can the corporation use ultra vires as a defense?   _____

25. Brown Corporation enters a contract with Bob, a builder. The contract is of a kind that is ultra vires for Brown.

   a. If neither side has performed, can Bob enforce the contract if the corporation raises an ultra vires defense?   _____

   b. If both sides have performed, can Brown rescind?   _____

   c. If Bob has performed, but Brown has not, can Bob enforce the contract?   _____

MANAGEMENT AND CONTROL

26. At their annual meeting, the shareholders of XYZ Corp., a publicly held corporation, voted to fire President and hire Jones as new general manager at $100,000 per annum. Are these resolutions effective?   _____

27. Does "statutory close corporation" status depend entirely on the existence of a specified number of shareholders?   _____

28. Small Corporation is a statutory close corporation with five shareholders, who are also the five directors.

   a. May the five shareholders make a written agreement concerning distribution of dividends and election of officers?   _____

   b. One of the shareholders makes a permissible sale of one-half of his shares to an outsider. The share certificate indicates the existence of a written agreement concerning management. Is the transferee bound by the agreement?   _____

29. Is it ever permissible for a corporation to have only one director?   _____

30. May the board of directors remove a director?   _____

31. In most states, a director must own at least one share in a corporation of which he is a director. True or false?   _____

32. Under modern statutes, can the shareholders ever, **without cause**, remove a director before the expiration of her term?   _____

33. XYZ Corp. has seven directors, elected annually for one-year terms.

   a. If the shareholders' meeting elects directors for only six positions, does the incumbent in the seventh position continue to serve?   _____

   b. May the board of directors enter into a five-year employment contract with the general manager, thus binding future boards?   _____

   c. May the XYZ board delegate interim management decision-making authority to an executive committee composed of three of the directors?   _____

d. May five of the seven directors properly agree in advance as to how they will vote at board meetings?

e. At an unscheduled meeting, four members are present and make a decision by a three-to-one vote. The three absent directors subsequently waive notice and approve the minutes of the meeting. Is the board action valid under most statutes?

34. Even without prior agreement, a director is always entitled to reasonable compensation for ordinary services as a director. True or false?

35. By majority vote, the directors of Shield Corp., acting in good faith, reduce existing fire insurance coverage without investigating the value of the property insured, even though Shield was not in a position to self-insure. As a result, Shields sustains a major financial loss when the property is destroyed by fire.

a. Does the "business judgment rule" absolve the directors of liability for the losses?

b. Is each director who voted with the majority personally liable for the losses to Shield?

c. Are those who voted against the decision also liable?

d. If two of the directors were serving without pay, are they nevertheless personally liable?

e. If the directors relied on apparently sound reports by corporate officers (or on the advice of professional experts) that the property was "fireproof," are the directors relieved of liability?

36. Under most statutes, corporate officers are elected by the shareholders. True or false?

37. The president of Green Corp. hired three new employees as division managers without consulting the board of directors. On finding out, can the board cancel the employment contracts as unauthorized?

CONFLICT OF INTEREST IN CORPORATE TRANSACTIONS

38. Acme Corp. has nine directors, but four are absent from a meeting of the board. Director Donald, making full disclosure of all pertinent facts, offers to sell an office building to Acme. Donald's offer is accepted by a three-to-two vote, with Donald voting in favor. Under modern statutes—

a. Was Donald properly counted toward a quorum?

b. Was Donald's vote properly counted on the sale?

39. Same facts as above. Assume Acme buys the building from Donald, after full disclosure to the board, a proper quorum, and a disinterested majority vote of the board.

a.　At a later date, can the corporation rescind simply on the ground that the contract was made with an interested director? _____

b.　If the contract is later challenged as unfair in a shareholders' derivative suit, is the burden of proof on Donald to prove that it was fair to the corporation? _____

c.　If the shareholders **unanimously** ratify the contract, can Acme sue to rescind for unfairness? _____

d.　If the contract is ratified by a **majority** of the shareholders, can Acme avoid it? _____

40.　On the same facts, **if** the contract had been unfair, and Acme sought damages, could Donald be held liable for more than the difference between the price paid by Acme and the fair market value of the building? _____

41.　Red Corp. and Blue Corp. have a majority of directors in common. Is it ever proper for the two corporations to contract with each other? _____

42.　Winnie is a director of Textile Corp. The inventor of a new weaving machine, having offered it to Textile, also offers to sell it to Winnie.

a.　May Winnie buy the invention for her own business use while Textile is still considering the offer? _____

b.　If Winnie knows that Textile is financially unable to meet Inventor's price, may she buy the machine? _____

c.　If Textile makes a firm decision to reject the offer, may Winnie buy? _____

d.　If Winnie purchases from Inventor while Textile is still considering the offer, may Textile force Winnie to transfer the machine to Textile **at her cost**? _____

e.　If Winnie is on the boards of two different textile corporations, and Inventor directly approaches Winnie individually, may she choose to which corporation she will transmit the offer? _____

43.　Herbert is a director of Blank Corp. and has also served as Blank's secretary for five years.

a.　May Herbert properly vote on the amount of his own salary as secretary? _____

b.　If Herbert's salary is set by the disinterested directors, can it later be challenged in a derivative suit simply on the grounds that it is more than the average salary paid for similar positions in other corporations? _____

c.　If Herbert's salary is based on a percentage of corporate profits, is it automatically subject to challenge as a waste of corporate assets? _____

d.　If a disinterested board votes a substantial, but reasonable, increase in Herbert's salary, retroactive to the beginning of his service as secretary, can the corporation (*e.g.*, under a new board or as a result of a shareholder suit) recover the amount of the retroactive increase? _____

INSIDER TRADING

44. At common law, do directors and officers owe fiduciary obligations to individual shareholders to disclose inside information about the corporation when trading in its stock? _____

45. Do section 10(b) and rule 10b-5 of the 1934 Act apply to securities that are **exempt** from the registration and reporting requirements of the Act? _____

46. Virginia, a promoter of Round Corp., sold to Round, without full disclosure, property worth $20,000 in exchange for its issuance of shares having a par value of $35,000.

   a. Can Round sue Virginia under rule 10b-5? _____

   b. Can a shareholder of Round maintain a derivative suit against Virginia under rule 10b-5? _____

   c. If Round had paid Virginia $35,000 in **cash** instead of stock, could Round sue under rule 10b-5? _____

47. Can a plaintiff suing in state court on a state law claim join with it a 10b-5 claim arising from the same transaction? _____

48. Edgar, a shareholder of Circle Corp., brings an action seeking rescission of a just-completed merger of Circle into Square Corp., on the ground that Square made a false statement of a material fact in order to induce the shareholders' consent to the merger. Does rule 10b-5 apply? _____

49. Old Corp. issues a very optimistic press release that intentionally misstates material facts about its earnings. In reliance thereon, Davis buys stock. Also in reliance thereon, Edward, a shareholder, decides **not** to sell his stock. When the true facts are known, the stock falls sharply.

   a. Can Davis sue Old under rule 10b-5, even though he purchased his shares on the open market and not from Old? _____

   b. Can Davis seek either rescission **or** damages? _____

   c. Can Edward sue Old? _____

50. John is a director of New Corp. and knows that New has a new invention that will make its stock rise. Before any public announcement, John buys 1,000 shares directly from Thomas and also advises his neighbor, in confidence, to invest heavily in New stock because of the invention. The neighbor promptly follows John's advice.

   a. Can Thomas rescind? _____

   b. Is the neighbor liable under rule 10b-5? _____

51. Nondisclosure of a mere **possibility** may give rise to an action under rule 10b-5. True or false? _____

52. Is a corporate officer liable under rule 10b-5 for a merely negligent omission of a material fact in a corporate report, if a purchaser relies thereon to his detriment?

53. Franklin is vice president of Grand Corp., which is listed on the New York Stock Exchange and has 1,000,000 shares outstanding. In March, he bought 1,000 shares of Grand from Greg at $30. In June of the same year, he sold the shares at $45.

    a. Is Franklin liable under section 16(b) of the 1934 Act to disgorge the profit he made?

    b. Can Greg rescind or recover $15,000 from Franklin under section 16(b)?

    c. If Franklin's trading was *not* based on any inside information, does this affect his liability?

54. Regina is a director of Home Corp. In February, she sold 100 shares of Home at $12; in March, she bought 200 shares at $10; in August, she sold 200 shares at $10. Is Regina liable under section 16(b)?

55. Stone Corp. has 100,000 shares outstanding. Alice, who is neither an officer nor a director of Stone, sold all of her 25,000 shares in July at $10. In August, she purchased 5,000 shares at $8. Is she liable under section 16(b)?

56. Robert, the secretary of Wood Corp., is designated by Wood to represent its stock interest (less than 10%) in Rock Corp. by serving as a director of Rock. Can Wood Corp. be held liable for short-swing profits it derives from Rock stock under section 16(b)?

57. If an insider uses confidential information in *purchasing* stock of his corporation, but does *not* sell any stock in the corporation within six months of the purchase, can he be held liable either by the corporation or by the persons from whom he purchased?

VOTING BY PROXY

58. If shares are sold between the "record date" and the time of a shareholders' meeting, is the new owner entitled to vote the shares at the meeting?

59. If 100 shares are eligible to vote and four directors are to be elected by cumulative voting, a shareholder must have one-fourth of the shares (*i.e.,* 25 shares) to be able to elect one director. True or false?

60. In a corporation with cumulative voting, will reducing the size of the board or providing for staggered terms reduce the effective voting strength of a minority bloc of shares?

61. Is proxy voting permitted after a shareholder's death?

62. Shareholder Simon, owner of 10,000 shares, pledges 5,000 to X as security for a loan, and gives X an irrevocable proxy. Simon then gives Y a proxy for his other 5,000 shares. Simon, X, and Y all appear at the meeting to vote.

    a. May X vote 5,000 shares?   _____

    b. May Y vote 5,000 shares?   _____

63. The management of Ace Corp., whose shares are traded on a national exchange, solicits proxies for its annual meeting. Under the federal proxy solicitation rules, which, if any, of the following shareholder proposals is management required to include in the proxy solicitation materials?   _____

    (A) Nomination of directors with supporting statements.

    (B) A demand that the corporation take a public stand on foreign policy issues.

    (C) A proposal that would bind the board to replace a corporate vice president.

64. The management of Black Corp. solicited proxies for a vote on a proposed merger. The solicitation included several misstatements of material facts. The merger was approved.

    a. In a shareholder suit to rescind the merger, must the plaintiff-shareholder prove the *materiality* of the misstatements?   _____

    b. Must he prove that the merger approval *resulted* from the misstatements?   _____

    c. If the terms of the merger were fair to the corporation and the shareholders, can plaintiff still obtain relief?   _____

65. Following a proxy contest involving basic policy decisions of Alpha Corp., management loses in the voting.

    a. Can the corporation reimburse management for its expenses in the proxy contest?   _____

    b. Can the corporation reimburse the victorious insurgents?   _____

SHAREHOLDER AGREEMENTS

66. Is a pooling agreement among fewer than all shareholders in a close corporation valid?   _____

67. Will most courts enforce an agreement among shareholders that binds them in their actions as *directors*, if all shareholders are not parties to the agreement?   _____

68. A, B, and C, three shareholders in a close corporation, create a voting trust, transferring legal title in their shares to Thomas as trustee.

a.	Can A revoke before expiration of the term of the trust? _____

b.	Does the trust last as long as A, B, and C are shareholders? _____

c.	Can Thomas vote the shares in *every* shareholder vote? _____

TRANSFER OF SHARES

69.	Small Corp., a close corporation, has a provision in its articles that no shareholder may sell or transfer her shares without first giving the corporation, and then the other shareholders, a right of first refusal for 30 days.

a.	Is this restriction valid under most modern statutes? _____

b.	May Small exercise the option if the repurchase would impair its stated capital? _____

c.	If a shareholder dies, may Small insist on the right to repurchase from her legatee? _____

d.	If a shareholder, in violation of the restriction, sells her shares to a transferee with notice of the restriction, may Small refuse to recognize the transfer? _____

70.	Under modern statutes, if a corporation has a lien on shares, is a transferee without notice liable for the amount owed? _____

SHAREHOLDER RIGHTS TO INSPECT BOOKS

71.	At common law, did a shareholder have an *absolute* right to inspect corporate books and records? _____

72.	Under modern statutes, can the shareholders' right to inspect corporate books and records be eliminated by specific provision in the articles of incorporation? _____

73.	Is the objective of gaining control of a corporation through a proxy fight a "proper" purpose that justifies obtaining access to the shareholder list by insurgent shareholders? _____

CONTROLLING SHARES

74.	The majority shareholder of Beta Corp. causes the board of directors to declare an excessive—but lawful—dividend. Does a minority shareholder have standing to object, even though he too will receive the dividend? _____

75.	Minority shareholders in a close corporation actually owe a stricter fiduciary duty to other shareholders than do controlling shareholders of a publicly held corporation. True or false? _____

76.	Owen, the owner of 60% of the shares of Omega Corp., sells his Omega stock to Olive at a premium; *i.e.,* a price above market value. Must Owen share the premium with the other shareholders? _____

77. If a majority shareholder is selling his stock, may he, as part of the sale transaction, arrange for the incumbent directors to resign so that the purchaser can take immediate control?   _____

78. Sally, a majority shareholder in Epsilon Corp., sells her Epsilon shares to Louis at a price far above their fair value. Louis subsequently loots the corporate treasury.

   a. Can Sally be held liable to the minority shareholders?   _____

   b. If Sally is liable, is her liability limited to the minority's "share" of the premium she received?   _____

DERIVATIVE SUITS

79. The test of whether an action should be brought as a direct suit or as a derivative suit is the number of shareholders who claim to have been injured. True or false?   _____

80. The board of directors of Red Corp. has failed to sue for damages on a Red contract with another corporation, which the latter has breached. Jane, a Red shareholder, wishes to bring a derivative suit to enforce Red's cause of action.

   a. Must Jane first make a demand on the Red board of directors?   _____

   b. If a disinterested Red board rejects Jane's demand, can she still maintain her suit?   _____

   c. Must Jane also make a demand on the Red shareholders?   _____

   d. If a demand on the Red shareholders was required and the shareholders refuse to sue, may Jane maintain her suit?   _____

81. Must a derivative suit plaintiff always have been a shareholder at the time of the alleged wrongdoing?   _____

82. If a sole shareholder cannot file a derivative suit against former managers because he owned no stock when the wrongful acts occurred, may he instead instigate a suit by the corporation?   _____

83. If a corporate director is a defendant in a derivative suit, may the corporation's attorney represent the director?   _____

84. Is a corporation a necessary party to a derivative suit brought on its behalf?   _____

85. Is a jury trial ever available in a shareholder derivative suit in federal court?   _____

86. If a losing derivative suit plaintiff was required to post security for expenses, is the corporation automatically entitled to recover the amount posted?   _____

87. If a plaintiff-shareholder proves her derivative suit claim, will the court normally enter judgment in favor of the *corporation*?   _____

88. If a plaintiff-shareholder loses in a derivative suit against a third party, may the corporation later sue in its own name on the same claim? _____

89. Plaintiff in a derivative suit recovers a judgment against defendant directors.

    a. Is the plaintiff entitled to reimbursement from the corporation for his expenses? _____

    b. Are the losing directors entitled to indemnification by the corporation for damages assessed against them? _____

    c. If the plaintiff had lost, could the corporation reimburse the defendants for their expenses? _____

90. May a corporation properly provide insurance coverage for its officers and directors to protect them against personal liability or expenses in derivative suits? _____

CLASSES OF STOCK

91. If a corporation's articles authorize "preferred" stock, but fail to state what preferences the stock is entitled to, is it entitled to at least dividend and liquidation preferences? _____

92. The articles of Corporation Y provide for preferred stock with a "5%, cumulative, dividend preference."

    a. Must the directors pay the 5% dividend in a year in which funds are available? _____

    b. If no dividends were paid on the preferred in a given year, do the arrearages have preference over dividends on the common stock in a subsequent year? _____

AUTHORIZATION AND ISSUANCE OF SHARES

93. Once all of the authorized shares have been issued, may the board of directors authorize the issuance of more shares? _____

94. If a corporation repurchases shares and holds them as "treasury stock," does this affect the corporation's authorized or issued capital? _____

STOCK SUBSCRIPTIONS

95. Prior to the formation of Star Corp., A, B, and C each agree to subscribe to 100 shares of stock when issued at an agreed price. If A revokes before Star's incorporation is completed, can Star enforce the agreement against A? _____

96. Same facts as above. B paid 50% of the agreed price for her shares, with 50% balance due. If Star Corp. becomes insolvent, is B nevertheless liable for the balance owing on her subscription? _____

CONSIDERATION FOR SHARES

97. Which of the following shares have been lawfully issued by ABC Corp.? _____

    (A) 1,000 shares issued to Politician Paul as a gift?

    (B) 1,000 shares issued to Promoter Pat in exchange for her preincorporation services?

    (C) 1,000 shares issued to Promoter Pamela in exchange for her management services to be performed during the following two years?

98. May par value shares be sold by a corporation—

    a. For *less* than par value? _____

    b. For *more* than par value? _____

99. In April, Union Corp. issued to Arthur 100 shares of $10 par stock—marked "fully paid"—in exchange for property worth only $300. Can Union require Arthur to pay an additional $700 upon discovering the actual value of the property? _____

100. Same facts as above. Assume that in March, one month before the transaction between Union and Arthur, Creditor Cal extended $1,000 credit to Union. Assume further that in June, following the transaction between Union and Arthur, Creditor Cora extended $1,000 credit to Union. Union has now become insolvent.

    a. Can Cal sue Arthur for $700? _____

    b. Can Cora? _____

101. Same facts. Assume that Arthur, in May, sold his shares to Amos, who did not know of the watering.

    a. Under the majority view, can Cora still sue Arthur in July? _____

    b. Can she sue Amos? _____

102. Same facts. If both Arthur and the directors of Union believed in good faith that Arthur's property *was* worth $1,000 when it was exchanged for stock, is Arthur's liability changed? _____

PROMOTERS

103. Promoters Peter and Paul of Acme Corp. sell a warehouse to Acme that they bought for $30,000 and that has a fair market value of $40,000. In exchange for the property, they receive 5,000 shares of $10 par stock.

    a. If Peter and Paul have not made full disclosure as to the amount of their profit, may Acme rescind? _____

    b. If Acme chooses to sue for damages, how much will it recover? _____

104. Assume the same facts as above except that the stock received by Peter and Paul is **no-par stock**. If Acme chooses to sue for damages, how much will it recover? _____

105. Assume the same facts except that Peter and Paul were the **sole shareholders** at the time of the transaction.

   a. If only 5,000 shares have been authorized, does the corporation have a cause of action at common law? _____

   b. If the corporation has an authorized capital of 10,000 shares, and the issuance of the remaining 5,000 shares is planned as part of the original capitalization, will the corporation have a cause of action after the other shares are issued? _____

PREEMPTIVE RIGHTS

106. Did common law preemptive rights protect a stockholder against the dilution of her control by **any** new share issuances? _____

107. When a shareholder's preemptive rights have been violated by an issue of shares, his only remedy is to seek damages from the corporation. True or false? _____

UNDERWRITING

108. Can underwriters be held subject to the same liabilities as issuers for fraud in the sale of securities under federal law? _____

STATUTES REGULATING ISSUANCE OF SHARES

109. Can state blue sky laws validly require disclosure of information in connection with the issuance and sale of securities that is **not** required under applicable federal securities laws? _____

110. Can the Securities and Exchange Commission, under the 1933 Act, veto a proposed stock issuance if it is economically unsound? _____

111. Which of the following issuances or transfers, if any, are exempt from the registration requirements of the Securities Act of 1933? _____

   (A) Mr. Smith inherits 100 shares of X stock and sells them to his neighbor.

   (B) Y Corp. offers a new issue to only 20 persons, all of whom live in the same state and have financial experience and access to full information about Y.

   (C) Same facts as (B), but the 20 persons live in four different states.

   (D) Same facts as (B), but two of the offerees are brokers who intend to resell the stock to the public.

112. Can the purchaser of shares issued under a "private offering" exemption ever sell these shares **without registration?** _____

113. Orange Corp. knowingly files a false registration statement containing material misstatements. Ralph, without knowledge of the misstatements, buys 1,000 shares from Orange at the issuing price of $10. The stock goes down to $7 per share. Ralph promptly files suit.

    a. Is Ralph entitled to judgment against Orange, its directors, its underwriter, and the accountant who certified the financial portion of the registration statement? _____

    b. Must Ralph prove the elements of common law fraud? _____

    c. Must Ralph prove reliance on the misstatements? _____

114. Same facts as above except that Ralph, immediately after purchasing the shares, sold them to Cynthia at $10 per share. The price then went down to $7.

    a. Does Cynthia have a cause of action against Orange under section 11? _____

    b. Is Cynthia entitled to either rescission *or* damages from Orange? _____

115. Assume Orange had sold its stock by use of a material misstatement *other than* in its registration statement. Under section 12 of the 1933 Act—

    a. Does Ralph have a cause of action against Orange? _____

    b. Does Cynthia? _____

116. The purchaser of securities that were exempt from the registration requirements of the 1933 Act may nevertheless recover under the Act for material misstatements or omissions in connection with the purchase of such securities. True or false? _____

DIVIDENDS

117. Can common stockholders, by majority vote, compel payment of dividends, *if* sufficient funds are available? _____

118. Under most statutes, may dividends generally be paid out of stated capital if there are current net profits? _____

119. Corporation A sold 100,000 shares of its $20 par stock for $23 per share. Can the $300,000 later be available for dividends in most states? _____

120. Corporation B reduced the par value of its 100,000 shares of common stock from $12 to $10. Can it distribute the $200,000 as dividends in most states? _____

121. Corporation C owned real property with a book value of $200,000 based on its acquisition cost. The property is now worth $500,000. Can Corporation C pay dividends from the $300,000 increased value? _____

122. Can a director who votes for an illegal dividend be held **personally** liable for the amount distributed? _____

123. The directors of Acme Corporation all voted for an unlawful dividend, rendering Acme insolvent. Are the shareholder-recipients liable? _____

REDEMPTION AND REPURCHASES

124. If funds are available, does a corporation always have inherent power to redeem its shares? _____

125. Are redeemed shares ordinarily held as "treasury stock"? _____

126. May a corporation **repurchase** its shares on a selective basis (from certain shareholders and not from others)? _____

127. If a corporation contracts to repurchase its shares on an installment payment basis, is it enough that it has adequate funds available from a legal source on the date the contract is made (as distinguished from the dates each installment comes due)? _____

128. The directors of Gold Corp., knowing that shareholder X was planning a fight to unseat them, authorized the repurchase of X's shares at a premium. As long as a lawful source of funds was available, was their action proper? _____

FUNDAMENTAL CHANGES

129. The boards of directors of Red Corp. and Blue Corp. adopt a plan to merge Red into Blue. Neither corporation had any prior relationship with the other. Which, if any, of the following statements is correct under most statutes? _____

   (A) The merger must be approved by shareholder votes of **both** Red and Blue.

   (B) The debts and contract obligations of Red are automatically assumed by Blue upon completion of the merger.

   (C) Red is automatically dissolved upon completion of the merger.

130. Same facts as above. Assume that both Red Corp. and Blue Corp. had dissenting shareholders who complied with all the statutorily required procedures.

   a. Do the dissenting shareholders of both Red and Blue have appraisal rights? _____

   b. Can a shareholder who voted for the merger nevertheless exercise appraisal rights? _____

   c. Is the "fair value" for a dissenter's shares always the recognized market price at the effective date of the merger? _____

131. Green Corp. owns 90% of the stock of Brown Corp.; two individual shareholders each own 5% of Brown.

    a. If both boards of directors approve a "short-form" merger of Brown into Green, must both corporations' shareholders also approve? _____

    b. Do dissenting shareholders of Green have appraisal rights? _____

    c. Can Green eliminate the two minority shareholders by giving them cash instead of Green stock? _____

132. The board of directors of Gray Corp. contemplates a sale of "substantially all its assets" to Black Corp. for cash. Which of the following statements, if any, is correct under most statutes? _____

    (A) The shareholders of Gray must approve.

    (B) The shareholders of Black must approve.

    (C) In defining "substantially all" of Gray's assets, the determining factor is the percentage of gross assets to be sold.

133. The board of directors of Day Corp. wishes to acquire Night Corp., but fears opposition from a strong minority of its own shareholders. Day offers to buy Night's assets in exchange for Day stock with the proviso that Night will then vote on a plan of dissolution.

    a. Can the minority shareholders of Day object that they had no opportunity to vote on the transaction? _____

    b. If the sale has been consummated, can it be set aside? _____

134. If a board of directors unanimously approves a change in the articles of incorporation, is shareholder approval ordinarily also required? _____

135. May the state bring an action for involuntary dissolution of a corporation for abuse of its corporate authority? _____

136. Is a bankrupt corporation automatically dissolved? _____

137. If, after dissolution, directors conduct further business not reasonably incident to liquidation, can they be held personally liable for corporate debts? _____

138. If the assets of a dissolved corporation have been distributed while a creditor's timely claims are unsatisfied, the creditor can recover from the shareholder-distributees. True or false? _____

139. If controlling shareholders materially misrepresented the facts of a proposed merger so as to advantage themselves, can a dissenting shareholder exercise her appraisal rights under state law **and also** bring an action under federal securities acts? _____

140. Acme Corp. makes a tender offer to buy 60% of the shares of Star Corp. for cash.

    a.   Must the shareholders of both corporations approve? _____

    b.   After acquiring the Star shares, may Acme dissolve Star? _____

    c.   Must Acme disclose its plans for Star at the time it makes the tender offer? _____

ANSWERS TO REVIEW QUESTIONS

1. **NO** — Shareholder liability is usually limited to the amount of the investment, and only the corporation is liable on its debts. [§2]

2. **NO** — Except in extraordinary circumstances, shareholders have **no** power to manage and control; these powers are vested in the board of directors and the officers acting under the board's authority. This is a major difference between corporations and partnerships, because partners do have the right to participate in management. [§§4, 15]

3. **YES** — A corporation is a separate entity, whose existence can be perpetual and is unaffected by changes in the owners of its shares. This is another major difference between a corporation and a partnership. In a partnership, the death, withdrawal, or insolvency of any partner normally terminates the partnership. [§§5, 11-12]

4. **NO** — A corporation is a legal entity, but a partnership is not, even though the law sometimes treats partnerships as if they were legal entities. [§§1, 8]

5. **NO** — A limited partner, whose financial liability is limited to the amount of his investment, **may not** participate in the management of the business. [§§20, 24-25]

6. **YES** — In determining whether to "pierce the corporate veil" (*i.e.,* disregard the corporate entity and impose liability on shareholders for corporate obligations), the commingling of assets (treating corporate assets as if they were the shareholders' own assets) and lack of corporate formalities (no directors' or shareholders' meetings, and no corporate records) are major factors considered by the court. Both suggest the corporation is merely the "alter ego" of the shareholders and should be disregarded. [§§27-28, 30-31]

7. **DEPENDS** — Although DEF **was** maintained as a separate entity, some courts would permit creditors to disregard corporateness and reach the shareholders because DEF was undercapitalized; *i.e.,* Don, Ed, and Frank should have reasonably anticipated that $750 was inadequate capitalization to meet the obligations of DEF. [§§33-34]

8. **NO** — When this doctrine is applicable, the corporation's debts to shareholders are **subordinated** to its debts to outside creditors, but no additional personal liability is imposed on shareholders. (In effect, the debt owed to the shareholders is treated as additional investment capital.) [§§38-40]

9. **NO (both questions)** — The rule that the corporate form may be disregarded to avoid injustice is for the benefit of third parties, not the corporation; therefore, a corporation generally may not assert in its own name a claim or defense that belongs to a shareholder. (Note, however, that Beulah could **assign** her claim to XYZ Corp., in which case, it could assert same.) [§37]

10.a. **GENERALLY NO** — Although a few states require a specific statement, most do not, and some statutes (*e.g.,* Delaware) permit a purpose as general as to engage in any lawful activity for which a corporation may be organized. [§§44-46]

b. **NO** — Statutes commonly require the articles of incorporation to indicate the number of shares **authorized**. The number to be issued is usually decided at a post-incorporation meeting of the board of directors. [§§44, 48-49]

11.	**NO**	Incorporators file the articles and, if the statute does not provide that the initial directors be named in the articles, the incorporators hold an organizational meeting at which bylaws are adopted and directors are elected to serve until the first shareholders' meeting. [§§47-48]
12.	**NO**	The filing of the articles in proper form is required to create the corporation, but bylaws are usually adopted at a post-incorporation organizational meeting. Bylaw provisions may be regulated by statute, however. [§§43, 48-49]
13.	**(C)**	On the facts, it appears that White Corp., lacking sufficient compliance for "de jure" status, has met the conditions for "de facto" status—good faith, a colorable attempt to comply with a statute under which the corporation could have been formed, and actual use of corporate powers. Under modern law, the status of a "de facto" corporation can usually be challenged *only* by the state. In contrast, complete compliance with statutory requirements creates a "de jure" corporation, whose corporate status cannot be challenged by anyone. [§§53-54, 57-58]
14.	**FALSE**	Both the shareholders of a nominal corporation, having claimed corporate status in a transaction with a third party, and a third party who has dealt with the enterprise as if it were a corporation may be estopped from denying corporateness. [§§60-61]
15.	**DEPENDS**	Jurisdictions with statutes based on the old Model Act have abolished the de facto doctrine. However, under the Revised Model Act, only persons who *knew* there was no incorporation are barred from asserting de facto status. [§§68-69]
16.	**NO**	Even under the American rule, the corporation is not liable on promoters' contracts, unless the corporation adopts the contract. [§§75-80]
17.	**SPLIT**	Under the English rule, even corporate ratification will not create contractual liability (but the corporation may be liable in quasi-contract for any benefits obtained). Under the American rule, contractual liability *is* created by either express or implied ratification. [§§75-80]
18.	**YES**	Under both the English and American rules, Central may choose to enforce the contract. [§81]
19.	**DEPENDS**	If Perry had expressly disclaimed individual liability, he cannot be held. Otherwise, most courts will allow Manufacturer to enforce the contract against Perry, who may then have a right to indemnification by Central. [§§82-84]
20.	**YES**	Under modern law, courts broadly construe a corporation's implied power to do what is ***reasonably necessary to achieve its express purposes***, unless otherwise prohibited. Moreover, modern statutes confer many powers on corporations. [§§86-87]
21.	**NO**	Because participation in a partnership involves an impermissible delegation of managerial responsibility, in the past most courts held that a corporation could not enter into a partnership, absent specific authorization. (Modern statutes now specifically authorize this.) [§90]
22.	**YES**	Under the modern view, such gifts, if ***reasonable*** are permitted even without any showing of a direct benefit to the corporation. [§§91-97]
23.	**YES**	Any action outside corporate purposes and powers may be "ultra vires," regardless of its legality. [§98]

24.	**NO**	The corporation cannot rely on a disclaimer of its legal power to commit the particular act to avoid liability. [§§101-102]
25.a.	**YES (modern law)**	At common law, neither party could enforce an ultra vires executory contract. Under modern statutes, ultra vires is not a defense to an executory *or* executed contract. Under some circumstances, however, a shareholder may seek to *enjoin* performance. [§§104, 109-110]
b.	**NO**	The rule is the same at common law and under modern statutes. A fully performed contract, although ultra vires, is not subject to rescission. [§§105, 110]
c.	**NO (modern law)**	Under modern law, the ultra vires defense is *disfavored* even when one party has performed, but most statutes permit recovery in quasi-contract from the nonperforming party. At common law, the majority view denied the ultra vires defense to the nonperforming party in such a case. [§§107-108, 110]
26.	**NO**	Such management decisions are within the powers of the directors; shareholders have no *direct* control over the management of ordinary corporate affairs including the hiring and firing of corporate officers. (Some statutes, however, permit powers of management and control to be exercised by shareholders in a *close corporation*.) [§§118, 122, 127-129]
27.	**NO**	Most close corporation statutes impose additional requirements, such as identification as a close corporation in the articles of incorporation and restrictions on the transfer of shares. [§§120, 123-126]
28.a.	**YES**	Unlike an ordinary corporation, in which such an agreement would be deemed an improper infringement of the powers of the directors, written shareholder management agreements are generally permitted in close corporations. [§128]
b.	**YES**	Statutes frequently require a "conspicuous" notation of the existence of the agreement on a share certificate of a close corporation. If such a notation is present, a transferee takes subject to the agreement. [§§131, 136]
29.	**YES**	Many statutes authorize single-member boards, especially where there is only one shareholder. A few statutes authorize single directors for all corporations. [§138]
30.	**DEPENDS**	Under common law and the majority view, the board cannot remove a director, with or without cause. However, some modern statutes permit removal for cause. [§152]
31.	**FALSE**	However, unless prohibited by statute, the articles of incorporation or the bylaws may prescribe any reasonable qualifications for directors—including share ownership. [§139]
32.	**YES**	Unlike common law, which permitted removal only for cause, many modern statutes generally permit removal, without cause, by a vote of shareholders. [§151]
33.a.	**YES**	A director holds office until the term of office expires *and* a successor is elected and qualified. [§146]
b.	**YES**	Absent a prohibition in the articles of incorporation, a board may make a contract that extends beyond the directors' term of office. A future XYZ board could remove the general manager, but he would then have a cause of action for breach of contract. [§§148, 195]

c.	**YES**	It is common for a board to authorize day-to-day management by such a committee, although there are limitations on the committee's power to make certain decisions of a fundamental nature (*e.g.*, dividends, mergers, etc.). [§§162-164]
d.	**NO**	Fiduciary duties of directors require that directors be able to exercise free discretion in making corporate decisions. (Exceptions have been created for close corporations.) [§166]
e.	**YES**	Modern statutes reduce required formalities and permit waiver of notice before *or* after an unscheduled meeting. Furthermore, an action taken by a majority of the directors present is binding, *if* there was a quorum. A quorum is ordinarily a majority of the authorized number of directors. [§§156-158]
34.	**FALSE**	Generally, a director is not entitled to compensation for ordinary services as a director, unless compensation is provided for by the articles or by board resolution passed *before* services were rendered. However, a director may be entitled to compensation for authorized *extraordinary* services and for services as an officer or employee. [§§167-169]
35.a.	**PROBABLY NOT**	The business judgment rule protects a director who has made an erroneous policy decision in good faith *and* in the exercise of diligence. In the majority view, it does not protect a director who has acted negligently. [§§175-178]
b.	**YES**	Since the directors' action *caused* the loss, they are personally liable, and the liability is joint and several. Note that some statutes permit limitation or elimination of director liability absent bad faith, intentional misconduct, or illegal acts. [§§181-183]
c.	**NO**	If the director has recorded her dissent, then she is not liable. [§182]
d.	**YES**	Lack of compensation is ordinarily no defense. The director's fiduciary duty is not diminished by the fact that service is without pay. [§184]
e.	**YES**	*If* the reliance was reasonable *and if* the report or advice was within the competence of the person providing it, the directors have a defense to liability. [§§186-187]
36.	**FALSE**	Under most statutes, the major officers of a corporation are elected by the board, although some statutes permit election of officers by shareholders. [§195]
37.	**PROBABLY NOT**	The president of a corporation, by majority view, has *apparent authority* to make decisions and bind the corporation in transactions that are part of the ordinary course of the corporation's business. Hiring division managers is probably within that category. [§§203-204]
38.a.	**YES**	Most states permit an interested director to be counted toward a quorum (although a contrary result would have been reached at common law). [§§209-210]
b.	**NO**	Neither at common law nor under most statutes may an "interested" director's vote be counted on the transaction in which he has a personal interest. [§§209-210, 228]
39.a.	**NO**	Since there was full disclosure, most courts would require a showing of fundamental unfairness to the corporation. However, at common law such a contract was automatically voidable by the corporation. [§§211-216]

| b. | **YES** | The burden of proof is generally on the interested director, who must prove the fairness of the transaction. However, the burden may be shifted to the plaintiff in cases where the shareholders have ratified the contract. [§§217, 221-222] |

| c. | **NO** | Assuming full disclosure, unanimous shareholder ratification will preclude a suit by the corporation. However, if the corporation is insolvent, a creditor's suit may be possible. [§219] |

| d. | **DEPENDS** | Ratification by a disinterested majority may estop the corporation or at least shift the burden of proof to the plaintiff. Courts are split as to the effectiveness of an attempted ratification by an interested majority of the shareholders. [§§220-227] |

| 40. | **POSSIBLY** | The difference between price and fair market value would be the *usual* measure of damages. However, if Donald had purchased the building in order to resell it to Acme at an excessive price, some courts would penalize him by fixing damages at the difference between Donald's acquisition cost and the amount paid to him by Acme. Some courts may also order the interested director to repay his salary earned during the breach period, and others may assess punitive damages. [§§232-236] |

| 41. | **YES** | Modern statutes generally permit transactions between two corporations with interlocking directorates, *if* the transactions are fair and there is full disclosure. At common law, however, a transaction between Red and Blue was voidable at the option of either. [§§238-241] |

| 42.a. | **NO** | Since Textile was already considering the offer, this would be a clear usurpation of corporate opportunity and a breach of Winnie's fiduciary duty of loyalty. [§245] |

| b. | **DEPENDS** | Some courts hold that Textile's inability frees Winnie to take advantage of the opportunity. However, some courts would bar Winnie, on the rationale that her duty is to attempt to find the necessary financing for Textile. [§§251-252] |

| c. | **YES** | If Textile, fully informed, refuses the opportunity, there is no conflict of interest to prevent Winnie from proceeding. [§254] |

| d. | **YES** | Textile may compel a transfer of the machine and an accounting for any interim income or profits. If Winnie buys while the offer is a corporate opportunity and then sells the machine to Textile, Textile may recover Winnie's entire profit. [§§256-257] |

| e. | **NO** | Winnie may have to transmit the offer to both corporations. If she offers it to only one, she may be liable to the other. [§258] |

| 43.a. | **SPLIT** | Most states would not permit Herbert's vote to be counted to make up a majority vote, although some statutes provide otherwise. The effect of shareholder ratification would be the same as in any other case of an "interested director" transaction. [§260] |

| b. | **NO** | As long as the salary is reasonable, the fact that it is above market value for the services will not preclude application of the business judgment rule to protect both Herbert and the board of directors. The directors may, in good faith, believe that Herbert is worth more than an average secretary. [§§264-265] |

c.	**NO**	As long as the total compensation bears a reasonable relationship to the value of Herbert's services, there is no "waste." And, note that under such an arrangement, Herbert's interests would be more likely to coincide with Blank's interests than to conflict with them. [§§267, 275-278]
d.	**PROBABLY**	On general contract principles, past services are not ordinarily a legally sufficient consideration for the payment by Blank. A contrary result might be reached, however, if there was consideration (*e.g.,* the retroactive increase was expressly conditioned upon Herbert's remaining in the position for a specified period); or if it could be shown that the increase fell within the business judgment rule. [§§270-272]
44.	**NO**	The common law majority view was that no duty was owed. However, exceptions were recognized in many cases where "special facts" compelled disclosure (*e.g.,* in cases involving face-to-face dealing). [§§280-282]
45.	**YES**	Section 10(b) and rule 10b-5 apply to the purchase and sale of *all* securities. The only jurisdictional limitation to section 10(b) is the requirement that the "purchase or sale" must be effected by an instrumentality of interstate commerce. [§287]
46.a.	**YES**	Section 10(b) extends to any purchase or sale. "Sale" is construed broadly so as to include an original issuance by a corporation. [§§287, 315-319, 322]
b.	**YES**	If the corporation-seller does not act, a shareholder who meets the relevant procedural requirements can bring a derivative suit under 10b-5. [§323]
c.	**NO**	If there is neither a purchase nor sale of any *security,* the Act does not apply. [§314]
47.	**NO**	Federal courts have *exclusive* jurisdiction over rule 10b-5 actions. *Compare:* If plaintiff sues in federal court, he may, under the doctrine of pendent jurisdiction, join his state law claim in the federal action. [§§288-289]
48.	**YES**	"Purchase or sale" is broadly defined. The term includes the exchange of shares which occurs in connection with a merger. [§317]
49.a.	**YES**	Davis was a purchaser. It is not necessary that the defendant be either a purchaser or a seller. Nor is privity between defendant and the injured purchaser required. [§§313-314]
b.	**NO**	Davis is limited to damages, because the defendant corporation was not the seller. *If* Davis had bought from Old, rescission would be available. [§§329, 371-372]
c.	**NO**	Edward was neither a purchaser nor a seller within the meaning of the Act. "Aborted" sales are not sufficient. [§314]
50.a.	**DEPENDS**	If New Corp. is publicly held, Thomas can recover damages, but probably cannot rescind, since he can replace his stock. However, rescission is permissible if New Corp. is a close corporation. [§§366-370]
b.	**YES**	A tippee who knows or should know that the tipper breached his fiduciary duty to the corporation is liable under rule 10b-5. A tipper breaches that fiduciary duty by communicating inside information for personal gain. Tips to friends are treated as benefiting the tipper because they are the same as trades by the insider followed by gifts of the profits. [§§334-335]

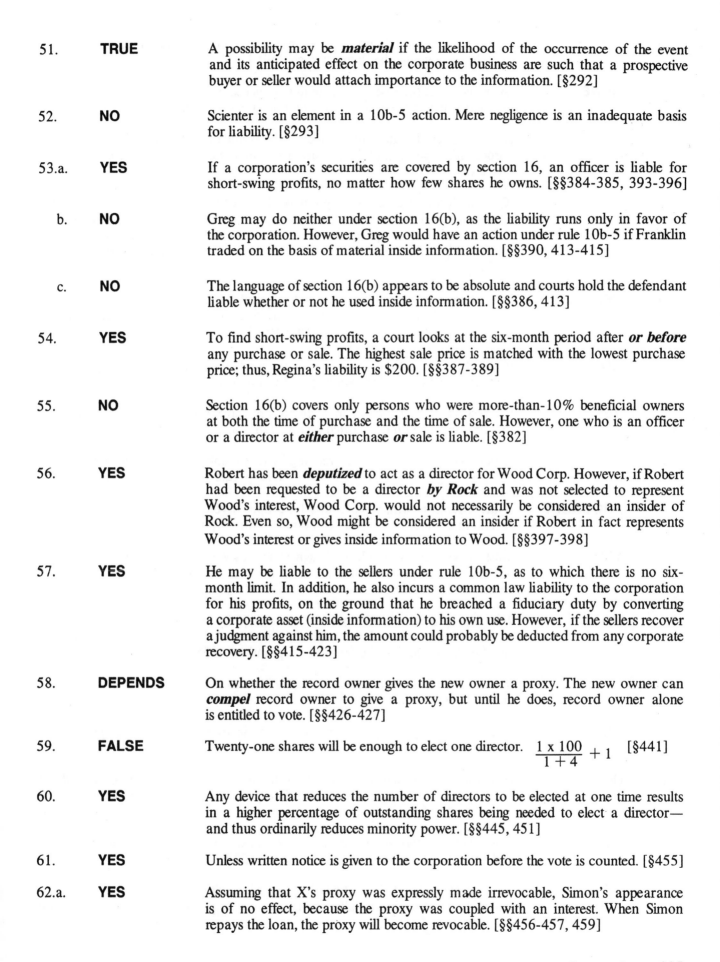

51. **TRUE**   A possibility may be ***material*** if the likelihood of the occurrence of the event and its anticipated effect on the corporate business are such that a prospective buyer or seller would attach importance to the information. [§292]

52. **NO**   Scienter is an element in a 10b-5 action. Mere negligence is an inadequate basis for liability. [§293]

53.a. **YES**   If a corporation's securities are covered by section 16, an officer is liable for short-swing profits, no matter how few shares he owns. [§§384-385, 393-396]

  b. **NO**   Greg may do neither under section 16(b), as the liability runs only in favor of the corporation. However, Greg would have an action under rule 10b-5 if Franklin traded on the basis of material inside information. [§§390, 413-415]

  c. **NO**   The language of section 16(b) appears to be absolute and courts hold the defendant liable whether or not he used inside information. [§§386, 413]

54. **YES**   To find short-swing profits, a court looks at the six-month period after ***or before*** any purchase or sale. The highest sale price is matched with the lowest purchase price; thus, Regina's liability is $200. [§§387-389]

55. **NO**   Section 16(b) covers only persons who were more-than-10% beneficial owners at both the time of purchase and the time of sale. However, one who is an officer or a director at ***either*** purchase ***or*** sale is liable. [§382]

56. **YES**   Robert has been ***deputized*** to act as a director for Wood Corp. However, if Robert had been requested to be a director ***by Rock*** and was not selected to represent Wood's interest, Wood Corp. would not necessarily be considered an insider of Rock. Even so, Wood might be considered an insider if Robert in fact represents Wood's interest or gives inside information to Wood. [§§397-398]

57. **YES**   He may be liable to the sellers under rule 10b-5, as to which there is no six-month limit. In addition, he also incurs a common law liability to the corporation for his profits, on the ground that he breached a fiduciary duty by converting a corporate asset (inside information) to his own use. However, if the sellers recover a judgment against him, the amount could probably be deducted from any corporate recovery. [§§415-423]

58. **DEPENDS**   On whether the record owner gives the new owner a proxy. The new owner can ***compel*** record owner to give a proxy, but until he does, record owner alone is entitled to vote. [§§426-427]

59. **FALSE**   Twenty-one shares will be enough to elect one director. $\dfrac{1 \times 100}{1 + 4} + 1$ [§441]

60. **YES**   Any device that reduces the number of directors to be elected at one time results in a higher percentage of outstanding shares being needed to elect a director— and thus ordinarily reduces minority power. [§§445, 451]

61. **YES**   Unless written notice is given to the corporation before the vote is counted. [§455]

62.a. **YES**   Assuming that X's proxy was expressly made irrevocable, Simon's appearance is of no effect, because the proxy was coupled with an interest. When Simon repays the loan, the proxy will become revocable. [§§456-457, 459]

b.	**NO**	Simon may revoke Y's proxy by express notification, by executing a new proxy, or as here, by voting the shares himself. [§454]
63.	**NONE**	(A) is incorrect because the rule requiring inclusion of shareholder proposals with management proxy solicitations does not apply to elections of directors. [§471]

(B) is incorrect because management may exclude proposals that are beyond the corporation's power to effect or are not significantly related to the corporation's business. [§471]

(C) is incorrect because a proposal need not be included if it purports to bind the board on a matter that is within their discretion, and not that of the shareholders. A purely advisory proposal, however, would probably be upheld. Note that the burden of proof is on management whenever it excludes a shareholder proposal. [§471] |
64.a.	**YES**	If misstatements or omissions are not material, there is no violation. A statement is material if the omitted fact would have assumed actual significance in the deliberations of the reasonable shareholder. [§§475-477]
b.	**NO**	If plaintiff proves that the misstatements were material, courts will assume that they may have affected the voting process and outcome. [§478]
c.	**YES**	Fairness is no defense when shareholders have been misled. Fully informed shareholders might have rejected even a "fair" proposal. [§482]
65.a.	**YES**	Management has the right to recover its reasonable expenses, whether or not it wins, as long as the controversy is over corporate policy, not personnel. [§488]
b.	**PROBABLY**	*If* the insurgents win, some courts have upheld voluntary reimbursement on the ground that a benefit has been conferred on the corporation. [§489]
66.	**YES**	Most modern cases uphold such agreements as valid contracts or as irrevocable proxies. However, some courts will not grant specific enforcement in case of breach unless all shareholders were parties. [§§493, 499]
67.	**NO**	When the agreement is not unanimous, the majority view is that it is unenforceable as an infringement on the discretion of the board. However, recent statutes and case law liberalize this rule for close corporations. [§§504-509]
68.a.	**NO**	A voting trust is usually irrevocable for its life, unless there is unanimous agreement to terminate it. [§513]
b.	**NO**	Statutes generally limit the duration of voting trusts. Most statutes provide for extensions. [§514]
c.	**NO**	Unless there is explicit authorization in the trust agreement, most courts will not allow the trustee to vote on extraordinary matters such as dissolution of the corporation. [§516]
69.a.	**YES**	Most statutes authorize restrictions on the transfer of shares *if* they are reasonable and are not total restraints on alienability. [§§524, 529]
b.	**NO**	A corporate right of first refusal in connection with a restriction on transfer of shares does not ordinarily alter the limitations on proper sources for repurchase of shares. [§534]

c.	**NO**	Absent a specific provision, restrictions may not be held to apply to involuntary transfers. Generally, stock transfer restrictions are narrowly construed. [§538]
d.	**YES**	A corporation may continue to recognize the transferor as the owner, *if the transferee had notice* (as here). [§§539-541]
70.	**NO**	Under the U.C.C., unless a lien is shown on the face of a share certificate, the corporation cannot enforce it against a bona fide purchaser who lacks notice of any restriction. The corporation must transfer the shares and recognize the new owner. [§§539-542]
71.	**NO**	The right was not absolute. The burden of proof was on the shareholder to show that the inspection was for a proper purpose. (Under most modern statutes, the burden is on the corporation to show an improper purpose.) [§§544-545]
72.	**NO**	Today, shareholder inspection rights are in most cases statutory. Considered fundamental, they cannot be eliminated by the articles. [§545]
73.	**YES**	The purpose is proper because it is related to the shareholder's legitimate interests in the corporation. [§§547, 549]
74.	**YES**	If the dividend distribution was designed to serve the interests of the majority shareholder and is harmful to the corporation, the controlling shareholder has breached his fiduciary duty to the minority shareholder. [§564]
75.	**TRUE**	*All* shareholders of closely held corporations owe each other the same duty of utmost good faith and loyalty that is owed by partners to each other. [§565]
76.	**NO**	Absent fraud, knowledge of purchaser's plan to loot, or other unfairness in the transaction, the majority view is that sale of control at a premium is not in itself a breach of a fiduciary duty. The seller need not account to the minority for the premium he has received. [§§572, 580-583]
77.	**YES**	This practice is permitted as long as the stock interest is large enough to give the purchaser effective control, so that he could have effected the changes immediately himself. However, the "sale" of directorships would be invalid if not connected with the sale of a stock interest large enough to carry effective voting control. [§§576-579]
78.a.	**PROBABLY**	If the seller of controlling shares knows or has reason to know that the transferee plans to deal unfairly with the corporation, the seller has breached her fiduciary duty. A price far above fair value should probably have put Sally on notice of Louis's intent. [§§583-586]
b.	**NO**	A seller who has breached her duty is liable to the minority shareholders either for their portion of the premium *or* for the actual damages caused to the corporation by the buyer, whichever is larger. [§587]
79.	**FALSE**	The critical questions are *who* suffered the injury—*i.e.,* the corporation or the shareholders—and to whom the breached duty ran. [§595]
80.a.	**YES**	A potential derivative suit plaintiff must first exhaust corporate remedies and a demand on the board of directors is an essential element of the cause of action, unless the shareholder can show that such a demand would have been futile. [§§599-601]

b.	**NO**	If a disinterested board has, in good faith, refused to act, courts will protect its exercise of business judgment and bar the derivative suit. [§604]
c.	**SPLIT**	Some states require demand only on the board of directors. Others require a demand on the shareholders if the act in question was within their power to ratify, but excuse the demand if such ratification were not possible. [§§614-615]
d.	**PROBABLY NOT**	If disinterested shareholders have refused to sue, they have, in effect, ratified the board's decision. If such ratification was within shareholder power, and was reasonable, the derivative suit is barred. [§622]
81.	**NO**	Contemporaneous share ownership is the *usual* requirement in most states. However, even in these states exceptions exist for a plaintiff who subsequently acquired his shares by operation of law (*e.g.*, inheritance), and some statutes waive the requirement when serious injustice would otherwise result. [§§625-629]
82.	**PROBABLY NOT**	If the sole shareholder is disqualified, equity may also bar suit by the corporation itself. [§630]
83.	**NO**	The director's interest is adverse to that of the corporation, so each must ordinarily have separate counsel. [§636]
84.	**YES**	The corporation *must* be joined as a party. The corporation is a defendant, even though its interests are ordinarily adverse to those of the other defendants. [§638]
85.	**YES**	Even though such suits are equitable in nature, the seventh amendment right to trial by jury applies to those issues upon which the corporation, as a plaintiff, would have been entitled to a jury. [§647]
86.	**NO**	Even where statutes provide that the defendant corporation, if it wins, may automatically move against the posted security, the court determines the amount of the award (usually limited to its reasonable costs and attorneys' fees). In some states, the security is available for defendant's costs only if the court finds that the plaintiff acted unreasonably in bringing suit. [§656]
87.	**YES**	Recovery usually goes to the corporation. However, if the corporation has been dissolved or if a corporate recovery would benefit shareholders not entitled to participate in it, the court may award payment directly to the innocent shareholders. [§§666, 671-673]
88.	**NO**	A judgment on the merits in a derivative suit is res judicata as to both the corporation and other shareholders. [§665]
89.a.	**YES**	The corporation must ordinarily reimburse the plaintiff because he has obtained either a "common fund" or some other "substantial benefit" for the corporation. He is entitled to his expenses, including attorneys' fees. [§674]
b.	**NO**	A director who has lost on the merits is not entitled to indemnification for the liability imposed. Otherwise, the recovery by the corporation would merely go right back to the defendant. [§§685-688]
c.	**YES**	In most states, reimbursement of a winning defendant is discretionary with the board, but some statutes require the corporation to reimburse a defendant who wins on the merits in a derivative suit. [§§680-681]

90.	**YES**	Many statutes permit such insurance, but they differ as to whether the coverage may extend to **any** liability or expenses. [§§689-691]
91.	**NO**	Any preferences must be **expressly set forth** in the articles. Otherwise, all classes of shares will be treated alike. [§§698, 704]
92.a.	**NO**	Unless the payment of dividends is expressly made mandatory, payment is within the discretion of the directors. If no dividend is declared on the preferred, however, no dividend may be paid on the common stock. [§§705-706]
b.	**YES**	Since the preferred shares are cumulative, both the current preferred dividend **and** all arrears take precedence over the common stock in any year. [§§705-706]
93.	**NO**	No further shares can be issued unless there is an amendment to the articles of incorporation authorizing a larger number of shares. The board of directors alone cannot amend the articles of incorporation; a shareholder vote is required. [§§713, 1034]
94.	**NO**	Treasury stock is considered as "issued" while in the hands of the corporation. The repurchase by the corporation does not affect the number of shares the corporation is authorized to issue. [§717]
95.	**NO (majority)**	Most courts at common law hold that, until the corporation comes into existence and accepts the subscription, a subscription is no more than a revocable continuing offer. A minority is contra, holding that the subscription is a binding contract among subscribers to become shareholders. [§§722-724]
96.	**YES**	Once accepted, the subscription is a binding contract, with no implied condition that the corporation will be solvent. And, Star's creditors may also enforce the contract as an asset of the corporation. [§§730-731]
97.	**(B) ONLY**	(A) is not lawful consideration because most statutes require that shares be issued in exchange only for money paid, property acquired, or labor done. [§733] (B) is lawful in most states, although some courts rquire that the "labor done" be done **after** the corporation is in existence (most, however, do not). [§733] (C) is not lawful because executory promises—whether for money, property, or future services—are not legal consideration for the issuance of shares under **most** statutes. [§734]
98.a.	**GENERALLY NO**	Except in special situations, a corporation may generally not sell its shares for less than par value, although the par value price may include underwriting commissions. Shares sold for less than par are "watered." [§§740-742]
b.	**YES**	Corporations frequently issue "low par" stock to provide financial flexibility, to create "paid-in" surplus, and to avoid watered stock problems. [§740]
99.	**NO**	Having issued the shares as "fully paid," Union is estopped to seek the additional payment from Arthur. But if fraud is involved it may sue to **rescind**. [§746]
100.a.	**NO**	At least under the majority view, based on a "misrepresentation" theory, a prior creditor (Cal) could not have been misled by the issuance of watered stock and therefore cannot compel the issuee to make up the difference. Under the minority "trust fund" theory, Arthur is liable to Cal. [§§749-753]

b.	**YES**	Under both the misrepresentation theory and the trust fund theory, Arthur is liable to Cora, who was a subsequent creditor. (Some courts that follow the misrepresentation theory would require Cora to show reliance when she extended the credit.) [§§749-753]
101.a.	**YES**	Although Arthur no longer owns the stock, he remains liable to a subsequent creditor, because he was a party to the original "deception." [§754]
b.	**NO**	Amos, as a transferee without knowledge, was not a party to any deception of creditors and is therefore not liable. [§755]
102.	**YES**	Most courts apply a "good faith rule" to preclude watered stock liability when there is no intentional overvaluation of property being exchanged for stock. [§§756-758]
103.a.	**YES**	Promoters owe a fiduciary duty to the corporation. Hence, if the promoters did not make full disclosure (either to an independent board of directors, *or* to all existing shareholders and to persons known to be planning to become shareholders), rescission is a proper remedy. [§§766-768, 775-776]
b.	**$10,000 (most courts)**	Most courts limit recovery to the excess of the price paid for the property over its fair market value (here, $10,000). Under some circumstances (*e.g.,* promoter acquired property for purpose of selling it to contemplated corporation), courts may allow recovery of the difference between the amount paid by the promoter for the property and the amount paid to him by the corporation (here, $20,000). [§§777-779]
104.	**NOTHING**	Since no-par stock generally does not have a set value, no amount of damages could be proved (except if the no-par stock had been assigned a stated value, in which event the result would be the same as in the previous question). [§781]
105.a.	**NO**	Where the promoters were the sole shareholders, the common law view was that the corporation had no cause of action, since full "disclosure" had been made to all shareholders. [§§769-771]
b.	**YES**	Most courts allow suit by the corporation on the rationale that the later, but planned-for, subscribers are among the stockholders to whom disclosure must be made. [§§772-774]
106.	**NO**	Preemptive rights at common law generally do not extend to the issuance of shares for property or services, the reissue of treasury shares, or the issue of previously authorized shares. [§§790-797]
107.	**FALSE**	The shareholder may seek to compel issuance of additional shares to himself or to have the new shares canceled if their holders have participated in the wrongdoing and shares are not available on the market. [§799]
108.	**YES**	Although underwriters, like issuers, have a "due diligence" defense. [§§866-869] Additionally, full disclosure of arrangements between issuers and underwriters is required by federal and some state laws. [§809]
109.	**YES**	The federal securities acts expressly do *not* preempt the field. Therefore, when issuing shares, a corporation must often satisfy both state and federal requirements. [§810]

| 110. | **NO** | The thrust of the 1933 Act is informational—*i.e.,* to compel disclosure, usually through the registration requirements. The SEC neither approves nor disapproves of proposed issuances. [§818] |

111. **(A), (B) and (C)**

(A) is exempt under the "casual sale" exemption. [§834]

(B) is exempt under the "private placement" exemption, assuming that each purchaser acquires the stock as an investment and signs a letter of intent to that effect; and possibly under the "intrastate offering" exemption as well. [§§839-850]

(C) is still exempt. The "private placement" exemption and the "intrastate offering" exemption are separate. Failure to qualify for one does not prevent qualification for the other. [§§839-850]

(D) is not exempt. The "private placement" exemption requires an intent by purchasers to acquire the securities *as an investment* (not for resale). [§842]

112. **YES**

SEC rule 144 now exempts limited resales under specified conditions. [§§844-848] Also, the purchaser may resell without registration if he has held the shares for a significant length of time and is a noncontrol person. [§848]

113.a. **DEPENDS**

Only Orange is absolutely liable. The others may avoid liability if they exercised due diligence with respect to those portions of the registration statement for which Ralph seeks to hold them liable. Note that the burden of proof of due diligence is *on the defendants.* [§§865-870]

b. **NO**

Section 11 of the 1933 Act requires only a showing of the materiality of the misstatement; *i.e.,* that it concerned a matter that would influence the decision of an average prudent investor. [§§859-860]

c. **NO**

Ralph need not prove his reliance on the misrepresentation nor that the misrepresentation caused the decline in price of the stock. [§861]

114.a. **YES**

Under section 11, *anyone* who acquired the securities without knowledge of the misstatement may sue; privity is not required. [§856]

b. **NO**

Cynthia is entitled only to damages. [§871]

115.a. **YES**

Issuers and dealers are liable for the use of any material misstatements or omissions, assuming the use of the mails or any means of interstate commerce. [§§873, 875]

b. **NO**

Section 12 liability runs only in favor of the original purchaser, not a transferee. [§874]

116. **TRUE**

Sections 12 and 17 apply to the offer or sale of *any* securities, whether subject to the registration requirements or not. [§880]

117. **NO**

Declaration of dividends is within the discretion of the board of directors. Absent an abuse of discretion, the shareholders have no power to compel declaration of a dividend. [§§889-890]

118. **NO**

If there is no earned surplus (*i.e.,* current net profits are offset by prior losses) and no other available surplus account, payment of a dividend would "impair capital." In most states, the current profit must be used to "repair" capital. Otherwise, the payment of a dividend might jeopardize creditors and preferred shareholders. [§§894-912]

119.	**YES**	The excess over par value is paid-in surplus, which is a lawful source of dividends in most states. Some statutes require that shareholders be notified if the source of a dividend is anything other than earned surplus. [§§916-917]
120.	**YES**	Assuming that it is not needed to repair the capital account, most states would permit dividend payments from capital reduction surplus. [§§918-920]
121.	**NO**	Most states do ***not*** permit unrealized appreciation in value of assets as a source of dividends. A few states do permit such use of revaluation surplus, especially if the asset is readily marketable (*e.g.*, listed securities). [§§922-924]
122.	**YES**	Unless absolved by good faith reliance on corporate financial statements, the directors are liable—at least up to the amount of injury to shareholders and debts owed to creditors. Liability is joint and several. [§§929-932]
123.	**YES**	When the corporation is insolvent, each shareholder is absolutely liable for the return of the amount of the dividend. ***If*** the corporation were not insolvent, shareholder liability would depend on notice. [§§934-937]
124.	**NO**	Redemption must always be expressly provided for in the articles of incorporation. In contrast, a corporation generally ***does*** have an inherent right to repurchase its own shares. [§§939, 948]
125.	**NO**	Redeemed shares are ordinarily canceled. Thus, the corporation, within the limits of the authorized number of shares, may issue new shares to replace the shares redeemed. [§947]
126.	**YES**	Unlike a redemption, which usually must be by lot or pro rata, a repurchase can be made selectively, subject only to limitations of fiduciary duty. [§§948, 963-964]
127.	**NO**	The availability of funds is tested by most courts ***when the payment*** (or each installment) ***is due***. Most states permit repurchase out of only those sources of funds then available for a cash or property dividend. [§957]
128.	**NO**	A redemption or repurchase must serve some ***bona fide corporate purpose***. Self-perpetuation in office, alone, would not satisfy this requirement. [§963]
129.	**ALL**	(A) is correct because most states require approval by an extraordinary majority—a two-thirds or a majority vote of the outstanding shares, not merely of the shares present at a meeting of both corporations. Further, some statutes require approval by each class of shareholders. [§§992-994]
		(B) is correct because the surviving corporation succeeds to the rights and obligations of the transferor by operation of law. No agreement is necessary. [§§988-989]
		(C) is correct because no further action is required to dissolve the transferor; it ceases to exist upon the filing of the merger certificate with the state. [§§986, 988]
130.a.	**YES**	A merger makes such fundamental changes in both corporations that, under most statutes, shareholders who reject the changes are entitled to force the corporation to buy them out. [§995]
b.	**NO**	A shareholder must have voted ***against*** the merger and also have met other procedural requirements in order to qualify for appraisal rights. He cannot vote in favor, assess the effects, and then change his mind. [§§979-982]

c.	**NO**	Other factors such as asset value and investment value will be weighed, as will temporary market-price distortions. Further, adjustments will be made for the effect of the merger on the market price. [§§970-978]
131.a.	**NO**	Approval is not required from *either* corporation's shareholders. In a "short-form merger" of a subsidiary into a qualifying parent, statutes generally permit simplified procedures. [§998]
b.	**NO**	In a short-form merger, the shareholders of the parent do not have appraisal rights. However, the shareholders of Brown, the subsidiary, would have such rights. [§§999, 1004]
c.	**YES**	Under most statutes, the surviving corporation may issue cash, securities, or other property to the subsidiary's minority shareholders, even if it results in a freezeout. [§1096]
132.	**(A) only**	(A) is correct; approval is everywhere required, although statutes vary as to the percentage vote needed. Sales made in the regular course of business, however, do not require shareholder approval. [§§1026-1027]
		(B) is wrong because no fundamental change in Black occurs, and hence approval by its shareholders is not required. [§1026]
		(C) is wrong because the test is whether the transaction will essentially terminate the transferor's business. Thus, the controlling factor is the percentage of *operating* assets sold. [§1032]
133.a.	**YES**	This is a classic de facto merger. The use of Day's stock for the purchase and the projected dissolution of Night suggests that the ultimate effects are those of a merger. A court may require the same shareholder vote as for a merger. (But note that some courts—principally Delaware—do not recognize the de facto merger doctrine). [§§1009-1012, 1018]
b.	**YES**	The boards of directors may be required to submit the plan as a merger to both sets of shareholders and to recognize appraisal rights of dissenters. [§1012]
134.	**YES**	Under most statutes, amendments to the articles must be approved by holders of a majority or two-thirds of the corporation's shares *and* by the board. [§1034]
135.	**YES**	However, dissolution is discretionary with the court, which may—depending on the seriousness and persistence of the misconduct—instead either suspend the corporation's powers or enjoin future misconduct. [§1062]
136.	**NO**	Dissolution requires affirmative action by the corporation itself or by the court. [§1050]
137.	**YES**	However, liquidation can be a long and complex process, so that courts may be hesitant to conclude that the business transacted was not incident to the liquidation. [§1064]
138.	**TRUE**	A creditor's claim is superior to that of shareholders. Each shareholder is liable up to the amount of assets he received in liquidation. [§§1065, 1068, 1071]
139.	**YES**	In this situation the appraisal rights are not an exclusive remedy. Depending on the nature of the transaction, the 1933 Act and/or the 1934 Act might apply. [§1084]

140.a. **NO** The Acme Board must authorize the transaction, but its shareholders do not vote unless Acme's articles must be amended. No offer is made to Star, *as a corporation*, and there is therefore no vote. Each Star shareholder, as an individual, may accept or reject the offer. [§1100]

b. **YES** As controlling shareholder, Acme may vote to dissolve Star. [§1098]

c. **PROBABLY** Various federal and state statutes now require the filing of information statements disclosing contemplated changes in the target corporation should the tender offer be successful. The federal statute (Williams Act) requires filing of such information with the SEC where the target corporation is subject to the reporting requirements of the 1934 Act or its securities are traded on a national securities exchange. [§§1111-1112, 1123-1136]

SAMPLE EXAM QUESTION I

In late 1988, Daniel Dollar, an accountant, and Peter Prop, a salesman, agreed to form a corporation, Wingtip, Inc., to engage in the business of selling private airplanes. The planes would be purchased from a major private airplane manufacturer under credit arrangements whereby Wingtip would pay only a small amount down, and the manufacturer would retain a security interest in the plane. The business would operate out of rented hangar and office space located at a local airport. It would have only one salaried employee, a bookkeeper-secretary. In lieu of salary, Wingtip's salespeople would work on a commission basis. Prop would generally oversee Wingtip's business, would hire the personnel, and would be Wingtip's president, but would not be compensated (except by way of dividends); he would devote only about 20% of his time to Wingtip's affairs. The parties estimated that to operate the business on this basis, Wingtip would need $4,000 in capital. Of this amount, $3,000 would be put up by Dollar and $1,000 by Prop. However, Dollar would take 60% of Wingtip's shares and Prop would take 40%, since Prop was to oversee Wingtip's business while Dollar was to be involved only in important policy decisions.

Wingtip was incorporated on January 2, 1989. Prop and Dollar put up the agreed amounts of cash, and 60 shares were issued to Dollar and 40 to Prop. Dollar then transferred five of his shares to his married daughter, Joan Green. Prop rented the hangar and office space, engaged the necessary personnel, made arrangements with a major private airplane manufacturer, and began Wingtip's business in the contemplated manner. Since Prop and Dollar were able to make major decisions between them, and since they were old friends, no formal board was ever designated, nor were formal officer elections ever held. Over the first six months of 1989, Wingtip broke even.

In July 1989, Prop learned that Flyout Corporation, a competitor of Wingtip, was going out of business, and was offering the 15 used planes in its inventory at a very low cash package price. Prop felt this was too good an opportunity to pass up, and signed a contract with Flyout, on Wingtip's behalf, as its president, to purchase the 15 planes for $150,000. Prop realized that Wingtip could not pay this amount, but he was sure he could make the necessary credit arrangements. However, when Dollar learned what Prop had done, he refused to go along with the deal, and informed Flyout that Wingtip would not buy the planes. Flyout then brought an action for breach of contract, naming Wingtip, Prop, Dollar, and Green as defendants.

Assume that Flyout's suit is meritorious and that the judgment will be in the $20,000 range. Discuss the liability of Wingtip, Prop, Dollar, and Green.

SAMPLE EXAM QUESTION II

In 1988, Oliva purchased a new highway ice cream stand for $15,000, the list price of the building and equipment. In the same year, Allen opened a new hot dog stand, at a cost of $15,000, on adjoining property. After four years, Oliva and Allen decided to combine, and to continue personally operating the stands. Without the aid of an attorney, Oliva formed the Cream Dog Corporation with an authorized capital of 50 shares of $1,000 par common stock. Pursuant to statute, she filed articles of incorporation with the secretary of state, but due to inexperience, failed to comply with the statutory requirements of local filing and proper publicity of the incorporation. Oliva told Rollins, one of her suppliers, of everything that she had done. Rollins offered Oliva $30,000 for the ice cream stand. Despite the fact that a number of independent appraisers had just valued Oliva's business at a maximum of $27,000, Oliva refused.

Oliva transferred the ice cream stand to the corporation, in exchange for 30 shares of stock marked "fully paid." On behalf of the corporation, she offered Allen 15 shares for the hot dog stand. Oliva stated only that she was entitled to the greater share because her ice cream business had been making the greater profit. On the other hand, Oliva argued, Allen's business was worth no more than its original cost. Allen agreed with Oliva on the value of his business, but disagreed as to the valuation of Oliva's business. As a compromise, Oliva agreed to have the corporation issue 20 shares to Allen, marked "fully paid," in exchange for his hot dog stand. Allen agreed that these shares be recorded on the corporation's books as having been issued in exchange for $15,000 worth of property, and that Oliva handle all of the legal and accounting details. Oliva and Allen both became directors of Cream Dog.

Shortly thereafter, having examined the corporate financial statements, Rollins began to sell supplies to both of the Cream Dog stands. Subsequently, Cream Dog became insolvent, and Rollins obtained a judgment against it for $10,000. He is the sole creditor who remains unsatisfied.

Advise Rollins of his rights against Oliva and Allen.

SAMPLE EXAM QUESTION III

Machine, Inc. was organized in 1983 by Bilker to manufacture small tools. Its authorized stock was as follows: 6% Nonvoting Preferred—1,000 shares at $100 par value; Common—200,000 shares at $1 par value. Bilker then owned some machinery that he had purchased from Abel and Cane in 1982 for $40,000. It had a present market value of about $30,000. Bilker transferred this to Machine in exchange for 40,000 shares of common stock. Several days thereafter, Machine issued 30,000 shares of common stock each to Abel and Cane, who each paid $35,000 cash. A few days later, a half dozen investors bought all the preferred stock for $100 per share.

At the first shareholders' meeting, Bilker, Abel, and Cane were elected as Machine's three directors. They continued to be elected annually as such until December 25, 1988, when Abel died. The next shareholders' meeting is scheduled for January 15, 1989.

Machine's business had not done well from the outset. For several years, Bilker had unsuccessfully attempted to interest some outsiders in buying some of Machine's unissued common stock. Early in 1988, the board became interested in diversifying Machine's business by acquiring control of the Crafts Company, a lawn furniture manufacturer. Crafts had just recently been purchased for $50,000 by Kanine Corporation, all of whose stock was owned jointly by Cane and his wife Nina. Bilker and Abel were unaware of the identity of Kanine's shareholders.

At a Machine's directors' meeting of April 1, 1988, at which Abel was unable to be present due to illness, the directors voted unanimously to buy Crafts from Kanine in exchange for the 100,000 shares of unissued Machine common stock.

When Abel died, he bequeathed his Machine common stock to his nephew, Doltless. Doltless also owns 100 shares of Machine preferred stock, which he purchased in January of 1988 from an original owner.

Doltless wishes to be elected to Machine's board and to redress any legal wrongs done to the corporation. He seeks advice as to what, if anything, can be done toward these ends, and how he should go about doing it. Discuss fully.

SAMPLE EXAM QUESTION IV

Consolidated Orange Products, Inc. ("CO") is a corporation engaged in freezing and canning orange juice and other fruit juices and food products. It has eight plants located nationwide. CO's stock is listed on the New York Stock Exchange. Article IV(3) of CO's certificate provides for cumulative voting.

In connection with CO's forthcoming annual meeting, Donald Deem, a CO shareholder, has submitted the following proposals for inclusion in CO's proxy materials:

1. To amend CO's bylaws to provide that any director may be removed by the shareholders without cause.

2. To amend CO's bylaws to provide that whenever CO proposes to construct a new plant, it shall first prepare an impact statement showing the effects of the proposed plant on the environment (including details on air, water, and thermal pollution, if any), a copy of which statement shall be sent to each of CO's shareholders.

3. To amend CO's bylaws to provide that no new plant shall be constructed without shareholder approval.

Discuss whether these proposals, or any of them, must be included in CO's proxy materials.

SAMPLE EXAM QUESTION V

Hardback Corporation is engaged in the book publishing business. Hardback has 2,000 shares of common stock issued and outstanding; of these 1,000 shares are owned by Denise Dure, and 1,000 by Stanley Stray. Dure oversees marketing strategy, and the development and maintenance of author relations; Stray oversees the administrative, financial, and editorial side of the business. Dure and Stray had operated Hardback as a partnership from 1976 to 1989; in 1989 they incorporated for tax reasons. Hardback's board consists of Dure, Stray, and Wright, a senior employee.

Dure has learned that Stray proposes to sell his stock in Hardback to Lawrence Light. Light is a wealthy playboy who has always wanted to have an interest in a publishing house. Dure knows him, does not particularly like him, and thinks very little of his business ability. Although Dure and Stray never entered into a formal shareholders' agreement, Dure feels that a sale of stock by Stray would be contrary to what was understood, even if not made explicit, in the Dure-Stray relationship.

Dure now seeks advice on whether she can prevent Stray from selling to Light, and if not, whether there are any arrangements she can make, or steps she can take, to protect her economic interests against Light's lack of skill and judgment.

(Assume that Dure cannot afford to buy Stray's shares at the price Light is willing to pay.)

SAMPLE EXAM QUESTION VI

Jax, Inc. was incorporated in 1988 with 2,500 shares of common stock at a par value of $100 per share authorized. Of those, 2,200 shares of Jax stock have been issued and are outstanding. From 1982 through 1987, Jax incurred net operating losses totaling $80,000. At the end of 1988, the corporation had net earnings of $25,000 for that year. The Jax board of directors, consisting of A, B, and C, met on February 16, 1989, and unanimously voted to declare a cash dividend of $10 per share on outstanding stock.

Pursuant to a bylaw authorizing the board to appoint officers and committees, at the February meeting A, B, and C also unanimously voted to create an Executive and Finance Committee composed of B, C, and W. W was not a director or officer of Jax, but was a shareholder. The bylaw permitted, and the board resolution provided, that the Committee would have all the powers of the board of directors.

On June 15, 1989, the board authorized the purchase by Jax of 200 shares of Jax stock, held by D, at a price of $95 per share. D had indicated he was ready to sell them at that price to a competitor of Jax.

On July 18, 1989, the Executive and Finance Committee directed Jax to issue 100 shares of previously unissued stock to E, as "fully paid" shares in return for E's promissory note to Jax in the sum of $7,500. Such stock was issued to E for his note as described.

On August 31, 1989, as president of Jax, A wrote to F, a shop superintendent employed by the company who was retiring on his 65th birthday, as follows:

> "In light of your years of faithful service to this company since it was established, I have decided that upon your retirement today, Jax will pay you a monthly pension of $300 for the rest of your life, so long as our financial condition warrants it."

X, a Jax shareholder, seeks advice as to the legality of:

1. The declaration of the cash dividend.

2. The appointment of the Executive and Finance Committee.

3. The purchase of shares from D.

4. The issuance of the 100 shares to E.

5. The promise to F to pay him a monthly pension.

Discuss.

ANSWER TO SAMPLE EXAM QUESTION I

1. **Liability of Wingtip:** Wingtip's liability depends on whether Prop had authority to make the contract with Flyout on its behalf. There is nothing to indicate that Prop had **actual** authority. Wingtip's business plan called for the planes to be "purchased from a major private airplane manufacturer under credit arrangements whereby Wingtip would pay only a small amount down. . . ." Prop was to oversee Wingtip's business, but Dollar was to be involved in "important policy decisions." Certainly, a major deviation as to financing, source of supply, and quality of aircraft seems to be an important policy decision, which Prop had no actual authority to make. The issue then is whether Prop had **apparent** authority, or **power of position**.

An initial question in considering apparent authority is whether Prop was president of Wingtip. Although it had been agreed between Prop and Dollar that Prop would be Wingtip's president, he was never formally elected to that office. Nevertheless, Prop should be deemed Wingtip's president, at least as to third parties, and probably even within the corporation. It is characteristic of a close corporation that formalities are not rigorously followed. Prop and Dollar, who owned all but five shares of Wingtip's stock, explicitly agreed to Prop's being a president, and in all probability Green either acquiesced, or was represented in corporate affairs by Dollar.

Assuming that Prop was Wingtip's president as to third persons, he would have a president's **apparent authority** (power of position) as to those persons. There are several competing rules as to a president's apparent authority. An older rule, now discarded for all practical purposes, is that a president has no more authority than any other director, but the two rules that continue to have support are (i) that the president has power to bind the corporation to contracts within the ordinary course of its business; and (ii) that the president has power to bind the corporation even to contracts of an "extraordinary" nature, provided, at least, that the contract is one the board could authorize or ratify. Under the second rule, which is less widely accepted, Wingtip would be bound. Under the first rule, Wingtip's liability is less certain.

Since this situation concerns apparent authority, presumably the issue is whether the transaction would appear to be in the ordinary course when viewed from the perspective of the third party—here, Flyout. The amount involved may very well have indicated to Flyout that the transaction was not in the ordinary course, particularly since Flyout, as a competitor, may have been familiar with Wingtip's business.

On the other hand, Wingtip was engaged in the business of selling airplanes, and it seems reasonable for Flyout to assume that the president of such a corporation would have authority to buy airplanes for resale. Therefore, Wingtip should be held liable on the contract.

2. **Liability of Prop, Dollar, and Green:** Even if Wingtip is liable on the contract, Flyout would also seek to hold Wingtip's shareholders liable (since Flyout will recover a judgment of $20,000, and Wingtip has assets of only $4,000). Normally, of course, a shareholder's liability is limited to his or her investment in the corporation (a shareholder has no individual liability for the corporation's debts).

However, two factors in this case might justify "piercing the corporate veil" and holding the shareholders individually liable. One is the failure to follow normal corporate formalities. Shareholders' and board meetings were not held, and officers were not elected. However, while lack of such formalities is often pointed to in piercing the veil cases, it normally would not suffice to justify individual liability in itself, especially in a close corporation (if only because it is seldom connected with the plaintiff's loss).

A very important factor is the possibility that Wingtip was undercapitalized. It is true that Wingtip was able to break even for six months. Nevertheless, $4,000 does not seem like sufficient capital for engaging in the kind of business Wingtip set up (particularly considering the kind of personal injury liability that might be involved in such a business). Few cases have rested individual liability solely on the ground of undercapitalization, but in this case a lack of formality is present as well.

It is also arguable that a contract creditor is in a weaker position than a tort claimant to base recovery on this theory, since he goes into the situation knowing that he is dealing with a limited liability enterprise, and had a prior opportunity to investigate the enterprise's resources. However, the better view is that even a contract creditor is justified in expecting that the entity with which he deals will be capitalized to absorb the consequences of predictable business events.

Assuming individual liability would be imposed in this case, the next question is which shareholders should be liable? Again, there are conflicting rules. Under one rule, all the shareholders would be liable as partners. Under a second, only the individual who actually conducted the transaction—Prop—would be liable. Under a third rule, which is probably the soundest rule, only the corporation's *active managers* would be liable—Prop and Dollar.

ANSWER TO SAMPLE EXAM QUESTION II

1. Defective Incorporation
The first issue is whether Oliva and Allen are insulated against personal liability despite the defects in the incorporation process (failure to file locally and properly publicize filing). Three questions must be asked:

(a) Was a *de jure corporation* formed despite these failures? The answer to this question is almost certainly no. For a de jure corporation, there must be substantial compliance with the statute. These are more than insignificant defects.

(b) Was a *de facto corporation* formed? Some modern statutes appear to eliminate the de facto doctrine. Assuming that Cream Dog's state of incorporation does not have such a statute, it is a close question whether Cream Dog is a de facto corporation. Clearly there was a good faith actual use of the corporate existence. The issue then is whether there was a good faith, colorable attempt to comply with the statutory requirements for incorporation. Since the defects were due to inexperience, the good faith test is met. Moreover, the most essential step, proper filing of the original articles, was taken.

(c) If, however, the omitted steps are found to be too important for the enterprise to be a de facto corporation, the next question is whether it constitutes a *corporation by estoppel* as against Rollins? (That is, will Cream Dog be treated as a corporation for purposes of transactions with Rollins?) Statutes that put an end to the de facto doctrine may or may not have a comparable effect on the estoppel doctrine.

Assuming the applicable statute does not have such an effect, there is a strong case for applying the doctrine. Rollins dealt with Cream Dog as if it were a corporation. Since he had actual notice of the attempted incorporation, there was no causal relationship between the failure to file and properly publish (both of which may be seen as provisions directed toward giving notice) and the loss resulting to Rollins. All parties were proceeding on the premise that the liability of the owners was limited by due incorporation. Therefore, the doctrine may be applied, and Oliva and Allen may be insulated from personal liability.

(Note that even if Oliva is liable, Allen might argue that he should not be held personally liable, on the ground that he did not participate in organizing the corporation, and the court should only hold liable the person responsible. It seems doubtful that this is a good defense because Allen was also a director and, therefore, responsible for corporate activity. Many courts even impose liability on shareholders where a corporation is defectively formed.)

2. Watered Stock
The second issue concerns watered stock. Most states require that par value shares be sold for at least par. If they are not, creditors can require, upon bankruptcy, a stockholder who has not paid par (at least on an original issue, such as is involved here) to pay the difference between what he originally paid and par. The theory behind the par value rule is that creditors have a

right to rely upon the corporation receiving capital equivalent to the par value. The only creditor (Rollins) examined the balance sheet, and undoubtedly saw that the corporation did not receive par. Thus, in those states that require reliance to be proved by a creditor before he can recover, it seems doubtful that Rollins can prove reliance. (Some states, however, presume creditor reliance, and would put the burden on the defendant to prove that Rollins did not rely.) Other states do not require reliance. They treat the corporation's stated capital as a "trust fund" for creditors, and permit all creditors to recover irrespective of reliance.

Assuming that Rollins can recover if the stock was issued for less than par, was there such an issuance here? From the facts, Allen received $20,000 par value stock for property worth no more than $15,000 (under any theory of value), so Allen owes $5,000. Thus, Rollins may recover the $5,000 from Allen.

Rollins will have a more difficult time arguing that Oliva's stock was watered (*i.e.,* that her property was overvalued), since Rollins himself offered her $30,000 for it. Under the majority rule, watered stock liability exists only for **intentional** overvaluation of assets received by the corporation. If, as appears to be the case here, the parties believed in good faith that the property was equal to par value, the stock is not watered.

Therefore, Rollins will be limited to any corporate assets still available and Allen's $5,000 to satisfy the claim.

ANSWER TO SAMPLE EXAM QUESTION III

1. Doltless's ability to be elected to the Machine's board will greatly depend on whether there is cumulative voting. In some states cumulative voting is mandatory; it is permissive in the rest, usually existing only if so provided in the articles or bylaws. Assuming it exists in this case, with 200,000 voting common shares outstanding, Doltless would need 50,001 shares to elect one director:

$$\frac{200,000}{3 + 1} + 1 = 50,001$$

As things presently stand, Doltless will be unsuccessful because he owns only 30,000 shares. However, there are several routes he might pursue to improve his situation.

Doltless could attempt to assert preemptive rights in the 100,000 shares issued Crafts. Since Abel (Doltless's predecessor in interest) held 30% of the common stock at the time, if Doltless were successful, he would get an additional 30,000 shares. This would give him enough to elect a director. This assumes preemptive rights exist (in some states they exist unless negated by the articles; in other states, the opposite is true).

These 100,000 shares were authorized and issued, and the general rule is that there are no preemptive rights therein (the rationale being all shareholders knew that 200,000 shares were previously authorized and they had no right to rely on more than their percentage of that). But, in this case, five years have passed with the original percentage existing. It might well be argued that after this period of time the original issue had terminated. In fact, in some states, statutes provide a limited time, *e.g.,* two years, for the original issue after which preemptive rights again attach. Furthermore, there is the doctrine that if originally authorized stock is subsequently sold for expansion purposes, rather than just raising additional working capital to be used in the original business, preemptive rights attach. That would seem to be the case here. However, Doltless will fail in this preemptive rights approach because preemptive rights do not apply if the stock is issued for property rather than cash. It should also be clear that preferred stock has no preemptive rights.

Alternatively, Doltless could seek to get the issuance of the 100,000 shares to Crafts rescinded. If he were successful, it would take only 25,001 shares to get a director elected, and his 30,000 shares would be more than sufficient.

At the meeting of April 1, only two directors were present, Bilker and Cane. Cane was clearly an interested director vis-a-vis the Crafts transaction, due to his holdings in Kanine. As a director, he was necessary for a quorum. This alone might make the transaction voidable at common law, as would the fact that he voted for the deal. Under statutes like New York's and California's, the quorum issue is not determinative, nor is Cane's vote, despite the fact that it was a determinative vote. The transaction would not be voidable under modern statutes unless it is unfair. Failure to make full disclosure to an independent board renders the transaction unfair.

If the action to rescind is held to be a derivative suit since it alleges injury to the corporation, most jurisdictions would require Doltless to be a contemporaneous owner. As an owner of preferred (who would have a general interest in the integrity of the corporation's assets), he would meet this requirement. Even as an owner of common, it would seem that he could qualify under the exception for shares devolving by operation of law (here, inheritance). Historically, the contemporaneous ownership requirement existed to prevent the buying of lawsuits by strikers (the reason for the rule has no application here).

Some states have statutes that require the plaintiff-shareholder to post security to indemnify the corporation for expenses. If there is a minimum percentage requirement (*e.g.,* 5% in New York), Doltless would be excused. In other states (*e.g.,* California), security rests within the discretion of the court. Doltless's action will benefit the corporation, so here too he would be excused.

Demand on directors, generally required in all states, should be excused here because it would be futile. Cane is interested and that leaves only Bilker. Demand on shareholders (a prerequisite in most states "if necessary") might be required, especially because it would be simple and inexpensive and might result in Bilker joining the suit and making it more effective. The wrong (voidable board action) might also be considered subject to shareholder ratification. Cane would clearly cast his 130,000 votes against the suit, but since this is an **interested** vote, it clearly should not bar suit.

If Bilker casts his 40,000 votes against suit, this arguably could be a decision of a majority of the disinterested shareholders, having full disclosure, that the suit was not in the corporation's best interests. This might be held to be a reasonable judgment given Machine's alleged need for diversification by purchase of Crafts. (But some courts might hold the transaction void and thus incapable of shareholder ratification. *Note:* This might excuse shareholder demand altogether.) Or, some courts might find that there just are not enough disinterested shareholders, since Cane owns 65%; or, because Bilker might be a defendant in another suit by Doltless (*see* below), his vote might be considered interested; or there is the possibility that Bilker can be divested of 10,000 of his shares (*see* below), thus removing his edge over Doltless.

There are other possibilities in respect to the Crafts transaction that would provide redress to the corporation, but would not enhance Doltless's voting position.

It appears clear that Crafts's "true value" was much less than the $100,000 worth of par value stock paid for it (but this rule is a minority view). Perhaps, under the majority "good faith" theory, it could be argued that it was a reasonable business judgment for the board to believe that the value to Machine was $100,000, but this is unlikely due to Cane's interest in the matter and the recent market valuation of $50,000.

Usually, only creditors can recover for watered stock. However, an occasional case has permitted enforcement by the corporation, when it needs the money (such as the case here). Since this is the corporation's cause of action, the suit would be derivative, thus presenting the issues discussed above.

Apart from the par value rule, Cane's failure to disclose his interest in the transaction would be considered a breach of his fiduciary duty resulting in damages for the corporation (if not rescission, as discussed above). The corporation would at least be entitled to the difference between the value of the stock issued and the value of the assets received. It might even be possible to force Cane to disgorge his entire profit as a penalty and deterrent, for breach of fiduciary duty. This again, would be a derivative suit.

The nondisclosure by Cane in connection with his "purchase" of stock from Machine, and his consequent breach of fiduciary duty would also appear to give Machine a cause of action under rule 10b-5, assuming some use of the mails or interstate commerce. Doltless could bring a derivative action for this, and this federal action would excuse him from any state security for expense requirements.

There is a possible argument that Cane appropriated Machine's corporate opportunity when he caused Kanine to purchase Crafts. This argument depends on facts not available—was Machine actively seeking diversification at the time? In what capacity did Cane learn about Crafts's availability? To the contrary, the facts appear to indicate that Kanine bought Crafts before Machine decided to diversify. Since Crafts was therefore not even in Machine's "line of business," the argument would seem to fail. But if an action lies, it is derivative since it was the corporation's opportunity.

Finally, there is Bilker's 1983 sale of machinery to the corporation. Again, under either valuation test, Bilker's stock appears to be watered to the extent of $10,000. (The fact that Cane and Abel paid $10,000 over par value would not appear to cure the defect. This would be a premium over par value and was probably so recorded. As such, it would not be so permanently "locked in" for the benefit of the corporation and its creditors.) But, again, most states would hold the corporation estopped from bringing suit since it was a party to the contract. Doltless was not a contemporaneous owner for purposes of a derivative suit, and he might well be barred by a statute of limitations. But if Doltless could counter all these hurdles, he probably would be more benefited by a suit to rescind 10,000 shares. The corporation, however, clearly would be better off if damages were recovered, and, after all, it is the corporation's cause of action.

Bilker was a promoter in 1983. As such, he was obliged to disclose his profits on the transaction. Although he was the sole party in interest at the time, it was clearly contemplated that other shareholders were to be brought in immediately. Under the better rule, disclosure should have been made to them. It may well be that Cane and Abel will be held to have had disclosure because of their prior dealings with Bilker in respect to this very machinery. Thus, Bilker's duty as to them was satisfied. But there is no evidence that the 1983 purchasers of preferred had any knowledge or disclosure of Bilker's profits—and they had a real interest in the integrity of the "cushion" or assets that Machine had.

Thus, as to them, it would appear that Bilker violated his duty of disclosure, thereby affording a common law cause of action to the corporation for his gain (also under rule 10b-5), which was at least $10,000: the difference between what he got, and what he gave up. But the suit is derivative, Doltless is not a contemporaneous owner, and what about the statute of limitations? Even if there is no contemporaneous ownership requirement, Doltless may be barred because he is Able's successor, who may have been estopped because of knowledge.

ANSWER TO SAMPLE EXAM QUESTION IV

Proposal 1: CO is governed by the proxy rules, since its stock is listed on the New York Stock Exchange. Proxy rule 14a-8 provides that management must include a timely filed shareholder proposal in the corporate proxy materials, unless the proposal falls within an exclusion in rule 14a-8. The only exclusion that might be applicable to Proposal 1 is rule 14a-8(c)(1), which allows management to omit a shareholder proposal if "under the laws of the issuer's domicile [it is] not a proper subject for action by security holders."

The issue is whether the proposed bylaw conflicts with CO's certificate. If it does, Proposal 1 would not be a proper subject for shareholder action, since in case of conflict between certificate and bylaw, the bylaw falls. Article IV(3) of CO's certificate provides for cumulative voting. This provision would be undercut by removal without cause, since the majority shareholders could eliminate minority-elected directors seriatim, by removing each one without cause. Then each vacancy could be filled by an election, for a single director, in which the minority could not effectively cumulate its votes.

It is true that under the cases the mere fact that a certificate or bylaw amendment weakens cumulative voting does not render it invalid, but Proposal 1 seems to cross the line—not only weakening cumulative voting, but effectively destroying it. Many statutes bar removal of a director if the votes against removal would be sufficient to elect the director through cumulative voting. On this basis, the proposed bylaw would be invalid if adopted, and the proposal to adopt it would, therefore, not be a proper subject for CO's shareholders.

Proposal 2: Proposal 2 raises several problems under 14a-8. First, it can be argued that Proposal 2 is not a proper subject under state law as infringing on the powers of the board to manage the corporation's business. But Proposal 2 only requires a report. The decision whether or not to build a plant would still be in management's hands. (However, it could be argued that the *manner* in which decisions are made is itself a management function.)

Second, rule 14a-8(c)(7) permits management to omit a proposal if it deals with a matter relating to the conduct of the ordinary business operations of the issuer. Certainly, Proposal 2 deals with the conduct of business operations. Since the addition of a plant would be a major undertaking, it is not clear that it relates to the conduct of "ordinary" business operations, but for this purpose any decision within the general framework of CO's business would probably be regarded as "ordinary." However, the relation of Proposal 2 to business operations is only indirect.

The bylaw would not regulate how management operates the corporation's business; it would not even set parameters for management's decisions; all it would do is direct that when a certain type of decision is proposed, management must send the shareholders information concerning the proposal. While the decision could go either way (since the proposed bylaw would increase the flow of information to shareholders, which is the object of the proxy rules, and since it gives no direction or recommendation concerning how CO's business should be conducted), it should not be deemed to fall within the 14a-8(c)(7) exception.

Finally, the proxy rules allow management to omit a proposal if it deals with a matter that is not significantly related to the issuer's business or is beyond the issuer's power to effectuate. However, Proposal 2 is within the power of CO to effectuate, and it seems to be significantly related to CO's business (since it deals with closely relevant externalities of CO's operations). Proposal 2 must be included in CO's proxy materials.

Proposal 3: Unlike Proposal 2, Proposal 3 directly regulates the allocation of powers over CO's business, by shifting the power to approve new plants from management, where it would normally be located, to the shareholders. Statutes sometimes provide that the business of a corporation shall be managed by the board, unless the certificate otherwise provides. However, Proposal 3 does not call for amendment of the certificate, and the statutory provision vesting management in the board cannot normally be varied (at least outside the context of a close corporation), except insofar as the statute explicitly permits. Proposal 3 may be omitted from CO's proxy materials.

ANSWER TO SAMPLE EXAM QUESTION V

1. **Prevention of Sale:** Corporate stock is normally freely transferable, absent an agreement to the contrary. Dure's major argument for preventing Stray from selling his shares would be based on the fact that such a sale "would be contrary to what was understood, even if not made explicit, in the Dure-Stray relationship." More specifically, Dure would claim that Hardback is really a joint venture, in which the prior "understanding" was preserved, notwithstanding adoption of the corporate form. There is some support in the facts for this position, since Hardback was operated as a partnership from 1976-1989, and was incorporated only for tax reasons. Certainly such an implicit understanding would probably be reasonable in almost any close corporation.

However, it is doubtful that a court would view this kind of implicit understanding as sufficient to override the well-entrenched rule that corporate stock is freely transferable, particularly where the circumstances do not indicate that the sale violates any fiduciary obligation that Stray might owe Dure. Thus, Dure probably could not restrain Stray from selling his stock to Light.

2. **Protection of Dure's Interest:** Whether there are any arrangements Dure can make, or steps she can take, to protect her economic interests against Light's lack of skill and judgment, the first point is to note that Dure's position is not as bad as she might think. The mere fact that Light holds stock will not, in itself, give Light any voice in corporate management, since the power to manage the corporation's business is in the board, not the shareholders. Light's holding would, of course, give him a voice in *shareholder* matters, but that would probably not be very significant as to the corporation's day-to-day affairs. In any event, with only a 50% interest Light would not be able to take any effective action as a shareholder, unless Dure concurs.

The immediate question, then, is whether Light could get a seat on the board. Since the directors are elected by the shareholders, and since Dure holds 50% of the stock, again the answer seems to be no (at least for the short range). Assuming Light could not cumulate his votes, the most votes he could give any one candidate, including himself, is 1,000. Dure could also cast 1,000 votes for any one candidate, and therefore if Dure does not vote her shares for Light, the result of any election would be a tie. In that case, a new (also futile) election would have to be called, and the old directors would hold over. The old directors, of course, are Dure and Wright. Assuming Wright stayed on the board and did not side with Light, Dure would have a quorum for board action and probably could get the board to vote as she wished. Thus, at least for the short term, Dure probably has no great reason for alarm.

In the long run, however, such a posture might not be viable. Several statutes provide for the appointment of a provisional director if the directors are divided, but these would be inapplicable because Hardback's *directors* would not be divided. However, under the hypothesized facts, Light might be able to obtain involuntary dissolution on the ground of deadlock at the shareholder level (although some courts are unwilling or reluctant to grant this remedy in the case of a prosperous corporation, particularly where the deadlock does not threaten the prosperity). But while dissolution might be undesirable to Dure, it would probably be even more undesirable to Light, who could not carry on a similar business, as could Dure. (Alternatively, Dure might seek dissolution herself, on the theory that she could effectively take over Hardback's business on the dissolution sale, since Light would be in no position to do so. However, if Dure sought dissolution herself, she would be accountable to Light for Light's share of the prospective business opportunity, if she purchased the business, and probably this would also be true in a custodial dissolution as well.)

Taking into account the bargaining power of each party, Dure is probably in a position to strike a bargain with Light under which Light would get some, but limited, participation in business decisions of Hardback. Such limited participation might satisfy Light, since he is after all, only a dilettante. Since Hardback is a close corporation, such an agreement would probably be valid at common law, and if Hardback is incorporated in a state with special close corporation legislation, the articles could be amended to qualify it as a statutory close corporation, and ensure the enforceability of such an agreement.

ANSWER TO SAMPLE EXAM QUESTION VI

1. **Cash Dividend:** In most states, Jax would not be legally permitted to declare a cash dividend. As of the end of 1987, Jax's capital was impaired in an amount of $80,000 (its accumulated operating losses). The $25,000 net earnings in 1988 is ordinarily not available for dividends, but must instead be used to repair the impairment of capital. As of the end of 1988, Jax has no surplus (assets in excess of liabilities and stated capital), which is usually required for the payment of dividends. Rather, it still has a deficit of $55,000. Creditors are entitled to rely on the fact that, before dividends are paid to shareholders, the corporation's assets must exceed its liabilities and capital.

Some states, however, permit the payment of "nimble dividends." Under this rule, dividends may be paid to the extent of current net profits (profits during the preceding year or two), even though capital is impaired (*i.e.*, even if there is no surplus). Under this rule, Jax could pay its declared $22,000 dividend.

In California, Jax could pay the dividend as long as after such payment its total assets were at least 1-1/4 times its total liabilities, and its current assets were at least equal to its current liabilities. Since the figures are not available in respect to these matters, one cannot say whether Jax's dividend would be permissible in California.

In any event, even in California or a nimble dividend state, Jax could not legally pay the dividend if it were insolvent or would thereby become insolvent. Jax is obviously not insolvent in the bankruptcy sense, *i.e.*, its liabilities do not exceed its assets, since it has capital of $165,000. However, insolvency includes inability to meet debts as they mature, and as to this the facts are incomplete.

2. **Appointment of Committee:** Virtually every statute contains provisions allowing the board to create committees, and delegate thereto certain of the board's powers. However, the composition and powers of the Jax Executive and Finance Committee conflict with those statutory provisions in two respects. First, the statutes typically limit committee membership to directors, and W is not a director. Second, the statutes typically carve out certain powers that cannot be delegated, and here the Jax board delegated all its powers. It can therefore be argued that the Jax Executive and Finance Committee was not validly created and constituted, and its actions are void.

As to the first point, however, unless the relevant statute provided that executive or finance committees consist of at least three directors, the Jax committee could have been constituted of only B and C. Therefore, any action (such as the issuance of stock in this case) in which B and C concurred, might be deemed valid notwithstanding W's participation. Similarly, as to the second point, the fact that the Jax committee was vested with more powers than was legally permissible should not necessarily make invalid the exercise of a power that could be legally delegated, and the issuance of stock is a power that can be delegated to an executive committee under most statutes.

3. **Purchase of Shares:** Under both common law and statute, corporations are empowered to repurchase their own shares. However, the general rule is that the same conditions that are prerequisite to the payment of dividends must also be met before a corporation may repurchase its own shares (*i.e.*, the corporation must have a surplus at least equal to the amount of the repurchase). Here, the repurchase amount is $19,000. Jax has no surplus whatever. Even in a "nimble dividend" jurisdiction, there is only $3,000 of current net profits remaining after the February 16 dividend declaration. As for the "California rule," the facts are not known, as indicated above. Thus, it would seem that Jax cannot legally repurchase from D.

Many states do make certain exceptions to this rule and permit a corporation to repurchase its shares out of capital, under designated circumstances. Here, D will sell to a competitor if not to Jax, but this is not within the exceptions to the general rule.

4. **Issuance of Shares:** The issuance may be illegal on two separate grounds. First, most states require that par value shares be originally issued by the corporation for at least par value. Here, Jax issued previously authorized, but unissued stock, at $75 per share, despite the fact that it was $100 par. Unless the jurisdiction has special procedures for such issuance at less than par, this issuance is illegal.

Even though the shares were improperly issued for less than par, the general rule is that neither the corporation, nor a shareholder in a derivative suit, can sue E for the balance up to par. Jax, having issued the shares as "fully paid" in an arm's length transaction, is ordinarily estopped to claim otherwise. However, if Jax were to become insolvent, certain of its creditors may be able to sue E for the difference between par and what E paid for the stock.

Second, most states have constitutional or statutory provisions that a corporation may issue its shares only for "money paid, labor done, or property actually acquired." E's unsecured promissory note (assuming it is not secured by adequate collateral), is **not** lawful consideration for these purposes. Unless this is a minority jurisdiction that permits a corporation to issue its shares in exchange for a promise to pay in the future, the issuance to E may be considered void and subject to cancellation by Jax.

5. **Pension for F:** It would appear that A, as president of Jax, has authority to compensate corporate employees, like F, in the usual and regular course of the business. Further, since there is no indication that there is any conflict of interest in respect to this transaction, A cannot be held liable for this promised pension, as long as the payment involves a matter of reasonable business judgment. Nonetheless, neither officers nor directors may "give away" or "waste" corporate assets, absent unanimous shareholder approval. Pursuant to this doctrine, it has often been held that agreements by the corporation to pay for past services is a waste of corporate assets on the ground that the corporation has received nothing in exchange. Furthermore, since F has given no consideration for the pension, F cannot enforce this promise against Jax.

On the other hand, some courts have held that a corporation may pay reasonable bonuses or pensions to employees for past services, if approved by a majority of the shareholders. (But there is no evidence of shareholder approval here.) In addition, some states have statutes that specifically authorize the board to provide pensions in recognition of past services. (But the pension here was promised by Jax's president and not by the board. Thus, unless this is a jurisdiction that grants the president authority to do any act that the board could authorize, the pension cannot be sustained on this approach.)

TABLE OF CASES

Collins v. Morgan Grain Co. - §723
Commonwealth Title Insurance & Trust Co. v. Seltzer - §580
Continental Securities Co. v. Belmont - §§615, 619
Coombes v. Getz - §1047
Corning Glass Works v. Lucase - §93
Costello v. Fazio - §41
Crane v. Anaconda Co. - §545
Cranson v. IBM - §§62, 69
Credit Bureau Reports, Inc. v. Credit Bureau of St. Paul, Inc. - §551

D.A. McArthur v. Times Printing Co. - §79
David v. Southern Import Wine Co. - §80
DeBaun v. First Western Bank & Trust Co. - §585
Deibler v. Chas. H. Elliott Co. - §457
Diamond v. Oreamuno - §416
Dirks v. SEC - §§302, 332-339
Dodge v. Ford Motor Co. - §§92, 890
Donahue v. Rodd Electrotype Co. - §565
Doran v. Petroleum Management Corp. - §840
Dottenheim v. Murchison - §§391, 627
Duane Jones Co. v. Burke - §258
Duffy v. Loft, Inc. - §435
Dunlay v. Avenue M Garage & Repair Co. - §794
Dunnett v. Arn - §580
DuPont v. Bell - §753
Dupuy v. Dupuy - §348
Durfee v. Durfee & Canning, Inc. - §217

E.K. Buck Retail Stores v. Harkert - §493
Easton National Bank v. American Brick & Tile Co. - §753
Edgar v. MITE Corp. - §§1124-1127, 1131-1134
Edwards & Hanley v. Wells Fargo Securities Clearance Corp. - §346
Eisenberg v. Flying Tiger Line, Inc. - §596
Eliasberg v. Standard Oil Co. - §221
Elkind v. Ligget & Meyers, Inc. - §§374, 375
Erie Railroad v. Tompkins - §774
Ernst & Ernst v. Hochfelder - §§293, 330, 481
Erskine v. Chevrolet Motors Co. - §85
Escott v. Barchris Construction Corp. - §868
Essex Universal Corp. v. Yates - §§578, 579
Estate Counseling Service, Inc. v. Merrill Lynch, Pierce, Fenner & Smith, Inc. - §354
Everett v. Transnation Development Corp. - §149

Farber, State *ex rel.* v. Sieberling Rubber Co. - §173
Farris v. Glen Alden Corp. - §§1010, 1012
Feder v. Martin Marietta Corp. - §§398, 402
Federal United Corp. v. Havender - §1048
Financial Industrial Fund, Inc. v. McDonnell Douglas Corp. - §331
Financial Investment & Rediscount Co. v. Wells - §646

Flanagan v. Jackson Wholesale Building Supply Co. - §71
Fletcher v. A.J. Industries, Inc. - §675
Fliegler v. Lawrence - §229
Ford v. Magee - §162
Foremost-McKesson, Inc. v. Provident Securities Co. - §§405, 406
Framingham Savings Bank v. Szabo - §77
Francis v. United Jersey Bank - §§175, 178, 182, 184
Francis I. duPont & Co. v. Universal City Studios - §§974, 976
Frank v. Anthony - §149
Freeman v. Decio - §416
Friedman v. Altoona Pipe & Steel Supply Co. - §550
Fridrich v. Bradford - §374

GAF Corp. v. Milstein - §1105
G. Loewus & Co. v. Highland Queen Packing Co. - §762
Gaines v. Haughton - §§477, 478, 480
Galef v. Alexander - §603
Galler v. Galler - §§122, 505
Gearhart Industries, Inc. v. Smith International, Inc. - §1120
Geddes v. Anaconda Copper Mining Co. - §1040
General Aircraft Corp. v. Lampert - §1106
General Bonding & Casualty Insurance Co. v. Moseley - §735
General Rubber Co. v. Benedict - §597
General Time Corp. v. Talley Industries - §548
Gerard v. Empire Square Realty Co. - §159
Gerdes v. Reynolds - §§583, 585, 587
Gerstle v. Gamble-Skogmo, Inc. - §481
Giant Portland Cement Co., *In re* - §427
Gilbert v. Burnside - §205
Gilligan Will Co. v. SEC - §835
Gimbel v. Signal Companies - §1073
Glazer v. Glazer - §505
Globe Woolen Co. v. Utica Gas & Electric Co. - §216
Globus v. Law Research Service, Inc. - §882
Goldberg v. Meridor - §324
Goodman v. Ladd Estate Co. - §115
Goodwin v. Aggasiz - §281
Gottfried v. Gottfried - §889
Gould v. American-Hawaiian Steamship Co. - §481
Grace Securities Corp. v. Roberts - §949
Graham v. Allis-Chalmers Manufacturing Co. - §182
Gratz v. Claughton - §388
Gray v. Harris Land & Cattle - §527
Green v. Occidental Petroleum - §354
Guth v. Loft, Inc. - §§250, 258
Guttman v. Illinois Central Railroad - §707

Haberman v. Tobin - §652
Hall v. Geiger-Jones Co. - §811

sale or transfer of control, §§571-588
  corporate action, §580
  equal opportunity doctrine, §§573-574
  fraud and nondisclosure, §581
  general rule, §§572-574
  sale of office, §§576-579
  to looters, §§582-588
directors. *See also* Conflict of interest; Directors; Insider
      trading
promoters, §§73, 765-783. *See also* Promoters

FRAUD
anti-fraud provisions. *See* Securities Act of 1933
blue sky laws, §§811-817
piercing corporate veil, §29

FUNDAMENTAL CHANGES, §§968-1136
amendment of articles, §§1033-1049. *See also* Articles of
      incorporation
controlling shareholder power, §§1072-1094. *See also*
      fiduciary duties
de facto mergers, §§1009-1021
dissolution, §§1050-1062. *See also* Dissolution
liquidation, §§1063-1071. *See also* Liquidation
mergers and consolidations, §§986-1025. *See also* Mergers
      and consolidations
sale of substantially all assets, §§1026-1032. *See also* Sale
      of substantially all assets
tender offers, §§1095-1136. *See* Acquisition of stock

GH

GOING PRIVATE TRANSACTIONS, §§1086-1089
GUARANTEES, §89

I

INDEMNIFICATION
derivative suits, §§685-691
directors, §§678-691, 881-882

INSIDER TRADING, §§279-424
See also Rule 10b-5
common law duty of disclosure, §§280-283
  "special facts" approach, §282
  to shareholders, §§280-283
common law liability, §416
  rule 10b-5 compared, §§422-424
  section 16 compared, §§417-421
remedies, §§350-379
  application, §§359-376
    closely held corporations, §§360-364
    government, §§376-379
    publicly held corporations, §§365-375
  damages, §§352-370
    benefit of bargain, §353
    out-of-pocket, §§352-354
    restitutionary relief, §§355-358
  injunctive, §377
  rescission, §§356-357
rule 10b-5, §§285-379. *See also* Rule 10b-5
  elements of plaintiff's action, §§292-300
    diligence, §§347-348
    materiality, §292
    reliance, §§296-300
    scienter, §§293-295

jurisdiction, §§288-290
nondisclosure, §§286, 301-311, 331
persons liable, §§321-349
  insiders, §§303, 321-328
    temporary insiders, §339
  non-insiders, §§329-330
    aiders and abettors, §§340-346
    pari delicto defense, §§347-349
    tippees, tippers §§332-338
  remedies, §§350-379
    application, §§359-376
      closely held corp., §§360-364
      government, §§376-379
      publicly held corp., §§365-375
    potential, §§351-358
  securities covered, §287
  standing, §§312-320
  statute of limitations, §291
section 16, §§380-424
  generally, §§382-411
    disclosure, §§382-384
    liability, §§385-411
    objective theory, §410
    subjective theory, §411
  insiders, §§392-406
    beneficial ownership, §§399-401
    deputization, §398
    director, §397
    officer, §§393-396
    relatives, §400
    time status is determined, §§402-406
  purchase and sale, §§407-411
    "garden variety," §407
    unorthodox, §§408-411
  rule 10b-5 compared, §§412-424
  securities affected, §381
  short swing profit, §§387-389
  who may recover, §§390-391
Securities Exchange Act of 1934, §284
  generally, §284
  jurisdiction, §288
  rule 10b-5. *See* Rule 10b-5, above.
  section 16. *See* Section 16, above.
statute of limitations, §291
venue and service, §290

INSPECTION OF RECORDS
See Directors; Shareholders
**INSURANCE AGAINST DERIVATIVE SUIT
      LIABILITY,** §§689-691
INTERLOCKING DIRECTORATES, §§238-244
ISSUANCE OF SHARES
See also Preemptive rights
blue sky laws, §§811-817. *See also* Blue sky laws
consideration. *See* Consideration
federal regulation, §§818-887. *See also* Securities Act
      of 1933
generally, §§714-717
state regulation, §§811-817. *See also* Blue sky laws
stock subscriptions. *See* Stock subscriptions
underwriting, §§806-809

JK

JOINT VENTURE, §19

L

LIABILITY
  directors
    criminal, §194
    defenses, §§184-188
    due care, §§181-183
    illegal dividends, §193
  insider trading. *See* insider trading
    rule 10b-5, §192
    Securities Act of 1933, §191
  limited, §2
  partnership, §§9, 18
  promoters. *See* Promoters
  shareholders, §51
LIMITATION OF ACTIONS
  See Statute of limitations
LIMITED PARTNERSHIPS, §§20-24
LIQUIDATION, §§1063-1071
  creditors' rights, §§1068-1071
  management, §1064
  nature of, §§1063
  shareholders' rights, §§1065-1067

M

MANAGEMENT AND CONTROL, §§116-278
  centralized, §4
  directors. *See* Directors
  officers. *See* Officers
  partnerships, §15
  shareholders' rights, §§116-136. *See also* Fiduciary duties;
        Shareholders
    close corporations. *See* Close corporations
    generally, §116
MEETINGS
  directors'. *See also* Conflict of interest
    noncompliance, §§159-161
    notice, §156
    organizational, §49
    quorum, §157
    voting, §158
MERGERS, §§986-1025
  appraisal rights, §§969-987
    exceptions, §§1003-1007
    procedure, §§979-985
    valuation of shares, §§970-978
  consolidations, §987
  de facto mergers, §§1009-1021
  statutory mergers, §§986-1008
    board approval, §991
    consolidation, §987
    effect, §§988-990
    generally, §986
    shareholder approval, §§992-1008
      appraisal rights, §995
        exception, §§1003-1007
      class voting, §994
      exclusivity, §1008
      percentage required, §993
      short form, §§996-999
      small scale mergers, §§1000-1002
  triangular mergers, §§1022-1025
    conventional, §1023
    reverse triangular merger, §1024

voting and appraisal rights, §1025
MINORITY RIGHTS
  See Fiduciary duties; Voting rights

N

NIMBLE DIVIDENDS, §§897-898, 904
  See also Dividends
NO-PAR VALUE STOCK
  See Par value
NOTICE
  director's meeting, §156
  noncompliance, §§159-161

O

OFFICERS
  See also Control persons; Directors
  authority, §§196-205
    power to bind corporation, §§203-204
    president, §§201-205
    ratification, §200
    types of authority, §§196-200
  casual sales, §§834-837
  conflict of interest. *See* Conflict of interest
  duties, §206
  election, §§48-49, 195
  insider trading. *See* Insider trading
  suits by, §692
ORGANIZATIONAL MEETINGS, §§47-49
  bylaws, §§48-49
  directors, §§48-49
  election of officers, §§48-49
  issuance of shares, §§48-49
  notice, §156
ORGANIZING THE CORPORATION, §§42-71
  articles of incorporation, §§43-46. *See also* Articles of
        incorporation
  corporations by estoppel, §§59-63
  de facto corporations, §§56-58
  de jure corporations, §§53-55
  organizational meetings, §§47-49. *See also* Organizational
        meetings

P

PAR VALUE, §§740-759. *See also* Shares; Watered stock
  articles of incorporation, §45
PARTNERSHIPS, §§6-25
  authority, §16
  defined, §8
  dissimilarities, §§8-18
  duration, §11
  governing by agreement, §15
  joint ventures, §19
  liability, §§9, 18
  limited partnerships, §§20-24
  management and control, §15
  ownership of assets, §17
  participation and corporate power, §90
  profit and loss, §11
  transfer of interest, §10
PERPETUAL EXISTENCE, §5

Notes

Notes

Notes

Notes

Notes

Notes